DATE DUE

D1068369

RELIGION, TERRORISM AND GLOBALIZATION. NONVIOLENCE: A NEW AGENDA

RELIGION, TERRORISM AND GLOBALIZATION. NONVIOLENCE: A NEW AGENDA

K.K. KURIAKOSE
EDITOR

Nova Science Publishers, Inc.
New York

NOTICE TO THE READER

The Publisher has taken reasonable care in the preparation of this book, but makes no expressed or implied warranty of any kind and assumes no responsibility for any errors or omissions. No liability is assumed for incidental or consequential damages in connection with or arising out of information contained in this book. The Publisher shall not be liable for any special, consequential, or exemplary damages resulting, in whole or in part, from the readers' use of, or reliance upon, this material.

This publication is designed to provide accurate and authoritative information with regard to the subject matter covered herein. It is sold with the clear understanding that the Publisher is not engaged in rendering legal or any other professional services. If legal or any other expert assistance is required, the services of a competent person should be sought. FROM A DECLARATION OF PARTICIPANTS JOINTLY ADOPTED BY A COMMITTEE OF THE AMERICAN BAR ASSOCIATION AND A COMMITTEE OF PUBLISHERS.

LIBRARY OF CONGRESS CATALOGING-IN-PUBLICATION DATA
Religion, terrorism, and globalization : nonviolence : a new agenda / K. K. Kuriakose, editor.
    p. cm.
Includes bibliographical references and index.
ISBN 1-59454-553-7
1. Violence--Religious aspects. 2. Terrorism--Religious aspects. 3. Nonviolence--Religious aspects. 4. Globalization--Religious aspects. I. Kuriakose, K. K.
BL65.V55R465   2005
205'.697--dc22   2005020872

Published by Nova Science Publishers, Inc. ✦New York

CONTENTS

PREFACE

By the end of the last Millennium and especially after the terrorists attack of the World Trade Center in New York City in 2001, the question "Is it possible for a religion to promote terrorism or violence?" was asked from many corners of the world. This question adds to the issue of the growing political/religious upheaval caused by terrorism that has challenged human security globally in recent years. The questions continue: If religion stands for peace and conflict resolution, how can a religion support violence? In addition, the relationship of religion and violence and the growth of terrorism in Palestine, troubles in Ireland, Al Qaeda and other Muslim extremist involvement in terrorist activity, lead people to wonder if religion can justify the murder of innocent people. Ironically, it is a time when many use religions not only to justify violent actions, have credited their religion as the origin of inspiration for terrorist activities. The issue is not only a political concern but also a challenge to world religions.

The culture of violence has gained a religious coloring in modern days. With a destructive technological impetus, the question arises: Is there abuse of religious teachings? Is their any religious basis for violence and war? Then follow questions about the purpose of religion and the significance of concepts of peace and non-violence. As some find justification for war and violence in their religion, an inquiry must be made about the influence of religious scriptures on peace.

My involvement with the Fellowship of Reconciliation, a pacifist organization and my professional inquiry into Gandhian philosophy and moral education, inspired me to address the challenge of the critical situation of religions' history. Longtime research for the publication of my book *Nonviolence: The Way of the Cross* (Xulon Press, 2004) developed my continued curiosity on what world religions teach about peace and nonviolence. I was inspired to explore the heritage of peace concepts in World Religions and for this laborious task I decided to approach scholars from different religious traditions.

The post World War II era has been marked by rapid technological change that has become the basis of modern globalization. There has been a revolution electrified by technological advancement in information and social communication, and the establishment of an infrastructure paralleled by a growing consciousness of world realities, such as oppression, human rights violations and above all the threat to human security by war, violence and terrorism, ecological disaster, and calamites. The challenges posed by the market-oriented globalization has economically benefited only a minor population around the world, and those countries that have been overlooked have had mixed feelings about the process. Globalization has had a varied impact on political, social, cultural, and religious behavioral systems.

Globalization prescribed a new role for religions in defining the moral fabric of political communities. People accepted technological change but hesitated to embrace any social or cultural change, as they believed that globalization damaged their religion, customs and traditions and these were more important than material development. The Internet and the market-based globalization led to a global culture of multi-polar world of fragmented groups of religions, cultures and ethnicities. People failed to understand the core of religions and their religion has been used to justify struggles for national identity, or worse, violence. For others such an understanding of religion helped only for the growth of religious fanaticism or communalism. Further, modern globalization supported the development of communalism in some regions and became the source of uncontrolled violence and the growth of terrorism.

Globalization supports the spread of a violent culture. The process of globalization has two faces: it brings cultural-spiritual crisis and it creates material insufficiency. Human dignity and human value is neglected in this technological culture. Market-oriented globalization exploits the masses and then the majority of the material resources benefit only a low percentage of the world population. Economic injustice causes mass poverty, insecurity, oppression, humiliation and these different faces of human rights violations all lead to violence. The insecurity that spreads harms both the individual and social fabric of the people. Some people who benefited from globalization, like Osama bin Laden, subsidize their wealth for the growth of communalism or terrorism. On the other hand, religious fundamentalists, including Christians, justify war. In addition, there is shocking news of violence, including school shootings, in the media every day.

From this context of violence and globalization we have moved forward with a culture of violence and the abuse of religious teaching. Humanity needs a way out. Humanity needs an evolution in human thinking and has to seek a belief system that honors the concepts of truth, peace and nonviolence and the essence of religious and cultural heritage.

The tragic situation of modern humanity is that most of the world population is unaware of or neglects the consensus of nonviolence within their human behavior system. The concept of nonviolence should be a basic understanding of each individual as well as for the greater community. It is necessary for a peaceful existence, locally and internationally. It is not a sense of passiveness; rather it is an affirmative action. The concepts and practice of nonviolence are a moral force within an individual that can combat offences, coercions, stress, egoism, oppression and humiliation. The culture of nonviolence becomes then a force in the growth of a community that enriches its political, social and cultural dimensions.

This volume attempts to comprehend the concepts of nonviolence and peace within different religious and cultural traditions. This work, you will discover, is intended to be a means of renewing and discovering the cardinal teachings and practice of peace and nonviolence in different religious/ cultural traditions. The concept of nonviolence teaches humanity of the irreparable damage done to our planet as well as the morally corrupting impact of violence and war on human beings across cultures. To address the situation with the principle and practice of nonviolence in our age is the challenge before the global community.

There are many proponents who have accepted nonviolence in their struggle for a better world. Among them were Mahatma Gandhi, and Martin Luther King, Jr. Gandhi found *ahimsa* as the core value in his experiments with truth, organizing community life, and later in political struggle against the British and the Indian independence movement. He explored the insights of nonviolence from the religious scriptures, especially from Hindu philosophy and enriched it from other World Religions. "Love your enemy," a key concept of the Sermon on the Mount, and Jesus' teaching to "love your neighbor as thyself" enriched his concepts of nonviolence. Gandhi applied the strategy of nonviolence personally, in his family, in his community, and then in political life. In the struggle with the British he adopted nonviolence and its derivative *satyagraha*, as a powerful weapon to undermine the imperialistic structure and to build up an ideal community in India. Like Gandhi, Martin Luther King, Jr. accepted the religious ethics of "love" and "justice" in the civil rights movements in the United States. He found the concept of nonviolence quite necessary in order to reform human calamities and turmoil with the principles of human dignity as it seeks for equality and classlessness. Both Gandhi and King found that the practice of nonviolence ultimately helps to develop ideal and peaceful communities locally and internationally.

This book is comprised of seven chapters. Chapter one offers a conceptual framework that underlies the basic issues behind religion and violence and the issue is discussed under the title "Does Religion Cause Violence?" Chapters two through five are articles addressing the concepts of peace and nonviolence in Hinduism, Buddhism, Islam and Christianity. In this section there are also articles on Gandhi and on the Native American experience of nonviolence. Chapter six discusses the concept of nonviolence within the context of the war on terrorism. And the articles in the last chapter seek for a new world order as well as for the possibility of a culture of peace and recommend a relevant educational pedagogy at this point.

In this inquiry, scholars from different religious/cultural traditions joined together to contribute a varied perspective on nonviolence within cultures. They share with readers more effective ways of integrating the concepts of nonviolence and peace. I commend the contributors for their time, energy, and their intellectual commitment to explore the richness found in sacred writings and traditions within the themes they undertook. The ideas provided by the contributors shall be shared with others, with the hope that they will build a more peaceful global community. This is the only intention behind this humble attempt.

ACKNOWLEDGMENTS

Many individuals have offered their thoughts and wisdom in helping to create this volume and I would like to thank each of them. First of all, I thank the contributors who added significantly to this book. They gave valuable resources of time, cooperation and prompt communication throughout the various stages of this project. In addition my thanks to Professor Vincent Cornell, head of Fahd Center for Middle East and Islamic Studies at the University of Arkansas in Fayetteville, AR, for writing an enlightening and meaningful introduction for this book.

I wish to extend my sincere appreciation to a few people who supported this project from the beginning. Rev. Fr. M..C. George of Kottayam, India, deserves my gratitude for his support. I would like to extend special thanks to Professor Frederick Denny at Colorado State University in Denver, CO, for sharing information and for finding learned contributors at the initial stage of this project. I am grateful for the stimulating discussions with Rev. Peter Strand, pastor of Ridgefield Presbyterian Church in New Jersey, and Professor Paul Keim at Goshen College in Goshen, IN; both helped clarify my insight on pacifist consensus at many points. Rev. T. Kenjitsu Nakagaki, Buddhist Chaplain at Columbia University in New York, enriched my knowledge of peace and nonviolent concepts in Buddhism. I would be remiss if I failed to highlight the friendship of my colleague Samuel Cordero, at Teachers College, Columbia University, New York who provided me with intellectual liveliness at many crossroads of this work.

I am also indebted to Jodi Mathews at St. Vladimir's Seminary in Crestwood, NY. She did a laudable job assisting in the editing process, monitored a myriad of details, coordinated activities, suggested improvements, and kept things running smoothly and punctually in order to complete this volume.

Finally, my thanks to Nova Science Publishers, New York, for their inspiring support for shaping this book's present form.

CONTRIBUTORS

Joseph Chuman teaches courses in religion and human rights in the Graduate School of Columbia University and in the honors program at Hunter College of the City University of New York. He has also taught human rights at the United Nations University for Peace in San Jose, Costa Rica. He received his doctorate in religion from Columbia University. Dr. Chuman has published over a hundred articles in newspapers, journals of opinion and encyclopedias. Among them have been articles on "Ethical Culture" for the *Encyclopedia of American Social Movements*, published by the M.E. Sharpe Company and *Encyclopedia of Contemporary American Religion*, published by MacMillan, for which he also contributed an article on "Agnosticism." An article on "Non-religious Beliefs" was also published in MacMillan's *Encyclopedia of the Future*. For over thirty years, Joseph Chuman has served as the professional leader of the Ethical Culture Society of Bergen County in Teaneck, New Jersey. Ethical Culture is a congregational movement which affirms the dignity of all people in a humanistic and non-theological context. Dr. Chuman is a community activist who has worked primarily in the areas of human rights and the protection of civil liberties. Most recently he has founded a temporary sanctuary for asylum seekers who are released from federal detention centers prior to their hearings in immigration court.

Professor Vincent Cornell is a summa cum laude graduate of the University of California, Berkeley. He received his Ph.D. in Islamic Studies from University of California Los Angeles in 1989. He has taught at Northwestern University (2 years), the University of Georgia (1 year), and Duke University (9 years). Since July 1, 2000 he has been Professor of History and Director of the King Fahd Center for Middle East and Islamic Studies at the University of Arkansas. He has published two major books: *The Way of Abu Madyan* (Cambridge: The Islamic Texts Society, 1996) and *Realm of the Saint: Power and Authority in Moroccan Sufism* (Austin, Texas: University of Texas Press, 1998). His pre-modern interests cover the entire spectrum of Islamic thought from Sufism to philosophy and Islamic law. He has lived and worked in Morocco for nearly six years, and has spent considerable time both teaching and doing research in Egypt, Tunisia, Malaysia and Indonesia. He is presently working on four book projects: (1) He has a contract with Praeger Press to edit a five-volume set entitled, *Voices of Islam*. (2) He is finishing a translation of volume 8 of 'Allama Tabataba'i's Qur'an commentary *al-Mizan fi Tafsir al-Qur'an* for the Alevi Foundation. (3) He is preparing a critique of contemporary Islamist reform movements tentatively entitled, *Islamic Modernism and the Myth of Authenticity*. (4) He is also preparing a second critique of Islamism tentatively entitled, *The Roots of Islamic Totalitarianism*. His most recent publications are on Islamic theology and philosophy: "Religion and Philosophy" chapter for *World Eras Volume 2: The Rise and Spread of Islam 622-1500*, (Susan L. Douglass, ed. [Farmington Hills, Michigan: The Gale Group/Manly Inc., 2002]). He has also written about the challenge to Islam of the terrorist attacks of 9-11-01: "A Muslim to Muslims: Reflections after September 11," in Stanley Hauerwas and Frank Lentricchia, Eds. *Dissent from the Homeland: Essays after September 11* (Durham, N.C. and London: Duke University Press, 2003), pp. 83-94.

Dr. Charlotte Coté is an Assistant Professor in American Indian Studies at the University of Washington in Seattle. Dr. Coté is a member of the Nuu-chah-nulth Tribe situated on the West Coast of Vancouver Island in British Columbia, Canada. She graduated with a Ph.D. from the University of California at Berkeley. Her dissertation focused on the Makah and Nuu-chah-nulth whaling tradition. Her areas of academic interest are Native sovereignty, treaty rights, contemporary indigenous whaling, and Indian law and policy. Her research covers both Canadian and U.S. issues related to Native people. Dr. Coté has published articles on Indian sovereignty in Canada and the United States, Makah and Nuu-chah-nulth whaling, and the Northwest Coast Guardian Spirit Complex. She is currently working on a book that examines the political, social, economic and spiritual importance of contemporary indigenous whaling.

Perry L. Glanzer, Ph.D., is an assistant professor in the School of Education at Baylor University in Waco, Texas. His research and teaching interests include moral education, the relationship between religion, education and politics, and the philosophy of education. He has written various articles addressing these topics for journals such as *Journal of Church and State*, *Journal of Moral Education*, *English Journal*, *Phi Delta Kappan*, and *Religion and Education*. He also recently authored *The Quest for Russia's Soul: Evangelicals and Moral Education in Post-Communist Russia* (Baylor University Press).

Daniel G. Groody is currently an Assistant Professor of Theology and the Director of the Center for Latino Spirituality and Culture at the Institute for Latino Studies at the University of Notre Dame. A Catholic priest and a member of the Congregation of the Holy Cross, he has spent many years working in Latin America, particularly along the U.S.- Mexican Border. He was also the director of two international conferences at Notre Dame, including "The Option for the Poor in Christian Theology" and "Migration and Theology," and he is currently working on various books on the subjects of faith, justice, globalization and immigration. He is the author of *"Border of Death, Valley of Life: An Immigrant Journey of Heart and Spirit,"* which has been translated into multiple languages. He holds a B.A. from the University of Notre Dame in the Great Books (Program of Liberal Studies), a Masters of Divinity and a Licentiate in Sacred Theology and Master of Divinity degrees from the Jesuit School of Theology, and a Ph.D. from the Graduate Theological Union. He is also the executive producer of various films and documentaries, including "Endless Exodus" and "Dying to Live: A Migrant's Journey." He teaches courses in U.S. Latino Spirituality, inculturation, Christian Spirituality and Social Justice. He has lectured both in the United States, Latin America and Europe and is currently working on a book tentatively called, "Walking Humbly, Living Justly: Following Christ in a Globalized World."

Hugh Talat Halman, PhD. Duke University (2000), is Research Assistant Professor of Religious and Islamic Studies at the University of Arkansas, Fayetteville, dually appointed in the Program in Humanities and the King Fahd Center for Middle East Studies. He is currently a Fulbright Scholar (2004-5) teaching at the State Islamic University of Indonesia (UIN Syarif Hidayatullah) in Jakarta and researching the interreligious milieu of Southeast Asia. His research has focused on hermeneutical and historical dimensions of Sufism and contemporary Turkish-Islamic Sufi culture. He has contributed to the forthcoming *Encyclopedia of the Modern Islamic World* and *Holy People: an Encyclopedia*. His dissertation, "Where Two Seas Meet: The Quranic Story of Moses' Journey with al-Khidr as a model of Spiritual Guidance in Sufi Quran Commentaries" (Duke, 2000), explored hermeneutical traditions of teachings about master-disciple relationships exegeted from Quranic discourse.

Zayn Kassam is Associate Professor of Religious Studies at Pomona College, Claremont, California and is also on the faculty at Claremont Graduate University, Claremont, California. A graduate of McGill University (Ph.D 1995), she teaches courses in Islamic philosophy, mysticism, gender and literature as well as a course on philosophical and mystical texts from a comparative perspective. She has been honored with a Wig Award for Distinguished Teaching at Pomona College, and has lectured widely on gender issues in the United States, Canada, and Britain. Her published articles include: "Muslim Women Writers in South Asia"; "Our Worlds and His: Naguib Mahfouz's Palace Walk"; "Mindfield or Minefield: Teaching Religion in a Multicultural Classroom"; "The Individual and Notions of Community"; and others dealing with ethics and gender. She is currently working on two books, one on aspects of Quranic interpretation in medieval Islamic philosophy, and one on gender issues in the Islamic world.

Paul Keim is professor of Bible, Religion and Modern and Classical Languages at Goshen College, a Mennonite college located in Goshen, Indiana. His area of specialization is Old Testament and Ancient Near Eastern languages and civilizations. He completed his undergraduate studies at Goshen College, his M.Div. at Associated Mennonite Biblical Seminary, and his Ph.D. at Harvard University. He has taught at Indiana University (Bloomington, IN) and the College of Charleston (SC). He was the academic dean at Hesston College (KS)for two years and at Goshen College for four years before returning to fulltime teaching at Goshen. Prof. Keim is married to Julie, an Expressive Arts therapist, and they have three children.

Karikottuchira K. Kuriakose, is a native of South India. His area of specialization is Theology, Ethics and Nonviolence. He has been involved with the activities of Fellowship of Reconciliation. He began research at the Christian Institute for the Study of Religion and Society in Bangalore and also worked for the Church Relations Committee of the Senate of Serampore College. He received his Ed D from Teachers College, Columbia University, New York. His dissertation focused on Gandhian philosophy. Since 1996 he has taught at the College of New Rochelle, New York, and has written articles on "Multiculturalism", and "Youth and Culture." He has published a book entitled *Nonviolence: The Way of the Cross* (Xulon Press, 2004). Another effort in the works is *Value and Character Education*, due for publication by summer 2006.

Thomas Mockaitis is Professor of History at DePaul University, where he chaired the department from 1997-2000. He earned a BA in European History from Allegheny College in Meadville, PA, and his MA and Ph.D. in Modern British and Irish History from the University of Wisconsin-Madison. Professor Mockaitis co-edited *Grand Strategy and the War on Terrorism* (London: Frank Cass, 2003) with Paul Rich. He is the author of *British Counterinsurgency: 1919-1960* (London: Macmillan, 1990), *British Counterinsurgency in the Post-Imperial Era* (Manchester: U. of Manchester Press, 1995), and *Peacekeeping and Intrastate Conflict: the Sword or the Olive Branch?* (Westport, CT: Praeger, 1999). He has received two major grants from the United States Institute of Peace. He has lectured at the U.S. Marine Corps Command and Staff College and the Canadian Forces Staff College and presented papers at the Pearson Peacekeeping Center (Canada), the Royal Military Academy Sandhurst (UK), and at conferences co-sponsored with the Military Science Department of the Austrian Ministry of Defense. As part of a team of terrorism experts affiliate with the Naval Post Graduate School's Center for Civil-Military Relations, he has co-taught courses in Romania, Malta, Hawaii, and California. He was appointed Eisenhower Chair at the Royal Dutch Military Academy for the fall of 2004. A frequent media commentator on terrorism and security matters, Dr. Mockaitis has appeared on Public Television, National Public Radio, and various Chicago radio and TV stations. He appears regularly as a terrorism expert for WGN TV News (Channel 9). An Elder at Winnetka Presbyterian Church and a member of the Presbytery of Chicago Peacemaking Committee, he coauthored (with Barbara Batten) the denominations adult education study, *Just Peacemaking* (Louisville, KY: PC (USA), 2002).

Gabriel Moran is Director of the Program in Philosophy of Education at New York University. He also teaches international ethics in the International Education Program. He has a PhD in religious education from the Catholic University of America. For the past forty years he has been a leading author in the field of religious education. His works have been translated into many languages. He has written essays on force, violence and war for several edited collections and journals. His books include *A Grammar of Responsibility* (1996) and *Both Sides: The Story of Revelation* (2002).

John McGuckin is a priest of the Orthodox Church (Patriarchate of Romania), who came to America from England in 1997, where he was a Reader in Patristic and Byzantine Theology at the University of Leeds. Upon arrival he assumed the position of Chair in Early Church History at the renowned school of Union Theological Seminary in New York. His academic career began with the study of Philosophical Theology at Heythrop College, a Pontifical Athenaeum, from 1970-72, and from there he read for a Divinity degree at the University of London, graduating with First Class Honors in 1975. For his doctoral researches at Durham University (1980), he studied the politics and theology of the early Constantinian era, with a thesis on the thought of Lucius Caecilius Lactantius, the emperor Constantine's pacifist Christian tutor and political advisor. Prof. McGuckin was elected a Fellow of the Royal Society of Arts in 1986, and a Fellow of the Royal Historical Society in 1996. He is the author of fifteen books of historical theology, including: *The Transfiguration of Christ in Scripture and Tradition* (1986); *St. Cyril of Alexandria: The Christological Controversy* (1994); *At the Lighting of the Lamps: Hymns from the Ancient Church* (1995, and repr. 1997); *St. Gregory of Nazianzus: An Intellectual Biography* (2000)—Nominated for the 2002 Pollock Biography Prize; *Standing in God's Holy Fire: The Spiritual Tradition of Byzantium*

(Orbis, 2001); *The Book of Mystical Chapters* (Shambhala, 2002); and *The Westminster Handbook To Patristic Theology* (2004). He has published numerous research articles in scholarly journals ranging in subject matter from New Testament Exegesis to Byzantine Iconography, though mainly centered on the thought of Origen of Alexandria and the fourth to fifth century Greek Christian theologians. In 1994 his first collection of poetry, *Byzantium and Other Poems*, was published. Prof. McGuckin has served as visiting professor and guest lecturer in many universities and colleges in England, Ireland, Greece, Romania, Ukraine, Italy, and the United States. In 2003 he was invited by the Royal Norwegian Academy to serve as an International Research Fellow at the Academy's "Center For Higher Studies" in Oslo. There he formed part of a team of international specialists considering the elaboration and development of principles of aesthetics in early Christian culture-formation. He is currently working on a study of the significance of aesthetics as a medium of discourse between Christian and non-Christian writers in Late Antiquity. He teaches Graduate- level courses as a faculty member of both Columbia University's Religion Department and Union Theological Seminary, and he also serves as a priest in a small Orthodox parish in Manhattan.

Ven. T. Kenjitsu Nakagaki is the head resident minister of New York Buddhist Church - Jodoshinshu (Shin Buddhist) Temple and chairperson of the Eastern District Buddhist Ministers Associations of BCA. Nakagaki is also current president of the Buddhist Council of New York, UCM Buddhist Chaplain at Columbia University, adviser of the American Buddhist Study Center and active in interfaith community such as Interfaith Center of New York, Religions for Peace, Interfaith Alliance. He is author of "New York Bozu Indo o Aruku" (Gendai-shokan Publisher in Japan). He was ordained in 1980, and came to USA in 1985 as oversea minister from Hongwanji Mother Temple, Kyoto, Japan. Nakagaki graduated from Ryukoku Univeristy in Kyoto (B.A,) majoring in Buddhist History in 1983, graduated from California State University, Fresno (M.A.) majoring in Linguistics in 1994.

Vanessa Rebecca Sasson has been teaching Comparative Religion in the Liberal Arts Department of Marianopolis College since 1999. She is also a lecturer of Comparative Religion at McGill University and runs regular Interfaith Graduate Seminars there every year. She finished her Ph.D. in 2003 with a comparative study of the birth mythology of Moses and the Buddha, which she is now revising for publication with Sheffield Academic Press. She is also currently putting together, along with Jane Marie Law, an edited volume about fetal mythology and embryology, entitled *Imagining the Fetus*. Outside of her academic life, she can be found in the boxing ring, where she has been for almost a decade.

Noel Sheth, S.J. is President of Jnana-Deepa Vidyapeeth, Pontifical Institute of Philosophy and Religion, Pune, India. He also teaches Indian Philosophies and Religions. He was a former Rector of Papal Seminary in Pune. He is a Gold Medallist of the University of Pune, having secured a First Class First in Sanskrit-Pali in his M.A. there, and his Ph. D from Harvard University. On several occasions he has chaired sections of the World Sanskrit Conferences and his name is in the Who's Who of Sanskrit Scholars of India. He has been awarded numerous scholarships and prizes from different institutions. He has been honored with "Dr. Sam Higginbottom Award for the Best Principals of India, 2004-2005," which was conferred on him by the All India Association of Christian Higher Education (AIACHE). He is a member of several learned bodies, such as the Bhandarkar Oriental Research Institute and the Heras Institute. He is a member of the Rectors' Committee and the Administrative Council of the International Federation of Catholic Universities (IFCU) and a member of the Executive Committee of the International Conference of Catholic Theological Institutions (COCTI). He has been widely published in various journals. His publications deal with the exegesis of Sanskrit texts, on Hinduism, Buddhism and on comparative theology. His book, *The Divinity of Krishna*, is mentioned in the Bibliography under "Krishnaism" in the prestigious *Encyclopedia of Religion*, edited by Mircea Eliade.

Liyakat Takim A native of Zanzibar, Tanzania, Professor Liyakat Takim teaches a wide range of courses on Islam in the Department of Religious Studies at the University of Denver. He has published over 30 articles/entries in various journals, books, and encyclopedias. In addition, Professor Takim has translated four books and has recently completed a book titled, *The Heirs of the Prophet: Charisma and Religious Authority in Islam*. His book has been accepted for publication by SUNY press. He is currently translating volume four of 'Allama Tabatabai's voluminous exegesis of the Qur'an. Professor Takim has taught in American and Canadian universities and has lectured in various parts of the world. A well-respected scholar in the Muslim community, his current research examines reformation of Islamic law in contemporary times.

Dr. Tony L. Talbert, Associate Professor in the School of Education at Baylor University, is a qualitative and ethnographic researcher whose teaching and research areas of expertise include: qualitative and ethnographic research design and analysis; democracy education; peace education; and social justice education. Dr. Talbert refers to his field of research as Education As Democracy which integrates democracy, peace, and social justice education into a focused discipline of qualitative and ethnographic inquiry examining teacher and student empowerment through activist engagement in political, economic, and social issues confronting education. Dr. Talbert is pleased to discuss: qualitative and ethnographic research design and analysis; distinctions between democratic movements (e.g., market democracy vs. popular democracy); alternatives to war-centric curriculum and practice in public schools and society; traditions of dissent within democratic societies; interactive peace and democracy teaching strategies and resources; and, the role of activism within education and society. Dr. Talbert can be reached at (254) 710-7417 or Tony_Talbert@baylor.edu.

Norberto Valdez received his MA and PhD from the University of Wisconsin, Madison. He is Assoc. Prof. of Anthropology and Chicano/Latino Studies, Colorado State University. His family roots are in southern Colorado and Native communities of northern New Mexico. His teaching and research interests include: globalization and development theory; Third World and Latin American rural and Indigenous populations and human rights; impacts of free trade agreements in Mexico and Central America; immigrant rights and political economy; and Chicana/o cultural transformations in the U.S. Southwest. He has published a book about "Ethnicity, Class, and the Indigenous Struggle for Land in Mexico" and has written articles on Chiapas and autonomy struggles, issues of land reform and unequal development in Guerrero, Mexico and on community justice and police relations. Dr. Valdez is currently doing field research in the Chiapas and Cancun area of southeastern Mexico, western highlands of Guatemala, and Atlantic coast of Costa Rica to assess community responses to Plan Puebla-Panama, CAFTA, and other free trade aspects of corporate globalization. He is also working on another book (to be published 2005 with co-authors William Timpson and David Giffey) entitled *From Battleground to Common Ground: War Veterans and Peace Activists Share Stories About Transformation and a Deeper Democracy* (Madison, WI: Atwood). Dr. Valdez is also doing research for an upcoming piece, "Globalization, Free Trade, and the Immigration Reform Debate In the U.S."

Katherine K. Young, James McGill Professor, teaches in the Faculty of Religious Studies and is a member of the Centre for Medicine, Ethics, and Law. She publishes in three fields: Hinduism, ethics (Hindu ethics, comparative medical ethics, and social ethics), and gender and religion. She has co-authored *Hindu Ethics* (1989) and has coedited *Religion and Law in the Global Village* (2000). On the topic of non-violence and violence, she has published a chapter called "Hinduism and the Ethics of Weapons of Mass Destruction" in *Ethics and Weapons of Mass Destruction: Religious and Secular Perspectives*, edited by Sohail H. Hashmi and Steven P. Lee (2004). She is currently writing a book on the peaceable ideal of manhood in the cultures of Indian Brahmans, orthodox Jews, Mennonites, and Swedes. She has written for the *Encyclopedia of Bioethics* (Macmillan) and six chapters for the forthcoming *A History of Medical Ethics (Cambridge University Press)*. On the topic of gender, she has collaborated with Arvind Sharma on twelve books on women in world religions and has co-authored with Paul Nathanson *Spreading Misandry: The Teaching of Contempt for Men in Popular Culture* (2001) and "Legalizing Misandry: from Public Shame to Systemic Discrimination against Men" (forthcoming 2005).

INTRODUCTION: QUESTIONING RELIGION, PROBLEMATIZING VIOLENCE, AFFIRMING LIFE

Vincent J. Cornell

King Fahd Center for Middle East and Islamic Studies
University of Arkansas

Throughout the twentieth century, it was commonplace— even a cliché— in Western countries to blame religion for the violence among nations and peoples. This secular prejudice has persisted into the new millennium, despite the fact that the greatest wars and genocides of the twentieth century had little or nothing to do with religion. Few if any historians would claim that the First and Second World Wars, the Korean and Vietnam Wars, or the Cambodian and Rwandan genocides, were caused by religion. And even though the other great genocides of the twentieth century, that of the Armenians by the Turkish state and the Holocaust perpetrated by the Nazis on the Jews of Europe, involved religious minorities, blame for these atrocities has usually been laid at the feet of racism or nationalism, which are secular in origin. Even during the Balkan conflict of the 1990s, when warring nationalities often broke along religious lines, observers could not agree on which identities were more important: Were they the ethno-nationalistic identities of Croat, Serb, or Bosniak, or were they the religious identities of Roman Catholic, Orthodox, or Muslim?

Clearly, if the number of corpses produced is any measure of the truth, secular ideologies have caused far greater suffering in the modern world than has religion. However, despite this conclusion, the secular prejudice against religion remains.[1] Secularists still see each occurrence of religious violence or bigotry as proof that religion is at the root of violence and intolerance. This prejudice can even be found among those who are well acquainted with nonviolent traditions in world religions. The Indian-born doctor and self-help guru Deepak Chopra, who once expressed the wish that he could be "right up there" with religious leaders such as the Dalai Lama, the Buddha, and Jesus, recently condemned religion as a major cause

---

[1] See, for example, sociologist Peter Berger's comment. "I don't want to be a crude empiricist, but it seems to me you could start making body counts. In this century, I think the godless have a slight moral edge, but if you take all of history, I'm not so sure." In Adam B. Seligman, *Modest Claims: Dialogues and Essays on Tolerance and Tradition* (Notre Dame, Indiana: Notre Dame University Press, 2004), p. 61.

of world violence during a promotional tour for his book, *Peace is the Way*: "Religion has become divisive, quarrelsome, and idiotic. Religion is the reason we have all this conflict in the world. We have squeezed God into the volume of a body and the span of a lifetime; given God a male identity, and ethnic background; made him a tribal chief and gone to war." Chopra went on to say that the solution to religious violence is to conceive of God as female, because women are more nurturing, caring and loving than men: "The human male has become the most predatory animal on our planet. It's time that we embrace the feminine face of God."[2]

Apart from his New Age and feminist references to the Goddess and divine femininity, Chopra's comments reflect a critique of religion that has changed very little in the last 350 years. The key to this critique is the Enlightenment notion of empirical reason, which refuses to place ultimate truth-value in inherited beliefs or traditions. In his *Essay Concerning Human Understanding* (1690), John Locke graded assertions of truth on a scale of probability that was based on the rules of legal evidence. Knowledge based on religious tradition or revelation was, for Locke, low on the scale of evidential probability. The farther from the actual event, the weaker evidence becomes. Religious traditions or doctrines cannot be taken as evidence for their truth, he argued, because there are no longer any eyewitnesses to verify the claims on which religious doctrines are based. Since the claims of revealed religions could not have the highest degree of truth-likelihood, they could not attain factual certainty. Instead, they could only attain "moral certainty." For this reason, Locke suggested that religious beliefs be held with "tempered firmness." In other words, religious beliefs should be "tempered" by the understanding that no religious conviction can attain full empirical or rational demonstrability. Since religious beliefs are only private convictions and not empirical facts, there is no rational justification to impose them on another person or group of persons. This skepticism about the certainty of religious knowledge formed the basis for Locke's argument for a pluralistic Christianity in his *Letter Concerning Toleration* (1685-9).[3] In the hands of American political theorists, such as Benjamin Franklin and Thomas Jefferson, it formed the basis for a truly interreligious pluralism. "God has bestowed reason as the umpire of Truth," said Jefferson in 1814.[4] Later, in his 1821 *Autobiography*, Jefferson explicitly affirmed the notion of universal religious toleration, saying that religious freedom "meant to comprehend within the mantle of its protection the Jew and the Gentile, the Christian and Mahometan, the Hindoo and infidel of every denomination."[5]

The reason why Locke and other Enlightenment thinkers subordinated faith to reason was because Europe had just emerged from over two centuries of bloody conflict that was precipitated by the intolerance of the Protestant Reformation and Catholic attempts to suppress it. Foremost in Locke's mind was the fear of what he termed "religious enthusiasm"

---

[2] "Interview: 10 Questions for Deepak Chopra," *Time*, Vol. 165, No. 4, January 24, 2005, p. 10.

[3] This work was first written as *Epistola de Tolerantia* in Holland in the year 1685. Initial Latin and English translations were published in 1689. On John Locke's epistemology and views on religion, see Nicholas Wolterstorff, *John Locke and the Ethics of Belief* (Cambridge: Cambridge University Press, 1996) and Henry G. Van Leeuwen, *The Problem of Certainty in English Thought, 1630-90* (The Hague: Martinus Nijhoff, 1963). A summary of Locke's views on epistemological certainty can also be found in Ronald A. Kuipers, *Critical Faith: Toward a Renewed Understanding of Religious Life and its Public Accountability* (Amsterdam: Vrije Universiteit Amsterdam, 2002), pp. 10-43. Parts of the above paragraph paraphrase Kuipers' conclusions on pp. 19-20.

[4] Thomas Jefferson, *Collected Works*, Memorial Edition, 14:197.

[5] Ibid, 1:67. This statement was made as part of a debate over a bill for the establishment of religious freedom in the state of Virginia.

— today we would call it "religious fanaticism"— that gave rise to all "the Bustles and Wars, that have been in the Christian World, upon account of Religion."[6] At the beginning of the twenty-first century, in the wake of religiously inspired acts of terrorism in New York, Madrid, Bali, and Israel, and the spread of religious fundamentalism from the Christian West to Islam and now to Hinduism and Buddhism, it seems to many observers that the world has embarked on a new and equally dangerous path of "religious enthusiasm." In fact, the present situation is potentially more dangerous than it was in the seventeenth century because religious "enthusiasm" is no longer confined to just one civilization. For Samuel P. Huntington, religious conflict is a major component of the "clash of civilizations" thesis, which replaces the nation state with civilizational blocs that are largely defined in religious terms.[7] Despite numerous attempts to refute Huntington's thesis, his model of conflict between "the West and the rest" has enjoyed remarkable staying power. Recent disputes between the proponents of democracy and partisans of Islamic integrism in the Middle East and South Asia and between proponents of "Western" and "Asian" values (which Huntington would call "Confucian values") in China and Malaysia illustrate that in some contexts, at least, Huntington's concerns may be justified.[8]

In Islam, the potential for violence is not only found in the conflict between what Huntington calls the "universal" values of the secular West and those of traditional religion. Throughout the Islamic world, the rise of identity politics and the competition for power within nation states has redrawn religious boundaries and has led to increased religious sectarianism in countries where a real, if formally unacknowledged pluralism once existed. In a recent article in *The New Yorker*, the Sunni Iraqi politician Adnan Pachachi recalled an Iraq "in which no one knew who was Sunni and who was Shiite. The new wave of identity politics is often blamed on outsiders— variously, Iranians, Arabs, or Americans. Every Iraqi can name a sibling or a cousin in a mixed marriage."[9] Many Iraqi intellectuals view the pre-Baathist era of the 1950s, when religious traditionalists and secular nationalists coexisted without ideological conflict, as a golden age of toleration that may be lost forever. Majid al-Sary, an Iraqi Shiite politician who believes, like Jefferson, that reason is the arbiter of truth, characterized the struggle for peace as a struggle against the resurgence of religious ideologies in Iraqi political life: "The [Iraqi elections of January 30, 2005] showed the strength of religious ideas here. I will stay and fight those bad ideas. It's changing from a fight against violence and explosions to a new category—thoughts."[10]

A category of believer that Huntington overlooked in his "clash of civilizations" **thesis** is the democratic religious pluralist, who seeks to build bridges between the West and traditional **religions** by appealing to universal human values. In his book, *What's Right with Islam*, Imam Feisal Abdul Rauf, who heads a major Islamic center in New York City, attempts to harmonize the values of Islam and the Enlightenment by tracing the roots of civil society to Abrahamic monotheism.[11] As part of his argument, he cites two fundamental

---

[6] Locke, *Letter Concerning Toleration*, quoted in Kuipers, *Critical Faith*, p. 17.
[7] See Samuel P. Huntington, *The Clash of Civilizations and the Remaking of the World Order* (New York: Touchstone Simon and Shuster, 1997)
[8] Ibid, pp. 184-206
[9] George Packer, "Letter from Basra: Testing Ground," *The New Yorker*, February 28, 2005, p. 45.
[10] Ibid
[11] See Imam Feisal Abdul Rauf, *What's Right with Islam A New Vision for Muslims and the West* (San Francisco: Harper Collins, 2004), pp. 11-40. Abdul Rauf's view of the Abrahamic roots of civil society echoes that of Karl Jaspers in *The Origin and Goal of History* (New Haven, Connecticut: Yale University Press, 1953).

principles of capitalism— the idea of usury as excessive interest and the concept of the corporation— as sources of world economic prosperity and hence of moral good.[12] As sources of moral good, these capitalist innovations are Islamic in spirit, if not in origin. By Islamizing Martin Luther's redefinition of usury and by introducing a legal concept that is not found in traditional Islamic law, Abdul Rauf tries to demonstrate how reason in the service of human interests can transcend the limitations of traditional religion. In doing so, he embraces the notion of utility espoused by Enlightenment thinkers such as Adam Smith, Jeremy Bentham and Thomas Jefferson. According to Utilitarianism, whatever promotes human happiness is good, whether or not it is mandated in a religious text. Abul Rauf's project can thus be seen as a redefinition of Islam in Enlightenment terms, in that reason is made the umpire of tradition in the pursuit of human happiness. In his attempt to construct a Reformed Islam on liberal democratic foundations he resembles the Jesuit theologian John Courtney Murray (1904-1967), who advocated a reformed Catholicism based on the liberal concepts of the separation of church and state, limited government, and religious freedom.[13] It remains to be seen whether Abdul Rauf's version of Reformed Islam will result in the revision of long-held principles, as Murray's American Catholicism did at Vatican II, or whether its non-traditional origins will render it unacceptable to the rest of the Muslim world.

However, the path away from violence and toward a more peaceful form of religious interaction involves more than just the acceptance of a new world order and the reform of civil society. Sometimes, the causes of religious violence are counter-intuitive. For his book, *The Colors of Violence*, the Indian psychiatrist Sudhir Kakar interviewed Hindu and Muslim participants and leaders of the Hyderabad communal riots of 1991, in which scores of Muslims and Hindus were killed in spasmodic orgies of retaliation. As part of his research, he prepared a questionnaire that elicited the moral limits imposed by each community upon itself. Kakar's findings indicate that religious violence often involves a complex interplay of social and psychological factors that may go against normative religious teachings. For example, the mere prospect of a Muslim girl going to the cinema with a Hindu boy elicited a more agitated response among Muslims than the prospect of a Muslim girl marrying a Hindu boy. This flies in the face of the fact that marriage to a non-Muslim is forbidden for women in the Qur'an, whereas going to the cinema or appearing in public with a non-Muslim is not forbidden as such. Nearly one third of Muslim respondents reacted to the prospect of a Muslim girl going to the cinema with a Hindu boy by saying that they would "have the girl killed, expecting the parents to quietly poison her, bury her alive, or themselves commit suicide."[14] It is such violent responses that are most strongly condemned by Islamic law and scripture, not the behaviors they are meant to prevent. Kakar's findings illustrate the important point made by Joseph Chuman in the present volume: That it is essential to separate "the religious factor from other dynamics— economic, political, ethnic, psychological and ideological— that comprise the matrix from which violence is spawned."[15]

For social theorists of religion such as Bruce Lincoln, the matrix is everything when it comes to the causes of religious violence. In a recent article, "Theses on Religion and Violence," he puts forth fourteen points that propose to answer why religious violence is

---

[12] Abdul Rauf, *What's Right with Islam*, p. 3
[13] The implicit comparison with Reformed Judaism in this paragraph is intentional.
[14] Sudhir Kakar, *The Colors of Violence: Cultural Identities, Religion, and Conflict* (Chicago and London: The University of Chicago Press, 1996), p. 135.
[15] Joseph Chuman, "Does Religion Cause Violence?" p. 24 below.

caused and why, once it begins, it is so difficult to stop.[16] Lincoln dismisses the psychopathological explanation of religious violence as holding "relatively little theoretical interest." Instead, he argues that the cause of religious violence is more or less the same as the cause of violence in general: It is competition over scarce resources. However, violent competition is not only over material resources. It may also be over non-material goods such as prestige, dignity, or justice. When a "non-material maldistribution" of resources is perceived as an injustice, and when religious discourse recodes a violent response to injustice as a righteous deed or sacred duty, the condition for religious violence is established. Lincoln is careful to note that no religious tradition is more or less inclined than any other to make arguments of this sort. He also notes that the politics of identity may exacerbate the tendency to promote violence in a religious community by recasting self-interest— which is criticized as selfishness in most religions— as group interest, such that it becomes a moral duty or a holy cause. The most dangerous situations occur not when the disadvantaged seek power, but when those who already enjoy disproportionate power persuade themselves through religious arguments that their exploitation of the disadvantaged other is "benevolent, meritorious, or holy."

A recent trend in moral philosophy has been an increased openness to the insights offered by the social sciences. This openness has provided benefits in two directions, by opening philosophy and theology to the results of empirical studies, and by reconnecting the social sciences to their philosophical roots. But whether Lincoln gets us any farther in understanding the root causes of religious violence than philosophers or theologians might have done is open to question. First of all, his fourteen theses appear to be irrelevant to the very events that he claims gave rise to them— the murder of Dutch filmmaker Theo Van Gogh and the American assault on the Iraqi city of Fallujah. Lincoln's refusal to consider seriously the psychological dimension of religious violence eliminates at the outset what may be the most useful explanation for the murder of Van Gogh. According to most accounts, Mohammed B., the Dutch-Moroccan arrested for the murder, was a culturally well-integrated second-generation Dutch Muslim who only turned radical when the projects he proposed failed to receive funding from the Dutch government. If these accounts are true, the perceived injustice that prompted his violence had more to do with the Freudian concept of "the narcissism of small differences" than it did with the unequal resources model used by Lincoln.[17] As for the American assault on Fallujah, apart from the fact that the city was a center of Jihadist opposition to the U.S. occupation of Iraq, it had nothing directly to do with religion at all. Certainly, there are important questions to be asked about the religious background of American political moralism and the policy, followed by the present U.S. administration, of evangelizing "freedom" throughout the world. But this is an ideological issue that is not addressed by Lincoln's functionalistic explanation of religious violence, whose theoretical roots lie not in the philosophy or theology of religion, but somewhere in the sociological hinterland between Marx and Weber.

Up to this point, our discussion of religion and violence has focused mostly on the issue of tolerance, and the problem of intolerance as a cause of religious violence. This is to be expected, because most investigations of religion and violence since the terrorist attacks of

---

[16] Bruce Lincoln, "Theses on Religion and Violence," *ISIM Review*, Leiden, The Netherlands, number 15, spring 2005, p. 12.

[17] See Seligman, *Modest Claims*, p. 60. This term comes from Freud's *Civilization and its Discontents*.

September 11, 2001 have revolved around the related problematics of tolerance and the negative image of the unbeliever, whether it is the infidel without or the heretic within. Major investigations of these questions have recently been undertaken by the office of the Archbishop of Canterbury (between Christians and Muslims), the Shalom Hartman Institute in Jerusalem (among Christians, Muslims, and Jews), and the Elijah Interfaith Institute (among Christians, Muslims, Jews, Hindus, and Buddhists), to name just a few. However, the articles that are presented in this volume also remind us that the problem of tolerance, although it is crucially important to the maintenance of world peace, is only one of several issues that are related to the question of religion and violence. The articles by Kenjitsu Nakagaki on "The Practice of *Ahimsa* in Buddhism," Katherine Young on "Non-Violence and Peace in Hinduism," Charlotte Coté on "Nonviolence and Conflict Resolution in Native American Traditional Systems of Justice," and other contributions take the investigation of religion and violence in important new directions. These include questions of internal power dynamics, the desire for social harmony, the concept of just war and ethical arguments against killing, the role of the state in creating the conditions for violence. the role of compassion and the elimination of pain and suffering, and the role played by ideological approaches to the question of violence, such as pacifism, ascetic world-denial, and mysticism.

One reason why theological issues have not been more widely discussed in studies of religion and violence is because of an aversion to polemics and apologetics. As Bruce Lincoln correctly observed, within each religious tradition one can find justifications for and against violence. For example, Hugh T. Halman's article on nonviolence in Islam cites several verses from the Qur'an that call for the peaceful resolution of conflict, such as: "Repel [evil] with what is better. Then the one between whom and you was hatred shall become as it were your friend and intimate" (41:34).[18] However, despite the existence of this and other verses in which God calls humanity to "the Abode of Peace" (10:25), Islam does not contain a systematic doctrine of nonviolence that can be compared to the Buddhist concept of *ahimsa*. This fact can all too easily lead an apologist for Buddhism to assume a condescending attitude toward Islam by maintaining that the lack of an explicit doctrine of nonviolence in the Qur'an somehow makes Islam more of a problem than Buddhism. This in turn leads the apologist for Islam to fall back on a "Me too" response to the Buddhist critique, in which one cites a laundry list of verses that ostensibly prove that the "real" spirit of Islam is both tolerant and nonviolent.

There are several problems with such religious one-upmanship. The first is that this practice is misleading, both for the person who tries to take the moral high ground and for the person who tries to play catch-up. In the example given above, the Buddhist apologist who presents an idealized version of Buddhist nonviolence ignores recent examples of violence committed by Buddhists, such as sectarian murders in the Tibetan community, violence by Sinhalese Buddhists against Tamils in Sri Lanka, and violence by Buddhist authorities against Muslims in southern Thailand. A more accurate approach would be to acknowledge that the realities of all religions, including Buddhism, do not always measure up to their ideals. Faced with a discrepancy between theory and practice, the Buddhist apologist is forced to resort to the same strategy as the Muslim apologist, whose claim that "Islam means peace" is belied by suicide bombings whose practitioners believe that their acts of terror will earn them a reward

---

[18] Hugh T. Halman, "Four Voices for Nonviolence and Peaceful Coexistence in South and Southeast Asia," p. 203 below

in heaven. Both apologists have no recourse other than to fall back on the claim that their violent co-religionists are not following "real" Buddhism or "real" Islam and that the essence of each religion is nonviolent.

But this response begs another set of questions. Even if Buddhism and Islam were essentially nonviolent, is it reasonable to assume that the only sincere Buddhists are monastic members of the *sangha* or that the only sincere Muslims are Sufis or liberals? Is there not a more basic problem, which has to do with the question of "Religion and Violence" itself? Can theory be separated from practice to such a degree that only ideals are discussed and realities are ignored? And what about differences of opinion within each tradition? Is there only one normative response to the question of "Islam and Violence," "Buddhism and Violence," or "Christianity and Violence?" If this is the case, are we not creating a new, albeit more peaceful and liberal, form of fundamentalism? To paraphrase the Turkish sociologist Nilüfer Göle, do we not run the risk of creating a parody of traditional religion by overemphasizing individual markers of moral identity, such that there is a rupture with traditional expressions of religion and a turn toward assimilation with the more "reasonable" ideals of secular modernity? Are we not merely avowing, "Islam is beautiful" or "Buddhism is beautiful" in the same way that we redefine cultural identities by avowing, "Black is beautiful" or "Women are beautiful?"[19]

The contributions to this volume attempt to answer many of the most difficult questions concerning religion and violence. At the same time, they chart a normative course toward new, more hopeful theological and moral perspectives that highlight the nonviolent aspects of each religious tradition. They avoid the pitfalls of the apologetic, "Me too" approach discussed above by implicitly acknowledging that in many cases, a turn toward an ethic of nonviolence requires a new approach to theology. This new theology requires a reconceptualization of the religious other in terms of a religious humanism that builds on traditional roots but moves in directions not contemplated by the majoritarian viewpoints of the past. Where the question of religious tolerance is concerned, a number of observers, such as Adam B. Seligman, have concluded that the way to this new humanism may be found in mystical perspectives that modern approaches to religion have dismissed as irrational.[20] According to Seligman, the value of mystical traditions is that they stress an "epistemic modesty," a sort of epistemological humility the leads the religious practitioner to restrain her desire to use moral and theological judgments as justifications for coercion.[21] In a remarkable and often overlooked passage from *Rights of Man*, Thomas Paine posits a similar type of humility as fundamental to the liberal democratic notion of freedom of conscience:

> Man worships not himself, but his Maker; and the liberty of conscience which he claims is not for the service of himself, but of his God. In this case, therefore, we must necessarily have the associated idea of two beings, the mortal who renders worship and the immortal being who is worshipped. Toleration therefore places itself not between man and man, nor between church and church, nor between one denomination of religion and another, but between God and man; between the being who worships and the being who is worshipped; and by the same act of assumed authority by which it tolerates man to pay his worship, it presumptuously and blasphemously sets up itself to tolerate the Almighty to receive it...

---

[19] Nilüfer Göle, "Islam as Ideology," in Seligman, *Modest Claims*, pp. 91-94.
[20] Seligman, *Modest Claims*, p. 119.
[21] Ibid, pp. 20 and 140.

Who art thou. vain dust and ashes. by whatever name thou art called. whether a king. a bishop. a church. or a state. a parliament or anything else. that obtrudest thine insignificance between the soul of man and his Maker? Mind thine own concerns. If he believes not as thou believest, it is a proof that thou believest not as he believeth. and there is no earthly power that can determine between you.[22]

There is a world of difference between Thomas Paine's theological justification for tolerance and Bernard de Mandeville's (1670-1733) suggestion in *The Fable of the Bees* that one should tolerate another because one might need his assistance at some future time. For Mandeville, who practiced what J. B. Schneewind has termed "mathematical morality," virtue no longer exists as a meaningful ideal.[23] Instead, virtue is explained away as part of a behavioral calculus in which the moral actions of man are performed for the sake of self-interest alone. Similar utilitarian arguments for enlightened self-interest have been made in the pursuit of non-violence. Utilitarianism changed the Golden Rule from "Do unto others as you would have them do unto you," to "Do not do unto others, lest they do unto you." While this is practical advice, it is hardly a moral precept.

For Paine, however, one refrains from doing violence to the person who does not share one's values not out of fear of retaliation, but simply because one is not God. One does not "tolerate" or suffer another to be different; rather, one accepts difference as part of God's plan. Epistemic modesty is found in the realization that since none of us is God we all share in the same limited knowledge of the truth. In a similar vein, the Spanish Sufi Ibn 'Arabi (d. 1240) said, "You are the one who becomes manifest to yourself, and this gives you nothing of [God] . . . You do not know other than yourself."[24] In the Abrahamic religions, the same logic that authorizes the acceptance of diversity prevents believers from doing violence to other human beings. In Islam, the concept of epistemic modesty means that to kill, harm, or punish another because of her beliefs is an act of arrogance, for such actions require the human being to arrogate to himself one or more of the characteristics of God.

According to Noel Sheth's article on the nonviolence of Mahatma Gandhi, Gandhi's practice of *ahimsa* reflected the concept of epistemic modesty through compassion, humility, and the acceptance of all religions and cultures.[25] Gandhi viewed nonviolence as an essential part of human nature, a natural virtue that is a consequence of the theological doctrines of the oneness of being, belief in God, and the interdependence of all living things. On the level of practice, nonviolence also involves the moral doctrines of universal brotherhood and the innate goodness of humanity. Gandhi's teachings remind us that a religious approach to nonviolence must be founded on a life-affirming theology and an optimistic view of human potential. This optimism is a key element in the mystical traditions of most world religions.

At the end of the fifteenth century, a Sufi from Granada named Ali Salih al-Andalusi (d. ca. 1508) outlined a theology of human potential that is relevant both to the question of

---

[22] Thomas Paine, *Rights of Man* (New York: Doubleday, 1961), p. 324, cited in Ibid, pp. 115-116.

[23] See J. B. Schneewind, *The Invention of Autonomy: A History of Modern Moral Philosophy* (Cambridge: Cambridge University Press, 1998), pp. 323-329. Schneewind uses the term "mathematical morality" in reference to Samuel Clarke (1675-1729), but it is equally applicable to Mandeville.

[24] William C. Chittick, *Imaginal Worlds: Ibn al-'Arabi and the Problem of Religious Diversity* (Albany, New York, 1994), p. 163. The passage comes from *Futuhat* (IV 421.34).

[25] Noel Sheth S. J., "The Nonviolence of Mahatma Gandhi," p. 59 below.

religion and violence and to the establishment of an ethic of nonviolence.[26] For Andalusi, theologies that push the envelope of normative religion do not undermine religion; rather, they complement formal religion by opening up the pragmatic perspective of the Law to the possibility of transcendence. The legalism of formal religion is necessary for maintaining the theological and ethical boundaries of the religious community. This perspective starts from a premise of weakness or inadequacy in the human being that must be overcome by training and discipline. This is why exoteric approaches to religion stress sincerity and personal effort and require outward conformity to the divine command. According to Andalusi, the epistemology of formal religion is nomocentric, in that it sees the Law as the ultimate criterion of knowledge, and is epitomized by the phrase, "We hear [and obey]." Insofar as it is meant to establish the limits of belief and practice, exoteric religion endorses the use of sanctions as a means of boundary maintenance.

Mysticism and the theology of human potential honor the same virtues as do exoteric theologies, but they proceed from a different premise. Rather than focusing on what people cannot do, they give greater attention to the transcendental potential of the human spirit. They start from the premise that human beings are by nature fully prepared to fulfill their role as God's vicegerents on Earth. The development of the spiritual person thus becomes a matter of education and character formation, rather than of mere training and discipline. For this reason, mysticism and the theology of human potential rely more on the pedagogies of love and nurturance than on disciplinary training, and concentrate on the inward assimilation— without rejecting the outward practice— of divine commands. Their epistemology is logocentric, in that it is based on a direct and unmediated knowledge of the divine Word. Whereas the exoteric practitioner of religion follows the dictate, "We hear [and obey]," the mystic or theologian of human potential responds, "We have witnessed [and understand]."

The optimism that characterizes Andalusi's theology of human potential is a result of the religious believer's ability to "see" and hence to understand God's will from a wider, universal perspective. This is why, according to Andalusi and apparently Gandhi as well, exoteric perspectives on religion need the transcendental leaven of esoterism as much as esoterism needs the water of exoterism to ground religious practices. Nonviolence, if it is to be made integral to religion, must be located within a tradition that goes beyond exoterism, yet remains fully rooted in the scriptures and doctrinal sources of religion itself. In Islam, this nonviolent perspective sees self and other as part of the same unity, according to the Qur'anic verse: "Oh humankind! Keep your duty to your Lord, who created you from a single soul, and created its mate from it and from whom issued forth many men and women. So revere the God by whom you demand rights from one another and revere the rights of the wombs" (4:1). From an exoteric point of view, the duty to revere the rights of the womb applies to biological kinship, such that Muslims must revere the duties and obligations of family membership before all else. But in a theology of human potential, this duty also refers to the greater kinship of the human species, since all of humankind, as the children of Eve, are born from the same womb. This wider duty pertains irrespectively of whether the other is one's biological kin or belongs to another race or religion.

---

[26] The discussion that follows is based on Abu al-Hasan Ali Salih al-Andalusi, *Sharh rahbat al-aman* (Rabat: Bibliothèque al-Hasaniyya, manuscript number 5697, 970/1562-3), pp. 4-20. The only discussion in print on Andalusi's doctrines can be found in Vincent J. Cornell, *Realm of the Saint: Power and Authority in Moroccan Sufism* (Austin, Texas: University of Texas Press, 1998), pp. 213-218.

However, the Qur'an does not only discuss duties, it also establishes a concept of rights, which are part of God's gift of grace to humanity. The bestowal of rights is a function of divine mercy, as expressed in the verse, "My mercy encompasses everything" (7:156). The concept of universal rights under God and the requirement to emulate God by applying mercy before any other duty provide another opening for an ethic of nonviolence in Islam. This opening to nonviolence is widened even further when it appears in the context of a theology of human potential. The most basic right in the Qur'an is the right to life: "Do not take a human life, which God has made sacred, other than as a right; this He has enjoined upon you so that you might think rationally" (6:151). The command to "revere the rights of the wombs" in verse 4:1 above alludes to another basic right, that of human dignity. If we are all born from the same womb, we are all brothers and sisters before God and hence can demand from each other the right to be treated with respect. Finally, the Qur'an affirms the right of free choice, without which the concept of divine judgment would be meaningless: "The truth is from your Lord. So whosoever wishes shall believe, and whosoever wishes shall disbelieve" (18:29). This is the "freedom of conscience" which Locke, Jefferson, and other Enlightenment thinkers advocated. In moral terms, it is the right to believe what one will; in legal terms, it is the right, not just to be right, but also to be wrong.

Several of the authors in this volume contribute to the discussion of religion and violence in ways similar to that just suggested, by identifying resources in different religions that promote nonviolence through the affirmation of life, dignity, freedom, and mercy. Even Joseph Chuman, who is primarily concerned with religion's potential for violence, acknowledges that external dynamics, and not essential religious teachings, are most often responsible for precipitating religious violence in specific contexts.[27] Neither violence nor nonviolence is endemic or essential to any religion. As Thomas Paine reminds us, violence and intolerance tend to occur when something external— whether ideology, nationalism, legalism, narcissism, or some other form of -ism— "obtrudes its insignificance between the soul of man and his Maker."

The task in formulating an interreligious approach to nonviolence is thus twofold: We must heed Joseph Chuman's warning not to romanticize religious traditions by "claiming for them a benevolence that they do not frequently merit in practice."[28] However, those who still believe in the truths conveyed by religion should not simply capitulate to the Enlightenment conception of reason as the only path to rationality. The religious person should not forget that, as a unique combination of spirit and matter, the human being is a *pontifex*, a builder of bridges between worlds. Beneath the differences that obtain between religious doctrines, sacred laws, and worldviews, all human beings share the same transcendental nature; all have access to the "words," be they divine or human, which allow them to communicate across conceptual divides. Because the human being is a bridge-builder, it is unreasonable to assume that differences are insurmountable or that new theologies stressing peace and human potential cannot be formulated. If scholars and practitioners of different religions cannot come to an understanding, it means that one or both of them are lacking in spiritual insight, or that one or both of them are in error. If only one party is in error, there is still the chance that the other is not in error, and that their doctrines may be reconciled. If both parties are in error, it means that the Enlightenment critics of religion may have been right in assuming that faith

---

[27] Chuman, "Does Religion Cause Violence?" p. 24 below.
[28] Ibid, p. 37 below

is a treacherous path to the truth. The stakes in this debate are high— so high, in fact, that the very relevance of religion as a means to the realization of human potential is in question. However, the challenge put to religion by the Enlightenment may be severe, but it is not unfair. For among the rights bestowed upon us by God, the right *not* to understand is nowhere to be found.

SECTION I

In: Religion, Terrorism and Globalization
Editor: K.K. Kuriakose, pp.15-30

ISBN 1-59454-553-7

Chapter 1

DOES RELIGION CAUSE VIOLENCE?

Joseph Chuman
Columbia University, New York, NY

THE INTERNATIONAL RELIGIOUS RESURGENCE

Among the most dramatic and unpredicted phenomena of the past thirty years has been the resurgence of religion on the world scene. Defying secularization theorists who predicted that religion would increasingly retreat to the margins of society in the wake of industrialization, modernization and scientific development, religion has returned with energy born of four centuries of relative privatization and rejection from the political sphere. Not only has religion challenged the presumptions of the liberal secular state, it has forced itself on the world with paroxysms of violence which have dashed the hopes that the close of humankind's bloodiest century would usher in a new epoch of peace.

Clearly not all violence is fomented by religion, nor is religion a salient factor in much of the world's recent conflicts. The wars raging in Congo, in which up to four million people have perished, are waged along primarily tribal lines and reflect brute power struggles, in which religious difference plays no significant role. The Shining Path guerillas of Peru engaged in terror, as do Basque separatists and narco-terrorists in Colombia, but religion is not a factor in this violence.

Nevertheless, the fusion of religion and politics has found expression in each of the world's historical religions. In India, Hindu nationalists seek to replace the official secular ideology of the state with the doctrine of "Hindutva" and a new explicitly Hindu constitution. The result has been an invigorated outbreak of mass violence targeting the Muslim minority, and to a lesser extent directed at Christians. In Sri Lanka, the government dominated by Sinhalese Buddhists has been embroiled in an egregiously terroristic struggle with the Tamil Hindu minority, a conflict sanctioned by sectors of the Buddhist priesthood. In the West Bank, religious Messianists comprise the trenchant hard core of the settler movement as suicide bombings and Israeli retaliation remain continual occurrences of that tragic conflict. While power sharing has diminished Catholic-Protestant strife in Ulster, the peace is fragile and sporadic violence remains a looming possibility. In the United States, the rise of politicized evangelical and fundamentalist Christianity has moved the political landscape far to the right. Though the Christian right has not been violent on the domestic scene, it has provided the context within which members of extremist fringe groups have been empowered to murder doctors providing abortions and has given sanction to violence-prone militia groups touting racist and anti-Semitic propaganda. On the American foreign relations front, Christian evangelicals comprise the largest constituency for the invasion of Iraq, in part legitimating that support via theological rationales linked to Armageddon End Times scenarios.

It is the awakening of politicized Islam, especially since the Iranian revolution of 1979, that has evoked new challenges and has spurred thinking about role of religion in the international political theater. The list of violent acts against American targets, or perceived surrogates of Western hegemonic interests, committed in the name of Islam is long - from the assassination of Anwar Sadat by the Egyptian Islamic Group in 1981, though the killing of foreign tourists at Luxor in the 1990s to the state sponsored terrorism of Iran, to the Islamic Jihad groups in the Occupied Territories. With Hizbollah in Lebanon and the brutal and terroristic civil war sustained by fundamentalists in Algeria, the list grows to include post 9/11 assaults in Bali, Tunisia and Morocco. Inclusive of attacks on American identified targets both at home and abroad have been the first assault on the World Trade Center in 1993, bombings in Riyadh, Saudi Arabia in 1995, the Khobar Towers attack in 1996, the destruction of United States embassies in Tanzania and Kenya in 1998, the USS Cole in Yemen in October 2000, culminating in the destruction of the World Trade Center and assault on the Pentagon.

The latter unprecedented attack on America launched the "war against terrorism", the pursuit of the Al Qaeda network worldwide, and the routing of their Taliban hosts in Afghanistan while providing justification for the invasion and occupation of Iraq.

In great measure the return of religion reflects a crisis of modernity and dissatisfaction in broad sectors of the developing world with the failure of the liberal secular state to sustain adequate standards of living and provide a framework of hope for more bountiful futures. It's a condition severely aggravated by the disparities wrought by rapid globalization. In the Arab world, in particular, the promise of Western secular governments has transmogrified into oppressive military dictatorships in many cases sustained by American support. Secularism, touted as a vehicle toward development in the early phases of the post-colonial era, is now perceived as a looming vestige of imperialism. Despair with secular government, both liberal and Marxist, originating in the West, has inspired the call for cultural liberation rooted in religion and movements to replace secular nationalism with various agendas propounding religion-based nationalism.

THE QUESTION OF RELIGION AND VIOLENCE

With the demise of hostilities following the collapse of the Soviet Union in 1991 and the end of the Cold War, theorists see the alliance to religion and its resurgence as filling the vacuum of political loyalties, thus establishing a new framework governing international relations. According to political theorists such as Samuel Huntington and Mark Jurgensmeyer, we are confronting "a clash of civilizations" and a "new Cold War" replacing the paradigms of bi-lateralism and the policy of containment that dominated relations between the West and the Soviet bloc for the past half-century.[1] Religion is the anchor of this new framework, for as Huntington alleges, "religion is the central characteristic of civilizations..."[2] suggesting that religion is a dominant engine of violence.

The religious resurgence and the growth of violence and terror committed in religion's name bring into relief the issue of religion's dynamic relationship to violence. The specific question of whether religion causes violence is the focal inquiry of this essay, recognizing that in these times we cannot avoid placing the religious factor in the forefront of analysis if obstacles to peace are to be overcome.

We are confronted straightaway with the knotty problem of teasing out the religious factor from other dynamics – economic, political, ethnic, psychological and ideological – which comprise the matrix from which violence is spawned. Human motivation is never mono-causal, but is a product of a complex of dynamics and contexts. Is religion a root cause of violence? Does it function primarily as a legitimator of violence, the causes of which are rooted in other dynamics? Or in violence between different religious groups, does religion serve merely as marker identifying the boundaries between groups? In short, is religion an effective cause of violence, or is its role epiphenomenal?.

In this regard, the typology presented by political theorists, Andreas Hasenclever and Volker Rittberger is instructive. They sketch three possible roles in assessing religion's place in violent conflict. *Primordialists* see religion as an important independent variable in spurring violence. "Collectives at the national as well as international level tend to form alliances around common cosmologies and tensions arise and escalate primarily between alliances with different cosmologies."[3] The primordial view, so described, coheres with "the clash of civilizations" hypothesis. For *instrumentalists*, religious differences can aggravate arenas of conflict, but conflict is "rarely if ever caused by them." Violence would have been caused in any event, driven by economic and other factors. For *moderate constructivists*, religion is a motive force in engendering violence – or forestalling it. Religion provides legitimation when other factors are present in violence prone situations, and religious leaders can either provide that legitimation or withhold it. Instrumentalists and moderate constructivists both agree that political and economic forces are primary in the fostering of inter-group violence. And both concur that wars cannot be initiated without leadership elites. Yet for the latter, appeals to religious rhetoric and motivations are not unlimited. According to Hasenclever and Rittberger, while instrumentalists "...suggest that, ultimately, determined leaders can manipulate religious traditions at will and that the justification of violence is at best rhetorical but not a substantial problem, moderate constructivists insist that religious traditions are intersubjective structures that have a life of their own."[4] In other words, religion is an "intervening variable" whose influence can lead to violence or to peaceful accommodation.

This cluster of issues raises a second core problem: In order to assess the power of religion to motivate violence, we must ask how religion operates in the lives of its adherents. I

---

[1] Samuel P. Huntington, *The Clash of Civilizations* (Cambridge: Cambridge University Press, 1999) Mark Juergensmeyer, *The New Cold War?* (Berkeley and Los Angeles, 1993).

[2] Huntington, p. 47.

[3] Andreas Hasenclever and Volker Rittberger ,"Does Religion Make a Difference? Theoretical Approaches to the Impact of Faith on Political Conflict"in Fbio Petito and Pavlos Hatzopoulos, eds. *Religion in International Relations* (New York: Palgrave MacMillan, 2003), p. 108.

[4] ibid., p.104.

have found that in many contemporary discussions of religion, there is often neglect of the functional nuances of religion. Many commentators impose upon the category of religion an implied monlithicism that neglects the reality that religion is highly differentiated force from religion to religion, from adherent to adherent and within the hearts and minds of individual believers. The nuanced and differentiated nature of religion, I contend, is a prerequisite for understanding its relationship to violence.

RELIGION, THICK AND THIN

Religious and secular dispositions and actions comprise a dynamic mix in both individuals and collectives. There is a descending slope from the pervasively religious to the secular with innumerable intervening gradations, though no human behavior can be construed as purely religious or wholly secular. Within highly religious traditional cultures the intrusion of practical concerns, inclusive of strategies for survival, mercantile activity, and the pursuit of prevailingly pragmatic interests etc., ensure the infusion of non-religious modes of thought and behavioral motivators. Contrawise, even the most secular of individuals and cultures harbor values that transcend empirical verification and rational analysis, and so in the wider sense can be understood as religious, though not so named. Consequently, the determination of religion as a root cause of violence, or its prevailing cause, requires an analysis of the pervasiveness of the religious factor amid a range of intersecting motivators within individuals and groups.

The ability of religion to serve as a substantial resource of human behavior is a theme richly explored in the social sciences. Freud's polemical assault on religion as the leading competitor with the scientific weltanschauung, and its role in providing consolation in the face of existential hardships, bespeaks its inspirational power.[5] For Clifford Geertz religion is "a system of symbols which acts to establish powerful, pervasive, and long lasting moods and motivations in men by formulating conceptions of a general order of existence and clothing these conceptions with such an aura of factuality that the moods and motivations seem uniquely realistic."[6] The motivational factor of religion and its realism is such that "It alters, often radically, the whole landscape presented to common sense, alters it in such a way that the moods and motivations induced by religious practice seem themselves supremely practical, the only sensible ones to adopt given the way things 'really' are."[7] For Mircea Eliade, the human being is a *homo religiosus* who strives to live primordially in a sacralized cosmos. Within the consciousness of the religious person of archaic societies the religious sphere is the "really real", the realm of power which he is propelled to seek.[8] And for Emile Durkheim, religion is a dynamic concept fueled by the collective power of the group on which the individual depends.[9]

---

[5] See especially Sigmund Freud, *The Future of an Illusion* (Garden City: Anchor, 164) ch. 7and *New* Introductory *Lectures on Psychoanalysis,* lecture xxxv.

[6] Clifford Geertz, "Religion as a Cultural Symbol" *The Interpretation of Cultures* (Basic Books: 1973) p. 90.

[7] ibid., p.122.

[8] The dichotomization of reality into sacred and profane space and time is foundational to Eliade's theory of religion. See Mircea Eliade, *The Sacred and Profane* (San Diego, New York. London: Harcourt Brace and Company, 1987.

[9] Emile Durkheim, *The Elementary Forms of the Religious Life* (New York: Collier Books, 1961).

It is significant to note that the definitions and descriptions of religion of these classical thinkers are drawn from traditional societies, and not from the advanced industrialized world which has experienced pervasive secularization. Under the force of modernization, the religious element will be diluted by other motivators, and its role significantly pushed to the background. Yet, as these thinkers have clearly established, religion, as expressed prevailingly through myth and ritual, can serve as a powerful root cause motivating behavior. This power results, moreover, from religion's ability to banish chaos and its resultant anxiety, while locating the individual within the framework of an ordered universe. The question I now turn to is whether religion is inherently violent or contains combustible elements which readily burst into violence with requisite stimulus.

For many theorists, there are elements distinctive to religion that make it especially dangerous. Borrowing from the theologian, Paul Tillich, Lloyd Steffen identifies religion with that which is ultimately transcendent. Because religion incorporates ultimacy at its core it "opens up a realm of power like no other."[10] "Religion can motivate and sanction violence, having the power sufficient to legitimate harmful acts in a realm of ultimate meaning and through ultimate authority."[11] While ultimacy can point humans beings toward the good, and be a potent source of human flourishing, for Steffen, religion turns malignant when ultimacy is identified with absolutism. The Absolute, which is all encompassing, envelops both the good and all that opposes the good. When absolute evil becomes ultimate, hatred, destruction and violence take on religious meaning. A discrete religion which appeals to the Absolute also becomes the locus for the assertion of its own positive identity to the exclusion of those deemed to be "outsiders." Hence religion becomes the venue *par excellence* for dividing good from evil, those blessed by God from the accursed, the saved from the damned, the believer from the heretic. This capacity to create divisions between communities renders religion a powerful agent in fomenting xenophobia and xenophobic violence. When religious minorities reside within a dominant culture their juxtaposition, coupled with differences in worldviews, can grow fractious as a result of cognitive dissonance that emerges between the groups. Moreover, absolute justice is divine justice, and no power commands with the authority and power of one's commanding God. The divine mandate to slay the infidel is poised to resist compromise and subordination to any earthbound requirement.

For Sigmund Freud, religion is essentially violent. Freud made use of the leading social science of his day, borrowing from the thought of Charles Darwin, James Frazier and Emile Durkheim, among others. Though his theory of religious origins is dated, it finds a place in the canon of the sociology of religion.

Freud envisions a primal horde living under the rule of an authoritarian father, who appropriates the females of the tribe.[12] The brothers arise to slay the primal father whom they subsequently cannibalize. Motivated by guilt, the brothers establish a totem, which they both venerate and fear, while creating a taboo against incest. For Freud religion is an edgy affair. Religious devotion is aligned with the repressive moral functions vested in the superego that heighten intra-psychic tension and seek release. Behind religion, and masked from the contemporary believer in metaphor and symbol, is the act of the primal parricide. At its core, religion is driven by aggression and violence.

---

[10] Llloyd Steffen, *The Demonic Turn* (Cleveland: The Pilgrim Press, 2003) p.39.
[11] ibid., p. 37.
[12] Freud's most elaborate rendering of his theory of religious origins is found in *Totem and Taboo* (W.W. Norton and Company. Inc: New York, 1950).

Rene Girard carries forward the Freudian approach to religion. For Girard the dynamics of aggression and sex are replaced by mimetic desire. As he notes, "Two desires converging on the same object are bound to clash. Thus, mimesis coupled with desire leads automatically to conflict."[13] Whenever the disciple borrows from his model what he believes to be the 'true' object he tries to possess that truth by desiring precisely what the model desires. Whenever he sees himself closest to the supreme goal, he comes into violent conflict with his rival."[14] The purpose of religion is to divert this violence-laden desire and render it harmless. Speaking of religious practice, Girard concludes, "The idea of ritual purification is far more than mere shadow play or illusion. The function of ritual is to 'purify' violence, that is to 'trick' violence into spending itself on victims whose death will provoke no reprisals."[15] Again, we observe that religion is played out in symbolic form cloaking its fundamentally violent character.

Moving beyond essentialist theories to the manifest content of religious myth, it is noted that the scriptures of world religions are replete with values that are life and peace affirming, while in other places they invoke martial metaphors, military conflict, and divinely sanctioned killing. The Ten Commandments prohibit murder. (Exodus 20:13). The Book of Psalms enjoins believers to "Depart from evil, and do good; seek peace, and pursue it." (Psalms 34:15). The Hebrew prophets Micah and Isaiah describe Messianic times as period wherein "they shall beat their swords into pruning hooks: nation shall not lift up a sword against nation, neither shall they learn war anymore." (Micah 4:3, Isaiah 2:4).

In The New Testament, Jesus is a messenger of peace. "Blessed are the peacemakers, for they shall be called sons of God." (Matthew 5:9). "...if anyone hits you on the right cheek, offer him the other as well." (Matthew 5:19). "For he is our peace, who has made us both one, and has broken down the dividing wall of hostility..." (Ephesians 2:14).

But we find in both the Jewish and Christian scriptures passages that can be employed to justify violence and war making. In the Hebrew bible, it is written, "the Lord is a warrior." (Exodus 15:3). After the Israelites enter the Promised Land under the leadership of Joshua, God commands the extermination of the resident population inclusive of "men and women, young and old, oxen, sheep and donkeys" thus giving license to divinely sanctioned genocide (Josh. 6:21). In Exodus and Deuteronomy, the children of Amalek are defined as Israel's perpetually enemy, "The Lord's war against Amalek is from generation to generation" (Ex 17.14,16; Deut. 25.17-19). Despite later interpretation, the Gospel is not wholly pacifistic. Jesus proclaims that he had "not come to bring peace to the world, but a sword" (Matt 10:34). The final text of the Christian canon, the Book of Revelation, is a kaleidoscope of phantasmagoric images centered on apocalyptic war between the legions of the blessed and the legions of Satan culminating in final judgment and the establishment of a new heaven and earth.

In Islam, *jihad* or striving, is a central aspirational concept of Muslim life. Those who portray Islam as a religion of peace will underscore a spiritual interpretation of *jihad* as striving for a moral and virtuous life in submission to the will of God. Such spokespersons will invoke Muhammad's proclamation on returning from battle. "We return from the lesser *jihad* to the greater *jihad*." Or when referring to martial conflict, will invoke the Koran's commitment to defensive war. "And fight in the way of God with those who fight you, but

---

[13] Rene Girard, *Violence and the Sacred* (Baltimore and London: Johns Hopkins University Press, 1977) p. 146.
[14] ibid., p. 148.
[15] ibid., p. 36.

aggress not: God loves not the aggressors." (2:190) But Mohammed is not solely an administrator and prophet. He is also a military leader who vanquishes neighboring tribes. (e.g 8:6). Citations drawn from the Koran have also been used to justify *jihad* for expansionist and aggressive purposes, including terrorist assault on the stated enemies of the Islamic *ummah*. "When the sacred months have passed, slay the idolators wherever you find them, and take them, and confine them, and lie in wait for them in every place of ambush." (9:5) In Islam, as with all the traditions, text and mythos can be employed for multiple purposes and are endowed with multiple meanings that elude definite interpretation from which there can be no dissent. Words, in the final analysis, are sanctioned by their use.

The Vedas, the most sacred scripture of Hinduism, has warriors calling on the gods to engage in their own violent conflicts. Perhaps the most beloved of Hindu epics, the *Bhagavad Gita* is a military saga that validates *dharmic* responsibility for killing. Buddhism is arguably the most pacifistic of all the great religions, yet, violence is permitted under certain limited circumstances. The Pali Chronicles of Sri Lanka, which have assumed scriptural significance, tell of the battles waged by early Buddhist kings.[16]

In times of relative tranquility, when religious cultures are not pressed by economic austerity or political challenges, military myths can be read metaphorically as inspirational sources by which to engage in spiritual struggle. In times of stress, by contrast, material otherwise interpreted metaphorically can be transmogrified into a call for literal violence against external enemies. As Mark Juergensmeyer reminds us, religious war is cosmic war. [17] It is violence tied to divine command, and what would otherwise be interpreted as a merely political cause, becomes a sacred cause, an eternal cause to which all other interests are subordinated. The cosmic character of religious warfare also accounts for its often-expressed dramatic and symbolic manifestation.

The discussion until this point has been of "thick" religion, implying that religion is a root motivator of human behavior, inclusive of violent behavior. Yet, central to my thesis is the assumption that religion is never of this unalloyed character. It is always intermixed with practical and secular concerns that dilute its strength. This political fact suggests that heterogeneous cultures require and are based upon the infusion of secular values to remain viable, orderly and cooperative. In a globalized world, experiencing the "universalization of particularisms",[18] this interpenetration of non-religious values into religious life at virtually all levels has become inescapable. Religious cultures are today increasingly, and in many instances, pervasively, exposed to forms of economic organization, bureaucratic management, high technology, and political discourse inclusive of the secular and universal values of human rights which emerge, in great measure, from outside those cultures and carry a prevailing instrumental and non-religious valance. The contemporary religious resurgence is, therefore, in great measure, reactive to the imposition of globalized values, with which it is inextricably interdependent. This ensures, that however ostensibly parochial the religious reaction, and however intense, resurgent forms of religion and the communities inspired by them lack the organic character of traditional religion. They are ineliminably infused with secular values, diminishing the univocal power of religion in motivating behavior.

---

[16] Juergensmeyer, *The New Cold War?* p. 158.

[17] ibid., pp. 156-163.

[18] See Robert McCorquodale and Richard Fairbrother, "Globalization and Human Rights" in *Human Rights Quarterly* 21.3 (1999) p. 724.

Political scientist, Benjamin Barber, has speculated on the dialectics of globalization and the reactions it has spawned in the form of communal and religious resurgence. In Barber's analysis, the forces of modernization, Westernization and globalization, the forces of "McWorld", are inseparably yoked to the emergent parochial backlash, termed "Jihad." Yet, the phenomenon of contemporary reactive religion is not pre-modern, for it is ineluctably apiece with the dynamics of modernization.

> Jihad stands not so much in stark opposition as in subtle counterpoint to McWorld and is itself a dialectical response to modernity whose features both reflect and reinforce the modern world's virtues and vices – Jihad *via* McWorld rather than Jihad *versus* McWorld.[19]

The interpenetration of the new communalism with the dynamics of modernity ensures that religion is more accessible to transformation, more unstable, more of an elective and contractual phenomenon than organic. This mitigating factor opens the possibility for evolving accommodation with the values that make for cooperation and peace, which I explore at the conclusion of this essay.

The role of religion within the psychological framework of the individual roughly parallels the situation involving collectives. Human personalities as well as groups harbor sentiments that are differentiated in their structure.[20] Religious thoughts and emotions can be complex and held by the believer in ways that encompass reflection, criticism and reworked interpretation. While religion claims to be the most comprehensive of interest systems, it is not the only interest system that drives and inspires behavior. Human beings, as noted, are motivated by physical needs and employ pragmatic strategies necessary to ensure survival, as well as modes of ratiocination that have little to do with religion. While the culture in which an individual lives out his or her life may be deeply influenced by religion, the processes and dynamics of mercantile activity, domestic maintenance and the manipulation of the accessories of the workplace may bear little relevance to religious values per se. They are primarily secular in content, and serve, no less, to inform the personalities of individuals. Moreover, we may speculate that if the religious impulse is rooted in human temperament, no less is the impulse toward skepticism, all of which tends to mitigate the power of religion as a motivator.[21]

Beyond the operation of religious dynamics within the personalities of individual believers, a point that needs greater attention is that the appropriation of a religious identity differs in intensity from person to person. The affirmation of a religious identity can imply deep commitment to a religious life, inclusive of belief, ritualized behaviors and deference to religious authority, reinforced by immersion in a thick religious culture. On the opposite end of the belief spectrum, a religious identity may signify little more than a formality that is passively held. In such cases, religious motivation for behavior may be small or not appreciably existent.

The assessment of whether religion "causes" violence, rests, therefore in great measure on whether the subject is religious in the "thick" or "thin" sense. Without positing that

---

[19] Benjamin Barber, *Jihad vs. McWorld* (Balantine Books: New York, 1996) p. 157.
[20] See Gordon W. Allport The *Individual and His Religion*, ((MacMillan Publishing Co., Inc.: New York, 1974) pp. 65-71.
[21] Speculation on the innateness of skepticism has been discussed by the contemporary science writer and atheist, Natalie Angier. See "Confessions of a Lonely Atheist", *New York Times Magazine*, Janaury 14, 2001.

religious is epiphenomenal in motivating action, including violence, I conclude that in most cases we need to look for ulterior dynamics – economic, political, ethnic, historical and especially the pursuit of power-- as the primary sources for violence between peoples, including war. The causal role of religion in conflict is, as suggested, dependent upon the pervasiveness of religion in the culture and the actors involved. My conclusion is that religion can be a contributing cause of violence, but more often serves as a legitmator of violence, which springs from other sources. Religious differences, can, moreover, be manipulated by elites to further justify violence. Whereas religion can identify the differences between groups, by demarking their respective shared cosmologies, religion requires the "spark" of underlying, more materially based causes in order to burst into violence.

This analysis moves me away from the primordialist camp, and closer to the position of moderate constructivists. Here the observations of Hasenclever and Rittberger are again useful.

> Moderate constructivists...propose to view religion as an intervening variable, i.e., as a causal factor intervening between a given conflict and the choice of conflict behavior. In this way, the impact of religious traditions on conflict behavior is deeply ambiguous: They can make violence more likely, insofar as a reading of holy texts prevails that justifies armed combat; on the other hands, they can make violence less likely, insofar as a reading of holy texts prevails that delegitimizes the use of violence in a given situation or generally.[22]

RELIGION -- UNIVERSAL, PAROCHIAL AND ROMANTIC

The salience of the religious factor in current politics, and its fretful role as a legitimator of violence, raises the crucial question of the relative potentials for religion as an agent for inter-group cooperation, and as a force for peace. My analysis to this point suggests that religion can be a substantive dynamic in bending political conflicts in the direction of active violence or its avoidance - and we would hope, optimally, toward brotherhood and cooperation. Yet, to the extent that religion can be teased out as an independent variable, we may appropriately ask whether the religious factor is weighted more toward one end of the spectrum than the other. Even if we allow for the secularizing dynamics, both individual and collective, underscored by the "thinning" tendencies wrought by the influences of modernization and globalization, my own assessment of the role of religion is that it more readily allies itself with the forces of violence than with those of cooperation and peacemaking.

Religious apologists ubiquitously put forward the socially and ethically salutary values of the historical traditions –the affirmation of human dignity, their commitment to brotherhood, their prophetic commitments to the poor, marginalized and disenfranchised. In these times of vehement polemical assault on secularism, religion is positioned as providing salvific and necessary structures of meaning. The rise of religion out of the despair of secular culture allows for the wielding of great rhetorical and effective power in both the developed and developing world. In the American context this has resulted in a progressive dismantling of

---

[22] Hasenclever and Rittberger, p. 115.

the "wall of separation" between church and state, and attendant disenchantment with secular government.

I do not gainsay the universal values of religion and their propensity to foster respect and brotherhood necessary for a peaceful world order. Nor do I underestimate the central importance of religious values and teachings in shaping culture, often toward beneficent social ends. The inspiration of the "*philosophia perennis*" has notably served to motivate the activism of stewards of the prophetic tradition yielding for humankind its most noble exemplars.[23] It is often -- and correctly -- noted that it is a mistake to identify religion with extremism and fundamentalism.

At the same time, I maintain the resurgence of religion on the contemporary scene has caused many, both religious apologists and secular critics outside the traditions, to romanticize religion while claiming for it a benevolence that it does not frequently merit in practice. The promotion of religion in our times suffers from intellectual essentialism. Too often religious teachings (frequently cherry picked from scriptures for apologetic purposes) are upheld at the expense of more penetrating critiques of how these teachings function when deployed through the necessary media of social practice. In short, religious teaching, if it is to find expression in the real world, cannot avoid being molded by political concerns and psychological processes, dynamics beholden to the vagaries of the quests for security and power.

As a broad generalization, religious belief, and practices related to it, are strewn between two opposing poles: The universal pole, reflected in the noble teachings of the traditions, constitutive of brotherhood, respect for the sacredness of all human beings, commitment to tolerance and regard for the stranger; the opposing pole, which conduces toward the communal and the parochial, toward the longing to feel at home with others who share common histories, values and ways of life.

For Durkheim, communal bondedness is constitutive of religion, and it is defined by the function of uniting people of common belief into a group. Religion is revelatory of humankind's social nature to which it seeks to give expression. As Durkheim observed,

> The really religious beliefs are always common to a determined group, which makes profession of adhering to them and of practising the rites connected with them. They are not merely received individually by all members of this group; they are something belonging to the group, and they make it a unity. The individuals which compose it feel themselves united to each other by the simple fact that they have a common faith. [24]

For contemporary theorists, such as Robert Bellah, religion serves as a source of social solidarity strengthened through an evocation of common memories. [25]In Juergensmeyer's view, those sharing religious belief are bound through a common "ideology of order" reinforced by the appeal to a transcendent, absolute and unchanging realm. As he notes,

---

[23] One cannot understand the political activism of Mohandas Gandhi apart from his commitments as a devout but reforming Hindu. Likewise, Martin Luther King's political mission can only be adequately grasped through an understanding of his rootedness in the African-American Baptist Church. For a treatment of the religious sources of Gandhi's political philosophy, see Dennis Dalton, *Mahatma Gandhi* (Columbia University Press: New York, 1993). For a brief sketch of King's intellectual and religious sources see James Cone, "The Theology of Martin Luther King, Jr." *Union Theological Quarterly Review* volume xl, number 4, 1980.

[24] Durkheim, p. 59.

[25] Robert Bellah et al., *Habits of the Heart* (Perennial Library: New York, 1985) p. 114.

"Members of these communities...share a tradition, a particular world-view, in which the essential conflict between appearance and deeper reality is described in specific and characteristically cultural terms. This deeper reality has a degree of permanence and order quite unobtainable by ordinary means."[26] For Juergensmeyer, secular nationalism can play this role, and so in the modern context competes with religious loyalties. Yet, one can legitimately argue that when it does so, secular nationalism, to that extent, functions religiously.

The unifying and identity building power of religion cannot be underestimated. For the Christian devotee, engaging in the rite of the Eucharist binds the believer together with all of his co-religions in space and time. Vertically she is united with all Christians everywhere; and with all fellow believers extending from the Last Supper to the Second Coming. The resonance of such ritual with the mythopoeic propensities of mind and imagination serve to strengthen the power of communalism all the more. Human beings are narrative beings who dwell in their narratives. The ability of religion to satisfy the existential needs for meaning, identity, rootedness in an absolute and unchanging reality and for social solidarity are explicative of its appeal and power in creating communal cohesion.

These centripetal vectors of religion are directly proportional to its ability to separate insiders from outsiders, and intensify the divisions between those blessed by God and those who are damned. The stage is set, as noted, for xenophobia, and when ignited by the political and economic tensions, violence. In threatening environments, even small differences can be magnified to serve as causes for inter-group strife.

In contrast to these dynamics, the positive resources found in religious teachings, which work to engender respect across parochial lines, I argue, are relatively weak. It should be noted, moreover, that there is no "religion-in-general." There are only specific religions with their distinctive ways of life, and concrete values rooted in their specific cultures. [27] Hence, all commitments to universal values, by necessity, are perceived from *within* religious communities and are winnowed, and often diverted by values and concerns that are themselves parochial. In this sense, it is perhaps not surprising that when religious groups have agitated for religious freedom, it is most often for sake of the group itself; the freedom of other religious communities have mattered far less. Despite the fact that it is undertaken with universalistic rhetoric, the ecumenical project initiated by many faiths in the past three decades is often tentative and fragile. And the religions, for the most part, have been slow to adopt the international human rights agenda, premised, as it is, on universal values. In the final analysis, the religions, for the most part, are interest groups, which, more often than not, are governed by the impulse to protect their respective turfs.

---

[26] Juergensmeyer, *The New Cold War?* (University of California Press: Berkeley and Los Angeles, 1993) p. 26.
[27] For a discussion of the misplaced value of "religion-in-general" within the debate over foundations for human rights, see the international legal theorist Louis Henkin, "Religion, Religions and Human Rights" *Journal of Religious Ethics* volume 26.2 fall, 1998.

THE TRANSFORMATION OF RELIGION INTO A FORCE FOR PEACE: DIALOGUE, DEVELOPMENT AND DEMOCRACY

Globalization, as its critics note, has further widened the disparities between the wealthy and the desperately poor. It has favored neo-capitalist accumulation and broadened the hegemonic presence of Western values. But despite backlashes that have revived religious cultures, it has ensured that all cultures have been brought closer together and have been increasing permeated with modernizing elements. The Princeton scholar of religion, Cornel West, has noted that all cultures are a product of "radical hybridity" and this is especially true under the forces of globalization currently operative.[28] The purity of "culture", in my view, is itself another romantic fallacy very much in evidence among contemporary critics and activists. If globalization is defined by the spread of economic markets, it is no less defined by the pervasiveness of new communication technologies and the salience of the human rights culture together with its attendant universal norms. These elements can work to assuage the insular forces that set the stage for the transmogrification of religion into a catalyst for violence.

My argument to this point has been that as a discrete social and psychological phenomenon, the power of religion to bind people into an "in" group is a more powerful motivator than the universalizing values found in the traditions. But, as noted, these respective religious potentials can become resources for war or peace dependent on the political and economic environments in which the religious culture is played out.

This analysis, therefore, opens the door to strategies that will help ensure that the religions can be harnessed as peacemakers, as opposed to the divisive markers and influences that have enabled inter-group violence, war and genocide. Among these strategies are the pursuit of dialogue among the religions, the fostering of economic development, especially as it benefits the poor and marginalized sectors of society, and the strengthening of democracy, on both national and local levels.

By invoking these secular strategies, I am not asserting a secular ideology as hegemonic. My thesis recognizes the continuously coextensive and mutually interactive relationship of religion and secular values. What I do maintain is that in a pluralistic world in which religious communities are drawn closer together, and religious distinctiveness is highlighted, such communities need to be girded with zones of liberality My conclusion is that only secular values can to that job.

The proximity of cultures in our time makes inter-religious dialogue both possible and necessary. If we avoid economic reductionism and accept that religious teaching can serve as an independent resource for human action, as my analysis allows, then dialogue within a respectful framework can serve a positive purpose. While such dialogue is most often carried forward by intellectual elites, the proliferation of NGO's on the international scene has ensured that much productive dialogue can and, does go on the grass roots level. The economist, Amartya Sen, reminds us that tolerance, for example, is by no means an exclusively Western value.[29] Values inherent in one culture, on further investigation, can be understood to have parallels in other cultures, and at times even origins outside one's culture.

---

[28] For a discussion of the hybridization of culture within the dialectics of multiculturalism, see Cornel West *Prophetic Thought in Postmodern Times* (Monroe, Maine: Common Courage Press, 1993) p. 2ff.

[29] Amartya Sen, *Development As Freedom* (Anchor Books: New York, 1999) p.235.

Values and cultural possessions, through processes of natural accretion, are and can be grafted from one culture to another without condescension or debasement of the receiving culture. Culture, inclusive of religion, is not a static, but a dynamic phenomenon, and religions change owes as much to external influences as it does to deliberate adjustment within traditions. Dialogue can assuredly be one of these salutary external influences. In the domain of inter-religious dialogue, if we wish to ensure that practices emerge which are consonant with human rights, we are best situated, as Daniel Bell suggests, if we can build on those local resources that promote those values. [30] I would argue that constructive dialogue cannot go on in many instances unless Western interlocutors are willing and able to understand and accept that the values which make for peace within the local religious tradition. All of this presupposes a stance of openness, understanding and empathy, an environment that can work to nurture, both procedurally and substantively, a sensibility of respect and appreciation across religious lines.

Related to the call for inter-religious dialogue is the need for education within the denominations themselves. Here religious leadership needs to evoke the positive resources for peace making in order to move the traditions away from parochial preoccupations and toward an orientation adaptive to a global pluralistic environment. The teachings of all the historical religions manifest the conceptual and moral frameworks of universalism and holism with regard to the creation and the unity of humankind. Hinduism espouses a common human origin, and has been especially pluriform in its acceptance of paths, including atheism, which can lead to liberation. Compassion lies at the center of Buddhist virtues, and like Hinduism, sees its specific doctrine as a vehicle amongst others which conduce to spiritual ends. Clearly, the monotheistic faiths have thicker boundaries that define insiders and exclude others. Yet, all, as noted, have a universal pole which can serve as a basis for tolerance and inter-group harmony. In Judaism, man is made "in the divine image" (Genesis 1:27) and the Talmud teaches that "the righteous of all nations shall have a share in the world to come." (Tosefta Sanhedrn 13:2) In Christianity, the parable of Good Samaritan (Luke 10:29-37) and the Golden Rule (Matthew 7:12) speak to regard for the stranger. In the Koran, sura 2:256 teaches "Let there be no compulsion in religion."

Contemporary religions bear the task within our globalized world, which have brought the diverse faiths closer together, to raise the profile of their positive resources that affirm peacemaking. A reverence for life needs to supersede preoccupation with doctrinal issues which work to strengthen divisions among the faiths. All religions have leaders and reformers who speak to the more universalizing elements in their traditions. Often these representatives have been the minor voice. Whether the press of the dangers humankind confronts in the contemporary world will move these representatives into dominant positions within their faith communities remains an open question. Much depends on leadership within the religions and dynamics outside of them. My thesis entails that changes in the underlying economic and political ground and the infusion of liberalizing forces which come from outside of the religious realm are necessary to enable the salutary forces in the religions to gain more traction. But how religion is interpreted and transmitted by religious elites, especially in critical moments, is also deterinative.

---

[30] Daniel A. Bell, "The East Asian Challenge to Human Rights: Reflections on an East West Dialogue" *Human Rights* Quarterly, volume 18.3 1996.

Endemic poverty and economic injustice are breeding grounds for political instability and the emergence of autocratic regimes. When the capabilities of people who yearn for economic advancement are thwarted, the seeds are sown for religious extremism and demagoguery, which can ripen into violence. Though the Marxist critique of religion has proven to be too reductionist, it remains nevertheless true that the quashing of dignity, and of hope in an a more bountiful and equitable future, can lead people to turn toward the parochial realms of religious tradition and transcendental realities as alternative sources of meaning. Such conditions, as noted, can be exploited by religious elites and bent in violent directions.

A direct correlation between poverty and inequality and religious violation is admittedly not self-evident. It has been pointed out that Africa and Latin America also suffer broad reaching economic dislocations, yet religious violence on those continents is relatively rare. It has also been noted that Osama bin Laden is a millionaire, and that the perpetrators, of the September 11, 2001 terrorist assault on the World Trade Center and the Pentagon, with few exceptions, were from middle class families for whom economic opportunity was not foreclosed. But the economic status of these individual actors does not nullify the importance of poverty and equality as the fertile ground from which violence is spawned, in combination with religious sanctions interpreted by religious elites. My thesis is that religious violence is a product of a combination of elements of which grievances resulting from economic disparity and depravation are active agents.

Juergensmeyer in his cross cultural study of religious violence has noted the correlation between social marginality rooted in conditions which lead to economic dead ends, and the vulnerability of young men, in particular, to be lured into acts of religious violence. He notes:

> In the cultures of violence that have led to religious terrorism, the anxieties of all young men – concerns over careers, social location and sexual relationships – have been exacerbated. Experiences of humiliation in these matters have made them vulnerable to the voices of powerful leaders and images of glory in a cosmic war. In Palestine, for example, where the unemployment rate among young men in their late teens and early twenties has hovered around 50%, economic frustration has led to sexual frustration. Without jobs, which is usually a prerequisite to searching for a wife in traditional societies, they cannot marry. Without marriage, in strict religious cultures such as that of of Palestinians Arabs, they cannot have sex. The Hamas movement has provided a way of venting the resulting frustrations in a community that supplies a family and an ideology that explains the source of their problems and gives them hope. [31]

Juergensmeyer has documented analogous situations among fighters in the Islamic Resistance Movement in Algeria and movements for Sikh empowerment in India.

While poverty and economic disparity of themselves do not cause violence in religious communities, it is difficult to conclude that without these factors serving as contextual dynamics, religious teaching conducing to violence could be sustained. My views concur with Oliver McTernen in his following observation:

> Inequality does matter and needs, therefore to be addressed to avoid the danger of communal strife in multifaith/multicultural societies as well as to lessen the risk of global terrorism.

---

31 Mark Juergensmeyer, *Terror in the Mind of God* (University of California Press: Berkeley and Los Angeles, 2000) p. 191.

Extreme poverty, social injustice, unemployment, illiteracy all contribute to the milieu that can provide both a trigger and a fertile recruiting ground for high-minded and idealistic young religious entrepreneurs who believe that it is their sacred or religious duty to act on behalf of the downtrodden and to spearhead social and economic change. [32]

Amartya Sen, and the philosopher, Martha Nussbaum, have argued, economic development is itself a good, while it broadens the scope within which human capabilities and freedoms can flourish. If we wish to offset the potential of religion to become violent then we need to work to ensure that the future remains open to the possibility of economic advancement. This requires that the widening disparities of wealth wrought by globalization be hemmed by more equitable distribution of opportunities for development on local levels, that environmental despoliation be halted through a rational commitment to conservation and sustainability, and a world-wide ethos of human rights and dignity work to leaven the killing dynamics of the unfettered market. In these visionary endeavors the religions themselves can play a salutary role.

Related to the values issuing from economic development is the need to artfully promote the values of democracy. Democracy, in this regard, needs to be understood as not merely access to the formal rituals of the electoral process, though it must ineluctably include these. Rather, in the spirit of John Dewey, it is a commitment to a way of life that suffuses personality, as it gives shape to society. At the heart of the democratic character style as well as to democratic political structures is what the human rights theorist, Michael Ignatieff and others refer to as "agency." [33] At a minimum, agency presupposes a modicum of freedom, what Isaiah Berlin called "negative liberty"; the freedom to make choices, and the power to work to mold society and nature by the lights of one's personality. The ability to express one's agency, to actively participate in the world around oneself, like the promises of development, keeps before people the promise of a better future. Democratic participation is a wellspring of personal investment of the energies and hope that ward off the frustrations commensurate with political repression and autocracy. The liberating air sustained by freedom and democracy propels development, and it is of itself the best political environment serving to countermand religious extremism and violence.

CONCLUSION

Religion cannot merely be identified with its intellectual and scriptural traditions; neither solely with its teachings and doctrines. The religions function, to a greater of lesser extent, as the matrices in which people live out their lives, frame their consciousness, anchor their identities and solidify their communion with all fellow believers. While the cognitive elements of religion can be effective resources in motivating believers toward tolerance and peaceful acceptance of those who differ, the role of religion remains powerfully conditioned by the underlying economic and political environments in which all human life remains deeply rooted.

---

[32] Oliver McTernan, *Violence in God's Name* (Orbis Books: New York, 2003) p. 125.
[33] Michael Ignatieff, *Human Rights* (Princeton University Press: Princeton and Oxford, 2001) p.57.

The dangerous moment we are in, a moment in which we witness the fusion of religion and violence, provides the most ominous challenge to world peace for the foreseeable future. If it is true that human beings require frameworks of meaning which religion (and non-religious world views) provides, then it is no less true in these times, and especially in these times, that we need a resurgence of secular values manifested in the structures and content of civic society projected onto the international stage. Religious communalism, unassuaged by exposure to cultural diversity, devoid of the promises of economic justice and equality and drained of democratic resources is fated to take a dark, inward turn. If the great religious traditions are to fulfill their venerable hopes as beacons of peace and mutual co-existence, we need to forge a new blueprint providing a nuanced understanding of how religion dialectically responds to the realities in which it finds itself. It is out of such an understanding that state actors, non-government organizations and concerned citizens can frame enlightened policies in pursuance of a more peaceful world order.

SECTION II

In: Religion, Terrorism and Globalization
Editor: K.K. Kuriakose, pp.33-49

ISBN 1-59454-553-7

Chapter 2

THE NONVIOLENCE OF MAHATMA GANDHI

Noel Sheth, S.J.

Jnana-Deepa Vidyapeeth Pune, India

Although Mahatma Gandhi is known as the apostle of nonviolence (*ahiṃsā*), he never wrote a treatise on nonviolence. By nature he was a practitioner rather than a theoretician (Gandhi 1958-1988: *Collected Works*: 62: 224-225; henceforth as CW). He humbly admitted that he had no final word on it (CW 64: 225). In fact, he claimed that nonviolence was indefinable, that it was impossible to have a complete theoretical knowledge of nonviolence. It can only be understood through experience: we can merely catch glimpses of it as it unfolds in our life and actions (CW 71: 294). He was constantly experimenting, and his thought was continually evolving (CW 56: 128). Hence we have to sift through both his life and writings to get some idea of his understanding of nonviolence.

This article has three major divisions. The first part is expository, presenting Gandhi's concept of nonviolence in its varied hues and colors. In the second part, I give a critical appreciation of his understanding of nonviolence. The final part includes reflections on nonviolence and its contemporary relevance.

I. GANDHI'S UNDERSTANDING OF NONVIOLENCE

1. The Nature and Characteristics of Nonviolence

The Sanskrit word *ahiṃsā*, which is normally translated as 'nonviolence', literally means 'non-injury', 'non-killing'. It is made up of the negative prefix *a* and the noun *hiṃsā* (injury, harm, killing, destruction), derived from the verb *hiṃs* (to strike, hurt, injure, kill, destroy), which, in turn, is probably an abbreviated desiderative of the verb *han* (to kill, destroy, injure, strike down, conquer) (Whitney 1885: 205). In Indian tradition, although *ahiṃsā* is a negative term, indicating what one should not do (not injuring), it has a positive meaning too because it also involves positive acts of kindness, compassion, affection and love towards others.

Moreover, it includes not only physical or bodily nonviolence, but also vocal and mental non-violence (Tähtinen 1976: 56-59, 65-69).

For Gandhi too, nonviolence is not merely abstaining from physical injury or killing. "Non-violence means not harming anyone in thought, word or action out of ill will or selfishness" (CW 34: 437). For him, nonviolence was not merely negative; it was eminently positive. "It is a positive state of love, of doing good even to the evil-doer" (Chander 1945: 412). "We should learn to condemn evil but, at the same time, love the evil-doer" (CW 20:381). "Ahimsa means 'love' in the Pauline sense, and yet something more....Ahimsa includes the whole creation, and not only human. Besides, love in the English language has other connotations too, and so I was compelled to use the negative word. But it does not, as I have told you, express a negative force, but a force superior to all the forces put together" (CW 62: 200). He also refers to this 'love-force' as 'truth-force' (CW15: 249) and 'soul-force', as opposed to 'brute-force' (CW 14:379). On one occasion he proclaimed, "No other English term can express all the meanings of *ahimsa* which the word *innocence* expresses" (CW 18:265). Backianadan conjectures that Gandhi chose this word 'innocence' "since, positively it seems to connote pure love, simplicity, purity of intention, trust in others' good will; negatively an absence of hatred, duplicity and intent to hurt and destroy others" (1991: 79).

Thus, Gandhi's nonviolence went beyond Tolstoy's passive resistance. It is an active force of love (CW 48:407). In fact, it is all-comprehensive:

> "*Ahimsa* is not the crude thing it has been made to appear. Not to hurt any living thing is no doubt a part of *ahimsa*. But it is its least expression. The principle of *Ahimsa* is hurt by every evil thought, by undue haste, by lying, by hatred, by wishing ill to anybody. It is also violated by one's holding on to what the world needs" (Chander 1945: 404).
>
> "*Ahimsa* really means that you may not offend anybody, you may not harbour an uncharitable thought even in connection with one who may consider himself to be your enemy....For one who follows the doctrine of *Ahimsa* there is no room for an enemy: he denies the existence of an enemy" (Chander 1945: 405).

In dealing with one's opponent great care has to be taken to avoid violence of any sort. The antagonist is to be won over through gentle persuasion, not violence. Moreover, one's own nonviolence also prompts one to constantly reexamine and, if necessary, revise one's opinion, for it is possible that it may be false (Bondurant 1959: 33). While minimizing the disputant's error, one should magnify one's own error (CW 47: 244). One ought to refrain from giving unfavorable or unwarranted interpretations even to the motives of the opponent (CW 35: 104). One should seek an honorable solution, without harboring anger against the adversary; in fact, one should be ready to suffer the anger of the opponent, not returning tit for tat. One must even go to the extent of protecting the antagonist from insult and injury, even at the risk of one's life (Bondurant 1959: 39). Bondurant reports that some Indians refrained from taking action in the hot midday sun in order to spare their European opponents the torture of the scorching heat. And again, some others put off their agitation in order to give the Christian opponents time for the celebration of Easter (1959: 120, n). The whole point of such an exercise is not to humiliate the opponents, rubbing their noses into the ground, but to raise them up and give them face-saving opportunities.

Nonviolence can take on various forms. The subtle violence involved in hurting the feelings of others is, in Gandhi's view, far worse than gross murders: the latter are not so numerous compared to the incalculable instances of the daily loss of temper (CW 50: 205-206). Even laying down one's life for a cause, but out of anger, is useless; love should be the only motive (CW 66: 434). Rash judgments and generalizations about a person's character from a single instance and without conclusive evidence are also examples of violence (CW 72: 209). If one does not keep one's tools and implements in good condition, one goes against nonviolence. If, for instance, one meets with an accident due to keeping one's bicycle in ill repair, it is a sort of violence (CW 71: 153). Gandhi pointed out that even bad handwriting is an instance of violence, since it causes pain to others and betrays insufficient concern and love for others. He therefore laid down rules for good handwriting (CW 44: 374).

According to Gandhi, one should not be a vegetarian merely for health reasons, but for moral reasons. We must rise above our animal nature and live in accordance with our spiritual nature, abstaining from meat. He said that, if he were told that he would die if he did not have beef-tea or mutton, he would prefer death, for eating meat involved the killing of animals. He thought it was difficult to control one's passions, if one was a non-vegetarian: one becomes what one eats; the coarser the food, the grosser one becomes. On the other hand, he conceded that one might be very careful about one's diet and yet be passionate and violent, while a person who is broad-minded with regard to diet might well be non-violent (Gandhi 1959: 4, 18, 2-21, 24-26).

Theoretically, Gandhi was against the consumption of even animal products. While he asserted that the milk of animals is not necessary for human life and that we have a right only to our mother's milk, yet he himself did take (goat's) milk because he thought he needed it for his health and strength. He did not give it up, he said, because he could not afford to do so. He felt that from the cruel way in which honey was collected in India, one should avoid it on humanitarian grounds. But he himself did not abstain from honey. He admitted that he did not follow strict logic in this, but also rationalized that life was not governed merely by logic; it is an organic growth that must pay attention to many considerations. He realized that, in the strict sense of the word, even the eating of vegetables involves violence; but as long as he continued his physical existence, he could not do without them (Gandhi 1959: 4, 14, 22, 30).

We may mention here a special form of nonviolence, according to Gandhi, the practice of svadeśī. It means 'that which belongs or pertains to one's own region or country'. For Gandhi it meant concentrating on one's immediate "neighborhood", i.e., one's religion, one's institutions, one's local produce and industries, one's nation. He did not want to serve his distant neighbor at the expense of the nearest. He purchased foreign goods, but only those that did not hurt the Indian economy or the local artisans or industries. He considered it part of nonviolence to give preference to one's country's products for the sake of the progress of its inhabitants (Chander 1945: 537-539).

Nonviolence must flow into service of others. Gandhi gave shelter to a leper and attended to him personally, even dressing his wounds and massaging his body (Backianadan 1991: 155). For Gandhi, service took different forms. It included the promotion of nature cures, reduction of communal tensions, village betterment, the providing of basic education, and eradicating of social problems like caste and untouchability (Backianadan 1991: 221). We should not imagine that we are doing a great favor to the poor and the helpless by serving them. We are just paying back what we owe them. We must serve them with courtesy, respect and sincerity (CW 42: 43-44). Gandhi felt that it was the duty of everyone to render service.

Even sick people do service by thinking pure thoughts, expecting only a minimum of service from others, being cheerful and showing their love to those who serve them. Even devout meditation on God is a service (CW 52: 75).

Nonviolence does not consist merely in controlling one's own violent thoughts, words and deeds, but also in checking the violence perpetrated by other individuals and by society (Iyer 1973: 205). In this context, maintaining silence, without speaking out the whole truth, is cowardice (CW 83: 242). Similarly, one should not remain a silent spectator, even when one's enemy is being put to death. On the contrary, one ought to protect the enemy even at the cost of one's life (CW 83:259).

Nonviolence or love is not merely confined to the horizontal level, towards human beings. It involves also the love of God as well as sub-human beings. For Gandhi the love of God and the love of fellow human beings were two sides of the same coin. The latter was impossible without the former (CW 48: 411-412). Nonviolence also includes good will towards animals, birds and insects (CW 23: 24). Gandhi himself narrates a touching incident. He found a worm and a weevil in dates that he was eating. He gave them to his secretary, who absentmindedly put them in a washbasin. Later, when Gandhi got ready to wash his hands, he noticed that the worm and weevil had moved away and he breathed a sigh of relief. He saw God in that worm and weevil, he said. (CW 45: 20) Gandhi was truly sensitive to all life.

For Gandhi, nonviolence is to be exercised not only toward the individual, but also within the institutional or societal sphere. While one must willingly obey the laws of the state, even when they are inconvenient, one must respectfully disobey unjust laws that go against one's conscience. In so doing, one must be ready to suffer the punishments imposed by the state (Chander 1945: 396-397). The motivating force behind non-cooperation is love. Non-cooperation without love is not only empty; it is satanic (CW 21: 519). Non-cooperation is not a form of violence, even if it results in a certain amount of suffering to the wrongdoer, for one has recourse to it exclusively for the good of the evildoer (CW 23: 407).

In the Gandhian perspective, the ideal state has no political power, because there is no 'state'. In such a state everyone is one's own ruler, without being a thorn in the side of one's neighbor. It is a society based on nonviolent cooperation and peaceful co-existence (Dhawan 1946: 266-267). This is an ideal that all should strive for, even if we are unable to achieve it. Gandhi realized that it would be impossible for a government to be totally nonviolent; but he believed in the possibility of a state that was nonviolent to a large extent (Dhawan 1946: 274). He gave special consideration to minority views. According to him, total disregard of the minority by the majority smacks of violence (CW 33: 457-458).

The *Bhagavad- gītā* advocated violence, but Gandhi believed that nonviolence was also the religion of the warrior class (kṣatriya) (Chander 1945: 415). Those who are truly nonviolent do not need an army for their self-defense. A nonviolent army would fight against all injustice, but with "clean" weapons (CW 90: 503). Yet Gandhi declared that he would be ready to vote for those who wanted military training, since one could not force people to be nonviolent (CW 37: 271). Even though he tried to justify his earlier participation in the wars of Britain (Gandhi: 1944-1949: 1: 84-86, 99-102), he categorically asserted that war was "an un-mixed evil" and that he was "uncompromisingly against all war" (Gandhi 1944-1949: 1: 93, 100).

While not rejecting punitive measures altogether, he wanted punishment to be as non-violent as possible. Thus, for instance, while he accepted the need for police to carry arms or use tear gas, he was totally against capital punishment. The purpose is to reform the criminal, not to eliminate him. Given the existential situation, a police force is necessary, but it should be wholly nonviolent: the police should be servants, not masters, of the people. Ideally, they will use arms only rarely, and their police work will be primarily with dacoits and robbers. Actually they are reformers, not punishers. With the cooperation of the people, the police will be able to easily deal with the ever-decreasing disturbances in the nonviolent state (CW 72: 403).

Gandhi had first hand experience of life in jail. He was very critical of the treatment prisoners received. Prison authorities, he said, should be humane in their administration. The purpose of punishment is to reform the prisoners, but the sad fact is that it only brutalizes them (CW 23: 508-509). Just as hospitals cure physical diseases, jails are meant to treat mental illnesses. But, unlike hospitals, jails are very poorly maintained. If every prisoner were treated with kindness and sympathy, there would be fewer jails (CW 24: 224).

In Gandhi's view, self-suffering is an essential aspect of nonviolence. The self-suffering of Gandhi should be distinguished from the traditional practice of asceticism (*tapas*), which is for the good of the person who undertakes it. For Gandhi, the infliction of suffering on oneself is for the moral benefit of the world in general and, in particular, for bringing about a positive change in the person for whose sake the suffering is undertaken. It consists in overcoming the opponent by suffering in one's own person (Bondurant 1959: 27-28). Suffering goes beyond the rational defenses of the opponent and brings about conversion. "It is a divine law that even the most hard-hearted man will melt if he sees his enemy suffering in innocence" (CW 12: 187). "The appeal of reason is more to the head, but the penetration of the heart comes from suffering. It opens up the inner understanding in man" (CW 48: 189). It is in this spirit that Gandhi even undertook fasts unto death (CW 53: 460). Bondurant points out that, although the concept of self-suffering is difficult to acceptable for the Western mind, it paradoxically helps to achieve the dignity of the individual, which is highly prized in Western society (1959: 29).

Self-suffering, in the Gandhian understanding, is always coupled with courage and will power. It is not the last resort or weapon of the weak or cowardly person (Chander 1945: 417-418). It does not mean meek submission to the will of the evildoer; on the contrary one must resist the wrongdoer (Chander 1945: 412). Forgiveness does not spring from weakness, but from strength (CW 19: 401). Even in the case of violence, there is a brave violence, as when four or five men fight valiantly and die by the sword, and a cowardly violence, as when ten thousand armed men attack a village of unarmed people and decimate them (CW 88: 274). Gandhi even went to the extent of proclaiming, "I do believe that, where there is only a choice between cowardice and violence, I would advise violence" (cited by Nelson 1975: 72).

For Gandhi nonviolence was a creed, not a mere strategy or policy. However, he thought that a whole group of people could adopt nonviolence as a policy, without accepting it as a belief (CW 35: 457). Gandhi's secretary, Pyarelal, opined that even a nonviolent campaign based only on nonviolence as a policy could prove effective, provided the rules of nonviolent discipline and work were sincerely followed (Bondurant 1959: 103-104). Of course, those who merely accept nonviolence as a strategy could still use force in self-defense, but then they should honestly admit that they have merely adopted nonviolence as a policy and not a creed (cited by Iyer 1973: 196-197). Towards the end of his life, however, Gandhi realized that nonviolence as a policy could easily degenerate into a form of cowardice, into pseudo-nonviolence (cited by Iyer 1973: 199).

Nonviolence is related to Truth or God as means to the end. "To me Truth is God and there is no way to find Truth except the way of Nonviolence" (CW 32: 441). One cannot grasp Truth in all its comprehensiveness, but through nonviolence one will eventually reach Truth. This absolute Truth is reached gradually, through the intermediary steps of relative truths. These too are to be tested by nonviolence, which is the only way of discovering both relative as well as absolute truth (Bondurant 1959: 25). When there are divergent views, the truth is discovered through nonviolence and self-suffering. It should be noted that it is not necessary that the truth rests with only one of the many who hold different opinions; it may well be that they have all grasped the truth, but each in a limited way. Gandhi had no difficulty working together with those who disagreed with him. It is only when there is radical disagreement, that there is a need to win over the other through nonviolent means (Bondurant 1959: 31, 34). For Gandhi, *Satyāgraha*, i.e., insistence on Truth or Truth-force, is not a violent, physical force, but the 'force' of *ahiṃsā* or love (CW 42: 491).

2. Non-Violence Includes other Virtues and Qualities

In the Gandhian interpretation, the practice of nonviolence involves a number of virtues, qualities and attitudes or disciplines. Following are the main ones:

(1) Detachment: Taking his cue from the doctrine of selfless action propagated by the *Bhagavad-gītā* (e.g., 2.47), Gandhi linked detachment with nonviolence: "When there is no desire for fruit, there is no temptation for untruth or *himsa*. Take any instance of untruth or violence, and it will be found that at its back was the desire to attain the cherished end" (Desai 1948: 132). While granting that the Gītā could be interpreted to advocate war, he declared that years of experience had taught him that perfect renunciation of the fruits of one's actions was impossible without perfect nonviolence (Desai 1948: 133-134). It is well known that Gandhi himself lived a simple, frugal, self-sacrificing life.

(2) Compassion: According to Gandhi nonviolence is impossible to practice without compassion, and one is able to practice nonviolence only to the extent that one possesses compassion (CW 40: 192). Gandhi's heart went out to the poor, the downtrodden, and those in shackles. Identifying himself with the poor, he wore only a loincloth and built his house in a slum. Referring to the oppressed untouchables as Harijans or people of Viṣṇu (Gandhi was born in a Vaiṣṇavite family), he gave shelter to one of them in his own home. He urged his followers not only to physically touch the untouchables, but also to serve them with love (CW 22: 117-118). It should be noted, on the other hand, that he did not want to merely dole out food to the poor; he wanted to help them to stand on their own feet: "I do not wish to open free kitchens in India; on the contrary, I want to close them....I wish to make everyone self-reliant" (CW 25: 61). He urged his disciples to be strict with themselves, but liberal with others (CW 27: 235-236). On the other hand, he also held that one must sometimes be hard in order to be truly kind (CW 31: 446).

(3) Humility: Gandhi taught that nonviolence was humbler than even the mango tree, which bends low as it grows up. Instead of proving its own point, nonviolence, he said, lets all others prove their point of view (CW 34: 357).

(4) Acceptance of, and openness to, all religions and cultures: Gandhi's prayer for adherents of another religion was, "O God! give all Thy creation wisdom, so that each may worship and follow Thee according to his light and grow in his own faith"; and not "O God! give Thy creation wisdom, so that each may worship and follow Thee even as I try to do" (CW 57: 353-354). He believed in the equality of all religions (CW 51: 316-317). He declared, "I do not want my house to be walled in on all sides and my windows to be stuffed. I want the cultures of all lands to be blown about my house as freely as possible" (cited by Nelson 1975: 60).

(5) Celibacy: Gandhi believed that perfect nonviolence necessarily implied celibacy. Married people have to be more concerned about the welfare of their spouses and their families; they cannot practice universal love. If those who are already married live as if they were not married, i.e., as brother and sister, they will become free for universal service (CW 44: 68-69). Although married himself, he decided at the age of thirty-seven to abstain from sex and kept this resolution until his death. In order to test the power of his nonviolence, he experimented with sharing his bed with naked women to check whether he could remain chaste even in thought. He made this experiment publicly known and had to justify himself in the face of a lot of criticism (CW 87: 13-14, 89-92).

Gandhi's nonviolence, therefore, was concerned with all moral virtues. In this he followed the Jain view, which makes violence the root sin: all sins are in some way forms of violence, which is the basic sin.

3. Unavoidable Violence

Gandhi realized that perfect nonviolence was impossible as long as people had bodies. In such a state, perfect nonviolence was only a theory like Euclid's point or straight line (Gandhi 1944-1949: 1: 332). There is violence even in eating fruits. At this rate one would have to abstain from almost all kinds of foods, he said (CW 28: 240). He held that, if insects like ants, or animals like monkeys, dogs, or leopards harmed or adversely affected human beings, they could be driven away or even killed (CW 84: 230-231). He approved the killing of rabid dogs as the lesser of two evils. Things are not always what they seem, he explained: sometimes one has to resort to violence as the truest form of nonviolence (CW 31: 486-489). He put a calf to sleep when it was in pain and there was no chance of recovery. He considered this an entirely unselfish act (Gandhi 1944-1949: 1: 151). He was painfully aware he killed many organisms by the mere fact of his breathing. Similarly the use of antiseptics and disinfectants involved violence. He permitted snakes to be killed and bullocks to be driven away with a stick. A certain amount of violence is simply unavoidable as long as we are in the physical body, he said with regret (Gandhi 1959: 22). Although at one time he thought that a nonviolent woman did not need to defend her honor, since the power of her nonviolence and purity were enough to prevent the assailant from violating her (Gandhi 1944-1949: 1: 48), yet he later encouraged women to bravely defend themselves (Gandhi 1944-49: 2: 142). A woman is free to use every means that she can think of in order to defend her honor. Similarly a man who is witness to the assault should not be a passive spectator but, in the spirit of nonviolence, protect the woman even at the risk of his life (Gandhi 1957: 167-168). He also thought it was proper to dispatch a lunatic who went berserk, killing people with a sword, and no one dared to capture him alive (Gandhi 1957: 156). If his child were to get rabies, he would consider it his duty to take the life of the child in order to bring relief from the terrible agony (Gandhi 1957: 156). While Gandhi was not in favor of euthanasia for human beings, he did approve of it under certain conditions (Backianadan 1991: 93 and n. 347).

4. The Superiority of Nonviolence over Violence

According to Gandhi, violence is incapable of radically destroying evil. It only changes the form of evil (Gandhi 1944-1949: 2: 230). History teaches us, he said, that those who resort to violence even for a just cause ultimately fall prey to the very same disease of violence (cited by Iyer 1973: 198). Revolutions bring violence in their wake (Gandhi 1957: 164-165). Violence is very visible and palpable, while nonviolence is three-fourths invisible. It has a hidden and unconscious effect, which is far more potent, and it travels at great speed (CW 64: 222-223). Once nonviolence is established in one place, its influence spreads everywhere (CW 68: 29). Even when many lives are lost by resorting to nonviolence, in the long run this will result in less loss of life than if one had recourse to violence. Besides, such suffering is both ennobling and beneficial (Gandhi 1944-1949: 1: 49). Gandhi perceptively pointed out that violence did not change the adversaries and their perception of the truth, even if it subdued them (Parekh 1997: 52-53).

5. The Basis for Nonviolence

Gandhi was no systematic philosopher or theologian, and did not follow any one particular philosophical or theological system (CW 34: 91, 93). Yet, from his writings, we can cull out the following basic or foundational principles, on which he may be said to have built the edifice of nonviolence:

(1) He believed in the oneness of all reality: God and other beings in the universe are all one (CW 32: 218). All our souls are one; they differ only accidentally. Hence we cannot have any enemy and should be nonviolent towards all (CW 32: 189).

(2) He believed that as social beings we are interconnected and interdependent. Those who consider themselves independent cease to be nonviolent (CW 41: 345). Thus not only are we responsible for one another, but whatever we do affects one another.

(3) He believed that all human beings are brothers and sisters (CW 58: 50).

(4) For him nonviolence is essential to human nature. "Nonviolence is the law of the human race" (Gandhi 1957:154). "If mankind was not habitually nonviolent, it would have been self-destroyed ages ago" (CW 42: 363). As animals we are violent, but as spirit we are nonviolent. When we awaken to the spirit within, we cannot but be nonviolent (cited by Iyer 1973: 211).

(5) Gandhi believed in the innate goodness of human nature, which nonviolence, coupled with suffering, can evoke (CW 69: 70). A wicked person is temporarily debased, but deep down every human being is good (CW 45: 222).

(6) Nonviolence is based on belief in God: faith in God is itself the power behind nonviolence (CW 69: 226). Without trusting in God, that mysterious, supreme power or force, nonviolence is impossible (CW 76: 232).

These, then, appear to be the basic underlying principles of Gandhi's doctrine of nonviolence.

II. CRITICAL APPRECIATION

The unique contribution of Gandhi was to extend the concept of nonviolence from the individual and personal sphere to the social and political domain. He gave the traditional nonviolence of India a new orientation: he adopted it as a principle and technique for social and political change, as well as, religious reform (Bondurant 1959: 112). It is because of him that the word "nonviolence" has entered into the vocabulary of politics. Furthermore, he freed nonviolence from its cloistered confines and transformed it into a mass movement. For him nonviolence was the principle that governed his life in every sphere, domestic, institutional, economic, social and political (Bondurant 1959: 113). Although his nonviolence encompassed the social and political dimensions too, it remained eminently personal: it was aimed against evil, not against the evildoer. In fact, he went out of his way to ensure the well-being of the opponent.

Similarly asceticism, sacrifice, and suffering which, in the Indian tradition, were confined to the private life of an individual, were now brought into the public sphere of politics and society. They became a means not only for personal salvation, but also for social and political welfare. Suffering became a means of bringing about a change of heart in the opponent (Bondurant 1959: 113-115). Gandhi departed from tradition by teaching others to seek to protect the opponent from harm, even at the risk of one's life (Bondurant 1959: 119). Gandhi was also unique in distinguishing between nonviolence as a creed and as a policy, as well as between the nonviolence of the strong and the weak (Iyer 1973: 192).

Gandhi's nonviolence strove to keep a healthy balance between self-identity, self-respect, self-worth and honor on the one hand, and openness, inclusiveness, and dialogue on the other hand. He was able to stay clear of self-righteousness, fanaticism, and bigotry (Parekh 1997: 94-95). Nonviolence was not to be limited to action alone; it also extended to words and thoughts. Although he was not totally free from utopianism and romanticism, he succeeded to a large extent in keeping his feet firmly rooted in reality. "Unlike sentimental humanists Gandhi identified enemies and showed who to fight against, but unlike conventional revolutionary theorists he also saw them as potential partners in a common struggle" (Parekh 1997: 96).

For Gandhi, nonviolence is not just for an elite coterie, but it can be practiced by all, even the masses. "If truth be not a monopoly of the few why should nonviolence, its counterpart, be otherwise?" (CW 43: 309). However, possessing a sense of realism, he felt he could not expect the masses to practice nonviolence in thought; he would be satisfied if they practiced it in word and deed (CW 76: 333). Nevertheless, the fact remains that thousands of people voluntarily entered prisons; they were beaten and killed, without their raising even a finger in self-defense. Thousands of women collected contraband salt without harboring any hatred.

Thousands of farmers revolted against agrarian evils without bearing any ill-will (Gandhi 1944-1949: 1: 279). Gandhi's secretary Pyarelal asserted that it was possible to run a nonviolent movement among the masses merely by their accepting it as a policy, not a creed, provided they followed the leaders who practiced pure nonviolence (Bondurant 1959:103-104). With this in mind, it is interesting to report that in sociological studies of three Gandhian movements (Bardoli, Rajkot, and Pardi), it was found that it was the masses, and not so much the leaders, who practiced nonviolence as a creed (Nakhre 1982: 72-73, 96-102).

For nonviolence to be successful in the political and social sphere, it is not necessary to accept the Hindu world-view. It has proved successful in other religious traditions and social milieus. For example, although Islam and Hinduism differ in many important points, and there was a world of difference between the relatively mild-mannered Indian and the hot-blooded Pathans (Bondurant 1959:132, 141-142), a Pathan named Khan Abdul Ghaffar Khan, more fondly known as the Frontier Gandhi, organized a very effective nonviolent movement called the Khudai Khidmatgar or the "Servants of God" (Bondurant 1959: 131-144). Martin Luther King, who was a Christian, adopted and adapted Gandhi's method of nonviolence in his Civil Rights Movement in the United States of America. Nonviolent approaches are being tried out in several other parts of the world. Calling the Chinese his brothers and sisters, the Dalai Lama wants a nonviolent solution to the autonomy of his homeland Tibet, and, in agreement with history, assures the Chinese that Tibet will continue to remain linked with China. In South Africa, Nelson Mandela did not hold any grudge against the Whites even after being incarcerated for twenty-seven years. When he became president, Mandela invited his White jailor to the inauguration (Gandhi 1999: 400-401). In 1995 South Africa's new democratically elected parliament set up the Truth and Reconciliation Commission, headed by Nobel Laureate Archbishop Desmond Tutu. Its purpose was to bring about peace and reconciliation. The commission gave ample opportunity for both White and Black perpetrators of political crimes to confess to the truth of their atrocities and receive amnesty and reconciliation, and for the victims to experience healing through forgiveness. In an interview with Frank Ferrari, the Archbishop reveals the benefits that accrued from this venture to both victim and perpetrator (Ferrari 1997: 13-18). Striking a note of hope for the future, Archbishop Tutu declares in his book, *No Future without Forgiveness*, "No problem anywhere can ever again be considered to be intractable.... Our experiment is going to succeed because God wants us to succeed.... God wants to show that there is life after conflict and repression that because of forgiveness there is a future" (1999: 282). It is important to remark that the Archbishop replaces 'retributive justice' with 'restorative justice'. In retributive justice criminals are punished for the sake of vengeance rather than to prevent them from commuting future crime or to reform them. Restorative justice, on the other hand, promotes reconciliation between the victim and the perpetrator. While it seeks to do justice to the victim, it also restores harmony.

Gandhi exclaimed that he would lose all interest in life if he did not believe he could attain perfect love on earth (CW 14:146). He valued it so much that he asserted that it could not be bartered away even for independence (CW 75: 220-221). On the other hand, in a more realistic mood, he realized that perfect nonviolence is not attainable like Euclid's point or straight line (Gandhi 1944-1949: 1: 332). "Although Gandhi was an absolutist in regard to his faith in *ahimsa* as a creed, he was clearly willing to make qualifications....He valued *satya* [truth] even more than *ahimsa*, justice even more than abstention from violence, courage more than mere non-participation in war" (Iyer 1973: 202). What was important for him was the spirit of nonviolence, and not blindly following the letter of the law.

Even though Gandhi did make exceptions, for him the principle of nonviolence was never wrong. He said, for instance, that if violence did break out after his death, people should conclude that it was because his violence was imperfect or even non-existent (CW 59: 420). Gandhi did allow exceptions, but these were due to unavoidable circumstances, human weakness, and lack of courage. Although these anomalies were part and parcel of reality, he did not nuance his theory accordingly and integrate them into his doctrine. "Rather than insist on a pure theory and permit impure practices, the more sensible thing would have been to legitimise and regulate the latter by making space for them within the theory itself" (Parekh 1997:101).

In some respects Gandhi tended to be an utopian. His critique of the state, his advocacy of a politically mature citizenry, his insistence on humane ways of treating criminals, and, so forth, all have inspired people in different countries. Yet, his dream for a totally nonviolent state, and a nonviolent army and police force appear to be too idealistic. A certain amount of coercion from the state is both necessary and wholesome.

As a matter of fact, one may say that, in a certain sense, Gandhi's nonviolence does contain an element of force or coercion, or at least influence or moral pressure or persuasion. It does not advocate physical force, but it does have power, even if it is not violent, aggressive power. After all, it is not for nothing that Gandhi referred to nonviolence as "soul-force". No doubt there is a world of difference between nonviolent coercion and violent coercion. In the former case, there is a willingness to undergo self-suffering, while in the latter there is a deliberate inflicting of suffering on the adversary. In the case of nonviolent coercion, even though no harm is intended and efforts are made to minimize it, still a certain amount of moral pressure is exerted on the mind and will of the antagonist. This pressure is exerted not only through the use of reason but also through self-suffering, and non-cooperation or civil disobedience. Non cooperation may cause inconvenience and loss to the opponent. Of course, this is nothing compared to the excessive harm caused by violent coercion (Bondurant 1959: 9-11). Linked with this idea of moral coercion, or pressure on the adversary, is the possibility of Gandhi's having imposed nonviolence on his followers. Although, theoretically, Gandhi never wanted to coerce his followers, there may have been occasions when the power of his personality as well as conviction left some of his followers with practically no alternative but to follow suit. As Iyer puts it, "It is, of course, very difficult to draw the line between persuasion and intimidation'... 'between entirely peaceful and forceful conversion when no physical force or material inducement is used" (Iyer 1973: 209). What must be borne in mind, however, is that even this minimum pressure is not directly intended and, most importantly, is motivated by love, not hate. This slight coercion is admitted as a necessary evil in order to obtain a greater good.

Gandhi's nonviolent approach to the resolution of conflict appealed both to the reason as well as the heart. It was concerned not only with eliminating the conflict, but also mending and promoting the relationship between the opponents. However, Gandhi did not realize sufficiently that there need not be unanimity of views even among honest and sincere persons. E.g., some look upon euthanasia and war as morally sinful, while others think they are justified under certain conditions. Now it is true that Gandhi also appealed to the heart, through self-suffering. Many indeed are moved by suffering, but Gandhi did not pay attention to the fact that, depending on whether one considered the suffering deserved or not, the reaction could be different. The Jewish holocaust did not prick the consciences of some of the Nazis. Some Americans suffered no twinge of conscience when the bomb was dropped on Hiroshima, because they thought the Japanese deserved it. Moreover, while it is true that human nature is basically good, the fact is that some people are so pathologically warped that they are practically impervious to any wholesome influence on the mind or the heart (Parekh 1997: 59-60).

Gandhi felt that, after his conquests, Hitler would find himself as empty-handed as Alexander did. Europe should have dealt with him in a non-violent manner. In this case, even if Hitler might (but only might) have taken possession of the European countries, he would have done so without bloodshed and the loss of lives (Gandhi 1944-1949: 1: 310-312). As for the Jews, he thought they too should have offered only non-violent resistance, and he compared their plight to that of the Indians in South Africa, saying that the Jews were in a better position to offer nonviolent resistance than the Indians in South Africa (Gandhi 1944-1949: 1: 184-187). In response, the Jewish philosopher Martin Buber penned a letter to Gandhi, pointing out that there was a world of difference between the Jews in the concentration camps and the Indians who were restricted to certain areas in S. Africa, and that the nonviolence of the Jews was to no avail: "a diabolic universal steam-roller cannot thus be withstood" (1963: 139-141). The managing editor of *The Jewish Frontier* wrote, "A Jewish Gandhi in Germany, should one arise, could 'function' for about five minutes until the first Gestapo agent would lead him, not to a concentration camp, but directly to the guillotine" (Gandhi 1944-1949: 1: 499). Gandhi, on the other hand, believed that even Hitler could be influenced by non-violent action (Gandhi 1944-1949: 1: 364), that nonviolence would certainly bear fruit, even if it be after the lifetime of the sufferers (Gandhi 1944-1949: 1: 235). However, it is doubtful whether non-violence can always be effective in a brutal, totalitarian regime, against "a diabolic universal steam-roller", as Buber put it (Parekh 1997: 60).

On one occasion, when asked whether it was possible to administer violence in a spirit of love, Gandhi denied it point blank. But he proceeded to mention the incident where he put a calf to death because it was lame, full of sores, unable to eat, and breathed with difficulty. This action, he said, was nonviolent because it was a totally unselfish act since it had no other purpose than to relieve the poor calf from its excruciating pain (Gandhi 1944-1949:1: 151). Gandhi rules out the possibility of unselfish violence. In this context, it is appropriate to quote the words of Buber, in the above-mentioned letter to Gandhi: "I do not want force. But if there is no other way of preventing the evil destroying the good, I trust I shall use force....We should be able even to fight for justice but to fight lovingly" (Buber 1963:146). If nonviolence can be rooted in love as well as in hate (as in the nonviolence of the weak, as Gandhi himself emphasized), there can be a violence fuelled by hatred and a violence springing from love as, for example, when parents scold their children out of love. We have seen that Gandhi accepted the possibility of eliminating a lunatic who had run amuck and could not be captured. Now Gandhi referred to Hitler as "an obviously mad but intrepid youth" (Gandhi 1944-1949: 1:184). But, unlike in the case of the insane person, he did not want violence to be used against Hitler. It is true that, in the example of the single lunatic, the matter would have ended with dispatching that person; whereas in Hitler's case, violence would have generated counter violence. Nevertheless, one may say that Gandhi need not have insisted only on one method to the exclusion of others. "Different circumstances require different responses, and violence might sometimes achieve results that nonviolence is either incapable of or can achieve only at an unacceptably high price in human suffering" (Parekh 1997: 61).

III. REFLECTIONS ON NONVIOLENCE AND ITS CONTEMPORARY RELEVANCE

Gandhi asserted that nonviolence is not a meek submission to the will of the evildoer, but it means the pitting of one's whole soul against the will of the tyrant. He rightly held that true nonviolence comes from strength, not weakness. Although on rare occasions violence too can spring from courage, yet often enough we observe in our daily life that it is frequently the weak, e.g., those who experience a sense of inferiority complex, who try to dominate others. It is the truly great who are truly humble.

Christ teaches, "If anyone strikes you on the cheek, offer the other also." (Luke 6:29). This is no meek submission. There is tremendous strength and power in such an action. There are very few people who will dare to strike back at a person who offers the other cheek. In fact, such opponents are generally so taken by surprise that they lose their balance and poise as it were. The lack of physical resistance from the nonviolent person is so unexpected, that the adversaries become confused and helpless and do not know how to deal with this new situation. A secretary of General Smuts, who had imprisoned Gandhi in South Africa, confessed his helplessness to Gandhi, "I often wish you took to violence like the English strikers, and then we would know at once how to dispose of you. But you will not injure your enemy. You desire victory by self-suffering alone and never transgress your self-imposed limits of courtesy and chivalry. And that is what reduces us to sheer helplessness" (cited by Nelson 1975: 69). Moreover, when, contrary to their expectations, the antagonists experience kindness and compassion, it may move them to reflect on their actions and open their hearts to conversion.

On the other hand, if, instead of offering the other cheek, the person strikes back, we can be sure the fight will not stop there. Even if opponents are not physically strong enough to retaliate, they will strike back in other ways, like getting other people to do the dirty job, scheming against those persons, or speaking ill of them. Violence breeds violence.

Many a non-vegetarian does not feel anything when eating chicken or mutton or beef or pork because it is placed before us all dressed-up and camouflaged with sauce and curry. However, I am told that many who work in the slaughter houses just cannot bring themselves to eat meat because they see before their very eyes the severed heads and rivers of gushing blood and hear the blood-curdling screams of pain. But then, when one considers it from the Hindu point of view, the consumption of vegetarian food is equally violent. Gandhi's nonviolence towards animals and even plants was based on the Hindu belief in rebirth. An ignorant human soul can be reborn, for instance, in an animal body or a plant body. Essentially speaking, there is no difference between a plant, an animal, a human being, or a minor deity; the difference is only in degree. No wonder that Gandhi had qualms about eating even fruits and vegetables. He did not, however, go as far as the Jain religion, which believes that there are living, ignorant souls not only in plants, but also in so-called material things. The Christian tradition does not have to face this problem because it makes an essential distinction between humans, animals, and plants. Sub-human beings, according to Christian tradition, are to be used as means by human beings, who are ends in themselves. (This, of course, has landed Christianity into other problems, such as the conquest and exploitation of nature.) In any case, many a Christian and also many a Hindu, Buddhist, or whoever is unnecessarily violent towards insects and animals. I have seen people conversing with one another and, at the same time, even without being sufficiently aware of it, crushing underfoot some harmless ants (ones that do not bite) moving about on the floor. Such ants are not going to bring the building down, and yet we go merrily ahead, blissfully oblivious to the sacredness of life. In Christian Spain and countries that were colonized by Spain, we see the cruel sport of bullfighting. Briefly, I will describe how it came across to an amateur like myself when I watched it once on TV in Spain. The bull is systematically weakened by being pierced by lances and by three pairs of sticks with sharp barbed points that are hooked on to its neck and left hanging there, as blood trickles down its neck. The matador strides into the arena several times to tease the bull and make him see red. If the skillful matador succeeds, as he often does, in tiring out the bull and making it give up the fight, he slays it with a special sword, deeply piercing it between the bull's shoulder blades. And the crowd of spectators in the arena as well as those glued to their TV sets took sadistic delight in all this, loudly cheering *"ole"*. Maneka Gandhi, India's best-known animal rights activist, has chronicled atrocities by Hindus on animals like foxes, who are hunted during the festival of Makara Saṅkrānti, or on snakes, who are captured during the feast of Nāgapañcamī (Gandhi 1994: 73-78). One has only to browse through her books entitled, *Heads and Tails* and *The Second Heads and Tails*, to be stunned into disbelief at the senseless cruelty that is daily meted out to countless animals of various kinds to fish, coral, birds, and butterflies. Recently, an international organization called the People for the Ethical Treatment of Animals (PETA) shot incriminating footage in the Deonar abattoir in India, revealing the barbarous and inhuman treatment of animals before they are slaughtered (*The Indian Express* 2000: 2). More recently, the Indian Government's Committee for the Purpose of Control and Supervision of Experiments on Animals (CPCSEA) reported the miserable conditions under which horses are kept by the King Institute in Chennai, which manufactures anti-snake venom serum (*The Times of India* 2001: 6).

Many vegetarians do not realize that curds (yogurt) are non-vegetarian because of the live lactic bacteria in them. There are some who are stricter than most vegetarians in that they avoid even animal products like milk. Nowadays they are called vegans. In any case, modern life makes it very difficult for a strict vegetarian to avoid all contact with animal flesh and animal products. Many soaps are made from tallow, which is animal fat (Gandhi 1996: 70-71). Numerous brands of ice cream contain animal fat and a sort of glue produced by boiling down certain parts of animals (Gandhi 1994: 61). Why, even sweets that have silver or gold foil on them are not pure vegetarian fare: the thin sheets of silver or gold are placed between fresh bullock or buffalo intestines and repeatedly beaten to form the fine foil. In this process of course tiny bits of the animal gut mesh with the foil, and such sweets are even served in temples (Gandhi 1996: 68-70). Most of the booming business of cosmetics thrives on animal cruelty. All of us are aware of the sources of fur coats and bags made from live crocodiles, lizards, and snakes. We all know from where silk comes, even if we do not realize that some 20,000 silk moths are boiled alive to make just one kilo of silk. But perhaps few of us are aware that several types of talcum powder, lipstick and hair dye are made safe for human use by testing them on squirrel monkeys, in order to find out at which dosage these monkeys die. A number of aftershave lotions are made burn proof by testing them on the bare skin of guinea pigs after their hair is pulled off. Many a perfume is made from civet musk. The civet is whipped, so that when it is in pain it secretes its musk into its pouch. The latter is then forced open and scraped with a spatula. Musk is also obtained from musk deer, which are caught in spiked traps. And the litany continues with pearls from tortured oysters, fur from strangled rabbits, and so on and so forth (Gandhi 1994: 52-54).

The newspapers regularly report murders, rapes, and other violent crimes. But some of us can be blissfully unaware of other forms of violence in our society; in fact, we may not even see them as examples of violence. We may pride ourselves as being more civilized than people in ancient times. We think we are not as barbarous as the gladiators and duelists of old. But this is far from the truth. Take boxing, for instance. Here is a sport in which one human being physically hurts a fellow human being. They are "punished" and "knocked out", to use just a couple of the expressions so common in describing boxing. Not only are the boxers badly bruised and severely injured, some have even died in the ring. One has only to glance at the bloodthirsty spectators, the way they gesticulate, shout and cheer, and even go at each other: it just shows the extent of violence in our society. And this "civilized" sport is a multi-million dollar business! The same can be said of similar sports like wrestling, especially free-style wrestling. And it is all in the name of entertainment! Similarly, whether it is pigeon shoots in the United States, where up to 25000 pigeons are released and shot by shooters (*Times of India*, 1998: 11), or cock fights in Indian villages, we keep on brazenly amusing ourselves at the expense of animals.

Apparently, even plants have (rudimentary) feelings. Experiments have found that when we "talk to plants" and show them attention, they grow and flourish much more than plants that are ignored, even if these latter are given the same water, manure, and sunlight as the former. If in the hot summer we walk past a withering tree or a parched plant, do we pause for even a moment in sympathy, thinking of the poor plant thirsting for water? Some may think that these are ridiculous examples, but it is in such ways that we can develop sensitivity towards all life.

It is worth pointing out that nonviolence also benefits the agent of nonviolence. The Templeton Foundation recently funded a "Forgiveness Research Program". This research, led by the director of the program, Everett L. Worthington, Jr., has made it amply clear that forgiveness and reconciliation are good for the well-being not only of the soul, but also of the psyche and the body. In a program entitled "Eye for an Eye," which was telecast on May 16th-17th 1999, CNN, making a reference to forgiveness research, showed how rage and the thirst for revenge not only consume the soul and rob it of its inner peace, but also tear apart the body. Instead of hurting the hated person, it hurts oneself. Laboratory experiments have proved that in unforgiving conditions one's blood pressure, heart rate, and sweat rate shoot up. The conclusion is clear: revenge is not sweet, but bitter; while forgiveness and reconciliation take the hurt away. Moreover, experiments with chimpanzees indicate that there seems to be an evolutionary basis for forgiveness: it is vital for the survival of the species. There is now a scientific confirmation of what we have observed in daily life: have we not noticed an infuriated person becoming flushed? Have we not observed such a person's stammering speech and quivering lips?

Nonviolence in its complete and perfect form is surely utopian, but one cannot deny its importance and significance for the world of today, and if we choose to ignore it, our very survival is at stake. A nuclear war, for instance, will bring total destruction. In this nuclear age, the only way open to us is peaceful dialogue. Gandhi asked rhetorically, "Has not the atom bomb proved the futility of all violence?" (Gandhi 1994-1949: 2: 55).

What does the future hold for us? Our future lies in our children. Are we preparing them for peace or for annihilation? Some of the signs are definitely disturbing. Violence is on the increase in movies, TV programs, and·even comic books. One has only to enter a toyshop to see the great variety of toys related to war: toy guns, tanks, battle ships, bomber aircraft. So many computers and video games are also full of violence. We seem to be telling our children that war is fun, an enjoyable game.

While many children are being initiated into a culture of violence, some adults, on their part, decided to attack the apostle of non-violence himself. In 1998 a Marathi Play, entitled *Mī Nāthurām Godse boltoy* ("I am Nathuram Godse Speaking"), which glorified Gandhi's assassin, was playing to packed houses in Maharashtra, India. It was reported that the audience cheered and applauded with gusto (*The Indian Express*, 1998: 3). It should be noted that, yielding to the cries of protest from several quarters, the Government finally banned the controversial play. Nathuram Godse's bullet tried to silence the Mahatma, but his voice still speaks to us, challenging us to strive after nonviolence, especially during this International Decade of Peace.

BIBLIOGRAPHY

Anon., 1998. "To shoot or not to shoot pigeons?" *The Times of India*, Mumbai edition, August 23.

Anon., 2000. "PETA slaughters treatment of cattle at Deonar abattoir," *The Indian Express*, Pune edition, December 22.

Anon, 2001. "Institute fails to improve conditions under which animals are kept," *The Times of India*, Pune edition, January 8.

Backianadan, Joseph Francis, 1991. *Love in the Life and Works of Mahatma Gandhi*, Bangalore: Sterling Publishers and St. Peter's Pontifical Institute of Theology.

Bondurant, Joan V, 1959. *Conquest of Violence: The Gandhian Philosophy of Conflict*, Bombay: Oxford University Press.

Buber, Martin, 1963. *Pointing the Way: Collected Essays*, ed. and trans. Maurice Friedman, New York and Evanson: Harper Brothers, 1957; Harper Torchbook.

Chander, Jag Parvesh, ed., 1945. *Teachings of Mahatma Gandhi*, with a Foreword by Rajendra Prasad, Lahore: The Indian Printing Works.

Desai, Mahadev, 1946. *The Gospel of Selfless Action: The Gita according to Gandhi*, 1946; 4th impression 1956.

Dhawan, G. N., 1946.*The Political Philosophy of Mahatma Gandhi*, with a Foreword by S. Radhakrishnan, Bombay: Popular Book Depot.

Ferrari, Frank, 1997. "Forgiving the Unforgivable: An Interview with Archbishop Desmond Tutu," *Commonweal* 124(15), 13-18.

Gandhi, M. K., 1944-1949. *Non-violence in Peace and War*, 2 vols., vol. 1, 2nd ed., vol. 2, ed. Bharatan Kumarappa, 1949, reprint 1960, Ahmedabad: Navajivan Publishing House.

Gandhi, M. K., 1957. *Selections from Gandhi*, comp. Nirmal Kumar Bose, 2nd ed., reprint 1968, Ahmedabad: Navajivan Publishing House.

Gandhi, M. K., 1958-1988. *The Collected Works of Mahatma Gandhi*, 90 vols, plus Index Vol., Delhi: Publications Division, Government of India.

Gandhi, M. K., 1959. *The Moral Basis of Vegetarianism*, comp. R. K. Prabhu, Ahmedabad: Navajivan Publishing House.

Gandhi, Maneka, 1994. *Heads and Tails*, Mapusa, Goa: The Other India Press.

Gandhi, Maneka, 1996. *The Second Heads and Tails*, Mapusa, Goa: The Other India Press.

Gandhi, Rajmohan, 1999. *Revenge and Reconciliation: Understanding South Asian History*, New Delhi: Penguin Books.

Iyer, Raghavan N., 1973. *The Moral and Political Thought of Mahatma Gandhi*, Delhi: Oxford University Press.

Nakhre, Amrut W., 1982. *Social Psychology of Nonviolent Action: A Study of Three Satyagrahas*, Delhi: Chanakya Publications.

Nelson, Stuart, 1975. " Gandhian Concept of Non-violence," in *Facets of Gandhian Thought*, ed J. S. Mathur and P. C. Sharma, pp. 57-76.

Parekh, Bhikhu, 1997. *Gandhi*, Oxford: Oxford University Press.

Raikar-Mhatre, Sumedha, 1998. "Godse attacks Gandhiji; audience laps it up," *The Indian Express,* Pune edition, July 16.

Tähtinen, Unto, 1976. *Ahiṃs Non-violence in Indian Tradition*, London: Rider.

Tutu, Desmond Mpilo, 1999. *No Future without Forgiveness*, New York: Doubleday.

Whitney, William Dwight, 1885. *Roots, Verb-forms, and Primary Derivatives of the Sanskrit Language: A Supplement to His Sanskrit Grammar*, Bibliothek indogermanischer Grammatiken, Band 2 , Anhang 2, Leipzig: Breitkopf and Härtel; London: Trübner.

In: Religion, Terrorism and Globalization
Editor: K.K. Kuriakose, pp.51-61

ISBN 1-59454-553-7

Chapter 3

PRACTICE OF *AHIMSA* IN BUDDHISM

T. Kenjitsu Nakagaki

Buddhist Chaplain, Columbia University, New York

The concept of *ahimsa* or no killing and nonviolence is a difficult practice to adhere to even today. Since the Sept. 11, 2001 tragedy in New York, *ahimsa* has been challenged in our society. For Buddhists, *ahimsa* or nonviolence is an essential practice. I have been re-examining the meaning of *ahimsa* in Buddhism as I have participated in the many peace activities in New York. How important is *ahimsa* in Buddhism, especially in my particular tradition of Jodoshinshu Buddhism?

In this paper I would like to discuss the meaning of *ahimsa* in Buddhism, and try to show that it is at the core of Buddhism. It is closely linked to the fundamental concepts and practice of Buddhism. I would like to present the basic concept of *ahimsa* in Buddhism based upon the Buddhist scriptures from the *Theravada* and *Mahayana* sutras, because *Theravada* Buddhism and *Mahayana* Buddhism are considered to be the two main divisions of Buddhism.

First, I would like to briefly define the term *ahimsa*. *Ahimsa*[1] consists of two parts, that is, "*a*" plus "*himsa*." The "a" is a negative prefix, simply "no" or "not." And "*himsa*" is a derivation from the root "*han*", meaning "to kill" and "to injure." Therefore, *ahimsa* means "not to kill" and "not to injure."

Buddhism was founded by the Gautama or Shakyamuni Buddha in the 5th or 6th Century BCE in India. Based upon the enlightenment experience by Shakyamuni Buddha, the teachings were spread throughout India, then China and other Asian countries, and now all over the world. The main idea is based upon the interdependence or interconnectedness of all existence: therefore, everything is constantly changing. There is no self which exists totally independent and "Enlightenment" can be realized by true awakening to the universal nature of interdependence.

The Buddha-Dharma can be understood as "The Buddha's Teaching" as well as the "Teaching to become a Buddha." The Buddha's Teaching emphasizes the teachings personally taught by the Shakyamuni Buddha, which is emphasized by the *Theravada*

---

[1] Malasekera, G.P. *Encyclopedia of Buddhism.* 1961-65. (volume I, page 287)

tradition of Buddhism. Teaching to become a Buddha emphasizes the teachings that lead us to Enlightenment, which is stressed by the *Mahayana* tradition of Buddhism.

Theravada or "Way of Elders" is a surviving school of the older branch of Buddhism and focuses to this day on preserving and perpetuating verbatim the original words of the historical Buddha. The Four Noble Truths, which were emphasized as the main teaching of the Buddha, are an aspect of self-benefit. *Theravada* Buddhism spread to Burma, Sri Lanka, Laos, Thailand, Bangladesh, Afghanistan, and other places in South and East Asia.

Mahayana or "Large Vehicle" took the broader approach to spread the Teaching of the Buddha, following the heart or intention of the Buddha. Emphasized are the ideas of *upaya* or "Skillful Means," the Six *Paramitas*, and *Bodhisattvas* who decide to remain in the world of delusion because of the compassion for all beings, which are aspects of benefiting others. *Mahayana* Buddhism spread to China, Korea, Japan, Tibet, Vietnam and some other Asian countries.

In *Mahayana* Buddhism, we find different schools of Buddhism such as Zen, Pure Land, Nichiren, etc. Each school has developed its unique teachings, but we always find a common basic foundation of Buddhist teachings, as all of the Buddhist sects are based upon the Buddhist sutras or scriptures, which reveal the world of Enlightenment.

NATURE OF VIOLENCE IN BUDDHISM

Why did violence arise? It is anger, hatred and the feeling of revenge etc. that causes violence and war.

> *"He reviled me! He struck me! He defeated me. He robbed me!"* In those who do not gird
> *themselves up with this, hatred is quelled. In this world, hatred never yet has dispelled hatred.*
> *It is the absence of hatred that leads to peace. This law is ancient and will last forever.*
> *(Dhammapada[2], Chapter 1)*

This is a passage that I have used on many occasions at peace gatherings since the Sept. 11 tragedy. Whenever I am invited to Interfaith Peace gatherings in New York City or asked to share Buddhist perspectives on war with others, I always quote this passage. Attachment to anger and hatred need to be avoided from the aspect of the Buddhist teaching of *sunyata* or emptiness. Anger and hatred may be escalated when we are attached to them. Violence is not the answer to violence. Hatred is not the answer to hatred. This is the wisdom of the Buddha concerning anger, hatred and violence. Practicing *ahimsa* is the answer in the time of "*himsa*" or violence. Practicing patience as in the six *paramitas*, practicing compassion and loving kindness are the answer for Buddhist practitioners, when confronted by "*himsa.*"

The above quotation has played an important role in history and life. It was used when Japan lost World War II. When it was stated by Sri Lanka, Japan was able to avoid becoming a territory of another country.

It also played an important role in Japanese Buddhist history. It was the passage that guided young *Honen* into the path of the Buddha, a path which led him to create a new school of Buddhism, called *Jodoshu* or Pure Land Buddhism.

---

[2] Nakamura, Hajime. *Shinri no kotota, Kanko no kotoba.* Iwanami Shoten 1978 (page 10)

In the *Kamakura* Era in Japan, various new Buddhist sects were formed, such as *Jodo* (Pure Land) *-shu*, *Jodoshinshu* (Shin Buddhism), *Zen* (*Rinzai-shu*, *Soto-shu*, *Obaku-shu*) and *Nichiren-shu*. Among them, *Jodo-shu*, founded by *Honen Shonin* (1133-1212) was the first new school in Buddhism in the 12th Century. The story about *Honen* and why he began to walk the path of Buddhism and then created Pure Land Buddhism in Japan is well known.

When *Honen* was young, his father *Tokikuni Urum,a* was killed in front of *Honen*. Young *Honen* told his father that he would take revenge, *Tokikuni* said to *Honen* in his last words, "If you take revenge in *Gennai Akashi* [who killed *Tokikui*], his children will take revenge upon you later. There is no way to cease anger and hatred from generation to generation. I want you to learn the Buddha-Dharma and find a way to overcome such a cycle of revenge."

Ordained at the age of 15, *Honen* studied and practiced various paths of Buddhism for almost 30 years in order to find the answer to overcoming anger and hatred in ordinary people. Then, when he encountered the passage[3] of *Shantao*, a Chinese Pure Land master, he found the answer to be the path of *Nembutsu* to liberate us equally.

The *Nembutsu* is the path by which all sentient beings experience the Buddha's Boundless Wisdom and Compassion, particularly those who have suffered from the blind passions of anger, hatred, greed, and ignorance. It is this wisdom which makes us aware of suffering and pain arising from attachment to blind passions. It is this compassion which embraces the anger and hatred and transforms them into virtues.

Here, we see that the essence of the *Nembutsu* teaching in Pure Land Buddhism is deeply rooted in the idea of *ahimsa* found in the *Dhammapada*. Thus in Pure Land Buddhism, practicing the Nembutsu path means to practice *ahimsa*. *Shinran Shonin* (1173-1262) who was a disciple of *Honen*, and a founder of Pure Land Shin Buddhism stated:

> Those who feel uncertain of birth should say the Nembutsu aspiring first for their own birth in the Buddha Land. Those who feel that their own birth is completely settled should, mindful of the Buddha's benevolence, hold the Nembutsu in their hearts and say it to respond in gratitude to that benevolence, with the wish, "May there be peace in the world, and may the Buddha's teaching spread![4]

Practicing the *Nembutsu -Dharma* means to cultivate the mindful heart of "peace."

In terms of dealing with anger, the Buddha showed an interesting example when Brahmin *Bharadvaja* blamed the Buddha.

> Brahmin Bharadvaja angrily criticized the Buddha, who then said to him, "Brahmin, what do you think? Do your friends. Allies, relatives, or guests come to your home?"
> "Gautama. Yes, they sometimes come."
> "Brahmin, what do you think? Do you sometimes serve soup, or delicacies?"
> "Gautama, Yes, I do."
> "Brahmin, if they do not accept it, then to whom does the food belong?"
> "Gautama, if they do not accept it, it belongs to us."

---

[3] "Single-heartedly practicing the saying of the Name of Amida alone –whether walking, standing, sitting, or reclining – without regard to the length of time, and without abandoning it from moment to moment: this is called "the act of true settlement," for it is in accord with the Buddha's Vow." In particular, the last phrase "for it is in accord with the Buddha's Vow" moved *Honen* so deeply. He realized the *Nembutsu*, saying the Amida's Name, is the great path selected by the Buddha with Inconceivable Wisdom and Compassion in order to liberate all beings equally.

"That's correct. Brahmin. you criticized us even though we don't speak ill of you. You became angry at us who do not get angry. You became argumentative to us who are not argumentative. However. we do not accept it. Brahmin. therefore. it belongs to you...." (*Samyutta-Nikaya*, Chapter 7)[5]

AHIMSA FROM THE ASPECT OF PRECEPTS (*SILA*) IN BUDDHISM

Ahimsa is the first of five precepts or ten precepts that the Buddha taught - "do not kill."

The five precepts[6] are recited in Buddhists in *Theravada* tradition. The phrase "*Panatipata Veramani Sikkhapadam Samadiyami* (I observe the training rule to abstain from killing)" is the first precept of "do not kill" or *ahimsa*.

All beings fear violence; all fear death. If you take yourself as the measure, do not kill and do not let others kill. All beings fear violence; all love life. If you take yourself as the measure, do not kill and do not let others kill. (*Dhammapada*[7], Chapter 10*)*

Do not kill living beings. Do not let others kill. Do not allow others to kill. One needs to control violence toward all living beings whether they are strong and powerful in society or they are fearful and weak. (*Sutta-Nipata*[8], Chapter 2, #14*)*

"Do not kill" also includes "Do not let others kill." This means that Buddhism opposes any kind of killing. The Buddha Shakyamuni himself faced several wars. One of them was the dispute between *Kapilavatthu* and *Koli*[9] over irrigating water.

A long dry spell had persisted, causing the rivers to trickle little water, which in turn created irrigation problems. The two cities of *Kapilavatthu* and *Koli* saw struggles arising over the limited waters of the River *Rohini* flowing between them. The tight water situation caused the farmers of both banks to speak ill of those on the opposite bank until finally, armed with clubs and swords, blood was shed in the strife. When the Buddha heard this, he came to *Kapilavatthu* in time to position himself between the two opposing armies. The Buddha asked:

Why do you congregate here? Why are you about to engage in battle?
.....It was over water needed for irrigation
Compared to a human life, how valuable is water?
.....When comparing water to human life, the value of water was almost nil.
Why, then, is it for water, which has such little value, you all are trying to destroy invaluable human life?

[4] *Collected Works of Shinran.* Jodo Shinshu Hongwanji-ha 1997 (page 560)
[5] Nakamura, Hajime. *Akuma to no Taiwa,* Iwanami Shoten 1986 (page 128-129)
[6] Five precepts are:
  Panatipata Veramani Sikkhapadam Samadiyami I observe the training rule to abstain from killing.
  Adinnadana Veramani Sikkhapadam Samadiyami I observe the training rule to abstain from stealing.
  Kamesumicchacara Veramani Sikkhapadam Samadiyami *I observe the training rule to abstain from adultery.*
  Musavada Veramani Sikkhapadam Samadiyami I observe the training rule to abstain from lying.
  Surameraya Majjapamadatthana Veramani Sikkhapadam Samadiyami I observe the training rule to abstain from intoxicants. which cause heedlessness.
[7] Nakamura, Hajime. *Shinri no kotota, Kanko no kotoba.* Iwanami Shoten 1978 (page 28)
[8] Nakamura, Hajime. *Budda no kotoba (Suttanipata).* Iwanami Shoten 1984 (page 81)
[9] *Buddha-Dharma.* Numata Center for Buddhist Translation and Research 1984 *(*page 96)

After the Buddha intervened, it was settled. The Buddha was able to stop the people from killing each other. The Buddha practiced *ahimsa* even when the war was going on. The Buddha was *ahimsa* itself. He never participated in warfare, and he tried to prevent war.[10]

Precepts are one of the Three Learnings [11] of Buddhism, namely precepts, meditation and wisdom. All the practitioners of Buddhism should learn these three basic categories. They are considered to embrace all aspects of Buddhist doctrine and practice.

In *Mahayana* Buddhism, *sila* is one of six *Paramitas*[12]. The *paramitas* are the six kinds of practice by which bodhisattvas are able to attain Enlightenment in *Mahayana* traditions. *Paramita* means reaching or fulfilling the other shore of enlightenment.

A disciple of the Buddha shall not himself kill, encourage others to kill, kill by expedient means, praise killing, rejoice at witnessing killing, or kill through incantation or deviant mantras. He must not create the causes, conditions, methods, or karma of killing, and shall not intentionally kill any living creature.

As a Buddha's disciple, he ought to nurture a mind of compassion and filial piety, always devising expedient means to rescue and protect all beings. If instead, he fails to restrain himself and kills sentient beings without mercy, he commits a Parajika (major) offense. (Brahman Net Sutra[13])

In the *Mahayana* text, you see more detailed explanations of *ahimsa*, applied not only to ongoing wars, but also to removing conditions which may cause killing later. Trying to avoid hurting yourself as well as others is the precept that the Buddha established.

KNOWING YOURSELF

There is nothing more lovable than myself in all directions. In the same way, for other people, they themselves are most lovable. Therefore, treat not others in ways that you yourself would find hurtful. (Udana-Varga,[14] Chapter 5)

All beings fear violence; all fear death. If you take yourself as the measure, do not kill and do not let others kill. All beings fear violence; all love life. If you take yourself as the measure, do not kill and do not let others kill. (Udana-Varga,[15] Chapter 5; Dhammapada,[16] Chapter 10)

Buddhism centers around the Enlightenment Experience that the Buddha achieved through his deep meditation. To know who you are and what you are is essential in any form of Buddhism. Instead of looking outside, the Buddha emphasizes looking inside of ourselves.

---

[10] There was another incident in which the Buddha was directly involved. The Buddha intervened with the army of King *Vidudabha* of *Kosala* who attempted to attack the *Sakya* clan, the Buddha's original clan. The Buddha sat three times before the Vidudabha' army and was able to stop them, but at the fourth time, the Buddha was not there, because the Buddha saw the past deep karma that the *Sakya* clan had created. The *Sakya* clan was destroyed, and all of the people were killed.

[11] Sila (Precepts) are for stopping evil and practicing good. Dhyana (Meditation) is to practice concentration by calming down one's mind and body, and gaining single-pointedness without waving of mind. Prajna (wisdom) is to understand true reality of things and see things as they are.

[12] The six *paramitas* are *Dana-paramita* (giving), *Sila-paramita* (precepts), *Ksanti-paramita* (perseverance), *Virya-paramita* (efforts), *Dhyana-paramita* (meditation), and *Prajna-paramita* (wisdom)

[13] *Kokuyaku Daizokyo:* Kokumin Bunko Kankokai 1917 (Volume 3 Bonnmokyo page 7, 8)

[14] Nakamura, Hajime. *Shinri no kotota, Kanko no kotoba.* Iwanami Shoten 1978 (page 179)

[15] Nakamura, Hajime. *Shinri no kotota, Kanko no kotoba.* Iwanami Shoten 1978 (page 179)

[16] Nakamura, Hajime. *Shinri no kotota, Kanko no kotoba.* Iwanami Shoten 1978 (page 28)

Once one realizes the importance of himself or herself, one should be able to understand the importance of others.

There is a concept called "Buddha-nature" (*Buddhata* or *Tathagata-garbha*). It means that all sentient beings have the possibility or potentiality to be awakened and to become Buddha. Many times Buddha-nature is clouded by blind passions. Truly realizing one's Buddha-nature leads to the realization of the Buddha-nature of others.

> *Do not reflect upon missteps of others, their deeds and misdeeds, but rather look upon what you yourself have done and left undone. (Dhammapada, Chapter 4[17])*

"Knowing yourself" has two aspects. One is the enlightened quality of Buddha-nature, and the other is a deluded existence caused by blind passions. To know yourself means to realize what selfish and ill-willed beings each of us is. In Mahayana Buddhism, especially Buddhism in Japan, it is very important to be aware of ordinariness. We are ordinary beings who make many mistakes and do not know what is right and what is wrong. Master *Saicho* of the *Tendai* Tradition described himself as "lowest ordinary being Saicho." Master *Honen* of the *Jodoshu* Pure Land Buddhism called himself "foolish ignorant Honen-bo." And Master *Shinran* of the *Jodoshinshu* Buddhism called himself "foolish and stubble-haired Shinran."

Prince *Shotoku* (573-622) contributed a great deal to Buddhism in Japan, and clearly stated his policy based on *ahimsa*. Prince *Shotoku* was considered as the Shakyamuni Buddha in Japan. He is known for establishing a centralized government based on Buddhist principles. His ideals of government were stated in the "Seventeen-articles Constitution" written in 604 by Prince *Shotoku*. It begins with the importance of harmony, saying:

> Harmony is to be valued, and an avoidance of wanton opposition to be honored. All men are influenced by class-feelings, and there are few who are intelligent. Hence there are some who disobey their lords and fathers, or who maintain feuds with the neighboring villages. But when those above are harmonious and those below are friendly, and there is concord in the discussion of business, right views of things spontaneously gain acceptance. Then what is there which cannot be accomplished! (Article 1)[18]

We can see clearly in the Constitution the importance of harmony, and trying to avoid violence. How can this harmony be achieved? It is the teachings of the Buddha which can provide guidance. So, in Chapter 2, it says:

> Sincerely revere the three treasures. The three treasures: Buddha, Dharma and Sangha are the final refuge and are the supreme objects of faith in all countries. Can any man in any age ever fail to respect these teachings? Few men are utterly bad. They may be taught to follow it. But if they do not go to the three treasures, how shall their crookedness be made straight? (Article 2)[19]

Chapter 10 talks about the awareness of ordinary beings, who don't know what the true reality is all about and that they are deluded by their blind passions. When we are attached to

[17] Nakamura, Hajime. *Shinri no kotota. Kanko no kotoba.* Iwanami Shoten 1978 (page 17)
[18] *Jodoshinshu Seiten*, Hongwanji Shuppanbu 1988 (page 1433)
[19] *Jodoshinshu Seiten*, Hongwanji Shuppanbu 1988 (page 1433)

one view, we tend to become just, right, sage and/or wise, and consider others as unjust, wrong, evil and/or foolish. Human beings ultimately do not know what is just and what is right. Therefore, it is very important to attain enlightenment so that we can see things as they are. It is equally important for us to realize what we see is not necessarily ultimate truth, just, right, etc. Recognition of foolishness and ordinariness is very important wisdom that we should have within us.

> Let us control ourselves and not be resentful when others disagree with us, for all men have hearts and each heart has its own leanings. The right of others is our wrong, and our right is their wrong. We are not unquestionably sages, nor are they unquestionably fools. Both of us are simply ordinary men. How can anyone lay down a rule by which to distinguish right from wrong? For we are all wise sometimes and foolish at others. Therefore, though others give way to anger, let us on the contrary dread our own faults, and though we may think we alone are in the right, let us follow the majority and act like them. (Article 10)[20]

In my view, the above articles by Prince *Shotoku* are an example of profound wisdom based on the Buddhist teachings.

PRACTICE OF COMPASSION

How do we approach violence? It is by the practice of compassion or loving-kindness directed to any violence. Cultivating the mind of compassion will control anger, hatred and aggression, and from this sequence one will control violence that comes out of anger, hatred and aggression. This is seen throughout many Buddhist texts.

> May all beings be happy and secure; May their hearts be wholesome. Whatever living beings there may be, feeble or strong, tall, fat, or medium, short, small, or large, without exception, seen or unseen, those dwelling far or near, those who are born or who are to be born, may all beings be happy.(Sutta-Nipata,[21] Chapter 1, #8)
>
> Let none deceive another, not despise any person whatsoever in any place. Let him/her not wish any harm to another out of anger or ill-will. Just as a mother would protect her only child at the risk of her own life, even so, let him/her cultivate a boundless heart towards all beings. Let his/her thoughts of boundless love pervade the whole world: above, below and across without any obstruction, without any hatred, without any enmity. (Sutta-Nipata,[22] Chapter 1, #8)
>
> The Buddha's Mind is great compassion and loving kindness. It embraces sentient beings with unconditional benevolence. (Meditation Sutra on Amitayus[23])
>
> I became ill, because sentient beings are in suffering. (Vimalakirti Sutra,[24] Chapter 5)

Encouraging the performance of wholesome acts is very important in Buddha's teachings. *Metta* or the loving kindness meditation is essential in Buddhist practice. When the

---

[20] *Jodoshinshu Seiten*, Hongwanji Shuppanbu 1988 (page 1436)

[21] Nakamura, Hajime. *Budda no kotoba (Suttanipata)*. Iwanami Shoten 1984 (page 37)

[22] Nakamura, Hajime. *Budda no kotoba (Suttanipata)*. Iwanami Shoten 1984 (page 37, 38)

[23] *Kokuyaku Daizokyo*: Kokumin Bunko Kankokai 1917 (Volume 1, Kanmuryojukyo, page 18)

[24] *Kokuyaku Daizokyo*: Kokumin Bunko Kankokai 1917 (Volume 10, Yuimakyo, page 53)

Buddha talks about actions, there are three kinds of actions: action with the physical body, action with the mouth, and action with the mind. This is the practice of compassion, or cultivating the mind of loving-kindness for all beings. The practice of compassion or thinking of others' happiness, peace and well-being is based on the idea of the interdependence or interconnectedness of our existence. One exists because of everything else, and nothing exists independently. The benefits that Buddhism talks about are always of two aspects – self-benefit (or wisdom) and benefiting others (or compassion). Both are important.

Here, I would like to define compassion as it is perceived in Buddhism. Compassion as *maitri* (from the word "friendship"), and compassion as *karuna* (from the word "voice of suffering and pain") are two basic meanings. As friendship works on the same level, there are no hierarchical differences in compassion. It works on the level of equality with trusting each other and helping each other. From this, *maitri* means giving happiness to others equally. As we hear the voices of suffering and pain, share and understand the suffering and pain. From this, *karuna* means to get rid of suffering and pain. In addition to these two definitions, compassion also means joy and happiness as well as non-attachment.

You can see by definition that compassion and suffering are inseparable in Buddhism. Knowing the suffering and why there is suffering and how we can overcome the suffering is the wisdom of the Buddha. Once realizing this noble truth, one cannot help but act with compassion. Therefore, compassion should be understood as wisdom in motion. Theravada Buddhism tends to emphasize the Four Noble Truths, or self-benefit aspect, and Mahayana Buddhism emphasizes compassion or the aspect of benefiting others.

CONCERNING WEAPONS AND WAR

The practice of compassion is the path by which to overcome anger and hatred. Maintaining compassion in any situation may be difficult but we always need to practice it. How do we practice compassion in wars?

Look at the people who are fighting to kill. Their fears rose when they took weapons to attack. (Sutta –Nipata, [25] Chapter 4, #10)

First, do not carry any weapon to hurt others. This is so simple, yet once we get weapons, it is difficult to throw them away. Abolishing weapons will be the simplest way to stop wars. Having weapons also means possessing power to control others. All the fears come from existing weapons. Do not take any weapon from the start.

> *Bodhisattvas that abide in this stage are by nature completely free from the killing of living things. They are without brutality or the need to use weapons, and they do not harbor feelings of anger and resentment. With humility, they are full of good will and forgiveness towards living beings, only wishing for their welfare. These Bodhisattvas do not even have thoughts of distressing living beings, much less think of turning these thoughts into doing actual harm. (Avatamsaka Sutra,[26] Section of Ten Stages)*

---

[25] Nakamura, Hajime. *Budda no kotoba (Suttanipata)*. Iwanami Shoten 1984 (page 203)
[26] *Kokuyaku Daizokyo:* Kokumin Bunko Kankokai 1917 (Volume 8, Yuimakyo, page 208)

When a war happens, (the Bodhisattva) raises the mind of compassion, and teaches the sentient beings to settle on the foundation of no-fighting. If the great war happens, (the Bodhisattva) raises the mind of equanimity to embrace both ally and enemy, and with his/her high spirit, controls people's anger, and makes them peaceful and secured. (Vimalakirti Sutra[27], Chapter 8)

Keeping the mind of compassion and controlling anger in any situation, including in time of war, is essential in Buddhism. One needs to remember that we are all living beings who have precious lives whether they may be your ally or your enemy.

Wherever the Buddha comes to stay, there is no state, town or village which is not blessed by his virtues. The whole country reposes in peace and harmony. The sun and the moon shine with pure brilliance; wind arises and rain falls at the right time. There is no calamity or epidemic, and so the country becomes wealthy, and its people enjoy peace. Soldiers and weapons become useless; and people esteem virtue, practice benevolence and diligently cultivate courteous modesty. (Sukhavativyuha Sutra[28])

There are various symbols that Buddhism uses to signify compassion and enlightenment. One well-known symbol is the lotus flower. It is a symbol of enlightenment which transforms evil into virtue. The lotus does not grow on the plain ground (peaceful ground), but grows in the muddy pond of suffering and pain. In the end, violence and evilness need to be transformed into peace and virtuosity, because of the practice of wisdom and compassion.

In the story of the Buddha's enlightenment in Buddhagaya, Maras, or evil gods, attempted to stop the Buddha from becoming enlightened. They sent a great army to force the Buddha to move from his meditating under the Bodhi Tree. Mara's torrents of rocks, swords, and fire rained down upon the Buddha, but they were all transformed into a crown of flowers, and changed into scented powder. They were scattered all over the ground.[29] This story reveals the transformational nature of Buddha's teachings. Here, you see that the Buddha's path is the way in which to transform himsa, violence and weapons, into ahimsa, non-violence and peace.

King Asoka (circa 273-232 BCE), who created the largest territory of the Maurya dynasty in the history of India, was transformed from violence to ahimsa and peace by the teaching of the Buddha. After his conquest of Kalinga kingdom, he truly realized the tragic nature of wars, and governed the country with the spirit of ahimsa and compassion, taking refuge in the Buddha's teachings. He created rock-edicts and pillar-edicts in various places in his territories to let the people know about the Dharma in which King Asoka believed and encouraged the people to practice it.

Rock Edict XIII described the conquest of *Kalinga*:

The Kalinga country was conquered by King Asoka in the eighth year of his reign. One hundred fifty thousand persons were carried away captive, 100,000 were slain, and many times that numbers died. Immediately after the Kalinga had been conquered, King Asoka became intensely devoted to the study of truth, to the love of truth, and to the understanding of truth. King Asoka, conqueror of the Kalinga, is moved to remorse now. For he has left

---

[27] *Kokuyaku Daizokyo:* Kokumin Bunko Kankokai 1917 (Volume 10, Yuimakyo, page 88, 89)

[28] *Kokuyaku Daizokyo:* Kokumin Bunko Kankokai 1917 (Volume 1, Dimuryojukyo, page 73)

[29] *Buddha-Dharma*, Numata Center for Buddhist Translation and Research 1984 (page 27-30)

profound sorrow and regret because the conquest of a people previously involved slaughter, death, and deportation.[30]

King *Asoka* considered truth–conquest the most important conquest, instead of sword-conquest after the *Kalinga* war. Here the truth is the Dharma or Buddha's teaching.

The contents of the Edicts by King *Asoka* may be indexed[31] as:

a)   Forbidding slaughter of animals. Sacredness of all life.
b)   Establishments for the dispensing of medicine for men and for animals.
c)   Duties of royal executive officers. Instruction to be given by the Council.
d)   Practice of the Dharma.
e)   Appointment of Superintendents of the Dharma and their duties.
f)   Prompt dispatch of business of State.
g)   Equality of all men of all sects, except in their striving for perfection.
h)   Change in the nature of the king's pleasure.
i)   Virtue is better than ceremonies.
j)   Fame does not bring gain, but good deeds make one free from evil inclinations.
k)   The highest gift is the gift of the Dharma
l)   By tolerance of other sects one benefits one's sect.

King *Asoka* spread non-violence based upon the sacredness of all life. Rock Edict IV states:

> For many hundred years in the past, slaughter of animals, cruelty to living creatures, discourtesy to relatives, and disrespect for priest and ascetics have been increasing. But now because of King Asoka's practice of the truth, summoning the people to exhibitions of the chariots of the gods, elephants, fireworks, and other heavenly displays. King Asoka's inculcation of truth has increased, beyond anything observed in many hundreds of years, abstention from killing animals and from cruelty to living beings, kindliness in human and family relations, respect for priests and ascetics, and obedience to mother and father and elders ...[32]

We see the transformation from violence to nonviolence/peace when Buddhism enters different areas. Like the case of King *Asoka*, the Tibetan race used to be a war-loving race, but when Buddhism entered Tibet in the 7th Century, they became a peace-loving race. The *Huns* in China attempted to invade with an army, but they stopped or decreased their invasion when Buddhism entered among their people.

CONCLUSION

Understanding *ahimsa* in Buddhism leads one to explore the fundamental principles of Buddhism such as wisdom and compassion. It means that *ahimsa* is imbedded in the core

---

[30] Translation is from Nikam and McKeown, The Edicts of Asoka. University of Chicago Press, 1974
[31] According to *Encyclopedia of Buddhism*, Malasekera, G.P.1961-65 (Vol. II page 183)
[32] Translation is from Nikam and McKeown, The Edicts of Asoka. University of Chicago Press, 1974

teachings and practices of Buddhism. Learning the Buddha's teachings and practicing the Buddha's path naturally guides us to act and think based upon *ahimsa*. Though violence may never disappear from human history, we need to continue to make efforts to practice nonviolence, transforming violence into peace.

Recently there are movements of "Engaged Buddhism" which emphasizes that Buddhists should actively involve themselves in dialogue, social and political actions. Though such movements may still be small in scale, Buddhists definitely need to contribute more to the peace movement in this present world, as the teachings of the Buddha have a lot to offer in terms of nonviolence and peace. Buddhists should actively share their wisdom with others, actively participate in various opportunities for peace, and should be more responsible to our world as members of the whole human race, as members of the race of living beings.

May peace prevail on the earth. May all beings learn to respect all lives. May we all practice *ahimsa* and compassion. May all beings be happy, well and peaceful.

BIBLIOGRAPHY

Buddha-Dharma, Numata Center for Buddhist Translation and Research (1984)

Collected Works of Shinran, translated by Hirota, D., Inagaki, H., Tokunaga, M. and Uryzu, R.; Jodo Shinshu Hongwanji-ha (1997)

Inagaki, Hisao. *The Three Pure land Sutras*. Nagata Bunshodo Inc. (1994)

Kokuyaku Daizokyo: Tsuruta, K. Kokumin Bunko Kankokai (1917)

Jodoshinshu Seiten, Committee for compiling sacred texts. Hongwanji Shuppanbu (1988)

Nakamura, Hajime. *Gotama Buddha –shakuson no shogai-*, Sunjusha Inc. (1969)

Nakamura, Hajime. *Shinri no kotota, Kanko no kotoba*. Iwanami Shoten (1978)

Nakamura, Hajime. *Bukkyogo Daijiten*, Tokyo Shoseki Inc. (1981)

Nakamura, Hajime. *Budda no kotoba (Suttanipata)*. Iwanami Shoten (1984)

Nakamura, Hajime. *Akuma to no Taiwa*, Iwanami Shoten (1986)

Nikam and McKeown, *The Edicts of Asoka* . University of Chicago Press, 1974

In: Religion, Terrorism and Globalization
Editor: K.K. Kuriakose, pp.63-79

ISBN 1-59454-553-7
© 2006 Nova Science Publishers, Inc.

Chapter 4

WITHOUT RAISING HER FIST OR EVEN HER VOICE: SHIPRAH, PUAH AND GOTAMĪ'S NON-VIOLENT RESISTANCE TO INJUSTICE

Vanessa R. Sasson

Comparative Religion in the Liberal Arts Department of
Marianopolis College, Montreal, Quebec

In both the Hebrew Bible and the Buddhist Pali Scriptures, stories of injustice are laid out and various responses emerge. Perhaps the most famous such story in the Hebrew Bible is the story of Moses standing before the Pharaoh and demanding justice and freedom for his people. Buddhist literature explores injustice most often through the medium of the Jātaka tales – the stories of the Buddha's previous lives – in which the Buddha faced adversity of different kinds and attempted to respond in accordance with Buddhist principles. Female characters are similarly challenged in both literatures, but they are given significantly less treatment than the male characters. A few women have, however, emerged from the shadows. In the Hebrew Bible, two midwives faced a very difficult situation when the Pharaoh commanded them to kill the male Hebrew children at birth. In the Buddhist literature, Mahāpajāpati Gotamī was refused admission into the monastic order because she was a woman. These women were confronted with injustice, and they all rose to the occasion by fighting back without raising their fists, or even their voices. By looking at these women on their own and then comparatively, we will gain insight into each of their stories and will be able to reflect the story of one onto the other. We will also gain the opportunity to acknowledge their non-violence in challenging times.

THE EXODUS MIDWIVES

In the opening pages of the book of Exodus, we meet a Pharaoh who is desperately trying to control his raging Israelite population. Their numbers increased to the point that he feared they would eventually rise up against him and overtake his country (Ex. 1:10). He therefore set taskmasters over them, hoping that enslavement would both reduce his Hebrew demographics and keep the people under firm control. Miraculously, however, the Hebrew fertility rate was unaffected by his plan, and the Pharaoh soon found himself looking for further re-enforcements in his war against Hebrew fecundity. He chose two midwives, named Shiphrah and Puah in the biblical text, and commanded them to look upon the "two stones" (סינבא) when the Hebrew women gave birth, and "if it is a boy, kill him, but if it is a girl, you shall let her live" (Ex. 1:16).[1] These two heroic midwives chose not to obey his evil command, because, according to the text, they feared God (Ex. 1:17). When the Pharaoh asked them why they had refused to comply, they answered – mischievously perhaps – that Hebrew women were not like Egyptian women. They were so lively (היות) that they managed to give birth before the midwives even arrived. The Pharaoh apparently believed them.

One of the first questions that requires attention in this story is the question of who these midwives were. The text ambiguously describes them as תדלימה תירבעה. This can be translated either as "midwives of the Hebrews," or as "Hebrew midwives." The question we are therefore left with is, were they Hebrew or Egyptian? No clear answer presents itself, either by way of narrative logic, etymology, or archeological evidence, but it is generally assumed, by both scholars and the early rabbinic literature, that the women were Hebrew.

From the perspective of narrative logic, it would make less sense for the midwives to have been Egyptian than Hebrew. Were the midwives Egyptian, the Pharaoh would have been assuming that Hebrew women, in their moment of greatest vulnerability, would have been willing to entrust themselves to women who belonged to the community that was enslaving them. Surely most women would be suspicious of their enemy's help, particularly when faced with impending childbirth. The more reasonable possibility is that the midwives were Hebrew. Hebrew women would have trusted Hebrew midwives, (and history is replete with traitors who are willing to betray their own communities in return for some kind of material benefit). It is therefore more likely that the women were Hebrew. Of course, the plan was not a good one either way: asking midwives – women dedicated to helping bring life into the world – to kill the infants. But at least if the women were Hebrew, there is a greater chance that the plan would have succeeded.

Etymologically, the names of the midwives – Shiphrah and Puah – are generally believed to be of Semitic origin. Shiphrah is believed to mean "beauty" in Hebrew or a related Canaanite dialect,[2] and Puah has been linked to the Ugaritic epic of Aqhat, often translated as "girl" or "lass."[3] The names are therefore probably not of Egyptian origin, leading us to conclude that the midwives were indeed Hebrew. Greenberg, however, reminds us that many Egyptianized Semites were living in Egypt, especially among the menial and slave classes.

---

[1] The "two stones" are the subject of great controversy in biblical scholarship. No consensus has yet been reached about either the proper translation of the term or what it actually refers to. The most popular understanding is that the term refers to the birth stool upon which the mother rested while giving birth. See among others, Sarna, N. *The JPS Torah Commentary: Exodus* (Philadelphia: Jewish Publication Society, 1991), 7; and Hyatt, J. P. *The New Century Bible Commentary: Exodus* (Grand Rapids, Michigan: W. B. Eerdmans, 1971), 61.

[2] Propp, W. H. C. *The Anchor Bible: Exodus 1-18: A New Translation with Introduction and Commentary* (New York: Doubleday, 1998), 139.

[3] This reasoning is repeated consistently in almost all recent scholarship since Albright. See Albright, W. F. "Northwest Semitic Names in a List of Egyptian Slaves from the Eighteenth Century BC." *Journal of the American Oriental Society* 74 (1954): 222-233. There therefore seems to be consensus on the issue of the etymology. For a translation of the *Tale of Aqhat*, see Pritchard, J. B., ed. *Ancient Near Eastern Texts Relating to the Old Testament* (2nd ed. Princeton: Princeton University Press, 1955), 149-155.

The Bible records Egyptians with Semitic names, such as Hagar.[4] When two populations live side by side for an extended period of time, it is only natural that they eventually influence each other and borrow each other's names. It is therefore possible that the midwives were Egyptian women with Semitic names. Childs also believes that the midwives were Egyptian, but for an entirely different reason. According to the Bible, the reason the midwives eventually disobeyed the Pharaoh was because they feared God. As Childs points out, this reasoning appears in the text as a great surprise.[5] If the women were Hebrew, their fear of God would not be unusual. They must therefore have been Egyptian according to this reading. Jonathan Cohen points out, however, that this is not a strong argument, "since the text does not say *YHWH*, but rather *Elohim*; and anyone who believes in a deity, be it a false god or the true God, would fear taking the life of an innocent babe, regardless of what people they belonged to."[6] Cohen is right in my opinion. That the midwives suddenly feared God does not necessarily imply that they were Egyptian. Fear of any god should not be considered a remarkable feature of the story, particularly given the orders the women were expected to follow. And their fear of God may as easily be used as evidence that they were Hebrew, for fearing God in the context of a biblical story may almost surely suggest a fear of the biblical God. In other words, the midwives' fear of God does not help us in our quest for establishing their identity. We may therefore only assume that they were Hebrew based on earlier arguments, but we cannot state this with any certainty.[7]

The early post-biblical and rabbinic authors were almost unanimously convinced that the midwives were Hebrew rather than Egyptian women.[8] They were also convinced that these women were, in reality, Jochebed and Miriam – Moses' mother and sister.[9] The early interpretive literature regularly busied itself with associating unknown characters in the text with characters already well known. Such a midrashic method serves to close gaps presented in the biblical text and render whole what otherwise might appear as fragmented. By associating Jochebed and Miriam with the midwives, a loose end is tied and incorporated more fully into the biblical story.

This interpretive literature, however, does more than just tie up loose ends. It also leads us into the theme of this paper. In perhaps one of the first recorded cases of civil disobedience in Western literature, both Shiphrah and Puah refused to follow the orders assigned to them. These two women, who, according to the Bible, were responsible for the delivery of all the

---

[4] Greenberg, M. *Understanding Exodus: The Heritage of Biblical Israel* (New York: Berman House, 1969), 27.

[5] Childs, B. S. *The Book of Exodus* (Philadelphia: Westminster, 1974), 17.

[6] Cohen, J. *The Origin and Evolution of the Moses Nativity* (Studies in the History of Religions, volume 58. Leiden: E. J. Brill, 1993), 19.

[7] In a theological essay, Thomas Römer also argues that the midwives were Egyptian. He believes that their Egyptian background demonstrates that the biblical text had a universal approach, that the Hebrews were not the only people depicted as having been heroic. By having foreigners such as the midwives and Zipporah take positive roles in the narrative, the biblical authors were making the clear statement that people of all backgrounds could make moral choices. Although this is an inspiring interpretation of the biblical text, Römer unfortunately does not sufficiently justify why he believes the midwives were Egyptian other than as a result of his theological expectations. See Römer, T. "Péricopes: les sages-femmes du Pharaon (Exode 1/15-22)." *Etudes théologiques et religieuses* 2 (1994): 265-270.

[8] Among the exceptions are Josephus (*Antiquitates Judaicae* II:206) and the Septuagint.

[9] There are two exceptions to this rule: in Sotah 11b and Exodus Rabbah 1:13, Shiphrah is identified as Jochebed and Puah is identified as either Elisheba (Aaron's wife, and thus Jochebed's daughter-in-law), or Miriam. In identifying Puah as Elisheba, the text may have been attempting to solve the otherwise obvious problem of Miriam being too young to assist her mother in midwifery. According to Exodus Rabbah for instance, she was five years old at the time of Moses' birth (Exodus Rabbah 1:15).

Hebrew community's children – which in itself is rather spectacular[10] – refused to comply with the Pharaoh's schemes. Instead of bringing death upon the Israelites, they chose to give life, just as their careers suggested they should do. The biblical text explains that they chose to risk their careers, and probably even their lives, because "they feared God" (Ex. 1:17). These midwives proved themselves to be extraordinary women – heroes who chose to defy authority with both courage and cunning. Through faith in God, they found their way to a morality that gave them the determination required to challenge the injustice presented to them through non-violent means. The post-biblical interpreters would never have associated Moses' family members with these women had they been in any way negatively portrayed. It is therefore precisely because these otherwise unknown women are depicted as heroes that the early interpreters associated them with Jochebed and Miriam. Neither is given much of a role to play in the Exodus narrative (Jochebed especially); by linking these heroic midwives with Jochebed and Miriam, both women are given more prominent and exalting positions in the story.[11]

Our two midwives are therefore, according to the rabbinic literature, Moses' family members. Jochebed and Miriam single-handedly managed to temporarily counter the Pharaoh's attack on the Israelite nation. The early interpreters, of course, were not satisfied with having them simply disobey. Rather, they embellished and glorified the story in such a way that the midwives actually did everything in their power to ensure safe and healthy deliveries. Exodus Rabbah describes their actions as follows:

> Not only did they not fulfill his [the Pharaoh's] command, but they even went beyond this and did deeds of kindness to them. For those who were poor, the midwives would go to the houses of the rich to collect water and food and give them to the poor, and thus keep alive their children: this is what is meant by, AND THEY SAVED THE MEN-CHILDREN ALIVE. Further, AND THEY SAVED THE MEN-CHILDREN ALIVE – some children are liable to be born lame or blind or crippled, or require the amputation of a limb so that they may come out safely. So what did they do? They would pray to God thus: "Thou knowest that we have not fulfilled Pharaoh's command; for it is Thy command that we wish to fulfill. Lord of the Universe! Let the child come out safely, so that Israel finds no occasion to accuse us by saying: 'Behold, they have come out crippled, because they sought to slay them.'" God at once hearkened to their prayer and they were born safe and sound. R. Levi said: Why cite a minor matter? Quote rather one more important. There are some babes who would die at the time of birth or endanger their mothers, so as to die after giving birth. They, therefore, prayed to God, saying: "Lord of the Universe! Suspend their fate now and grant them their lives that Israel say not: 'They killed them.'" Therefore God granted their prayer, hence, AND THEY SAVED THE MEN-CHILDREN ALIVE.[12]

---

[10] This point has been noted by a number of scholars. It seems rather improbable that two women alone were responsible for the entire Israelite community, which, according to the biblical text had a population of more than 600,000 able-bodied men at the time of the exodus (Num. 1:45) Following Ibn Ezra, Sarna offers the suggestion that perhaps Shiphrah and Puah were overseers, or that their names were the names of particular guilds of midwives, rather than personal names. See Sarna, N. *The JPS Torah Commentary: Exodus,* 7.

[11] It is also not unreasonable to assume that the interpreters found satisfaction in eliminating any positive portrayal of Egyptian people.

[12] Exodus Rabbah 1:15 (translation by Rabbi Dr. H. Freedman and Maurice Simon. London: Soncino, 1977). A similar description of their good deeds can be found in the Babylonian Talmud, Sotah 11b.

According to these sources, Jochebed and Miriam went out of their way to ensure these delicate newborns a safe passage into the world. They brought food and drink to those families too poor to provide for themselves, and they regularly petitioned God to help them bring into the world babies who were whole and healthy. They showed kindness and care toward the very beings they were commissioned to kill. These extraordinary women were not arbitrary Egyptian midwives but Hebrew women deeply connected to Israel's salvation.

When the Pharaoh asked them why they did not do their jobs, they explained, in an incredibly sarcastic passage, that the Hebrew women were so strong, so "lively" (חיות), that they ended up giving birth before they could even get to them. As they said, "Hebrew women are not like Egyptian women" (Ex. 1:19). "Lively" is only one possible translation for the term חיות. Friedman translates it as "animal-like."[13] From his perspective, the midwives told the Pharaoh that Hebrew women were an entirely different kind of species. Unlike his own Egyptian community, they were strong and lively like animals. Driver disagrees with this translation, for he believes that it is unlikely that Hebrew women would have spoken so derogatively about their own people; rather, such a statement "would come more naturally from the lips of the Egyptians."[14] He translates the term as "prolific" instead, based on the assumption that the midwives were in fact Hebrew.

Whether the midwives were using the term positively or negatively, one of the significant features of this story is that the Pharaoh believed them. Since the Pharaoh abandoned his plans immediately after this conversation, and the women were not reprimanded and were even rewarded – as the biblical text later informs us – we may reasonably conclude that the Pharaoh was willing to believe the midwives' explanation.

The other significant feature of this story has to do with the method employed by the midwives to extricate themselves from an otherwise potentially dangerous encounter. The midwives are heroes because they refused to comply with the Pharaoh's decree. According to the post-biblical interpreters, their heroism extended to making herculean efforts to ensure that the Israelite babies emerged from the womb safely and in health. But the midwives saved *themselves* by lying to the Pharaoh. Presuming that Hebrew women were not different from Egyptian women, that they took time to give birth as all women do, the midwives lied to the Pharaoh in order to save themselves. They did not openly defy him by simply refusing to follow his orders outright. Rather, they pretended to agree and then subversively did otherwise. And when he asked them to account for their failure, they continued to deceive him. Obviously, their crimes were not great. In comparison with what the Pharaoh was attempting to do – and what he eventually accomplished – the midwives' deception is certainly not a crime. They survived their ordeal without seriously compromising their morality. That they lied in order to achieve this may certainly be understood as a necessary evil – or perhaps not an evil at all. Renita J. Weems argues that deception is the weapon of the powerless, as truth "is not defined by the powerful, but becomes the priority of the underclass to interpret and shape according to their own reality. The refusal to tell the "truth" becomes tantamount to the refusal to obey."[15] Deception may therefore be understood as their only

---

[13] Friedman, R. E. *Commentary on the Torah, With a New English Translation and the Hebrew Text* (New York: Harper Collins, 2001), 171. Friedman is not the first interpreter to suggest this translation. Propp traces this translation to Gressman, Ehrlich and Scharbert before him.

[14] Driver, G. R. "Hebrew Mothers: Exodus I:19." *Zeitschrift für die Alttestamentliche Wissenschaft* 67 (1955): 246-248.

[15] *Ibid.*, 29.

realistic way of surviving the Pharaoh's wrath while disobeying his command. Moreover, if he was willing to believe such a ludicrous statement, perhaps he deserved having it told to him! Nevertheless, if we are to scrupulously examine the behavior of the midwives, the fact remains that they lied. They did not harm any Hebrew mother or child. They chose not to kill but to save lives instead. For this they are heroes. But their record is not immaculate. They managed to save lives by doing violence to the truth. How much more impressive would they have been had they been willing to openly defy the Pharaoh instead?.

In an ideal world, the midwives would not have lied. They would have faced the Pharaoh squarely and courageously and refused to comply with his demands, regardless of the consequences. But, in an ideal world, they would never have been put in this situation to begin with. Shiphrah and Puah glide in and out of the biblical story quietly. After this one and only scene, we never meet them again. We know very little about them, who they were or where they came from, but we know that they managed to extricate themselves from a very difficult situation with cunning, intelligence and courage. Perhaps they could have acted with even greater courage, by refusing his demands rather than pretending to comply, and so perhaps they are short of the ideal, but they certainly succeeded in saving both themselves and countless newborns from an otherwise terrible fate without engaging in any physical violence, and for this they should be celebrated.

MAHAPAJAPATI GOTAMI

The injustice Mahāpajāpati Gotamī (henceforth, Gotamī) was asked to comply with represents a different kind than that which the midwives of the book of Exodus experienced. Gotamī was the Buddha's aunt and eventually his stepmother. We know a great deal more about her than we do about the Exodus midwives, but even so, the information is scarce in comparison with what we know about many of the male characters in either tradition. What is intriguing about Gotamī's story, however, is the source behind the injustice she encountered. Unlike the midwives who faced the injustice of an evil tyrant and foreigner, the injustice behind Gotamī's story came from the Buddha himself.

According to the Pali sources, Māyā, the queen of the Śakya kingdom in Northern India, gave birth to the future Buddha in Lumbinī garden. Seven days later, she died and her son was entrusted to her sister, Gotamī. The early sources provide a variety of different explanations for her death,[16] but they all agree on the timing. Gotamī raised the young Bodhisatta in her sister's place, and ostensibly became the only mother he ever knew. Despite the central role she must have played in his life, however, the scriptures are relatively uninterested in her. Short of a few exceptions,[17] Gotamī is marginalized by the literature.

---

[16] A number of explanations are provided by the early literature. For example, according to Buddhaghosa, her lifespan was simply exhausted (*Papañcasūdanī Majjhimanikāyaññhakathā*, iii 122.3); the Abhiniùkramaõasūtra argues that she died because she knew she would never again experience the joy she experienced while carrying the future Buddha inside her body (63); the Lalitavistara claims that she died because the mothers of all future Buddhas die seven days after giving birth, and they die because of a "split heart" (124). The most fascinating explanation, however, comes from the Mahāvastu, which claims that she died because it would not be fitting for the mother of the future Buddha to ever engage in love again. She therefore died in order to prevent any association with sexuality (ii 3).

[17] Gotamī appears sporadically throughout the canon, but her most important appearances, aside from the story of her ordination, are in the Therīgāthā (157-162) and the Gotamī-Apadāna. See Jonathan S. Walters for the

The most popular story about Gotamī is undoubtedly the story of her ordination.[18] Despite her marginalization, Gotamī remains famous and beloved for this one particular episode and is considered the spiritual ancestor of all Buddhist nuns as a result. The story begins a few years after the Buddha's awakening. King Suddhodana, the Buddha's father and Gotamī's husband,[19] eventually died, leaving Gotamī without a husband or a son to care for. She knew what her stepson had become and decided to follow in his footsteps. Leading a group of 500 similar-minded Śakyan women, Gotamī approached the Buddha and asked him for formal ordination and admission into the monastic order. In Hindu terms, her *dharma* to both her husband and her stepson were fulfilled, and she was therefore finally free to fulfill her *dharma* to herself.

The Buddha's answer to his aunt and stepmother has been a source of great controversy and debate over the years. I. B. Horner translates his answer as follows:

> Be careful, Gotami, of the going forth of women from home into homelessness in this *dhamma* and discipline proclaimed by the Truth-Finder.[20]

A more accurate translation of the Pali, however, can be found in Bhikkhu Ñāõamoli's work, *A Life of the Buddha*:

> Enough, Gotami, do not ask for the going forth from the house life into homelessness for women in the Dhamma and Discipline declared by the Perfect One.[21]

The Buddha did not explain why he refused her request. Rather, he simply refused her without further comment until she asked again. Gotamī asked the Buddha for permission three times, and each time the Buddha inexplicably refused.

Gotamī left the interview visibly distraught. Both the Vinaya and the Anguttara Nikāya passages describe her state with unusual emotional candor, as "hurt, upset, tearful and crying." These passages make it abundantly clear that Gotamī was not happy about the Buddha's decision. The child she raised, the one who eventually walked out of her life without any explanation or apology when he became an ascetic, now sat before her and refused her the one thing she is ever recorded as having asked him. She asked three times, and each time his answer was clear: Gotamī should not ask for admission into the order.

Although she was obviously upset by his behavior, the fascinating twist in the story is that Gotamī did not accept defeat. On the contrary, she defied his authority and continued to follow him despite his refusal. Even more radically, she and her companions shaved their heads, donned the ochre robes, and walked barefoot behind him to the gate of the hermitage in Vesālī, crying, with swollen feet and covered in dust. Gotamī was not happy about her exclusion, but she did not allow it to limit her entirely either.

Gotamī-Apadāna, particularly "A Voice from the Silence: The Buddha's Mother's Story." *History of Religions* 33 no 4 (1994): 358-379; and "Gotamī's Story" in *Buddhism in Practice* (ed. D. S. Lopez. Princeton: Princeton University Press, 1995), 113-138.

[18] The story appears in both the Vinaya (Cullavagga 10) and the Anguttara Nikāya (4:274-279).

[19] The king married both sisters.

[20] Cullavagga 10:1 (trans. I. B. Horner. Oxford: The Pali Text Society, 1997).

[21] Bhikkhu Ñāõamoli, *The Life of the Buddha* (Kandy: Buddhist Publication Society), 104. All other Pali translations mine.

Ānanda, the Buddha's chief attendant, eventually noticed the disheveled and ragged Gotamī and asked her why she was in such a state. She explained her situation to him and he offered to ask the Buddha himself for her admission into the order. He approached the Buddha and began the interview by telling the Buddha that his aunt was standing outside crying, with swollen feet and covered in dust. He then asked if women could be granted permission to enter the monastic order. He asked the Buddha this question three times, and just as before, the Buddha refused each time with the same formulation: "Enough, Ānanda, do not ask for the going forth of women…"

Although Ānanda is not often remembered for having been devious or particularly crafty, we may interpret his emphasis on Gotamī's disheveled state at the beginning of the interview as having been an attempt to awaken in the Buddha some compassion and perhaps even urgency to rectify an otherwise very unfortunate situation. When his strategy failed, he cunningly changed the direction of the conversation and tried again:

> "Bhante, having gone forth from the home life into homelessness in the Dhamma and Discipline taught by the Perfect One, are women capable of realizing the fruit of stream-entry or once-return or non-return or arahantship?"
> "They are capable, Ānanda."
> "If women are capable, Bhante, then since Mahāpajāpatī Gotamī has been of great service to the Blessed One when, as his mother's sister she was his nurse, his foster mother, his giver of milk as she suckled the Blessed One when his own mother died, it would be good, Bhante, if women could obtain the going forth."
> "Ānanda, if Mahāpajāpatī Gotamī accepts these eight capital rules, she will be ordained…"[22]

Ānanda realized that if the Buddha admitted that women were capable of achieving awakening, he could not then refuse them entry into the monastic order. Moreover, by emphasizing everything Gotamī did for the Buddha as a child, he reminded him of his filial obligation, thereby making it impossible for him to continue refusing her. In this way, Ānanda became the champion of women's rights, and is beloved by the bhikkhuni sangha in particular as a result. The monks, it seems, were not as enthusiastic about his involvement in these affairs. At the first council after the Buddha's death, they reprimanded Ānanda in this regard and asked him to admit his wrong-doing. Ānanda defended his decision to help women gain admission into the order, noting once again that the Buddha was indebted to Gotamī in particular for all that she did for him as a child. Eventually, however, he submitted to their authority and acknowledged a wrong-doing.[23] Nevertheless, nuns to this day continue to express gratitude to him for his efforts, and in Japan, Sōtō Zen nuns regularly perform a ritual in which they demonstrate their debt to him for his help in the establishment of a female monastic community.[24]

A number of questions emerge from this story, none of which are easily answered. The most obvious and most pressing, however, is why did the Buddha initially refuse to grant Gotamī, and women in general, admission into the order? What was his motivation? He obviously believed that women were capable of achieving awakening. Why, then, were they

---

[22] Cullavagga 10:1
[23] Cullavagga 11:1
[24] See Arai, P. K. R. "A Case of Ritual Zen: in Gratitude to Ānanda" in *Innovative Buddhist Women: Swimming Against the Stream* (ed. Karma Lekshe Tsomo. Richmond: Curzon, 2000), 123-129; and Arai, P. K. R. *Women Living Zen: Japanese Sōtō Buddhist Nuns* (Oxford: Oxford University Press, 1999), 105.

denied the context in which they could most easily do so? In recent years, scholars have suggested a number of explanations, from questioning the very historicity of the passage, to suggesting that he did not in fact refuse at all: he merely hesitated. Whatever answer one adopts, however, it is almost always the case that the answer is meant to explain what would otherwise appear as an injustice steeped in gender discrimination.

One of the more popular approaches to this passage has been to deny its historicity. So many inconsistencies and contradictions are embedded in the passage that it is rendered questionable in the minds of many. The historian E. J. Thomas, for example, questioned its authenticity by pointing out such problems as the fact that ânanda is portrayed as the Buddha's chief attendant at the time, and yet the passage also suggests that the event took place five years after the Buddha's awakening – before ânanda became his attendant.[25] Perhaps the most vocal proponent against the historicity of the story of Gotamī's ordination is Bhikkhuni Kusuma. Her unpublished doctoral dissertation is devoted almost entirely to this subject,[26] and her life, as she lives it today, is an expression of this view as she has taken the robes herself and become a Theravāda Bhikkhuni in Sri Lanka, despite serious political opposition. In an article entitled, "Inaccuracies in Buddhist Women's History,"[27] Kusuma provides an abridged version of her doctoral argument. She presents a series of inconsistencies in the story of Gotamī's ordination which she believes proves the historical inaccuracy of the passage. For example, she notes that, after Gotamī accepted the terms of her ordination, she asked how the other 500 women were to be ordained. She was told that they may be ordained by the monks. She herself, however, was not ordained in this way. When the newly ordained nuns told Gotamī that she was still unordained, she became confused and asked Ānanda nanda about her own ordination. Ānanda nanda approached the Buddha with this question and he replied that she became ordained when she agreed to his terms of ordination. The confusion behind this passage is evidence, according to Kusuma, that the passage makes little sense and could not be a historical account of the events.

Another excellent example provided by Kusuma has to do with one of the eight extra rules (aññha garudhamma) the Buddha required her to agree to for her ordination. One of these rules was that a nun must always bow to a monk, regardless of how senior she may be to him: "A nun who has been ordained even a hundred years must pay homage to, get up for, reverentially salute, and respectfully greet, a monk ordained that day."[28] Gotamī, however, asked ânanda to ask the Buddha how she should show respect to monks and nuns with regard to their seniority. As Kusuma points out, this passage makes little sense. She had already agreed to bow to monks regardless of questions of seniority. Why then, would she ask this question? This is an obvious discrepancy in the text which yet again points to its questionable historical status.

Alan Sponberg agrees with Thomas and Kusuma regarding the historicity of the passage, and argues that scholars tend not to take such contradictions seriously enough.[29] He examines an alternative version of the story preserved in a Sanskrit fragment that may have belonged to

[25] Thomas, E. J. The Life of the Buddha: As Legend and History (Delhi: Motilal Banarsidass, 1993), 110.

[26] Bhikkhuni Kusuma, "Bhikkhuni Vinaya" (Ph. D. diss. Pali and Buddhist University, 1999).

[27] Bhikkhuni Kusuma. "Inaccuracies in Buddhist Women's History" in Innovative Buddhist Women: Swimming Against the Stream (ed. Karma Lekshe Tsomo. Richmond: Curzon, 2000), 5-12.

[28] Cullavagga 10:1

[29] Sponberg, A. "Attitudes toward Women and the Feminine in Early Buddhism" in Buddhism, Sexuality, and Gender (ed. J. I. Cabezón. New York: SUNY, 1985), 13.

the Mūlasarvāstivādin canon[30] and notes a number of important differences between the Sanskrit and Pali versions that emerge. Perhaps one of the most striking is that the Buddha never refuses to grant Gotamī ordination. He offers it to her personally, but refuses to grant ordination to the women traveling with her. Convinced of the historical inaccuracies of the Pali version, Sponberg has chosen to look at the passage as a "document of reconciliation, as a symbolic, mythological expression of a compromise negotiated between several factions of the order, including the nuns and their male supporters."[31] In other words, according to Sponberg, this text is really about giving a mythological expression to a negotiation that needed to be worked through between the women and the men. Women could not simply settle into an ascetic community without some negotiation and discussion. The story of Gotamī's ordination, rather than being an historical account, is a creation of the imagination intended to help give voice to a process of discussion and reconciliation that was required for peaceful co-existence to be made possible.

A more popular approach to the text has been to interpret the Buddha's answer not as a refusal, but as a hesitation. Many scholars have argued that the Buddha did not want to refuse women the right of ordination, but that he needed to take the time to consider how to implement it without disrupting social mores too drastically. Kajiyama Yuichi, for example, has argued that the reason the Buddha "hesitated" before giving women the right to be ordained was not because

> women could not gain enlightenment, but because he had to deliberate on problems which
> might arise between the Order of monks and that of nuns, and between the Buddhist Order
> and the lay society. Gautama was as great an administrator as he was a religious sage. The
> hesitation or deliberation was quite natural on his part as the leader of a great number of
> disciples. We should not interpret this event as showing discrimination against women by
> Gautama because he never even as much hinted that a woman had not the same chance as a
> man to become an arhat, or that she was in any way unfit by her nature to attain nirvāōa.[32]

Padmasiri de Silva agrees in this regard, describing the Buddha as "a great sage and a great administrator and he acted with great caution."[33] He took his time to make his decision rather than act rashly. We find a similar argument from Lorna Dewaraja, who states that the Buddha probably hesitated because he wanted to retain public approval: "no religious or political leader, however broad his vision, can succeed if he forges ahead of the masses, completely ignoring public opinion."[34] The society of the time could not have accepted a community of female renunciants very easily, and so, according to these authors, he was acting cautiously, looking for the right moment to make his move. It should be noted, however, that I. B. Horner disagreed with these views. She lists a series of possible explanations for why the Buddha may have initially refused Gotamī's request, and argues that the least plausible explanation is that he did so because he wanted to appease the masses. The

---

[30] A translation of the fragment can be found in Diana Paul's *Women in Buddhism: Images of the Feminine in Mahāyāna Tradition* (Berkeley: Asian Humanities Press, 1979).

[31] Sponberg, A. "Attitudes toward Women and the Feminine in Early Buddhism," 16.

[32] Kajiyama, Y. "Women in Buddhism." *The Eastern Buddhist* 15 no 2 (1982): 60.

[33] De Silva, P. "The Concept of Equality in the Theravada Buddhist Tradition" in *Equality and the Religious Traditions of Asia* (ed. R. Siriwardena. London: Frances Printer, 1987), 91.

[34] Dewaraja, L. "Buddhist Women in India and Precolonial Sri Lanka" in *Buddhist Women Across Cultures: Realizations* (ed. Karma Lekshe Tsomo. New York: SUNY, 1999), 73.

Buddha did not have a habit of making decisions in the name of public opinion, and so there is no reason to suggest that he would have done so in this situation. As she says,

> there was much in the brahmanical institutions, such as prayers, rites, oblations and sacrifices, which revolted him. Nor did he show any signs of discouraging the formation of a Buddhist Order of Almsmen where the brahmins had none. Not even the most orthodox and ascetic among them had ever demanded to be bound together under a monastic system.[35]

In a discussion about the eight extra rules nuns were asked to follow, Nancy Auer Falk makes the comment that they did not oppress the nuns or hinder them in their most important pursuit – i.e. practicing the dhamma in order to attain liberation. Indeed, in her opinion, these extra rules were a far cry from the oppression women of the time normally experienced. Although she does not explore the story of Gotamī's ordination at length, we may well imagine that, in her opinion, the Buddha's initial refusal was not an injustice. On the contrary, given what women were accustomed to living with, his willingness to even engage in the conversation at all and his eventual acceptance of her request were extraordinary. She does, however, note in passing that the story of Gotamī's ordination and the Buddha's initial objections "must have cast a very long shadow on the nuns' endeavor."[36] Her views on the matter are therefore not entirely clear.[37]

Cornelia Dimmitt Church considers the message behind the story of Gotamī's ordination as ambivalent.[38] On the one hand, she believes that both the Buddha and Gotamī were convinced of the spiritual equality of women, and yet she also argues that there is a skepticism in the Pali Canon concerning women's abilities for self-discipline. In her opinion, women are treated like children. With the monastic life already an extraordinary challenge, there were serious questions about the ability of women to endure it. The Buddha was, after all, a man of his times, and he may have had reservations concerning the practical nature of a female order.

Almost all of the above interpretations are attempts at explaining what otherwise appears like a grave injustice. Whether one argues against the historicity of the passage, or one argues that the Buddha merely "hesitated" briefly in order to consider the practical implications of a female order, these scholars are all trying to explain the "Perfect One's" behavior. If we do not try to explain this passage, however, we are left with the glaring reality that the Buddha was not just with his aunt and stepmother. He refused her what he had already granted the men: a place to practice the teachings he had declared. She, however, countered his refusal with her own. She chose to defy his authority and followed him regardless. She did not enter the hermitage in Vesālī, but stood outside its gate, respecting to a certain degree his domain. But as Kate Blackstone argues, by shaving her head and donning the robes, she

---

[35] Horner, I. B. *Women Under Primitive Buddhism: Laywomen and Almswomen* (Delhi: Motilal Banarsidass, 1930), 113

[36] Falk, N. "The Case of the Vanishing Nuns: The Fruits of Ambivalence in Ancient Indian Buddhism" in *Unspoken Worlds: Women's Religious Lives* (ed. N. A. Falk and R. M. Gross. Toronto: Wadsworth, 2001), 203.

[37] Janice D. Willis argues along similar lines that the very fact that the Buddha was willing to create an order for women was radical. See her article, "Nuns and Benefactresses: The Role of Women in the Development of Buddhism" in *Women, Religion and Social Change* (ed. Y. Yazbeck Haddad and E. Banks Findley. New York: SUNY, 1985), 59-85.

[38] Dimmitt Church, C. "Temptress, Housewife, Nun: Women's Role in Early Buddhism." *Anima* 52 (1975): 53-58.

breached the symbolic parameters of the *sangha*. Mahāprajāpatī's fraudulent dress represents a very serious challenge to the integrity of the *sangha* and the validity of those who are truly ordained. In assuming the guise of a *bhikkhunī*, Mahāprajāpatī has undermined the care taken in the *Vinaya* to admit only those deemed suitable to represent the *sangha*. She has obliterated the distinction that separates the lifestyle of renunciation from that of householders. In so doing, she ruptures the integrity of those boundaries and introduces the possibility of contamination.[39]

From this perspective, Gotamī's actions, along with the women she led, represent a serious challenge to the Buddha's decision to initially bar her from the monastic community. She did not raise her voice to him, or adopt any violent methods against him, but she certainly refused to accept his refusal and found a way to express her disapproval to him clearly. Even if we agree that the Buddha did not initially refuse her but merely hesitated, she was still made to endure exclusion temporarily. She could not have known that he was "hesitating" and therefore this could have only caused her suffering – which is evidenced by her ragged and tearful state. One way or another, then, this story presents us with a story of injustice, and the women led by Gotamī resist this injustice openly, albeit non-violently, until the Buddha himself is forced to reconsider.

BRINGING THE STORIES TOGETHER

A number of similarities emerge from these different stories. Both the midwives and Gotamī were faced with a particular injustice and were expected to comply. Neither did. The midwives subversively defied the Pharaoh and, according to the rabbinic literature, they even made extraordinary efforts to help the babes into the world safely, while Gotamī openly defied the Buddha by taking on the appearance of a nun and following him to Vesālī despite his refusal to grant her ordination. All these women faced the injustices presented to them with courage, determination, and wit, and without physical violence of any kind.

These women also share an ability to co-operate harmoniously rather than compete with each other. The midwives acted in unison. Neither the biblical text, nor any of the early post-biblical writings report any disagreements or competitive behavior between them. The Pharaoh asked them to do something that challenged their ethical beliefs, and together they found a solution without betraying one another. Similarly, we find Gotamī leading 500 other Śakyan ladies, and no disturbance or competition is even hinted at. The Śakyan women allowed themselves to follow their leader, and she led them fairly and honestly. They co-operated, and together reached their goal. Although the Vinaya does record a slight disagreement between Gotamī and the others over the question of ordination procedure, the situation is resolved quickly and easily, and there is no reason to assume that it was a result of any negative feelings. It therefore appears to be the case that for both Gotamī and her followers, and for the two midwives, co-operation was central to their success.

This is noteworthy particularly given much of the vilifying material available in both religious traditions concerning women. Athalya Brenner, in an article entitled "Female Social

---

[39] Blackstone, K. "Damming the Dhamma: Problems with Bhikkhunīs in the Pali Vinaya." *Journal of Biblical Ethics* 6 (1999), 302.

Behavior: Two Descriptive Patterns Within the 'Birth of the Hero' Paradigm,"[40] argues that the most common portrayal of women in the biblical text is as hostile competitors rather than allies. Sarah and Hagar, Leah and Rachel, and Hannah and Peninah are all paired-off women who competed with each other rather than supported each other. Sarah went so far as to exile Hagar and her son Ishmael from her household, so threatened was she by their presence. Brenner argues that this kind of hostility is a typical pattern in the biblical text, as though the nature of women is to compete with each other, whereas male characters tend to be portrayed as being at least capable of reconciliation. Consider, for example, Jacob and Esau: although they began as competitors, they reconciled in the end; likewise for Joseph and his brothers, despite a brutal and potentially devastating beginning. Biblical women, on the other hand, tend to compete and remain competitive. Reconciliations are rare when women are involved. The midwives of the Exodus narrative, however, present an alternative. They did not even require reconciliation. On the contrary, they worked together to defy the Pharaoh, rather than competing with each other for the Pharaoh's pardon. As a unit, they resisted the injustice presented to them without violence.

A similarly negative portrayal of women can be found in the early Buddhist material. Liz Wilson, for example, in her book *Charming Cadavers: Horrific Figurations of the Feminine in Indian Buddhist Hagiographic Literature,*[41] has collected a number of passages in which decaying female corpses are used by the Buddha to develop a sense of revulsion for women's bodies. Numerous passages throughout the Pali Canon describe women as manipulative, cunning and evil. The Jātakas are filled with life lessons about the pitfalls women can lead men into. Although Buddhist literature also provides a number of inspiring passages about women, the difficult passages cannot be overlooked. For this reason, the co-operation between Gotamī and her followers should be read as a central feature of the story. She led them just as the Buddha led the male community, and they followed her without any evidence of reluctance or resentment. Indeed, in this regard, it may even be argued that the female community was more impressive than the male one: the Buddha found himself repeatedly threatened and challenged by disheartened or fallen monks – most notably by his cousin Devadatta. Gotamī, on the other hand, is not described by the literature as ever having been challenged by the nuns. She formed a community along with them, and together they were able to make a place for themselves in the Buddhist sangha. Their harmonious co-operation in this event challenges many of the stereotypes presented by the literature.

The two stories therefore clearly share a number of similar features. Differences, however, are also present, and these can be brought to light in particular when reflecting on the two stories together. As mentioned above, the midwives are certainly heroic in their cunning defiance of the Pharaoh's evil plans, but they are just a little short of the ideal. Rather than boldly facing the Pharaoh and refusing him outright, the midwives circumvented the issue. They lied to him when they pretended to accept his plan, and they lied to him when they explained why they failed to carry it out. Although their behavior remains courageous

---

[40] Brenner, A. "Female Social Behavior: Two Descriptive Patterns Within the 'Birth of the Hero' Paradigm." *VT* 36 (1986):257-273. This article is not only about the midwives, but about all the women in the story of Moses' birth.

[41] Wilson, L. *Charming Cadavers: Horrific Figurations of the Feminine in Indian Buddhist Hagiographic Literature* (Chicago: University of Chicago Press, 1996). See also her article, "The Female Body as a Source of Horror and Insight in Post-Ashokan Indian Buddhism" in *Religious Reflections on the Human Body* (ed. J. M. Law. Bloomington: Indiana University Press, 1995), 76-99.

because they managed to outwit him and save lives rather than take them, they could have become national heroes and perhaps could have even changed the tides of history had they chosen to refuse him outright instead. They would probably have done so at the expense of their own lives, but their martyrdom would have served as a powerful example of non-compliance in the face of evil.

Gotamī was much more forward in her resistance. Also with cunning, but much more directly, Gotamī challenged the Buddha with her presence and her appearance. She walked right up to his front door in Vesālī and silently demanded that he take note of her. She was not aggressive about it, she did not raise her voice or her fist, but she certainly demonstrated to him and to the entire community present that she would not allow herself to be excluded, and that she would take the robes whether he gave them to her or not. She defied him openly and clearly, and in the end, he was forced to concede. This was not a happy moment for her, however. She stood at the gate crying, her heart probably broken by his rejection, but she did not back down. She stood there, waited and protested until he opened the door to finally let her in. In this case then, the Buddhist women were more direct and more forward than the women of the Bible. Gotamī did not face the same kinds of potential consequences to be sure, but she certainly faced the injustice presented to her without a hint of submission.[42]

It must be noted that this parallel is unique. The stories are similar in their situations, the co-operation among the women, and the peaceful resistance employed by the heroes of these tales. But there are not many other parallels like this in the two early literatures. Buddhist literature is replete with stories of injustice and peaceful, non-violent resistance. Indeed, non-violence is one of the central pillars upon which the entire tradition rests. But this is not the case for the Hebrew Bible. The biblical text is rarely non-violent. Although there are a few episodes in which non-violence is hailed – consider, for example, the story of the wisdom of Solomon in I Kings 3 or the Book of Jonah[43] – for the most part, the biblical story is one of a violent reality. Many of the female characters engage in violent combat and behavior, and no apology is expected. The biblical story is one of humanity in all its color – violence and non-violence included. Buddhism is not often so open to the full spectrum of human behavior. Indeed, Buddhist literature provides numerous examples of non-violence taken to inhuman and fantastic extremes, with the Buddha in previous lifetimes or in his final rebirth choosing a non-violent response regardless of the consequences that may befall his person. This is not often the case in the Hebrew Bible. As Susan Niditch,[44] Regina Schwarz,[45] John Collins[46] and others have clearly argued, the biblical text makes no apology when it comes to violence. Violence belongs to the human experience, and it therefore belongs in the Bible.

This is perhaps the most important difference between the two religious traditions – namely, that the midwives are an exception to the rule, and that the story of Gotamī is not. By comparing these two stories, the differences between the priorities of the two religious

---

[42] Should one want to argue that the two stories cannot be compared precisely because the potential consequences of resistance were so drastically different, we might remember the numerous Jātaka tales in which the Bodhisatta was prepared and often did sacrifice his life for the benefit of another being. This is a popular theme in early Buddhist literature that cannot be overlooked.

[43] And even in these cases, the non-violent conclusions nevertheless emerge from threats of violence.

[44] Niditch, S. *War in the Hebrew Bible: A Study in the Ethics of Violence* (Oxford: Oxford University Press, 1993).

[45] Schwartz, R. M. *The Curse of Cain: The Violent Legacy of Monotheism* (Chicago: University of Chicago Press, 1997).

[46] Collins, J. J. "The Zeal of Phinehas: The Bible and the Legitimation of Violence." Journal of Biblical Literature 122 no 1 (2003): 3-21.

traditions come into view with great clarity. For one, the priority lies in painting an honest and often violent portrait of human history; for the other, it lies in raising the eyes to an inspiring, and perhaps often impractical, ideal.

BIBLIOGRAPHY

Albright, W. F. "Northwest Semitic Names in a List of Egyptian Slaves from the Eighteenth Century BC." *Journal of the American Oriental Society* 74 (1954): 222-233.

Arai, P. K. R. "A Case of Ritual Zen: in Gratitude to Ānanda." Pages 123-129 in *Innovative Buddhist Women: Swimming Against the Stream.* Edited by Karma Lekshe Tsomo. Richmond: Curzon, 2000.

Arai, P. K. R. *Women Living Zen: Japanese Sōtō Buddhist Nuns.* Oxford: Oxford University Press, 1999.

Bhikkhuni Kusuma. *"Bhikkhuni Vinaya."* Ph. D. diss. Pali and Buddhist University, 1999.

Bhikkhuni Kusuma. "Inaccuracies in Buddhist Women's History." Pages 5-12 in *Innovative Buddhist Women: Swimming Against the Stream.* Edited by Karma Lekshe Tsomo. Richmond: Curzon, 2000.

Bhikkhu Ñāõamoli. *The Life of the Buddha.* Kandy: Buddhist Publication Society, 1972.

Blackstone, K. "Damming the Dhamma: Problems with Bhikkhunīs in the Pali Vinaya." *Journal of Biblical Ethics* 6 (1999): 392-312.

Buddhaghosācariya. *Papañcasūdanī Majjhimanikāyaññhakathā.* Edited by I. B. Horner. London: The Pali Text Society, 1977.

The Book of Discipline: Vinaya Piñaka. Translation by I. B. Horner. Oxford: The Pali Text Society, 1996.

The Book of Gradual Sayings (Anguttara Nikāya) or More Numbered Suttas. Translation by E. M. Hare. London: The Pali Text Society, 1955.

Brenner, A. "Female Social Behavior: Two Descriptive Patterns Within the 'Birth of the Hero' Paradigm." *Vetus Testamentum* 36 (1986):257-273.

Childs, B. S. *The Book of Exodus.* Philadelphia: Westminster, 1974.

Cohen, J. *The Origin and Evolution of the Moses Nativity.* Studies in the History of Religions, volume 58. Leiden: E. J. Brill, 1993.

Collins, J. J. "The Zeal of Phinehas: The Bible and the Legitimation of Violence." *Journal of Biblical Literature* 122 no 1 (2003): 3-21.

De Silva, P. "The Concept of Equality in the Theravada Buddhist Tradition." Pages 74-97 in *Equality and the Religious Traditions of Asia.* Edited by R. Siriwardena. London: Frances Printer, 1987.

Dewaraja, L. "Buddhist Women in India and Precolonial Sri Lanka." Pages 67-77 in *Buddhist Women Across Cultures: Realizations.* Edited by Karma Lekshe Tsomo. New York: SUNY, 1999.

Dimmitt Church, C. "Temptress, Housewife, Nun: Women's Role in Early Buddhism." *Anima* 52 (1975): 53-58.

Driver, G. R. "Hebrew Mothers: Exodus 1:19." *Zeitschrift für die Alttestamentliche Wissenschaft* 67 (1955): 246-248.

Falk, N. A. "The Case of the Vanishing Nuns: The Fruits of Ambivalence in Ancient Indian Buddhism." Pages 196-206 in *Unspoken Worlds: Women's Religious Lives.* Edited by N. A. Falk and R. M. Gross. Toronto: Wadsworth, 2001.

Friedman, R. E. *Commentary on the Torah, With a New English Translation and the Hebrew Text.* New York: Harper Collins, 2001.

Greenberg, M. *Understanding Exodus: The Heritage of Biblical Israel.* New York: Berman House, 1969.

The Hebrew-English Edition of the Babylonian Talmud. Edited by Rabbi Dr. I. Epstein. London: Soncino, 1990.

Horner, I. B. *Women Under Primitive Buddhism: Laywomen and Almswomen.* Delhi: Motilal Banarsidass, 1930.

Hyatt, J. P. *The New Century Bible Commentary: Exodus.* Grand Rapids, Michigan: W. B. Eerdmans, 1971.

Josephus. *Jewish Antiquities.* Translation by H. St. J. Thackeray. Loeb Classical Library. Cambridge: Harvard University Press, 1930-1965.

Kajiyama, Y. "Women in Buddhism." *The Eastern Buddhist* 15 no 2 (1982): 53-70.

The Lalita Vistara: Memoirs of the Early Life of Sakya Sinha (Chs. 1-15). Translation by R. L. Mitra. Delhi: Sri Satguru Publications, 1998.

The Mahāvastu. Translation by J. J. Jones. Oxford: The Pali Text Society, 1976.

The Middle Length Discourses of the Buddha: A New Translation of the Majjhima Nikāya. Translation by Bhikkhu Ñāôamoli and Bhikkhu Bodhi. Boston: Wisdom, 1995.

The Midrash Rabbah. Translation by Rabbi Dr. H. Freedman and Maurice Simon. London: Soncino, 1977.

Niditch, S. *War in the Hebrew Bible: A Study in the Ethics of Violence.* Oxford: Oxford University Press, 1993.

Paul, D. *Women in Buddhism: Images of the Feminine in Mahāyāna Tradition.* Berkeley: Asian Humanities Press, 1979.

Poems of Early Buddhist Nuns (Therīgāthā). Translation by C. A. F. Rhys-Davids and K. R. Norman. Oxford: The Pali Text Society, 1989.

Pritchard, J. B., ed. *Ancient Near Eastern Texts Relating to the Old Testament.* 2nd edition. Princeton: Princeton University Press, 1955.

Propp, W. H. C. *The Anchor Bible: Exodus 1-18: A New Translation with Introduction and Commentary.* New York: Doubleday, 1998.

The Romantic Legend of øākya Buddha: A Translation of the Chinese Version of the Abhiniùkramaôasūtra. Translation by Samuel Beal. London: Trübner, 1875.

Römer, T. "Péricopes: les sages-femmes du Pharaon (Exode 1/15-22)." *Etudes théologiques et religieuses* 2 (1994) : 265-270.

Sarna, N. *The JPS Torah Commentary: Exodus.* Philadelphia: Jewish Publication Society, 1991.

Schwartz, R. M. *The Curse of Cain: The Violent Legacy of Monotheism.* Chicago: University of Chicago Press, 1997.

The Septuagint Version of the Old Testament: With an English Translation and with *Various Readings and Critical Notes.* London: Samuel Bagster and Sons.

Sponberg, A. "Attitudes toward Women and the Feminine in Early Buddhism." Pages 3-36 in *Buddhism, Sexuality, and Gender.* Edited by J. I. Cabezón. New York: SUNY, 1985.

Thomas, E. J. *The Life of the Buddha: As Legend and History*. Delhi: Motilal Banarsidass, 1993.

Vinaya Piñakaü: One of the Principle Buddhist Holy Scriptures in the Pali Language. Edited by H. Oldenberg. Oxford: The Pali Text Society, 1964.

Walters, J. S. "Gotamī's Story." Pages 113-138 in *Buddhism in Practice*. Edited by D. S. Lopez. Princeton: Princeton University Press, 1995.

Walters, J. S. "A Voice from the Silence: The Buddha's Mother's Story." *History of Religions* 33 no 4 (1994): 358-379.

Willis, J. D. "Nuns and Benefactresses: The Role of Women in the Development of Buddhism." Pages 59-85 in *Women, Religion and Social Change*. Edited by Y. Yazbeck Haddad and E. Banks Findley. New York: SUNY, 1985.

Wilson, L. *Charming Cadavers: Horrific Figurations of the Feminine in Indian Buddhist Hagiographic Literature*. Chicago: University of Chicago Press, 1996.

Wilson, L. "The Female Body as a Source of Horror and Insight in Post-Ashokan Indian Buddhism." Pages 76-99 in *Religious Reflections on the Human Body*. Edited by J. M. Law. Bloomington: Indiana University Press, 1995.

In: Religion, Terrorism and Globalization
Editor: K.K. Kuriakose, pp.81-93

ISBN 1-59454-553-7
© 2006 Nova Science Publishers, Inc.

Chapter 5

NON-VIOLENCE AND PEACE IN HINDUISM: IS THERE A CONNECTION?

Katherine K. Young
McGill University, Montreal, Canada

INTRODUCTION

A common mantra in Hinduism is "*aum* [the sacred syllable par excellence], *śāntiḥ (peace), śāntiḥ* (peace), *śāntiḥ* (peace)." It was originally found at the beginning of Upaniṣads. The Maṇḍukya-upaniṣad begins, for example, "O Gods (Devāḥ)! Auspicious sounds may we hear with the ears. Auspcious forms may we behold with the eyes. May we, full of praise of the Highest, enjoy, in healthy body with perfect limbs, our allotted years, (may we be) the beloved of the Gods. Aum Peace! Peace! Peace" (Nikhilananda trans. 1995, 1). For some Hindus, *aum, śāntiḥ, śāntiḥ, śāntiḥ* has been linked closely with the ethical principle of *ahiṃsā,* or non-violence. This chapter explores this link throughout Indian history with special reference to yoga at the individual level and peace at the societal level.

VIOLENCE AND NON-VIOLENCE IN PREMODERN HINDUISM

There is a pattern of violence and non-violence in premodern Hinduism. It could be viewed as thesis (agonistic, that is, constant warfare without regulation in the Vedic period), antithesis (radical rejection of warfare in the Upaniṣadic period), and, after a millennium of experimentation on how best to move beyond these problematic extremes, a synthesis (non-violence as the norm; violence as just war as the exception).

The Agonistic Vedic World and its Legacy

State formation has almost always been accompanied by the use of violence to establish polities not based on kin relations. This was true in ancient India as well. Although we know very little about how urban civilization began in the Indus Valley, we do know that conflict, violence, and perpetual crisis were central to the worldview of Vedic literature: the struggles between gods (*devas*) and anti-gods (*asuras*), sages and deities, sages and sages, sages and ordinary people, group and group (Gitomer 222). In religion, mock ritual attacks and ritualized verbal contests reflected the reality of constant warfare among nomadic tribes, which raided each other's herds and fought for control of pastures (Reich 145). Indra was the warrior god par excellence and chief god of the Vedic pantheon. Priests composed "power songs" to make the king victorious and compiled the Dhanur-veda (holy scripture on warfare). Warfare itself was sacralized and considered a religious ritual (*yajña*). The reward for death in battle was heaven.

Violence continued during the transition from tribal societies of the Ṛg-veda to early chiefdoms and kingdoms, which was accompanied by a second phase of urbanization, beginning in the Gangetic plain (about 1000-800 BCE). Because early chiefdoms and kingdoms competed for resources and dominion over local or regional domains, these early states were usually unstable. This constant violence was captured in maxims such as "big fish eat little fish," or "relative or no relative, crush the foes: conquer those who attack, conquer others by attacking" (Kauśītaki-brāhmaṇa XX.8.6). These societies, with their heroic views of fierce manhood, eulogized raw power and experienced it as sacred because of its dramatic hold on life and death. They harnessed and directed this power, their goals being to protect their lands and herds.

This agonistic orientation found expression in the great epic, the Mahābhārata (circa 200 BCE-200 CE). According toTamar Reich, this is based on "the triple equation of the sacred order (*dharma*) with sacrifice (*yajña*) *medha, vahni*), on the one hand, and with strife (*raṇa, āhava, yuddha*) on the other hand. In the text of the Mahābhārata itself, the bloody battle of Kurukṣetra is frequently compared to a sacrifice, because, as the story goes, a whole generation of warrior chieftains all but perished in it" (Reich 146) and the "idea that by sacrificing one can compete over chieftainship is of course the essence of the agonistic legacy" (Reich 160). Even the Brahmans (the intellectuals and priests) developed a taste for big-time power. In their epics, they tried to convince others that their magical power was superior to conventional military strength. Stories show them competing with warriors (kṣatriyas) with the power of an energy substance possessing fire-like qualities (*tejas*) and divine weapons (*brahma-astra*) that can be created from it (Whitaker 89-90). Rivalry between the two elites, Brahmans and Kṣatriyas, was common before caste rigidified and Brahmans, who composed the texts, made themselves superior to *Kṣatriyas*.

The Development of Ethics

Within the agonistic ethos, warriors gradually developed a code of morality. "Family honor or disgrace, protection or life or murder, possession of wives or adultery, possession of goods or stealing, truth swearing or false witnessing – all are the ken of the warrior class" (Smith 60). By the end of the Vedic age, this brought some order to tribal and then monarchical rivalries. That order made norms possible, and norms created ethics for the everyday (*pravṛtti*) world.

But for many people, warrior codes were not enough. They withdrew from society, becoming ascetics and criticizing violence. This gave rise to early Buddhist, Jaina, and Upaniṣadic views on non-violence (*ahiṃsā*). The word *ahiṃsā* – a compound from the desiderative form of the verbal root *han* (to injure or kill) with the negative prefix "a" – is found in Chāndogya-upaniṣad III.17 and elsewhere. In later scriptures, *ahiṃsā* was usually the first item in a list of ascetic values such as vegetarianism, celibacy, renunciation of possessions, and self-control associated with yoga. In this yogic context, *ahiṃsā* was connected with peace in the sense of an individual withdrawing from society, often to forest hermitages (*āśrama*s). This orientation of withdrawal for spiritual development became known as the perspective of *nivṛtti* (escape, abandonment, cessation) in contrast to the perspective of *pravṛtti* (action within the world).

Whether Brahmans became ascetics proper (and some had) or were just non-warriors whose mode of everyday behavior was non-violent by definition, they now faced the dilemma: Should they continue to uphold the warrior culture or encourage a shift to values that might initiate a more non-violent way of life for both society in general and brahmanical ritual (such as animal sacrifice) in particular? The general consensus was greater support for non-violence but how to achieved it was contentious. The conflict over means led to exploration through stories of possible resolutions. Some stories displaced the command for violence onto the gods/God (Smith 60; Gitomer 224). Some argued that war should remain, but that everyone should develop a spiritual state of equanimity, or detachment, in action (the message of Lord Kṛṣṇa to Arjuna in the Bhagavad-gītā). Some preferred silence in the face of conflict. And some argued that war should be eliminated altogether (Reich 168). Violence associated with animal sacrifice was particularly troublesome, because it was at the heart of Brahmanical ritualism and the Vedic worldview (just as warfare was at the heart of Kṣatriya identity).

The growing critique of violence was reflected in a Brahmanical attempt to shift power from the warriors to themselves. In the process, Brahmans changed royal imagery. They replaced literary images of the ferocious, tyrannical king with the just king who upholds *dharma* (from the verbal root *dhṛ*, to uphold) through righteousness and concern for the welfare of the people (*lokasaṃgraha*). This implied a stable and peaceful kingdom (although it acknowledged the need for defensive and offensive wars – ideally in someone else's territory – and fought by a new code of ethics that protected non-warriors and regulated battles between warriors. Brahmans as a class were interested in the ethics of non-violence and violence because as intellectuals and priests they did not participate in warfare (that was the prerogative by birth of the Kṣatriya caste), and yet they had to make sure that the warriors of their own kingdom did not act violently toward them and that they protected them from the aggression of enemy warriors.

The Rāmāyana introduces a concept of the king's social responsibility through the figure of Rāma: Kingship and Kṣatriya *dharma* were now to be premised on selflessness and compassion (II.101.30) to everyone rather than selfish aggrandizement of power, although the epic still refers primarily to one's own extended family or tribe. It replaces the agonistic code of warrior ethics with a concept of righteousness that is given transcendental, eternal authority, which can be accessed through personal conscience (II.101.19; II.16.53). And it encourages the king to have the yogin's equanimity in the midst of all conflicts. One passage even implies that to be righteous, king Rāma should give up warrior life and violence altogether because it is based on greed and tyranny (II.18.36 and II.101.20). This makes it seem as though the ethic of non-violence has been embraced at the heart of the warrior circle, although the story of the Rāmāyaṇa as a whole shows that Rāma has only renounced the old-style agonistic warrior worldview, for he stands ready to defend justice through violence.

> [T]his epic pits good (the god-king Rāma) versus evil (the demon Rāvana) in a kind of dharma-yuddha [just war]. In this head-on struggle, there is little moral ambiguity involved, no need for discussions of subtle rules. The battle is over the fact that Rāvana has abducted Sītā, Rāma's wife, which is an obvious moral wrong. It is assumed that Rāma, the embodiment of dharma, must answer such an obvious affront... [But], the scale of violence in this epic is limited. The battle is mainly between Rāma and Rāvana, and it is fought in the terrestrial realm, although extraordinarily powerful weapons are at times used, as in the Mahābhārata (Young 2004).

Much the same could be said for the Mahābhārata's perspective on war and peace, although this epic focuses much more than the Rāmāyaṇa on the moral dilemmas created by war and explores the topic of just war in detail. Here the image of the sage is transformed. Whereas withdrawal from society to search for enlightenment (*nivṛtti*) had been common in the Upaniṣadic period, now sages were to have a dharma focused on life in the world (*pravṛtti*) consisting of non-malificence (non-violence) but also beneficence (a social consciousness consisting of friendliness, compassion, and active work to care for *all* beings) (Mahābhārata XII.110.10; XII.237.19; XII.254.5). This dharma is nonetheless still intimately connected with yoga, for the sage is to have equanimity in his tasks. It is striking that the sage's dharma is explained in the Śāntiparvan (the chapter on peace). Other texts of the classical age stayed closer to the *nivṛtti* ideal; the Yoga-sūtra (2.20-31) summarizes, for instance, the sage's dharma as: "non-violence, truthfulness, non-stealing, celibacy, renunciation of possessions, and self-control." But some texts redefine the *nivṛtti* orientation by suggesting that everyone, not just sages, should embrace these ascetic values as the norm. This became known as *sāmānya*, or common *dharma* and *sādhāraṇa* or eternal *dharma*. *Mānava-dharma-śāstra* (10:63) refers, for instance, to non-violence, truthfulness, non-stealing, purity, and restraint of sense organs; and even *Kautīlya Arthaśāstra* (1:3:13), that masterpiece of pragmatic strategy for warfare, lists non-violence, truthfulness, purity, absence of envy, and forbearance as common and eternal values.

Still, a basic paradox remained with these *pravṛtti* and *nivṛtti* concepts. If the role of kings was to protect the people, then they could never become sages whose life was characterized by non-violence and compassion to all, because they had to be ready to use violence to uphold justice. Moreover, if non-violence was to be the common ethic, one eternally grounded, then the fact that the role of the Kṣatriyas necessitated violence meant that the ethic really could not be common.

Resolution: Non-Violence as Norm, Violence as the Exception

The result of our saga – a tale of thesis (endemic warfare and sacrificial violence) and antithesis (ascetic renunciation) – was synthesis: a common ideal (*sāmānya-dharma*), which is characterized by non-violence in the sense of noninvolvement in war and reinterpretation or rejection of animal sacrifice and meat-eating with, however, one important exception: support for violence in the context of just war by the warrior class.

By the end of the classical age, ethics had become embedded in norms of behaviour to order society and reduce friction conceptualized as *varna-āśrama-dharma*. They included duties that characterized one's identity by birth into one of the four major castes (*varna*) - Brahmans, Kṣatriyas, Vaiśyas, and Śūdras - or the myriad sub-castes (*jāti*), which were considered organically related to uphold societal order. They also included the four stages of life (*āśrama*) known as student, married person, partial renouncer, and full renouncer. *Ahiṃsā* was to be practiced by all groups except the Kṣatriyas. Although this view of dharma was portrayed as an ideal, reality was far more complicated because of social dynamism, whereby groups changed status (Śūdras, for instance, becoming Kṣatriyas) or gender distinctions that made the stages of life for men enumerated above different from those for women, and those of elite women different from those of other women.

The concept of war emerged from this transition profoundly changed. Only a just war was legitimate; its end and means, in other words, had to be just. There had to be legitimate reasons for war (self-defense after failing to secure peace in any other way); clarity (someone had to announce the war and the battle); and discrimination and containment. According to the latter, war had to take place only in restricted places, at restricted times, and with restricted people (those who were born into the warrior caste, the Kṣatriyas) so that Brahmans, the aged, women, children, peaceful citizens, the mentally ill, and the military support staff were not harmed. Ideally war should be restricted to a duel between two Kṣatriyas of equal status and ability. Finally, war had to be based on fairness and equality (warriors were equipped with proper arms and battles were fought according to a military code), and reconciliation after victory had to occur (Young 2004). Although the Mahābhārata refused to absolutize non-violence, it did promote noncruelty in war (Heitelbeitel 2001, 177-214). But this, too, had its exception. If the other side did not play by the rules of legitimate warfare, all stratagems to ensure victory were allowed.

With this new concept of dharma, Kṣatriyas could not withdraw and become sages because this would erode their role of protection of society. But they had access to the spiritual domain not only through the exercise of dharma but also the cultivation of yogic equanimity. This allowed the king to act in the world (the requirement of *pravrtti*) but also to move beyond the oppositions that characterize everyday life with a spiritual centeredness that negated the effects of karma.

This new Brahmanical concept of dharma helped Brahmanism to compete with Buddhism and Jainism, both of which developed the ascetic rejection of warfare and animal sacrifice into new monastic religions (even though they too sought the support of kings and Kṣatriyas in general by allowing dharmically conducted, non-cruel warfare as an exception to the ethical principle of *ahiṃsā*). In part, the new concept of dharma reflected the stabilization of kingdoms and the waning of the agonistic worldview as war became limited to special contexts. The history of actual warfare in India indicates, however, that new views of dharmic kingship, including the ruler's compassion for all, did not destroy the Kṣatriya heroic ethos from within, leaving society at large in a state of perpetual peace. Wars continued, although they were now conducted in a manner that brought greater security to ordinary people.

The plays of Bhāsa (circa third or fourth century) reflect this change in perspective. Duroyodhana, who epitomizes the agonistic, ruthless king in the Mahābhārata, is presented by

Bhāsa as reformed: "Having attained eminence by accumulating wealth, our Duryodhana gulped infamy through love of strife, but now serving dharma, he becomes a vessel of good deeds, and that same Duryodhana shines with new beauty (*Pañcarātra* 1.20 cited by Gitomer 227). To save the world and avert war, Duryodhana concedes half the kingdom, which he has righteously won!" (Gitomer 228). He goes beyond justice to generosity for the sake of everyone.

The new ethic of non-killing contributed to a debate over the ethics of sacrifice and meat-eating, too, which had been common in the pastoral economies of ancient and classical India. Should animal sacrifice be performed? Should animals be killed ritualistically? Should sacrificial meat be eaten? Should any meat be eaten? This debate is reflected in contradictory passages of Manu, the lawgiver, on this topic (Perrett 83). Gradually, vegetarianism took root in some circles. By the fifth century CE the Chinese pilgrim Fa-shien could claim that "no respectable person eats meat" (Perrett 86).

With greater social stability and the rule of thumb that nonviolence is the general ethical principle and violence and just war the only exception for violence, the *pravṛtti* orientation became more individual again and more yogic. The Nāṭyaśāstra (circa second century to fifth), drawing on the yogic or *nivṛtti* orientation, defines *śānta-rasa* as the absence of pleasure, pain, hatred, and envy and the presence of equanimity toward all creatures. By the ninth century, the Kashmiri savant Anandavardhana in his *Dhvanyaloka,* could say that the dominant aesthetic flavor (*rasa*) of the Mahābhārata is peace (*śānta*). Anandavardhana looked to Yudhiṣṭhira as the epic's exemplar of *śānta-rasa.* Because heroism and warfare dominate the epic, however, he rationalizes this choice of *śānta-rasa* by arguing that the antecedent to the *rasa* of peace is the stable emotion of disillusionment. According to Gary Tubb, in the Mahābhārata, the "more the insubstantial workings of this world (are seen to) turn out badly, the more a feeling of dispassion is produced" (Mbh. 12.168.4 cited by Tubb 186). The flavor of peace is brought about through suggestion, which extinguishes the dominant *rasa* of craving and makes happiness possible (Tubb 199): "The happiness produced by the extinction of craving (*tṛṣṇākṣayasukha*) to which Anandavardhana refers must exist outside the work [Mahābhārata], since the desires of the Pāṇḍavas pursue them to the very end ... [T]he experience of detachment is in fact the goal of the poem in Anandavardhana's interpretation" (Tubb 200). Here, Anandavardhana used the Mahābhārata not for a commentary on how to handle conflicts and war, a societal dilemma, but rather as a metaphor for the means to and goal of spiritual liberation. Once again, the *nivṛtti* orientation prevailed. In modern times, this metaphorical interpretation of the great Mahābhārata would be used by Gandhi, but within a perspective on non-violence that bridges *pravṛtti* and *nivṛtti*.

Personal and collective *ahiṃsā* remained closely linked in medieval times. The fact that some Brahmans and Vaiṣṇava sects practiced *ahiṃsā* in the context of ritual and were vegetarians helped to define these practices as elite behavior, which was imitated, in turn, by other upwardly mobile groups. The principle of non-violence gradually developed a solid basis in Hindu society as the spiritual ideal if not the practical reality. In the modern age, Gandhi had a major cultural tradition of non-violence on which to build.

NON-VIOLENCE, PACIFISM, AND THE
INDIAN STRUGGLE FOR INDEPENDENCE

Gandhi is known as the exemplar of non-violence par excellence. But was he an absolute pacifist? In this section, I will examine the evidence as it relates to these worldly (*pravṛtti*) and otherworldly (*nivṛtti*) perspectives.

Gandhi: A *nivṛtti* or *pravṛtti* Perspective?

Gandhi's identification with the yogic core of *sāmānya-dharma* led to a new chapter in the Indian history of violence and non-violence. His attraction to *ahiṃsā* was closely related to the yogic foundation of the lists of *sāmānya* virtues that usually began with *ahiṃsā*. For him, *ahiṃsā* was intimately linked with the yogic values of self-purification, fasting, sexual abstinence, and vegetarianism. After initial explorations into Westernized lifestyles during his years as a student in England and as a barrister in South Africa, Gandhi returned to India and his spiritual roots. Unlike most householders, he incorporated these yogic dimensions into his everyday life on the model of *vānaprastha* - the third stage of life in the classical *āśrama* scheme of four stages. This involved sexual abstinence (*brahmacarya*) and the practice of yogic disciplines but without the radical withdrawal of the ascetic renouncer (*saṃnyāsin*) from domestic life. Gandhi accommodated the original yogic core of the *sāmānya* virtues, which fostered a heightened spirituality and could therefore lead to the transformation of everyday life. He connected *ahiṃsā* with abstinence, especially from sex but also from drink, tobacco, drugs, and meat to create purity (*śauca*); fasting (*upavasa*); and non-materialism or spiritual poverty (*aparigraha*). Although this yogic orientation was still within the householder's domain and drew heavily on the Vaiṣṇavism of his family's tradition and his mother's spirituality, it was a Hindu idiom well-known to most Indians as an ideal and inspired ordinary people. Gandhi's *sāmānya-dharma* became an extraordinary expression of the ordinary life and laid the foundations for his eventual spiritual status as the great-souled one (*mahātmā*), a spiritual status that increased with his fasts to the point of death, the image of his lion-like but frail, loin-clothed body, his arduous marches about the country, and his equanimity in the face of enormous danger as he sought to quell violence.

Gandhi's Reinterpretation and Politicization of *sāmānya-dharma*

In his spiritual experiments, Gandhi drew not only on Hindu traditions but also on Jain ones (Gier 2004) and even the ascetic and mystical traditions of Christianity (via Tolstoy) and Islam. He hoped to inspire spiritual collaboration among members of the world religions in the quest for Indian liberation from colonial rule. But Gandhi also politicized the *sāmānya* virtues by incorporating them into his non-violent fight for Indian independence.

To do this, Gandhi had to remove the distinction between *sāmānya* virtues such as nonviolence as the norm and permissible violence (in the sense of just means and goals) as the exception (which made some wars permissible). He did this by arguing that struggles such as the fight for independence had to have not only just goals but also just means, and the only just mean was non-violence. To arrive at this position, Gandhi reinterpreted the Bhagavad-gītā - quite obviously a text about war - in allegorical terms as the "eternal duel between the 'forces of darkness and of light'" (Gandhi, *Harijan* 1936), an inner spiritual struggle. He argued also that Hinduism, as a living religion, constantly evolves; even his own understanding had changed through study of Hindu scriptures, exposure to other world religions, and thoughts about his own experience. To highlight this dynamism, Gandhi changed the conventional order of the *sāmānya* virtues and placed truth first, instead of *ahiṃsā* (although there were some traditional precedents for his order). He summed up his own spiritual quest as preeminently the search for truth (*sat*), an understanding that was related to his view that truth constituted the very nature of God. Truth was revealed through conscience, or the voice of God, within each person.

Now, consider *satyāgraha*. *Satyāgraha*, which means grasping and insisting on truth or acting with confidence that truth is on one's side, is a word that Gandhi created while in South Africa and mobilizing people of Indian origin to passive resistance against a new law that required them to be registered and fingerprinted. Gandhi connected *satyāgraha* as passive resistance with purification and penance, thus basing it in the yogic foundation of *sāmānya-dharma*.

Gandhi politicized other Indian religious practices as well. He turned fasting (*upavāsa*) into a political strategy, because both he and the British knew full well that should he die (and he certainly came close to doing so in the midst of several fasts), he would be perceived as a martyr. That would either mobilize his followers to new heights of activism or lead to uncontrollable riots. Both these would put pressure on the Raj to grant India her freedom. His long and difficult journeys by foot, on the model of the Hindu pilgrim (*yātrin*) or itinerant holy man (*sādhu*), were politicized as protest marches. People joined the inveterate walker and risked their lives against charges by the colonial police. Here is another example. Gandhi applied the spiritual principle of *naiṣkāmya-karmayoga* (the yoga of action without desire for its results) made famous by the Bhagavad-gītā to the struggle for independence. Gandhi capitalized on the traditional connotation of *ahiṃsā*. It meant not only not injuring or killing but also active compassion and love for the other, even in the most trying and dangerous circumstances. (This connotation was also made possible by the grammatical capacity of the compound, which fuses its distinct components - in this case, no desire to injure/kill, no maleficence - into a positive connotation, in which the meaning represents more than the sum of its parts (therefore, love, compassion, positive beneficence to all, in other words, *lokasaṃgraha*).

The million-dollar question was whether Gandhi's reinterpretation of *ahiṃsā* could be correlated with justice and peace and whether it could be the basis of an even more common ethic: a universal one. Martin Buber thought long and hard about this. In 1939, he read an article in which Gandhi compared South African treatment of Hindus to Nazi treatment of Jews and encouraged Jews in concentration camps to practise *satyāgraha*. Buber concluded that Gandhi's view was both tragic and comic; there could be no comparison between these two situations, and no one should demand martyrdom from a "diabolic universal steam-roller" which offered no hope of change (Buber 1939 cited by Estey and Hunter 1971, 146-147). Buber concluded "If I am to confess what is truth to me, I must say: There is nothing better for a man than to deal justly - unless it be to love; we should be able even to fight for justice - but to fight lovingly. I have been very slow in writing this letter to you, Mahatma. I made repeated pauses - sometimes days elapsing between short paragraphs - in order to test my knowledge and my way of thinking" (ibid 152).

Despite arguing against the moral position that Jews in concentration camps should be allowed self-defense, Gandhi did make room for violence in some contexts. In the Gītā Lord Kṛṣṇa's awareness that Arjuna's resistance to fighting (despite seemingly good reasons not to fight such as the fact that it would virtually destroy both sides of the royal family) was based ultimately on fear and cowardice rather than courage. Gandhi, too, was aware that inaction based on fear and cowardice was not real *ahiṃsā* and said: "Before he [a coward] can understand non-violence, he has to be taught to stand his ground and even suffer death in the attempt to defend himself against the aggressor who bids fair to overwhelm him. To do otherwise would be to confirm his cowardice and take him further away from non-violence. Whilst I may not actually help him to retaliate, I must not let a coward seek shelter behind non-violence so called" (Gandhi, *Harijan*, 1935). On another occasion, Gandhi was once asked: "'Supposing in the presence of superior brute force one feels helpless, would he be justified in using just enough force to prevent the perpetration of wrong?'... He answered: 'Yes, but there need not be that feeling of helplessness if there is real non-violence in you. To feel helpless in the presence of violence is not non-violence but cowardice. Cowardice must not be confused with non-violence'" (cited by Pyarelal 2:506). According to Gandhi, "It can certainly be said that to experiment with *ahiṃsā* in face of a murderer is to seek self-destruction. But this is the real test of *ahiṃsā*. He who gets himself killed out of sheer helplessness, however, can in no wise be said to have passed the test" (Gandhi in *Harijan*, 1946).

This exception to the principle of non-violence means that Gandhi was not a principled or absolute pacifist, even though on most occasions he argued against exceptions even for self-defense - a position more extreme than traditional Hindu ethics, which allowed self-defense as a reason for just war or for abortion when the mother's life is at stake.

There were several other situations in which Gandhi himself seemed to acknowledge the use of violent means, although he viewed this as the least of two evils.

His exhortation to the defenders to be wiped out to the last man in clearing Kashmir soil of the raiders rather than submit was even dubbed as 'Churchillian.' He had dared to advise, it was said, Churchill, Hitler, Mussolini, and the Japanese that they should adopt his technique of non-violence when they were likely to lose all. Why did he not give that advice to his friends in the National Congress when forsaking non-violence they sent armed resistance to Kashmir. Was it a case of being virtuous at others' cost? Gandhiji answered that in neither case had there been any lapse from his creed of non-violence. His Ahimsa did not forbid him from denying credit where credit was due even though the person to whom credit had to be given was a believer in violence ... As early as 1921, after deep thought, he had arrived at the conclusion that while a believer in non-violence is pledged not to resort, either directly or indirectly to violence or physical force in defence of anything, he is not precluded from helping men or institutions that are themselves not based on non-violence ... Even when both parties believe in violence there is often such a thing as justice on one side or the other ... 'It is permissible for, it is even the duty of, a believer in Ahimsa to distinguish between the aggressor and the defender ... (and to) side with the defender in a non-violent manner' (Pyarelal 2:502-503 referring to Gandhi's prayer speech Nov. 11, 1947).

One wonders why Gandhi was not more sympathetic with the plight of the Jews under Hitler.

Still, it is fair to argue that the Indian struggle for independence under Gandhi's leadership was far more peaceful than it might have been without his exemplary behavior and his reinterpretation of Hinduism. Violent revolution was certainly an alternative during these tumultuous times and had its leaders. It could well have become the mainstream movement in the struggle for Indian independence. Besides that, Gandhi himself checked many popular outbreaks of violence by his own charisma and by putting his life on the line in the name of non-violence.

But the catastrophic culmination of this struggle in Partition, when fifteen million people became refuges and between half a million and one million lost their lives, suggests that non-violence was by no means a clear victory on the ground, even though Partition was arguably beyond Gandhi's control, and that he felt betrayed in his final days by those who accepted it. He was shocked by the dropping of atomic bombs, too, on Japan. Gandhi said at the time, "Unless now the world adopts non-violence, it will spell certain suicide for mankind" and several months later opined "I regard the employment of the atom bomb for the whole sale destruction of men, women and children as the most diabolical use of science" (cited in Iyer ed. 2:13).

In short, I have argued that Gandhi was not a principled pacifist, although as the great-souled one (*mahātmā*) he combined the *nivṛtti* and *pravṛtti* orientations in a distinctive way.

INDEPENDENT INDIA: A REASSESSMENT OF NON-VIOLENCE AND SECURITY

The Gandhian legacy remained influential immediately after independence. India's first prime minister, Jawaharlal Nehru, promoted a political policy of nonalignment and in 1954 called for universal disarmament even as he supported the development of nuclear energy for peaceful uses. An early president, the philosopher-statesman Sarvepalli Radhakrishnan, promoted an image of Hinduism as the religion of peace (*śānti*) and tolerance (*tūlyatva*). But times were changing. National defense became a major problem, as India fought wars with Pakistan to hold on to to Kashmir and became engaged in a border conflict with China in 1962. First in 1965, then in 1974, and again in 1998, India tested nuclear devices and refused to sign the Nonproliferation Treaty.

Even before the 1998 bomb, some Hindu intellectuals were revisiting the Hindu and Gandhian legacies of non-violence and making another Hindu case for the just war - which arguably had long been the mainstream tradition in premodern India. In his essays, published posthumously under the title *Hindu Dharma*, the Sankaracharya of Kanci, Pujyasri Candrasekharendra Sarasvatisvami, reassesses the failures of the Indian experiment with *ahiṃsā* and argues for a just war theory similar to that of Buber.

First, he calls just war (and animal sacrifice) an exception to the general principle of *ahimsa*. Second, he places emphasis on the intention rather than the act. If violence is intended for the welfare of society and there is no hostility, it is permissible. Third, he argues that *samanya-dharma* is really required only for formal renunciates and functions merely as an ideal for the ordinary person. *Ahimsa* as a common value, moreover, should be understood as the absence of ill-feeling in all action. As such, it is optional. Fourth, he implies that violence in the context of a just war is no longer confined to the *ksatriya* caste and therefore acknowledges the modern reality of conscription. Fifth, he concludes that acts which 'apparently cause pain to others may have to be committed for the good of the world and there is no sin in them'" (Young 2004 citing *Hindu Dharma* 2000, 704).

The 1998 nuclear tests were called the "saffron bombs" or "Hindu bombs" by critics. They argued that these bombs had been tested because the Bharatiya Janata Party (BJP), which had the support of many Hindu holy men (hence the allusion to saffron, the sacred colour of ascetics) and was associated with Hindu fundamentalism, had endorsed the tests. Others pointed out that the nuclear program had been steadily if stealthily developing since China's nuclear test in 1964; it had hardly been invented by the BJP. This brought the Gandhians, along with leftists and others, onto the streets. In Gandhian style, they marched again for *ahiṃsā* but this time to a Buddhist pilgrimage site - Sarnath, where the Buddha first taught - rather than to a Hindu site. This venue avoided any Hindu overtones of the BJP and its allies. But one astute commentator pointed out that even the Buddha, when he was told that Ajatashatru of Magadha had attacked the Licchavi confederacy, commented that "perfect peace would never come until all the nations of the earth were equally mighty" (Malkani 1998). Given the public support and jubilation in the streets, it is clear that most Hindus supported Indian nuclear development.

CONCLUSION

Gitomer (232) sees the Mahābhārata as "a gap of ambiguity (or chaos, or meaninglessness) that rises within the episteme of the greater social discourse due to ruptures that occur in the 'political' order (that is, within the life of the polis)." Even Yudhiṣṭhira, the dharma king in the Mahābhārata - more Brahman in orientation than Kṣatriya - holds out the promise of a life without violence but is

> ... unable to receive his consecration, to reinaugurate the glorious dynasty of Kuru in any effective, lasting way. Only the radical strategy of junking every possibility of polity, destroying the earth's entire population and reconciling the combatants in heaven (note that this reconciliation takes place in heaven; the remaining life on earth is bleak, as the epic's opening attests) - only such a radical strategy will allow the book to end. And we know that the middle is infinitely expandable ... (Gitomer 232).

Gitomer sees this gap as the inevitable tragedy of human existence. For Gandhi and other followers of the nonviolent movement, Partition was a similar gap of chaos and meaninglessness due to an enormous rupture in the life of the polis. Like Yudhiṣṭhira, Gandhi had held out the promise of a life without violence but was unable to prevent the bloodbath of Partition. But in Gandhi's case, although he did not live to witness it, the rupture, violent though it was, moved quickly into a new age for India.

Are there any lessons to be learned from all this? Perhaps the wisdom is that these gaps of chaos can become fewer and more contained when inspired by the ethic of nonviolence for the many and an ethic of just war and deterrence as the exception. To say otherwise, puts social discourse in heaven and epic meta-time and takes human nature beyond tragedy, its very nature, altogether. Still, one could argue that righteous and contained war is a step in the direction of no war because it necessitates good reasons for war (thereby preventing some wars) and constrains the practice itself through rules. And maybe it goes much farther. If the ruler is to treat all beings as his family and see his *dharma* as bringing welfare to the world (*lokasaṃgraha*), he might well be inspired not to go to war except in the most egregious circumstances. There is hope, I think, in the concepts of *loksasaṃgraha* and *ahiṃsā* as ideals to work toward, step by step, building on more and more containment of violence, not categorical withdrawal from violence. As agonistic war became constrained to just war (in theory if not always in practice), and just war to just reasons and means (including nonviolence as the presumption with few exceptions), maybe the dharma of nonviolence developed from within the exercise of the containment of violence will allow progressively fewer episodes of violence, even just violence. This is a *pravṛtti-nivṛtti* perspective that involves us all, not just rulers, in embracing prudential sageliness in this life itself.

BIBLIOGRAPHY

Buber, Martin, 1971. "A Letter to Gandhi (1939)," in *Nonviolence: A Reader in the Ethics of Action.* Ed. George F. Estey and Doris A. Hunter. Waltham, MA: Xerox College Publishers.

Desai, Mahadev, 1946. *The Gita according to Gandhi.* Ahmedabad: Navajivan.

Deshpande, Madhav M., 1991. "The Epic Context of the Bhagavadgītā." *Essays on the Mahābhārata.* Ed. Arvind Sharma. Leiden: E.J. Brill.

Dhand, Arti, "The Dharma of Ethics, the Ethics of Dharma: Quizzing the Ideals of Hinduism." *Journal of Religious Ethics* 2002. 30.3 (2002):347-372.

Dikshitar, V.R. Ramachandra, 1948. *War in Ancient India.* 2nd ed. Delhi: Motilal Banarsidass.

Gandhi, M.K., *Harijan* (April 28, 1946) 106.

Gandhi, M.K., 1955. *Truth Is God.* Ahmedabad: Navajivan.

Gandhi, M.K., 1961. *In Search of the Supreme.* Ahmedabad: Navajivan.

Gier, Nicholas F, 2004. *The Virtue of Nonviolence: From Gautama to Gandhi.* Albany: State University of New York Press.

Gitomer, David, "King Duryodhana: The Mahabharata Discourse of Sinning and Virtue in Epic and Drama." *Journal of the American Oriental Society.* 112:2 (1992): 222-232.

Heitelbeitel, Alf, 2001. *Rethinking the Mahābhārata: A Reader's Guide to the Education of the Dharma King.* Chicago: University of Chicago Press.

Hiltebeitel, Alf, 1990. *The Ritual of Battle: Krishna in the Mahābhārata.* Albany: State University of New York Press.

Iyer, Raghavan, Ed. 1986. *The Moral and Political Writings of Mahatma Gandhi,* vol. 2 *Truth and Non-violence.* Oxford: Clarendon Press.

Katz, Ruth Cecily, 1990. *Arjuna in the Mahābhārata: Where Krishna Is, There Is Victory.* Delhi: Motilal Banarsidass.

Klostermaier, Klaus K., 1994. *A Survey of Hinduism.* Albany: State University of New York Press.

Malkani, K.R., "India, China and the Bomb." *Hinduistan Times.* 3 June 1998.

Nikhilananda, Swami, trans. 1995. *The Māṇḍukya Upaniṣad with Gauḍapada's Kārikā and Śaṅkara's Commentary*. Calcutta: Advaita Ashrama.

Perrett, Roy W., 1993. "Moral Vegetarianism and the Indian Tradition." *Ethical and Political Dilemmas of Modern India*. Eds. Ninian Smart and Shivesh Thakur. London: St. Martin's Press.

Pyarelal [Nair], 1956. *Mahatma Gandhi: The Last Phase.* vol.2. Ahmedabad: Navajivan.

Reich, Tamar C., "Sacrificial Violence and Textual Battles: Inner Textual Interpretation in the Sanskrit Mahābhārata." *History of Religions.* 41:2 (2001) 142-169.

Sarasvatisvami, Pujyasri Candrasekharandra, 2000. *Hindu Dharma: The Universal Way of Life*. Mumbai: Bharatiya Vidya Bhavan.

Sharma, Arvind,1991. Ed. *Essays on the Mahābhārata.* Leiden: E.J. Brill.

Sharma, Arvind, 1993. "Gandhi or Godse? Power, Force and Non-violence." *Ethical and Political Dilemmas of Modern India*. Eds. Ninian Smart and Shivesh Thakur. New York: St. Martin's Press. 15-29.

Smith, Mary Carroll, 1974. "Warriors: the Originators of the Moral Code in Ancient India." Preprinted Papers for the Section on Asian Religions –History of Religions. American Academy of Religion Annual Meeting.

Tallahassee, Fl: Florida State University.

Tubb, Gary A. 1991, "Santarasa in the Mahabharata." *Essays on the Mahabharata*. Ed. Arvind Sharma. Leiden: E.J. Brill.171-203.

Whitaker, Jarrod L., "Divine Weapons and *Tejas* in the Two Indian Epics." *Indo-Iranian Journal* 43 (2000) 87-113.

Young, Katherine K., 2004. "Hinduism and the Ethics of Weapons of Mass Destruction." *Ethics and Weapons of Mass Destruction: Religious and Secular Perspectives*. Eds. Sohail H. Hashmi and Steven P. Lee. Cambridge: Cambridge University Press. 277-307.

Young, Katherine K., 1990. "The Indian Secular State under Hindu Attack: A New Perspective on the Crisis of Legitimation." *Ethical and Political Dilemmas of Modern India*. Eds. Ninian Smart and Shivesh Thakur. Delhi: Chanakya. 194-234.

SECTION III

In: Religion, Terrorism and Globalization
Editor: K.K. Kuriakose, pp. 97-107

Chapter 6

GENDER VIOLENCE IN MUSLIM SOCIETIES

Zayn Kassam

Pomona College, Claremont, California, CA

The words *violence* and *Islam* often conjure up two images: political violence and violence against women. An example of the former is terrorist activity, such as the September 11th, 2001 attacks by Muslim suicide terrorists associated with al-Qaeda, by suicide bombers in Israel, the West Bank, and Gaza, by jihadists in Kashmir, and by Chechen rebels in Russia. All these illustrate violence by Muslims against non-Muslims under the rationale of opposing U.S. support for anti-Muslim regimes or in nationalist struggles for political control. But instances of Muslim political violence against Muslims include the government-abetted Janjaweed attacks on Black Muslims in the Sudan, the current attacks in Iraq on law enforcement officials, the Taliban's repressive policies against Afghan Muslims not considered "sufficiently Muslim," and Indonesian military actions against the residents of East Timor and Aceh.

The recent murder of Theo van Gogh,[1] a Dutch filmmaker, called attention to Muslim violence against non-Muslims and Muslims alike. Van Gogh was assassinated by an Algerian immigrant for directing a film written by Ayaan Hirsi Ali, a Somali refugee woman, who claims that violence against Muslim women is sanctioned in the sacred Muslim scripture, the Qur'an. In the film, verses of the Qur'an are written prominently in black on a naked female body, entirely shrouded in see-through black gauze and encased in a forbidding, opaque, black *chador* (outer garment). The beautiful, innocent, and sensuous young woman performs the *salat*, or ritual prayer, accompanied by *du'a* or supplicatory prayer, and complains to God that despite all she has done to follow His commands, His sacred words have been used to justify violence against her. Her uncle has sexually harassed her, her husband has beaten her, and this violence has been prolonged by her inability to leave home.

Van Gogh died for airing the issue of violence against Muslim women in a manner that desecrated the scripture of Islam—displayed on a nude woman's flesh—and flaunted the Muslim belief that God is just for both men and women. But perhaps the most easily recognized forms of Muslim violence against women are the forced veiling, or seclusion of

---

[1] http://news.bbc.co.uk/1/hi/world/europe/3974179.stm

women, honor killings, female genital surgery, and, wife or female battery. At worst, these acts are popularly understood as justified in the Qur'an. At best, they are considered extreme forms of fundamentalist Islam, such as that of the Taliban, who claimed that their treatment of women was in accordance with the dictates of Islamic law (*shari'ah*). The quandary media producers often face is how to avoid blaming Islam, while at the same time drawing attention to issues in which the chief perpetrators are Muslim. Support for veiling is often viewed as the mark of a Muslim fundamentalist, and by extension, a jihadist or violently predisposed individual. A symbol of Muslim male oppression of women, the practice has come to the fore in recent months as some European countries have moved to ban the wearing of the *hijab*, or head-covering, in schools and other public institutions. At times, Muslim majority countries like Iran in 1936 and Turkey in 1922 have, in an attempt to establish secularism or the separation of mosque and state, banned the use of the veil in public spaces. Soon after the Iranian revolution of 1978, when the Ayatollah Khomeini established an Islamic Republic, Iran's prohibition was rescinded in favor of compulsory veiling.

Honor killings have achieved international notoriety through such vehicles as the award-winning BBC documentaries *Murder in Purdah* and *Licence to Kill*, produced by Fiona Lloyd-Davies and researched and narrated by Olenka Frenkiel.[2] These programs first aired in March 2000 and investigated the custom in Pakistan. Perpetrators clearly articulate a link between honor killings and what they think the Qur'an prescribes as proper roles for women. Muslim women who step beyond these perceived prescribed limits do so at their peril, and Muslim men deem it a religious duty to uphold the honor and piety of their women at all costs.

Female genital surgery, deemed by African activists in Britain to be properly classified as torture, continues to be practiced in the Nile regions of Africa. It has also been reported in Southeast Asia and in transplanted African communities in Europe and the Americas. Although it is practiced by non-Muslims as well as Muslims in the Nile region, the Muslim rationale for the practice is found not in the Qur'an, but in the *hadith* literature, comprised of narratives of what the Prophet was thought to have said and done, as remembered by his associates and transmitted to posterity. According to *hadith* narratives, the practice ostensibly goes back to Abraham's command to Hagar to be circumcised in order to appease Sarah's wrath. Hence, the practice is often labeled *taharah*, or purification, and considered *sunnah,* or recommended religious practice.

Finally, female battery is rooted in the idea that a Muslim male has the right to discipline his wife or female members of his family in the manner of his choosing. This attitude is a feature of all traditional patriarchies, in which male honor can be compromised through the perceived misbehavior of female members of his family or clan. Scriptural justification for spousal violence is thought to be found in the infamous "wife-beating' verse, Q. 4: 34:

> Men are in charge of women, because Allah hath made the one of them to excel the other, and because they spend of their property (for the support of women). So good women are obedient, guarding in secret that which Allah hath guarded. As for those from whom ye fear rebellion, admonish them and banish them to beds apart and scourge them. Then if they obey you, seek not a way against them.[3]

---

[2] http://news.bbc.co.uk/1/hi/programmes/correspondent/909948.stm
[3] 4:34, translation found in Mohammad Marmaduke Pickthall, *The Meaning of the Glorious Koran: An explanatory translation* (New York: New English Library, n.d), 83:

Another documentary, *Beneath the Veil*, details the observations of a British Muslim woman, Saira Shah, returning to her native Afghanistan. She filmed under cover of the signature Afghan form of the *chador*, gazing through its meshed netting as if through the bars of a prison. The documentary shocked American audiences with poignant footage of three young children who had clearly been traumatized and perhaps otherwise violated when the Taliban stormed their house and killed their mother. Implicitly, the documentary also justified to Americans an ancillary moral reason for invading Afghanistan: not only should the Taliban be removed for refusing to hand over Osama bin Laden, but Afghan women should be granted basic rights to education, employment, and freedom of movement. The deafening silence that had long answered the pleas of women's groups working on behalf of Afghani women and children under the Taliban was now replaced by the deafening roar of artillery shells.

Similarly, the film *Osama*, produced and directed by Siddiq Barmak depicts the fate of a young girl whose mother dresses her up as a boy so she might support the family. When her sexual identity is discovered, she is not put to death, as dictated by the Taliban interpretation of Islamic law would dictate, but is married to an elderly *mullah* in a show of "compassion." The *mullah*, or religious expert akin to a priest, already keeps his several wives under lock and key. Both the documentary and the film chillingly reinforce popular notions of Muslim male misogyny, whose ill-treatment of women is thought to be rooted in the Qur'an and enshrined in Islamic institutions such as *shari'ah* law.

THE QUR'AN ON WOMEN AND ITS FORMATIVE RECEPTIVE TRADITIONS

Leila Ahmed has observed that men and women understand Islam differently, or they hear a different Qur'an.[4] Men hear a legal Qur'an in which women have curtailed rights and specific gender duties; men assume guardianship over women and expect obedience from them. Women, on the other hand, hear an egalitarian message in which they have moral agency, spiritual equality, and the guarantee of certain rights. The Qur'an demands moral uprightness from both men and women and holds both sexes accountable for their actions, rewarding or punishing them accordingly. However, in the social and legal context of the 21st century, there is no doubt that women are treated unequally. For instance, under family law provisions in many Muslim countries that draw upon *shari'ah* law, which is based in part upon masculinist legal interpretations of the Qur'an, women may inherit only half as much as their male relatives[5] and are restricted to monogamy while males may marry up to four women.[6] Women are subject to male guardianship of their affairs,[7] which includes the

---

4:34 Men are in charge of women, because Allah hath made the one of them to excel the other, and because they spend of their property (for the support of women). So good women are the obedient, guarding in secret that which Allah hath guarded. As for those from whom ye fear rebellion, admonish them and banish them to beds apart, and scourge them. Then if they obey you, seek not a way against them.

[4] In Leila Ahmed, *A Border Passage: From Cairo to America—A Woman's Journey* (New York: Penguin Books, 1999), 125.

[5] Qur'an, 4:11 ff.

[6] Qur'an, 4:3.

[7] Qur'an, 4:5.

ratification of marital contracts,[8] must don clothing that leaves only the face and hands uncovered in public, and their legal testimony carries half the weight of a male's testimony. Further, verse 4:34 in the Qur'an has been read by the male commentarial tradition to declare male superiority over women and male privilege in taking disobedient or rebellious women to task in stages of punishment ranging from separation to physical abuse. In the popular Muslim mind, this is the verse most likely to be appropriated for honor killings or punishment by death—by acid, by burning, or by shooting or stabbing. The Qur'an also recommends a hundred lashes[9] for men and women guilty of adultery. Adultery, however, is difficult to prove unless there are at least four witnesses to the adulterous act. Moreover, if a husband cannot produce witnesses, his wife may accuse him of bearing false witness or she may repent and be forgiven her transgression, although such a right is rarely accorded to women. Nonetheless, the question remains: is the Qur'an a misogynist document that devalues women?

In examining the status of women in Muslim societies, especially in connection with honor killings and other forms of violence against women, Riffat Hassan states that it is necessary to go back to the beginning—that is, to the founding narratives that have led to women's second-class citizens in Muslim societies. Although patriarchy did not originate with Islam, as argued by Ahmed and others,[10] how did the notion that women were created "from the male, for the purpose of the male," become entrenched in Muslim discourse and institutions, thereby enabling institutional gender discrimination? Hassan examines the Qur'an's creation narrative and hears, as many women do, the Qur'an's message of ontological and spiritual equality, in which both men and women are created from a single soul and there is no mention of the female as having been created from the rib of Adam.[11] The rib account of the creation of the first woman comes from Genesis 2:18-24, and, as Stowasser has shown in her masterful study of women in Qur'anic commentaries and the *hadith* literature, enters Muslim discourse through the efforts of the prodigious scholar al-Tabari (d. 923 CE) by way of Biblical traditions or lore (*isra'illiyat*), as well as through popular stories about the prophets (*qisas al-anbiya*). In her view, *isra'illiyat* literature played a pivotal role in Muslim juridical interpretations of gender-related verses in the Qur'an that were consistent with the social structures of Byzantine society, in which "the theme of 'woman's weakness' with its paradoxical twin, 'woman as threat to the male and society' dominated the Islamic scripture-based paradigm on gender throughout the medieval period."[12]

---

[8] Thus, for instance, although the Qur'an does not itself specify that women must have a male guardian who ratifies the *nikah* or marriage contract, the importance of the *wali* or guardian in concluding the marriage contract, which is properly a contract between the bridegroom and the bride's *wali*, cannot be overemphasized. Perhaps the role of the *wali* was inherited from pre-Islamic Arab society, and legitimated within Islamic law through a reading of 4:5 that included women among the "foolish" for whom a guardian was mandated. For the duties of the *wali* in the marriage contract, see *Encyclopedia of Islam* (Leiden, The Netherlands: E.J. Brill, 2001), "Nikah" CD-ROM Edition v.1.1.

[9] Qur'an, 24:2 ff.

[10] Leila Ahmed, *Women and Gender in Islam* (New Haven and London: Yale University Press, 1992), 33.

[11] Riffat Hassan, "Muslim Women and Post-Patriarchal Islam" in Paula M. Cooey, William R. Eakin, Jay B. McDaniel, eds., *After Patriarchy: Feminist Transformations of the World Religions* (Maryknoll, NY: Orbis Books, 1991), 44-45. See also Q. 4:1; 39:6; 7:189: "We created you (plural) from a single soul." Readings of the second person plural form vary from male and female from the point of view of feminists, to the diversity of peoples from the point of view of religious pluralists.

[12] Barbara Stowasser, *Women in the Qur'an, Traditions, and Interpretation* (New York: Oxford University Press, 1994), 23.

Why did medieval Muslims turn to Biblical lore and stories about pre-Muhammadan prophets for their edification and institutionalization? While the answer to such a question is complex, two factors are key: first, the Qur'an itself references Biblical figures and assumes that its audience is aware of who they are; and second, a *hadith* reports the Prophet as having said: "Pass on information from me, even if it is only a verse of the Quran; and relate traditions from the Banu Isra'il, for there is no restriction."[13] This report was understood as Muhammad himself recommending Muslims to ask their co-religionists, the Jews and the Christians, for details on Biblical figures, about whom they would know better. Further, as Muslim political power extended to empire over Byzantine and Sassanian territories, many institutional modes of governance were absorbed into the developing Islamic polity. So, for instance, Doumato has argued that Qur'anic laws pertaining to women were extracted in a manner consistent with the ways in which women in Byzantine territories were expected to behave.[14] Stowasser has shown how, for instance, the *hijab*, a physical curtain referenced in the Qur'an, became a portable curtain in the form of a veil. This was an emulation of upper-class Byzantine and Persian practices[15] symbolically marking the female as a "Good Woman."[16]

The medieval interpretation of gender in Muslim legal institutions, further inscribed in Muslim cultural productions such as commentarial, literary, philosophical, mystical, and theological discourses, have reinforced a patriarchal view of social arrangements that have produced structural gender inequities in Muslim societies. However, this is not simply a Muslim issue, but a wider religious issue. Were gender inequity not a global phenomenon, there would be no need for activism on behalf of women's suffrage access to social, educational, and legal institutions, or the right to contest patriarchal interpretations of scripture in all the world's faiths. Acknowledging the link or intersections between social institutions, discourses, and women's experience, Muslim gender scholars and activists have sought to identify the realities of Muslim women's experiences in their historical, economic, social, and legal contexts in which these realities are constituted, and have proposed alternatives for the future.

VIOLENCE AGAINST WOMEN

Of the many forms of violence against women, regardless of faith and geography, two merit special attention. These are: honor killings, and female genital surgery. The chapter concludes with a brief examination of structural issues, addressing which must form the cornerstone of activism aimed at reducing and ultimately eradicating violence against women.

---

[13] Quoted in F.E. Peters, *Judaism, Chrisianity, and Islam: The Classical Texts and Their Interpretation*, v. 2 (Princeton: Princeton University Press, 1990), 143.

[14] Eleanor Doumato, "Hearing Other Voices: Christian Women and the Coming of Islam," *International Journal of Middle East Studies*, 23 (1991), 177-199.

[15] Stowasser, *Women in the Qur'an*, 92 ff.

[16] Gerda Lerner, *The Creation of Patriarchy* (New York: Oxford University Press, 1986), 134, 139 where the veil is utilized circa 1250 BCE in Mesopotamia as a marker distinguishing respectable women who are under the protection of a male from disreputable women who were unprotected by men and therefore available. In both instances, class differences among women were defined in relation to men, with tighter sexual controls exercised on upper-class women as "the virginity of respectable daughters became a financial asset for the family."

Honor Killings

A feature of the classic patriarchy found in many parts of the world, including China, Latin America, and various Muslim regions, is the notion that women are the keepers of family honor, and by extension the guardians of tradition and religion.[17] From a very young age, a woman is socialized to bear this honor, expressed most saliently when she places her sexuality under the control of males, usually the family patriarch and more broadly her male relatives. As Abu-Odeh has argued, to define a woman's honor by her sexual behavior also shapes male identity, and has less to do with the woman than with male honor. This "derives from the struggle to retain intact the chastity of the women in the family, and this makes male reputation insecurely dependent upon female sexual conduct."[18] Examples of the tragic consequences of male honor "compromised" by female behavior, sexual or otherwise, can be found among places and cultural traditions as diverse as Muslim regions of Asia, in largely Hindu regions such as India, and in Buddhist/Confucian areas such as China as well as within Christian and indigeneous areas such as Latin America, and are not unknown in Europe and North America where they are more commonly understood under the rubric of spousal battery. Killing a woman for her perceived dalliances with men other than the one to whom she is formally contracted is called "honor killing" in regions like Jordan and Pakistan, and "dowry death" in regions like India. Both terms imply that something in the regional culture and religion legitimizes the practice.

However, Amnesty International reports on honor-killings in Pakistan suggest that economic motives may be a factor. Using acid, kitchen fires, or weapons to brutally eliminate a woman allows the man to marry again and accumulate more bride-wealth. Also, a man may kill a woman to settle an old score with other men, a practice known as *karo-kari*.[19] In this form of vigilante or tribal justice, the Islamic legal requirement to produce four witnesses to testify about the woman's sexual misconduct is rarely observed.

Just because Muslims use the Qur'an to rationalize honor killings, Islam cannot be held responsible for the practice. Rather, a cursory comparison of statistics suggests that the percentage of women in Pakistan subject to honor crimes is almost identical to the percentage of women in the United States who undergo spousal battery, sometimes resulting in death.[20] Reports also cite the inability of the police and court systems to deal with the issue. Problems range from poor police reception and response, to judicial apathy or even support for honor killings, making the justice system entirely ineffective in addressing honor killings. Moreover, legal loopholes allow perpetrators brought before the court to receive minimal sentences by claiming they were provoked to kill.

Asma Jehangir, a noted human rights lawyer in Pakistan whose office served as the stage for the honor killing of a client, Samia Sarwar, criticizes the state for failing to protect the

---

[17] Valentine Moghadam, *Modernizing Women: Gender and Social Change in the Middle East*, 2nd ed. (Boulder: Lynne Rienner, 2003), 118 ff.

[18] Lama Abu-Odeh, "Crimes of Honour and the Construction of Gender in Arab Societies" in Mai Yamani, ed., *Feminism and Islam: Legal and Literary Perspectives* (New York: New York University Press, 1996), 153.

[19] http://web.amnesty.org/library/Index/engASA330181999

[20] Intimate partner homicides are 3 per 100,000 according to a U.S. Department of Justice report for 2000 (see http://www.ojp.usdoj.gov/bjs/abstract/htus02.htm); 300 cases were reported for 1999 in Pakistan (see http://web.amnesty.org/library/Index/engASA330181999); the actual number is no doubt much higher. Another estimate suggests that 1250 women were killed in 2004. (*http://www.dawn.com/2005/01/17/local30.htm*).

lives of Pakistani women. He observed that the practice has nothing to do with Islam. Riffat Hassan further argues that until social mores and perceptions of women in Islamic discourse and legal institutions are changed, women will remain second-class citizens in Muslim societies. Hassan's academic activism examines the origins of the popular notion that women were created from the male for the purposes of the male, asserting to the contrary that the Qur'an suggests no such fiction. A study by Stowasser shows how the idea of woman as created from the Adam's rib was imported into Islamic discourse and that commentarial literature on the Qur'an, while paradoxically upholding women's moral responsibility and agency, blames women for social chaos (*fitna*) and constructs a female model based on Eve: sexually insatiable, responsible for Adam's disobedience to God, morally weak, and condemned to suffer the toils of childbirth.[21] Despite the fact that the Qur'an itself does not essentialize women in such a manner, it is clear that such imported views of women have justified violence towards women who are seen as being in need of guidance and control lest their natures get the better of them.

In the rhetoric surrounding honor killings, it is clear is that many Muslim men believe that the Qur'an gives men rights over women, including the right to discipline women, and such views are misused to justify violence against women. It is also clear that in many cases of Muslim violence against women, perpetrators are motivated by the hope of gain in economic and/or social capital. The phenomena of honor killings is made possible by social attitudes that consider women to be essentially expendable and by misapplied religious justifications, structural economic inequities, and an enervated justice system unwilling, unable, or unequipped to deal with the issue. In her efforts to address the complexity of honor killings, Riffat Hassan has created the International Network for the Victims of Violence in Pakistan (INRFVVP) to raise awareness of violence against women and raise funds for burn units, health care, medicine for burn victims, and shelters for survivors of attempted honor killings.[22] She has worked to convince General Pervez Musharraf that there is nothing Islamic about honor killings, which should be criminalized and handled by the justice system. In fact, Musharraf has done just that, and in recent months he has called for a review of the Hudood Ordinances, a set of laws initiated by a previous regime, in 1978 that greatly discriminate against women.[23] In January 2005, Musharraf moved to criminalize honor crimes, although without removing the legal option of retribution and blood money that could allow a perpetrator to go unpunished.[24]

---

[21] Stowasser, *Women in the Qur'an*, 28–30.

[22] INRFVVP@listserve.louisville.edu

[23] http://www.barnabasfund.org/News/Archive/Pakistan/Pakistan-20040716.htm

[24] http://www.csmonitor.com/2005/0120/p06s01-wosc.html, which reports: Social activists and opposition politicians say the government still needs to offset the Islamic law of *qisas* and *diyat* (retribution and blood money), which allows families of the deceased to either forgive the murderer or to ask for blood money in return. Since most honor killings are committed by brothers, fathers, or other kin, the perpetrators go unpunished after they are pardoned by other members of the family.

"So a son could forgive his father for murdering his mother, a mother could forgive her husband for killing their daughter, a father could forgive his brother and so on," says Saba Gul Khattak, executive director of the Sustainable Development Policy Institute (SDPI) and a women's rights activist.

Female Genital Cutting

Female Genital Cutting involves the removal of the clitoris and often the major and minor labia. Muslims may give it an Islamic rationale--so much so that recently the Shaykh of al-Azhar, the premier training institution for Muslim clerics in Egypt, announced that it is not in fact Islamic. The practice is most common along the Nilotic region in Africa, although it is also found in other parts of the world, such as Indonesia, Malaysia, and Sri Lanka. In the Middle East, according to Amnesty International, it occurs in Oman, Yemen, and the United Arab Emirates. In industrialized nations, it is typically confined to specific immigrant communities (it is unknown whether the 19th century practice of clitoridectomy for health reasons in Britain and in the USA has continued). (Women may, for aesthetic or other reasons, undergo labial reduction surgery at any number of clinics in the United States and the United Kingdom, as a recent Google search found.) Amnesty estimates that 135 million girls and women have undergone the operation, while 2 million are at risk every year. The surgery causes a host of health issues, including, in cases of infibulation, chronic kidney infections, kidney and bladder stones, reproductive tract infections, tumors, and the risk of heightened HIV transmission through intercourse. Often, without further cutting, intercourse or child delivery is impossible.

Female circumcision is thought to promote cultural identity, to restore a woman to her femininity by cutting out "male parts" such as the clitoris and labia, to abate female promiscuity by reducing a woman's sexual desire, and to enhance male sexual pleasure, although studies indicate that men prefer sexual partners who have not undergone the procedure. Aesthetic reasons have also been cited: a woman's genitals are thought to grow so much over time without the surgery that they would eventually come to hang between her legs. Other superstitions include the death of a male if his penis comes in contact with the clitoris, a notion extended to babies should their heads come into contact with the clitoris during birth. Some have argued fallaciously that without clitoridectomy, a woman cannot conceive.[25]

Although female circumcision is not mentioned in the Qur'an (nor is male circumcision), references suggest the practice was known to Muslims at the time the *hadith* pertaining to genital cutting were recorded, circa 200 years after the Prophet's death. Today, genital cutting is practiced by Muslims and non-Muslims alike, including Jews, Christians, and tribal peoples, but it is largely understood to be a Muslim practice, especially due to its prevalence in Egypt, Mali, Guinea, Gambia, Ethiopia, Eritrea, Sierra Leone, Somalia, and northern Sudan. Noor Kassamali argues that female circumcision, thought to have originated in Egypt, predates Islam by 2500 years and assumed an Islamic cast among practitioners who converted to Islam. In the regions where it is still practiced, it is often given a Muslim rationale, as evidenced by the reluctance of some Muslim clerics to disavow genital cutting.[26] In 1996 the Health Minister in Egypt banned all licensed health professionals from carrying out the

---

[25] http://www.amnesty.org/ailib/intcam/femgen/fgm1.htm#a3

[26] For instance, when in October 1994, the mufti of Egypt, Shaykh Muhammad Sayyid Tantawi declared that there is no Qur'anic basis for genital cutting, Shaykh Gad al-Haq Ali of al-Azhar, the premier educational institution in Egypt responsible for training the clergy, declared that "female circumcision is a part of the legal body of Islam and is a laudable practice that does honor to the women." Quoted in Noor Kassamali, "When Modernity Confronts Traditional Practices" in Herbert L. Bodman and Nayereh Tohidi, eds., *Women in Muslim Societies: Diversity Within Unity* (Boulder and London: Lynne Rienner Publishers, 1998), 43.

procedure. The ban has since been challenged in the courts, even though it has was upheld by the Shaykh of al-Azhar. Indeed, the reluctance of legislators to eradicate the practice seems to be rooted in a social desire to curb female sexuality. Kassamali contends that the attempt of religious leaders to moderate a woman's sexual desire is contrary not only to the Prophet's teaching but also to the Qur'an, which contains no reference to female circumcision. It appears in a few *hadith* of questionable authenticity, such as the *hadith* that reports, "Do not go in deep. It is more illuminating to the face and is preferable to the man." This *hadith* is not found in the highly regarded *hadith* collection of al-Bukhari.[27]

Ibn Kathir (d. 1373 CE) suggests that the practice was first ordered by Abraham. According to his account, Sarah, the wife of the patriarch Abraham, was given a slave-girl named Hagar by the Pharaoh of Egypt. Since Abraham and Sarah were childless, Sarah offered Hagar to Abraham in the hope she would conceive a child. Once Hagar became pregnant, her haughtiness aroused Sarah's jealousy, and Sarah vowed to cut "three limbs" of Hagar. Consequently, Abraham ordered Hagar to pierce her ears and to have herself circumcised.[28] Since Ibn Kathir bases his account of female circumcision on al-Kisa'i, a 9th century source, this suggests that during the 9th century, the practice of circumcision was identified with an Egyptian woman named Hagar.

Does the inclusion of such a narrative in Islamic sources make female circumcision an Islamic practice, especially given the importance of Hagar as the matriarchal progenitor of the Arabs, and whose descendant, Muhammad, would bring Arabs into the monotheistic fold? Ibn Naqib (d. 1368 CE), a Shafi'i legal scholar, says only this in his legal handbook, *Reliance of the Traveller*: "Circumcision is obligatory."[29] 'Umar Barakat's (d. 1890 CE), commentary on this statement expands on the definition of circumcision, adding the gloss: "for both men and women. For men it consists of removing the prepuce from the penis, and for women, removing the prepuce (Ar. *bazr*) of the clitoris." To this, the translator attaches: "(not the clitoris itself, as some mistakenly assert)." Sheikh 'Abd al-Wakil Durubi, Imam of the Mosque of Darwish Pasha in Damascus, Syria, adds: "Hanbalis hold that circumcision of women is not obligatory but sunna, while Hanafis consider it a mere courtesy to the husband."[30]

By 1890 CE, female circumcision was considered sufficiently Islamic for Barakat to add his gloss. Its existence is further acknowledged by Keller, the translator of the text, who apparently feels that the practice is abused enough to justify his defining the limits to which it should be extended, i.e., "not the clitoris itself." Esther Hicks notes:

> In Sudan (and Egypt), Shafi'ite law is predominant. This school of law holds the circumcision of girls to be obligatory (it is regarded as customary in the Malikite school and perceived as a 'good deed' for girls in the Hanafite school) (Dorkenoo, 1994:37). It is thus not surprising that laws prohibiting the practice of female circumcision in countries where the Shafi'ite school predominates will have little or no effect (Walther, 1993:79).[31]

---

[27] Ibid., 44.

[28] Barbara Freyer Stowasser, *Women in the Qur'an, Traditions, and Interpretation* (New York: Oxford University Press, 1994), 47.

[29] Nuh Ha Mim Keller, ed. and trans., *Reliance of the Traveller: A Classic Manual of Islamic Sacred Law* (Beltsville, Maryland: Amana Publications, 1999), e4.3, 59.

[30] Ibid.

[31] Esther K. Hicks, *Infibulation: Female Mutilation in Islamic Northeastern Africa* (New Brunswick: Transaction Publishers, 1996), 193.

Further research is needed to explain why male circumcision was extended to include female circumcision, clearly a local, pre-Islamic practice, in Islamic religious prescriptions.

Arguing that female circumcision was not an Islamic requirement at Islam's inception fails to address the issues facing Muslims in regions where it is now legally sanctioned, required, or recommended—all the more so since any challenges to Islamic law in post-colonial societies, whether mounted by Muslims or by non-Muslims, are tarred with the brush of "Western imperialism" or seen as promoting the culturally undermining agenda of Western feminists.

Certainly, Western feminists' tendency to sensationalize or sexualize female circumcision is counterproductive in its failure to acknowledge the structural economic, cultural, and health factors contributing to the practice. As Kassamali argues, "Unless the issues of dire poverty, hunger, illiteracy, and unhygienic conditions are addressed and there are simultaneous efforts to advance the status of women through economic and educational means, the impact [of attempts to eradicate the practice] will be marginal."[32] Kassamali states that legislative efforts alone cannot eradicate the practice; rather, culturally sensitive approaches present a better option. One example of this is to reduce the impact of female circumcision by symbolically nicking the genitals. Or activists can launch educational initiatives in conjunction with community leaders, the media, and with health organizations. Indeed, the Somali slogan created as part of activist efforts to eradicate the practice claimed: "it was not healthy, not clean, not Islamic and it did not guarantee virginity."[33] Such a slogan addresses the multi-dimensional contexts of the practice: women's health, cultural ideas of purity, religious sanctions or prescriptions, and cultural attitudes towards women's sexuality.

STRUCTURAL ISSUES

Honor killings and female genital surgeries are two examples of the complex factors involved in global violence against women, expressed in culturally specific forms in countries with Muslim majority populations. Any attempt to eradicate this violence against women, or any violence for that matter, must harness multiple strategies. Above all else, women need legal protection, such as the laws enacted in Sudan to limit the practice of genital mutilation. However, laws are not enough to reduce female circumcision or its health consequences, except where health groups combine with religious agents to educate, inform, and address cultural attitudes underlying the practice. Moreover, unless structural issues are addressed—issues like poverty, lack of access to health care and education, and economic roadblocks—gender parity will forever remain on the back burner. This cannot be done without examining the global economic and political systems and their impact on Islamic nations, a frequently negative effect that can tip the balance in favor of Islamist organizations that promise a just and fair society under their banner. In the search for nativist alternatives to dominant global economic, political and cultural systems, women's bodies will remain a battleground.

At the same time, Muslim activists are reconsidering the inscription of patriarchal attitudes and practices in legal and cultural codes, supposedly in the name of religion. The

---

[32] Kassamali, 51.
[33] Ibid., quoted on 52.

noted contemporary legal scholar Khalid Abou El Fadl suggests that *hadith* narratives demeaning women (and for that matter, people of non-Arab races) need scrutiny:

> If one adopts the faith-based conviction that the Prophet was not sent by God to affirm and legitimate conservative and oppressive power structures, traditions that affirm the hegemony of patriarchy would have to pass the strictest level of scrutiny. However, applying this level of scrutiny to these traditions would reveal that there were too many patriarchal vested interests circulating, advocating, and embellishing these types of reports.[34]

Amina Wadud and Asma Barlas have questioned popular cultural assumptions, as well as the Muslim scholarly tradition that reads verses in the Qur'an as sanctioning men's superiority over women, or asserts that women should be obedient to men, or may justify violence towards women should they fall out of line. Through challenging the meanings traditionally assigned to words in the Qur'an that could be read differently but still within the integrity of their lexical field, and by questioning the perception of God as a patriarchal father,[35] these scholars base their critique on an understanding of a God who is just towards both men and women. Such scholars challenge gender inequity that appears under the guise of religious authority through centuries of patriarchal readings of sacred text and their concomitant productions of gender-inscribed discourses and institutions. Some scholars have studied the impact of colonization on gender issues. Leila Ahmed has noted that "States in which Islamic groups have recently seized power and reinstituted Islamic laws have thus far invariably enacted laws imposing severe new restrictions on women and sometimes also laws resulting in savage injustice and inhumanity toward women."[36] She explains the phenomena thus: "The notion of returning to or holding on to an 'original' Islam and an 'authentic' indigenous culture is itself, then, a response to the discourses of colonialism and the colonial attempt to undermine Islam and Arab culture and replace them with Western practices and beliefs."[37] She suggests that the terms of the discourse on Islamic identity and authenticity were set by colonial discourses that identified Islam as backward and Muslim treatment of women as proof of that backwardness, thereby validating an inversion in Islamist discourse that views women's bodies, through their regulation by men, as the site of an authentic expression of Islam. While the impact of such discourses remains to be seen, the female body cannot be free from the threat of violence until certain structural religious, political, economic, and cultural factors are addressed.

---

[34] Khalid Abou El Fadl, *Speaking in God's Name: Islamic Law, Authority and Women* (Oxford: Oneworld, 2003), 246-7.

[35] See Amina Wadud, *Qur'an and Woman: Rereading the Sacred Text from a Woman's Perspective* (Oxford: Oxford University Press, 1999); and Asma Barlas, *"Believing Women" in Islam: Unreading Patriarchal Interpretations of the Qur'an* (Austin: University of Texas Press, 2002).

[36] Ahmed, *Women and Gender in Islam*, 232.

[37] Ibid., 237.

In: Religion, Terrorism and Globalization
Editor: K.K. Kuriakose, pp.109-120

ISBN 1-59454-553-7
© 2006 Nova Science Publishers, Inc.

Chapter 7

PEACE AND CONFLICT RESOLUTION IN THE ISLAMIC TRADITION

Liyakat Takim
University of Denver, Colorado

Since the events of September 11, 2001, Muslims have become aware that they cannot afford to live in impregnable fortresses and that living in a pluralistic milieu requires an active engagement with the "other." The events of September 11 also proved to the Muslim community that the silent majority syndrome has to end simply because Muslim acquiesce has encouraged an extremist expression of Islam. It is the extremists who have spoken on behalf of Islam as their acts of violence have drowned the silent voices of the Muslim majority. Hence, a discourse on the issue of peace and nonviolence within the Islamic tradition is to be welcomed. It is imperative to voice an opinion on an issue that is of major concern to millions of people, especially for a religion that has often been targeted as violent and militant.

In this paper, I will attempt to delineate the Qur'anic position on peaceful coexistence with the "other." In addition, I will examine the different modes of conflict resolution in Muslim societies in modern times. In the final section, I will discuss how dialogue can lead to peaceful coexistence and create an appreciation of the other.

PEACE AND CO-EXISTENCE IN THE QUR'AN

The Qur'anic view of peace and co-existence is interwoven with its view of a universal moral discourse that unites all human beings. According to the Qur'an, human beings are created with an innate disposition (*fitra*) that leads to knowledge of and belief in God. In fact, the Qur'an posits a universal morality for humankind that is conjoined to values ingrained in the conscience of all human beings (30:30). This suggests a universal, ethical language that all human beings can connect to and engage in. As the Qur'an states, "He (God) has inspired in [human beings] the good or evil [nature] of an act, whosoever has purified it (the soul) has succeeded, one who corrupts it has surely failed." (91:8-10). The Qur'anic concept of a universal moral order is thus grounded in the recognition of an innate disposition engraved in the human conscience. Through this notion, Islam embraced certain universal human values that could form the basis for interaction with a diverse "other."

The basis of such a universal moral order can also be traced to verses like the following, "Humankind, be aware of your duties to your Lord, who created you from a single soul, and from it created its mate, and from the pair of them scattered abroad many men and women (4:1)." The verse suggests a common genesis and unity of human beings based on God's creation. It also implies that human beings have to recognize and live with their differences. On the basis of universal guidance and a common human origin, the Qur'an posits the presence of an objective and universally binding moral standard that is accessible to all intelligent beings. A striking feature of the Qur'anic discourse is the emphasis on the capacity of human beings to use their innate intelligence to comprehend universal truths. It is on the basis of their innate capacity and shared moral values that human beings can deal with others based on the principles of fairness and equity.

A major obstruction to peace arises when human beings take upon themselves the task of judging and condemning others. This can engender an exclusivist attitude and lead to the marginalization and even extermination of the other. In this respect, the Qur'an insists that guidance is the function of God, and it is He alone who has the right to decide the "spiritual destiny" of human beings. The Qur'an categorically maintains that the ultimate fate of human beings be left to God, the true judge of human conduct. Not even the Prophet has the right to judge the ultimate fate of human beings. As it states, "Upon you [O Prophet] is the deliverance [of the message], upon us is the reckoning [of the deeds] (13:40)." In another verse, the Qur'an states, "Had God willed, they would not have been idolaters. We have not appointed you as a watcher over them, neither are you their guardian (6:107)." By elevating judgment to the divine realm, the Qur'an accommodates the space for coexistence on the human plane.

Fundamental to the Qur'anic conception of peaceful co-existence is the view that human beings are united under one God (2:213). They are to strive towards virtuous deeds (5:48), for the most noble person in the eyes of God is the one who is most pious (49:13). These and other verses command Muslims to build bridges of understanding and cooperation with fellow human beings so as to create a just social order.

ACCEPTANCE AND PROTECTION OF THE OTHER

Peaceful co-existence requires that people abstain from abusing and denigrating those who do not share their beliefs. Deriding and mocking others can often engender violence and hatred. Therefore, the Qur'an urges respect for the beliefs of others. The Qur'an further states, "Had God willed, they would not have been not idolaters; and We have not appointed you a watcher over them, neither are you their guardian. Abuse not those to whom they pray, apart from God, otherwise, they will abuse God in revenge without knowledge. So We have decked out fair to every community their deeds; then to their Lord they shall return, and He will tell them what they have been doing" (6:107-108).

Qur'anic tolerance extends protection not only to Muslims and the people of the book (*ahl al-kitab*) but even to strangers who openly declare idolatry. As it says, "If one of the idolaters seeks protection, then grant him protection so that he may hear the word of God, and after that, send him to a place of safety" (9:6). The verse instructs Muslims not only to protect but also to ensure that no harm comes to the idolaters when they leave Muslim territory, and to send them to a place of safety. The discussion above indicates that the Qur'an envisioned a diverse community that was united under common moral values. Human beings are to coexist in peace and harmony. Diversity and differences in faith were to be judged by God only since, "Isn't He (God) the best of judges"(95:8)?

Qur'anic verses allow warfare under specific circumstances and stipulate that Muhammad should accept peace overtures from the enemy (8:61). Verses 2:192-93 command the Prophet to cease hostilities if the enemy desists. In order not to transgress, Muslims are required to respond proportionally to the injury done to them. Even here, the Qur'an urges restraint by accepting blood money and forgiveness.

The Qur'an sanctions *jihad* to establish a moral order that will protect the welfare of the Muslim community against both internal and external enemies. The permission to engage in hostilities was a response to the threat posed by the powerful Meccan tribes. A prescriptive measure was needed to redress the harm and the wrongs suffered by the Muslims in the face of Meccan aggression. These divinely sanctioned campaigns were a response to the hostility of the Meccan pagans. The Qur'an does not state that force is to be used against all unbelievers; only those unbelievers who demonstrate their hostility to Islam by trying to undermine the Islamic polity and by persecuting Muslims are to be targeted. It is Meccan hostility, rather than their disbelief, that is the target of the Qur'anic verses on *jihad*.

The Qur'an does not accept the idea of unlimited or aggressive warfare. By the assiduous usage of the term *la ta'tadu* (do not transgress) in the context of warfare, it can be argued that the Qur'an qualifies *jihad* with a moral condition of restraint. It also exhorts Muslims to seek avenues of peace. Thus it restricts rather than gives free license to recourse to war.[1]

PEACE IN THE JURIDICAL LITERATURE

There has been limited discourse on peace in the exegetical and juridical literature. Most of the discourse was focused on warfare and the extension of the abode of Islam (*dar al-Islam*). For Muslim jurists, the discourse on peace was set in the context of a general theory, which presupposed that peaceful coexistence with a Muslim state was possible only when *dar al-harb* (the territory of non-Muslims) was subdued. Anything less than that was construed as seen as a compromise of Muslim ascendancy and an act of relinquishing power. This was in violation of the Qur'anic guideline of peaceful coexistence.

Furthermore, when Muslim jurists discussed peaceful coexistence with non-Muslims in the legal literature, it was in the context of certain measures that would allow for a temporary cessation of hostilities. Shafi'i jurists, for example, inserted between *dar al-Islam* and *dar al-harb* a third category, *dar al-sulh*, the abode of truce. *Dar al-sulh* refers to the territories where peace exists with an Islamic state based on treaties, alliances, and cooperation. During the

---

[1] There are other verses in which Muslims are seemingly encouraged to kill disbelievers wherever they are found. I shall deal with the "sword verses" later on.

period of the truce, *dar al-sulh* would have to pay the *jizya* (a tax levied on the people of the book) or cede a portion of its territory.[2]

According to al-Shafi'i (d. 820), the imam could contract the truce if the welfare of the Muslims required it. However, al-Shafi'i's theory only suspended, rather than eliminated, warfare. Based on the precedent established by the Prophet's agreement with the Meccan tribes at al-Hudaybiyya in 630 C.E., the truce could not exceed 10 years.

The jurists were also divided on the question of signing the period of the peace treaty. Malik b. Anas (d. 795) and Ahmad b. Hanbal (d. 855), two prominent jurists, supported the notion of an indefinite peace treaty as long as it served the interests of the Muslim community.[3] However, not all jurists recognized the existence of *dar al-sulh*. The Hanafis did not accept it whereas Ibn Taymiyya (d. 1328) argued against putting a restriction on the length of the peace treaty.[4]

The jurists conceived of another scenario for temporary peace. One of the most important aspects of *siyar*[5] was the guarantee of free passage or security *(aman)*, which any Muslim could grant to a visitor from *dar al-harb* (called *harbi*).[6] The *aman* is a pledge of security through which a non-Muslim would be entitled to protection for up to a year while he is in *dar al-Islam*. The holder of the *aman* (called *musta'min*) is not considered to be a *dhimmi*,[7] neither is he required to pay the *jizya*. The *aman* can be renewed at the end of the period if he agrees to pay the *jizya* and to become a *dhimmi*. The *aman* suspended, albeit temporarily, the state of hostilities.

Despite the focus on warfare in Muslim juridical literature, there have been many instances where Muslims have co-existed peacefully with non-Muslims. Indeed, to portray Islam as intrinsically violent and incompatible with Western values is to ignore Muslim engagement with and contribution to Western civilization. The tendency to view Islam through violence and militant lens distorts the view that Islam has a rich cultural heritage and precepts that necessitate co-existence with the other. Spain is a great example where Muslims co-existed peacefully with Christians and Jews. They also protected them and shared their scientific achievements with their counterparts. For much of Islamic history, Muslim societies have been remarkably open to the outside world.[8] Recounting such anecdotes in Christian-Muslim encounters serve two purposes; they not only destroy the myth of Islam as an intrinsically violent and militant religion but also provide a paradigm for co-existence and collaborative actions between the people of the two faith groups.

In the past, Muslims have tolerated and even protected minority groups, especially Jews and Christians, the people of the book. In ninth-century Baghdad, Hunayn ibn Ishaq, a

[2] Muhammad al-Idris al-Shafi'i, *Kitab al-Umm* (Beirut: Dar al-Fikr, 1990), 4:103-04.
[3] M. Raquibuz Zaman, "Islamic Perspectives on Territorial Boundaries," in *Islamic Political Ethics: Civil Society, Pluralism and* Conflict, ed. Sohail Hashmi (Princeton: Princeton University Press, 2002), 94.
[4] Khaled Abou El Fadl, "Between Functionalism and Morality: The Juristic Debates on the Conduct of War," in *Islamic Ethics of Life: Abortion, War and* Euthanasia, ed. Jonathan Brockopp (Columbia, University of South Carolina Press, 2003), 120.
[5] *Siyar* describes the conduct of Muslims in their relations with non-believers of enemy territory as well as with people with whom the believers had made treaties, who may have been temporarily or permanently in Muslims' land. In addition, *siyar* also describes the laws of conduct with apostates and rebels.
[6] There is a difference among jurists as to who can give the *aman*. See Majid Khadduri, *War and Peace in the Law of Islam* (Baltimore: The Johns Hopkins Press, 1955), 164-65.
[7] The *ahl al-dhimma* in the Qur'an and early history of Islam were the protected minorities, both Jewish and Christian, who had chosen not to convert to Islam.
[8] Eickelman, "Islam and Ethical Pluralism," in *Islamic Political Ethics*, ed. Sohail Hashmi, 118.

Christian, directed the translation academy when the classical Greek works and Hindu and Persian scientific treatises were translated to Arabic. The Caliph al-Ma'mun (d. 833) would send emissaries to Constantinople to bring back manuscripts written in Greek so that they could be translated. Greek works like Aristotle's *Rhetoric* and *Poetics* and Plato's *Dialogues*, were saved due to these translations. It was through the works of Avicenna (d. 1037) and Averroes (d. 1198) that Aristotelianism and neo-Platonism came into Europe.[9] Averroes' commentaries on Aristotle were indispensable to Thomas Aquinas (d. 1274) and Moses Maimonedes (d. 1204).[10]

Spain provides an excellent precedent where Muslims lived peacefully with Christians and Jews and shared their scientific accomplishments with them in the construction of a great civilization. Although treated as second-class citizens, the Jews of Spain were given religious liberty; they could run their own affairs based on their own laws. Cordoba was the center of a brilliant Jewish culture epitomized by Hasday b. Shaprut, a scholar and physician serving the caliphs 'Abd al-Rahman III and al-Hakam.[11] He was a Jewish physician in the Caliph's court, who, at various times, held important diplomatic and financial responsibilities.

Like Hasday, Isma'il b. Naghrila (d. 1056), known in Hebrew as Samuel the Nagid, was also a central figure in the Jewish community.[12] Bearing the Hebrew title *Nagid* (prince) he not only supported Hebrew poetry and Talmudic scholarship, but was himself one of the most accomplished men of his time in both fields.[13]

Christians and Jews were also involved in the Royal Court and in the intellectual life of Cordoba. Muslim-Christian interaction can be discerned from the following remark made by the Bishop of Cordoba, Alvaro. He stated regarding his Christian co-religionists, "...hardly one can write a passable Latin letter to a friend, but innumerable are those who can express themselves in Arabic and can compose poetry in that language with greater art than the Arabs themselves."[14] Other Christians served as administrators, financiers, physicians, artists, and craftsmen in the royal court.[15]

The discoveries by Muslim scientists were transmitted to the west. Cordoba's mosque was famed as a centre for higher learning on a par with Cairo and Baghdad and was the earliest medieval university in Europe. Major contributions were made in music, philology, geography, history, alchemy, chemistry, medicine, astronomy, philosophy, botany, mathematics, and agriculture.[16] Hellenism was largely reintroduced into Europe by way of Spain and Sicily. It was this phenomenon, which made the European Renaissance possible.[17] Such accounts are important to mention as they remind us of how, by adopting a nonviolent posture, Muslims, Jews and Christians established a brilliant civilization for posterity.

---

[9] Luce Lopez-Baralt, "The Legacy of Islam in Spanish Literature," in *The Legacy of Muslim* Spain, Salma Khadra Jayyusi ed. (Leiden: Brill, 2003), 1:509.

[10] James A. Bill and John Alden Williams eds., *Roman Catholics and Shi'i Muslims* (Chapel Hill & London: University of North Carolina Press, 2002), 101.

[11] Robert Hillenbrand, "The Ornament of the World: Medieval Cordoba as a Cultural Centre," in *The Legacy of Muslim* Spain, ed. Salma Jayyusi, 1:124.

[12] Raymond P. Scheindlin, "The Jews in Muslim Spain," *The Legacy of Muslim* Spain, ed. Salma Jayyusi, 1:190.

[13] Ibid. The Muslim rulers of Spain relied on Jews in diplomacy, finance and public administration, because the Jews could not aspire to ultimate political power. Thus, they posed a lesser risk to the political authorities.

[14] Robert Hillenbrand, "The Ornament," in *The Legacy of Muslim* Spain, ed. Salma Jayyusi, 1:115.

[15] Ibid. 123.

[16] Ibid. 122.

[17] Luce Lopez-Baralt, "The Legacy of Islam," in *The Legacy of Muslim* Spain, ed. Salma Jayyusi, 1:509.

PEACE AND CONFLICT RESOLUTION IN ISLAM

Many Muslims have questioned the formulations of the classical jurists, claiming that their interpretations are no longer binding in contemporary times. In particular, the scholars of al-Azhar, one of the oldest institutes of Islamic learning, have emphasized the social rather than militant dimension of *jihad*. According to them, *jihad* is a peaceful social struggle against illiteracy, poverty, and disease. They underline the peaceful nature of the Islamic message.[18]

Muhammad Shaltut, the rector of al-Azhar, asserts that Islam is open to pluralism. He also claims that the Qur'an does not require Muslims to resort to warfare when they proselytize. Fighting cannot be a part of the Islamic mission he argues, for the heart of Muhammad's mission is to bring good tidings and to warn humanity.[19] Since war is an immoral situation, Shaltut continues, Muslims are required to live at peace with non-Muslims.[20]

Muslims who have accentuated peaceful coexistence with non-Muslims have looked to the Qur'an as a legitimating source for their pronouncements. From its inception, Islam recognized the role of forgiveness in conflict resolution and combating violence. Thus, the Prophet is reported to have said, "God fills with peace and faith the heart of one who swallows his anger, even though he is in a position to vent it."[21] Muslims are urged to forgive especially when their rights have been violated and they are in a position to exact revenge.

Retaliation is a strictly defined legal principle that can perpetuate a culture of violence and a cycle of carnage. The Qur'an evidently wants to replace this with a culture of peace. While permitting retaliation, the Qur'an urges the victim to forgive and eschew revenge (2:178). To inject peace in a series of retaliatory measures requires forgiveness as a healing and empowering process so as to restore human relationship.[22]

Whereas a punitive response is often considered necessary when harm is inflicted, retribution is to be linked to a restorative process. Thus, verse 2:179 states that, "In [the law of] retribution is a source of life, O people of understanding." The verse invites people to replace the cycle of violence by considering retributive justice as a process of rehabilitation. In this way, the Qur'an is replacing death caused by retaliation with life through forgiveness.

Retributive justice, according to the Qur'an, should aim at redressing the wrongs by making the offender acknowledge responsibility and by encouraging the victim to consider alternatives to the perpetuation of violence through retribution.[23] The offender acknowledges the harm his acts have done so that a repaired relationship between the offender and victim can reinstate the dignity of both. Acknowledgement of injury inflicted is the first step in seeking forgiveness. Repentance and a genuine sense of remorse is another. The Qur'an also offers an alternative to violence by recommending the acceptance of blood money as compensation.

---

[18] Bassam Tibi, *The Challenge of Fundamentalism: Political Islam and the New World Disorder* (Berkeley: University of California Press, 1998), 58.

[19] John Kelsay, *Islam and War: A Study in Comparative Ethics* (Louisville: Westminster/John Knox Press, 1993), 40.

[20] Bassam Tibi, "War and Peace in Islam," in *Islamic Political Ethics*, ed. Sohail Hashmi, 183.

[21] Mohammed Abu-Nimer, *Nonviolence and Peace Building in Islam: Theory and Practice* (Gainesville, University Press of Florida, 2003), 67.

[22] Abdulaziz Sachedina, *The Islamic Roots of Democratic Pluralism* (Oxford: Oxford University Press, 2001), 105.

[23] Ibid., 112.

There is a clearly articulated preference in Islam for nonviolence and forgiveness over retribution. The Qur'an is also concerned about proportionality even in retribution. By stipulating appropriate levels of punitive response when attempting to restore violated rights or correct injustices, it regulates acts of retribution, for these should not exceed the extent of the original injury.[24]

On the part of the victim, forgiveness is preferred over retribution as he foregoes the moral right of demanding injury by inflicting more injury. As verse 42:40 states in this context, "... whoever forgives and thereby brings about a reestablishment of harmony, his reward is with God; and God loves not the wrongdoers." By his acceptance of compensation in the face of repentance and acknowledgement of the harm that the offender has inflicted, the victim demonstrates willingness to rehabilitate the offender in society. The victim is, in turn, rewarded by God.

Approaches to conflict resolution also appropriate religious values and traditional rituals of reconciliation. Scholars have also recognized the role that culture plays in conflict and peacemaking, and have affirmed the potential contributions of diverse institutions to conflict resolution. Cultural modes of reconciliation include acceptance of individual and collective responsibility of wrongdoing, attentiveness to face-related issues (public status, shame) and the achievement of restorative justice.[25] Muslims have delineated other processes for resolving conflicts in a peaceful manner. Conflicts are also resolved based on local customs such as public acts of repentance,[26] *sulh* (reconciliation),[27] and *tahkim* (arbitration).[28] Frequently, communal leaders and village elders facilitate a process of reconciliation. During this phase, the parties agree upon the outcome of the arbitration. If they publicly accept the outcome, then there is usually an amount of compensation to be paid, an amount that is determined before the public ceremony.

Islamic and Arab values are often used to resolve disputes. The traditional notion of '*urf* (customary law) functions as a mechanism for social control and cohesiveness, bringing the tribe's members together into a unified community. Such measures often help maintain social control. Administering an oath and offering testimony and evidence are other important methods of customary law. Tribal leaders use the Qur'an to administer the oath. It is believed that a false oath would have catastrophic effects on the person and or his/her family. The phrasing of the oath varies with the nature of the case involved.[29]

Recent measures in Iran have also tried to promote a nonviolent, peaceful image of Islam. Ayatollah Dr. Seyed Mohammad Bojnourdi, a former member of the Supreme Judicial Council in Iran, believes that when the 12th messianic Imam, the Mahdi reappears he will

---

[24] On the role of forgiveness as a tool in peace making and relationship building see Marc Gopin, *Holy War, Holy Peace: How Religion Can Bring Peace to the Middle East* (Oxford: Oxford University Press, 2002), 110-11, 129-130.

[25] Abdul Aziz Said, Nathan Funk, and Ayse Kadayifci, "Islamic Approaches to Peace and Conflict Resolution," in *Peace and Conflict Resolution in Islam: Precept and Practice*, Abdulaziz Said, Nathan Funk and Ayse Kadayifci eds (Lanham: University Press of America, 2001), 10.

[26] On the role of repentance in cultivating personality changes and humility see Gopin, *Holy War, Holy Peace*, 118-19.

[27] On the role of *sulh* in peace making see ibid., 136-37; George Irani and Nathan Funk, "Rituals of Reconciliation: Arab-Islamic Perspectives," in *Peace and Conflict* Resolution, ed. Said *et al.*, 183. The *sulh* rituals are often are conducted in public. See Gopin, *Holy War, Holy Peace*, 136.

[28] For details of this see, Gopin, *Holy War, Holy Peace*, 97; Ahmad Mousalli, "An Islamic Model for Political Conflict Resolution: *Tahkim* (Arbitration)," in *Peace and Conflict Resolution*, ed. Said *et al.*, 150-51.

[29] Mohammed Abu-Nimer, *Nonviolence and Peace Building*, 93.

guide mankind towards humanity and Islam through cultural means, reasoning, and logic instead of resorting to force.[30] This view is in contrast to the generally held view that when the messiah appears, he will fight and convert non-believers and those who oppose his mission.

Ayatollah Bojnourdi also believes that the current method of administering certain Islamic punishments weakens Islam and presents a distorted image of the religion to the world. He proposes that in the execution of Islamic punishments, it would be better to take advantage of the views of psychologists, sociologists and other experts. Bojnourdi further states that the Islamic penal code law is based on the principle of "elimination of obscene deeds." It is not mandatory, he argues, to resort to punishment if someone commits an offense, since the principle in Islam is based on correction and development of mankind. "The life style of the Holy Prophet (peace be upon him) and Imam 'Ali (the first Shi'ite Imam) attest to the fact that at the time of punishment, they would first resort to admonition and guidance in order to lead the convict to repent. In many cases, punishment would be averted if the offender repented."[31] Thus, in many cases of punishment, if the convict repents prior to the approval of the case by the court, the responsibility of the court to look into the offense would be dropped as well.

Bojnourdi further maintains that if the process for execution of penalty results in the denigration of Islam and causes the people, especially the youth, to demean the religion, then the process should then be revised so that no causes of such denigration would remain. If certain punishments such as flogging in public create a negative impression regarding Islam, such a practice should be abandoned. This is because the preservation of the dignity and prestige of Islam is the prime task and a duty that has priority over other obligations.

PEACE THROUGH DIALOGUE

One of the most potent ways to promote peace is by engaging in inter-faith dialogue. In its discourse with Christians and Jews, the people of the book, the Qur'an invites them to the notion of a shared religious community based on the belief in one God. Thus, the Prophet Muhammad is instructed to tell them, "Say! O people of the book! Come to a word common between us and you, that we serve none but God, and that we associate not aught with Him, and do not some of us take others as Lords, apart from God. And if they turn their backs, say, 'bear witness that we are Muslims'" (3:64).

The Qur'an also outlines the form that dialogue should take and the way in which it should be conducted. It suggests that Muslim interaction with the other should be accompanied with proper demeanor and attitude. As the Qur'an states, "Do not discuss with the people of the book except in the best way possible, apart from those who are unjust among themselves" (29:46). Furthermore, the Qur'an states, "God does not forbid you from establishing relations of generosity and just behavior with those who have not fought against you over your religion and who have not evicted you from your dwellings. God loves those who act fairly" (60:8). Verses such as these reflect the Qur'an's response to those who claim that it prohibits Muslims from interacting with non-Muslims.

---

[30] Based on an email I received from a friend.
[31] Ibid.

Historically, the Muslim encounter with Christians generated much debate, discussions, and even disputations between the parties.[32] As the parties argued for the preponderance of their distinctive theological points and tried to refute the arguments of their interlocutors, early Muslim-Christian encounters took the form of polemics rather than dialogue.[33] For example, Timothy, who was the head of the Nestorians in Iraq, had discussions with the 'Abbasid caliph al-Mahdi in 781 C.E.[34] Timothy had to respond to eight questions regarding various points of Christian beliefs. He was able to present a well-articulated and nuanced exposition of Christian theology.[35]

Most Muslim scholars were content to emphasize Christianity's deviation and corrupt beliefs and practices. Only a few scholars like al-Mas'udi (d. 956) and al-Shahrastani (d. 1153) were well versed in Christianity and had read the Christian scriptures in some detail. Later on, the Andalusian scholar Ibn Hazm (d. 1064) wrote a polemical tract, refuting Christian doctrines, especially those pertaining to the divinity of Jesus.[36] Al-Ghazali (d. 1111) also wrote a refutation of the divinity of Jesus.[37] As Hossein Nasr states, Jewish and Christian scriptures have rarely been studied seriously by the Muslims, and have often been subsumed under the category of abrogated texts or those which were interpolated by human beings.[38]

THE NATURE OF INTER-FAITH DIALOGUE

Dialogue is interwoven to the establishment of peaceful relations with others because it provides access to windows of understanding of how others define themselves and it challenges us to grow in our own faith through the experience of the other. It necessitates a shift in paradigm, asking us to embrace those we have previously excluded or demonized. We tend to exclude or marginalize others in different ways. These range from assimilation, abandonment, indifference, and domination of the other.[39] Exclusion is also conjoined with the distortion rather than simply ignorance of the other. As Miroslav Volf states, "it (exclusion) is a willful misconstruction, not mere failure of knowledge."[40]

---

[32] The Prophet Muhammad is reported to have met and discussed with Christians from Najran. See Muhammad b. Ishaq. *The Life of Muhammad*, trans. A. Guillaume (London: Oxford University Press, 1955), 179.

[33] For a summary of Muslim polemics against Christians in the early history of Islam see Montgomery Watt, *Muslim-Christian Encounters: Perceptions and Misperceptions* (London and New York: Routledge, 1991), 65-66. On the early Muslim-Christian debates and refutation of each other's arguments see Jacques Waardenburg, *Muslims and Others, Relations in Context* (Berlin: Walter de Gruyter, 2003), 136-40.

[34] Montgomery Watt, *Muslim-Christian Encounters*, 63.

[35] Jacques Waardenburg, *Muslims and Others*, 112. In response to a question posed by the 'Abbasid Caliph, the Assyrian patriarch is reported to have said that Muhammad had walked in the path of the prophets. See David Kerr, "He Walked in the Path of the Prophets: Toward Christian Theological Recognition of the Prophethood of Muhammad" in *Christian-Muslim Encounters*, ed. Y. Haddad and Wadi Haddad (Gainesville: University Press of Florida, 1995), 426.

[36] Montgomery Watt, *Muslim-Christian Encounters*, 65, 72.

[37] Ibid. 67.

[38] Seyyed Hossein Nasr, "Comments on a Few Theological Issues in the Islamic-Christian Dialogue," in *Christian-Muslim Encounters*, ed. Y. Haddad, 461.

[39] Miroslav Volf, *Exclusion and Embrace, A Theological Exploration of Identity, Otherness and Reconciliation* (Nashville: Abingdon, 1996), 75.
See also Liyakatali Takim, "From Conversion to Conversation: Interfaith Dialogue in Post-911 America," in *The Muslim World*, 94, no. 3 (2004): 343-357.

[40] Miroslav Volf, *Exclusion*, 76.

Exclusion often entails cutting of the bonds of humanity that connect us as moral human beings and can generate a wide range of emotional responses ranging from hatred to indifference and even cursing of or killing the other. The other emerges as an inferior being that must be either assimilated by being made like the self or subjugated to the self.[41]

Dialogue is the first step to accommodate or make space within oneself for the other. The challenge for both Muslims and Christians when they converse is to seek opportunities for interpretations that can make a community see the enemy in a new way. It is essential that we move away from defining ourselves over and above an enemy "other." This is an important measure to establish peaceful relationship. In this sense, I believe, that we need to go beyond tolerating or understanding the other.[42] More than ever, there is a need to embrace the other. This suggests a different function of dialogue, one that can bring the hearts - not just the minds - of the people together. Dialogue has become an effective act of affirmation, of listening, and of different hearts coming together. Muslims and non-Muslims have met to share their experiences of September 11, 2001 and to engage one another so as to help construct a more humane and just world.[43]

One of the major obstacles to reaching an understanding of the other is when we compare our ideals with the realities of the other. Viewed in this context, the violence perpetrated by members of one party is often contrasted with the ideals of peace and love of the other. A more appropriate basis of comparison is to contrast our ideals with theirs or our realities with the realities of those we dialogue. When communities compare their respective realities, they often discover that both of them have been unjust to each other, and, in the name of religion, have committed atrocious acts. Indeed, disputes between groups often arise when one party believes that it is the only injured group or victim and refuses to accept its role in the conflict. Dialogue provides the challenge and opportunity for both Muslims and non-Muslims to acknowledge that they have both inflicted and suffered much pain. For this to occur, dialogue needs to go beyond merely understanding the other; it has also to provide the platform for people to acknowledge and experience the pain of the other. As they relate their experiences in the past two years, their partners in dialogue have both communicated and internalized the pain. As a friend commented, "By internalizing the other's pain, dialogue enables me to view the other as a brother."

Given the realities after the events of September 11, 2001, dialogue can no longer be confined to a room where partners talk about peace and understanding. It must also confront the realities of hate, discrimination, and violence in society. Collaborative actions have become more important since September 11, 2001 as Muslims have realized that conversations with their non-Muslim friends ought to lead to shared commitment so as to address humanitarian issues that concern both communities. This sense of shared commitment and concern to address humanitarian issues has resulted in dialogue in action rather than mere conversation.

As Tariq Ramadhan correctly states, "One of the best testimonies that a religious or spiritual tradition can give of itself lies in acts of solidarity between its adherents and others.

---

[41] Ibid, 67.

[42] The root of the term tolerance comes from the medieval toxicology and pharmacology, marking how much poison a body could tolerate before it would succumb to death. See Omid Safi, "Introduction: The Times are A-Changing: - A Muslim Quest for Justice, Gender Equality, and Pluralism," in *Progessive Muslims: On Justice, Gender and Pluralism*, ed. Omid Safi (Oxford: Oneworld, 2003), 24.

[43] On specific steps toward building new relationship see Marc Gopin, *Holy War*, chapter 10.

To defend the dignity of the latter, to fight so that our societies do not produce indignity, to work together to support marginalized and neglected people, will certainly help us know one another better, but it will, above all, make known the essential message that shines at the heart of our traditions: never neglect your brother in humanity and learn to love him or at least to serve him."[44]

CHALLENGES FOR MUSLIMS IN CONTEMPORARY TIMES

Muslim discourse on war and peace has been defined primarily by the juridical literature. Especially after the events of September 11, 2001, we are witnessing a period of reinterpretation and redefinition of the notion of *jihad* in the Muslim community. It has been argued that the Qur'an offers a distinctly modern perspective on tolerance and respect in a multi-ethnic, multi-communal world.[45] The challenge for Muslims in contemporary times is to recover the tolerance and means for peaceful coexistence through the Qur'an rather than the juridical and exegetical understanding which were formulated to assert the subjugation of the "other" in a particular historical context. As they engage in a re-examination of traditional exegesis, the point of departure for Muslims has to be the Qur'an itself rather than the multi-faceted and multi-layered scholarly discourse that has accumulated since the eighth century.

The moral tenor of the Qur'an shows that it wants to engage humanity in a moral discourse where all human beings can connect with the Qur'an and with each other based on universal values. As Sohail Hashmi argues, there are few ethical works that outline the Qur'anic vision of coexistence or warfare. Muslims need to disentangle Islamic ethics from medieval Islamic law and re-examine the Qur'anic pronouncement on war and peace in light of its ethical axioms.[46] Thus, the challenge for Muslims is to draw on this Qur'anic vision so as to develop just interreligious and intercultural relationships in a world of cultural and religious diversity.

Muslims are also confronted with the challenge of contextual hermeneutics in dealing with the pronouncements of the Qur'an on specific legal issues like hostility and warfare. Verses on *jihad* must be understood taking into account the particular conditions of persecution and oppression in which they were revealed. Returning to the Qur'an and prophetic traditions in their proper historical context is often circumvented by the juridical interpretations that promoted the hegemonic interests of the Islamic state ignoring, in the name of Islam, the ecumenical and universal message of the Qur'an. Muslim scholars and jurists have to engage in hermeneutic and interpretive exercises to provide a coherent re-evaluation of classical formulations and to reassert the Qur'anic ecumenical and inclusivist vision of peace. Stated differently, Muslims need to go beyond the classical formulation on *dhimmis, siyar,* and non-believers. Boundaries have to be re-mapped since the delineation of *dar al-Islam* and *dar al-harb* is no longer applicable. Furthermore, Muslims must articulate a theory of international relations that will incorporate notions of dignity, freedom of conscience, rights of minorities, and gender equality based on the notion of universal moral values.

---

[44]Tariq Ramadan, *Western Muslims and the Future of Islam,* (Oxford, NY: Oxford University Press, 2004), 212.

[45] Eickelman, "Islam and Ethical Pluralism," in *Islamic Political Ethics,* ed. Sohail Hashmi, 115.

[46] Sohail Hashmi, "Islamic Ethics in International Society," in *Islamic Political Ethics,* ed. Sohail Hashmi, 148.

CONCLUSION

Peace requires changes in our worldviews. The quest for peace challenges us to reevaluate how we have viewed the other. It also necessitates a shift in paradigm, asking us to embrace those we have previously excluded or demonized. The challenge is to seek opportunities for interpretations that can make a community see the enemy in a new way. This is an important measure to establish peaceful relationship.

There is a concurrent requirement to move away from defining ourselves over and above an enemy "other." The starting point is to re-examine traditions that draw boundaries of exclusion and marginalization. Peaceful coexistence is only possible when we no longer see a group as the other but as a concrete human community with ancient values and norms. Ultimately, peaceful relations between human beings are grounded on a community's construction of an order based on egalitarianism, justice, and a concern for the moral and social well being of all its citizens.

Contemporary Muslims are confronted with hegemonic values of the past and the emerging political reality that often challenges the applicability of those values. The tension between the peaceful and militant strains of Islam can be resolved only through the reexamination of the specific contexts of the rulings and the ways in which they were conditioned by the times. This re-interpretive task demands that Muslims undertake the task of re-evaluating the classical and medieval juridical corpus.

In: Religion, Terrorism and Globalization
Editor: K.K. Kuriakose, pp. 121-141

ISBN 1-59454-553-7

Chapter 8

FOUR VOICES FOR NONVIOLENCE AND PEACEFUL COEXISTENCE IN SOUTH AND SOUTHEAST ASIA [1]

Hugh Talat Halman

University of Arkansas, Fayetteville, Arkansas

'Umayr wished them a good day – a salutation of paganism – and the Prophet [Muhammad] said: "God has given us a better greeting than thine, O 'Umayr. It is Peace. the greeting of the people of Paradise."[2]

INTRODUCTION

In this essay I discuss four exemplary practitioners of "Islamic nonviolence" from South and Southeast Asia. After first reviewing Islamic principles of peace in the Qur'an and prophetic precedents, I will discuss two recently deceased and two contemporary proponents of Islamic non-violence. Badshah Khan (Afghanistan), was one of Gandhi's closest associates. Bawa Muhaiyaddeen (Sri Lanka), was a Sufi Shaikh. Chaiwat Satha-Anand (Thailand) is a contemporary academic and theorist of nonviolence. And Aburrahman Wahid (Indonesia) is a leading political, religious, and intellectual figure.

All but Bawa Muhaiyaddeen have been leaders of social movements. Badshah Khan and Bawa Muhaiyadeen carried their non-violent witness to the extent of being vegetarians. In addition to contributing to a discourse and practice of Islamic non-violence, each further worked to promote a set of underlying conditions that can contribute to making non-violence a reality. As Abdurrahman Wahid has expressed this relationship, there is first a need to propose "frameworks offered in the hopes of alleviating…confrontational situations…[which]

---

[1] I wish to thank two institutions which supported this work: the Fulbright Foundation for a Teaching Grant in Indonesia (2004-5) and UIN Syarif Hidayatullah, Jakarta, Indonesia.
[2] Quoted in Martin Lings, *Muhammad: His Life Based on the Earliest Sources.* (Rochester, VT: Inner Traditions International, Ltd., 1983, pp. 157-158.

can serve as a first step toward non-violence."[3] At the outset it is useful to recognize that the discourse of Islamic nonviolence can be, and is, voiced through a variety of theoretical and terminological constructs. For example, recently Mohammed Abu Nimer has described a trend among some advocates of nonviolence to withdraw the literal Arabic term for nonviolence (*la 'unf*) and to replace it with the more active, "civic jihad," [4] This trend underscores a spectrum of continuing and emerging viewpoints on Islamic nonviolence. In order to introduce the four figures in this essay, it will help to begin by reviewing some of the principles of non-violence spelled out in the Qur'an and modeled in the exemplary precedent of the Prophet Muhammad's life (*sunna*).

THE QUR'AN AS A SOURCE FOR NONVIOLENCE

The Qur'an, like many other scriptures, addresses both warfare and peace. Certain veses of the Qur'an explicitly permit battles during the career of the prophet, while other verses spell out a long-range ideal of peace among different communities. The selections which follow will hopefully make clear that the Qur'an's long-term and primary vision is one of peace. Certainly this is the view of the four nonviolent practitioners profiled in this essay. Firstly, the Qur'an rejects killing outside of juridical contexts:

> For that cause [Cain's repentance over having murdered his brother Abel] We decreed for the children of Israel that whosoever killeth a human being for other than manslaughter or corruption on the earth, it shall be as if he had killed all mankind, and whoso saveth the life of one, it shall be as if he had saved the life of all mankind... (Qur'an 5.32; Pickthall translation)

While providing for the permissibility of warfare the Qur'an also decries aggression:

> Fight in the way of Allah against those who fight against you, but begin not hostilities. Lo! Allah loveth not aggressors. (2. 190)

The Qur'an here encourages humility and the ideal of offering unconditional and peaceful forbearance:

> And the servants of God Most Gracious are those who walk on the Earth in humility, and when the ignorant address them, they say "Peace." (25.63)

As might be expected, the Qur'an enjoins acting in peace toward those who believe and repent:

---

[3] Abdurrahman Wahid, "Islam, Nonviolence, and National Transformation," in Glenn D. Paige, Chaiwat Satha-Anand and Sarah Gilliant, ed. *Islam and Nonviolence* Center for Global Nonviolence, 2001, p. 56. Accesssed at: www.globalnonviolence.org October 2004.

[4] Mohammed Abu Nimer, "Nonviolence in the Islamic Context," *Fellowship Magazine* September/October 2004 (Fellowship of Reconciliation). Accessed at: www.forusa.org/fellowship/sept-oct-04/abu-nimer.html October 2004. Abu Nimer lists Khalid Kishtainy, Khalis Jalabi, Jawdat Said, and Imam Muhammad al-Shirazi as among those adopting the term "civic jihad" to replace the Arabic *la 'unf* because in Arabic the latter term carries connotations of passivity.

When those come to you who believe in Our signs, say, "Peace be unto you." Your Lord has inscribed for Himself (the rule of) mercy: surely, if any of you did evil in ignorance, and thereafter repented, and mended (his conduct). Lo! [God] is Oft-Forging, Most Merciful. (6.54)

The following three verses encourage Muslims to make peaceful gestures towards nonbelievers or the "enemy," transforming hatred into peace, friendship, and intimacy:

And if the enemy incline toward peace, then you incline toward peace and trust in God: for He is the Hearer and the Knower. (8.61)

Nor can goodness and evil be equal. Repel (evil) with what is better. Then the one between whom and you was hatred shall become as it were your friend and intimate. (41. 34)

And he saith: O my Lord! Lo! Those are a folk who believe not. Then bear with them and say: Peace. But they will come to know. (43.88-89)

God may even transform hatred into love:

It may be that Allah will ordain love between you and those of them with who you are at enmity. Allah is Mighty and Allah is Forgiving, Merciful. (60.7)

Nonviolence runs through the heart of this verse:

Only one will prosper who brings to God a peaceful and sound heart (*bi-qalbin salim*). (26.89)

Verses, such as the following, which speak of peace among Muslims, nonetheless reinforce nonviolence as a Muslim ethos:

This is the Way of your Lord leading straight. We have detailed the Signs for those who receive admonition. For them will be a home of peace in the presence of their Lord: He will be their Friend because they practiced (righteousness). (6. 126-127)

But Allah does call to the Home of Peace. He guides whom he pleases to a way that is straight."(10.25)

Peace – a word [of greeting] from a most merciful Lord. (36.58)

He it is who sent down Tranquility (*sakina*) into the hearts of the believers that they may add faith to their faith... (48.4a)

In addition to these explicit summons to peace, verses which establish the framework of peace among co-existing communities also belong to our consideration of Qur'anic precedents for nonviolence. Much of the discourse of nonviolence which follows addresses specific inter-communal crises. A key verse concerning such pluralism reads:

For each [community] We have appointed a divine law and a traced-out way. Had Allah willed He could have made you one community. But that He may try you by that which He hath given you (He hath made you as you are. So vie with one another in good works. Unto Allah ye will all return, and He will then inform you of that wherein you differ. (5.48b)

Similarly, common ground is a continuing theme:

And argue not with the People of the Scripture unless it be in (a way) that is better, save with such of them as do wrong and say: We believe in that which hath been revealed unto us and revealed unto you; our God and your God is One, and unto Him we surrender. (29.46)

Perhaps God's mercy, framed in a pluralistic context, crosses confessional lines:

Had Allah willed, He could have made them one community, but Allah bringeth whom He will unto His mercy. And the wrong-doers have no friend or helper. (42.8)

Finally the idea that every community has received a messenger from God, some of whose names are not known or mentioned in the Qur'an advances the case for a pluralistic context of nonviolence:

And messengers We have mentioned unto thee before and messengers We have not mentioned unto thee; and Allah spake directly unto Moses. Messengers of good cheer and of warning, in order that mankind might have no argument against Allah after the messengers. Allah was ever Mighty, Wise. (4.164-5)[5]

NONVIOLENCE IN THE PROPHETIC SUNNA

Throughout the Prophet Muhammad's career, he engaged in warfare only reluctantly. As Badshah Khan stressed, and we will discuss in more detail below, during the Prophet's Meccan years, he endured great suffering with a patience (*sabr*). Khan described the Prophet's *sabr* as his practice of nonviolence and equated it to what Gandhi called the power of truth (*satyagraha*). The Prophet viewed the three wars he fought during the Muslims' community's years in Medina as defensive wars and he awaited God's permission before he retaliated.[6] And as his Qurayshi adversaries subjected Medina to embargoes and blockades he was forced, for the sake of survival, to conduct raids to break through these restraints. In 628 with the truce and treaty of Hudaybiya, the Prophet abandoned warfare. In fact, many Muslims celebrate his conquest of Mecca as an act of nonviolent diplomatic negotiation. Entering Mecca, the Prophet cited the example of Joseph forgiving his brothers as he granted

---

[5] The idiom in most of the following verses "every community" (*kul umma*) establishes universality, inclusivity, and pluralism as a primary direction of Islamic discourse which takes precedence over divisiveness and animosity. cf. 10.48; 13.38; 14.4; 16.36, 63; 21.25; 35.24; 42.8

[6] Interestingly the verses of revelation sanctioning warfare (22.39-40) use the word "killing" (*q-t-l*), not *jihad* and explain this sanction as intended to protect all who worship One God, specifically in "cloisters, churches, oratories, and mosques."

amnesty to his Meccan tribesmen who had long persecuted and oppressed the nascient Muslim community.[7]

Muhammad's example reveals an absence of personal motives such as revenge, hate, and violence for violence's sake. In some Muslim perspectives, the Prophet exemplified warriorhood as a continual *inner* battle against egotism. Though Muhammad had many reasonable excuses for acting out of personal anger, hate, and revenge, he refrained from this course and constantly hoped and worked for a united and just political framework for a multiplicity of religious communities. In his initial charter of Yathrib (Medina) he affirmed the place of Jewish communities coexisting alongside Muslims in a covenant of mutual obligation.[8] Not only in word, but repeatedly in deed, the Prophet worked for peaceful coexistence.

The following are a number of salient quotes from the hadith literature in which the Prophet articulates the values of peace and nonviolence. In this first instance the Prophet affirms God's nature as peace and encourages invoking the divine name, "Peace:"

"Allahumma, Anta as-Salaam wa min Ka as-Salaam." "Our Lord, You are Peace and from You is Peace." (A traditional prayer often offered at the closing of *Salat*)[9]

Here the Prophet implies that the use of persuasion takes precedence over violence:

The best work of faith is to speak truth to an unjust leader.[10]

In a timely statement worthy of continued dissemination, the Prophet here made clear the rules of war and the limits of violence:

The Prophet, for example, instructed his fighting men that they must never kill old men, women, and children or anybody who merely utters the phrase, "There is no god but God," or even, "I give myself up to God."[11]

Here the Prophet places peace above rituals and practices:

Shall I not inform you of a better act than fasting, alms, and prayers? Making peace between one another: enmity and malice tear up heavenly rewards by their roots.[12]

---

[7] Cf. Lings, ibid. pp. 245-246; 297-303.

[8] Lings, ibid., 106-107.

[9] Quoted in Rabia Terri Harris, "Nonviolence in Islam: The Alternative Community Tradition." In Daniel L. Smith-Christopher, ed. Subverting Hatred: The Challenge of Nonviolence in Religious Traditions. Boston: Boston Research Center for the 21st Century, 1998, p. 113, n. 5

[10] Hadith, Sunan Abu Dawud 4330 (quoted in Harris, ibid.)

[11] Mishkat al-Masabih 838, in Harris, 1998: p. 106

[12] Quoted in Allama Sir Abdallah al-Mamun al-Suhrawardy, The Sayings of Muhammad. London: Pan-Islamic Society, 1905, p. 103

JIHAD AND HARB: SPIRITUAL EFFORT AND WAGING WAR

One of the important distinctions underlying the Prophet's practice of warfare is that between *jihad* and *harb* (war) and *qatl* (killing). In the Qur'an the term *jihad* is reserved for describing the effort of striving for righteousness and serving the needs of people and the society at large. In Quranic discourse *jihad* means striving for noble morality and piety which is called "*jihad* in the way of God."[13] The root verb *jahada* means "he struggled." To refer to warfare the Qur'an never uses the term *jihad*, but instead only uses the words warfare (*harb*) and killing (*qatl*). In the hadith literature[14] we find the term *jihad* used to refer to warfare because one type of *jihad* – the method of last resort -- involves military action. *Jihad* generally involves all types of moral and spiritual struggle to establish right action and morality in the way of God. In an everyday sense *jihad* most often involves nonviolent action. The famed Hanbali jurist Ibn Taymiyya (d. 728/1328), for example distinguished three types of *jihad* "by the heart, by the tongue, and by the hand" and advocated that *jihad* of the tongue and hand be carried out with understanding and patience.[15] In this comprehensive sense many have considered *jihad* to be an implicit "sixth pillar" complementing and supporting the first classic five pillars of Islam.[16]

Finally an important understanding of *jihad* involves the prophet's differentiation of two types of *jihad* as described in a famous hadith narrative. The Prophet Muhammad received companions returning from an expedition to Syria at Tabuk in the Autumn of 630 and explained to them that they had returned from the lesser *jihad* and were now to begin the greater *jihad* – *jihad al-akbar*. This greater *jihad*, he explains, is a *jihad* (divinely-sanctioned moral struggle) against the base parts of the soul or the self (*nafs*). This means working on taming and training the lower base passions while cultivating higher virtues. Later this would be refined into a system of introspection and self-scrutiny called the "reckoning of the soul" (*nafs al-muhasaba*) intended to prepare a person to accept God's forgiveness and strengthen one's heart for prayer.[17]

At the same time the Prophet also continued to clarify his peaceful objectives toward other communities. In 630 the Prophet made peace treaties with Christian and Jewish communities living along the gulf of 'Aqabah's north and eastern coast. And shortly before this the Prophet had conducted funeral prayers *in abstentia* for the Christian King (Negus) of Abyssinia.[18] These would strike one as the actions of a peacemaker, not a proponent of violence.

Considering these examples of the Prophet's policies on war and peaceful co-existence we can propose that many contemporary "Islam-ist" political ideologues, agitators, and

---

[13] For comprehensive treatments of this subject see Vincent Cornell, "Jihad: Islam's Struggle for Truth," *Gnosis* Fall, 1991; Reuven Firestone, *Jihad* (Columbia, S.C.: University of South Carolina Press, 1997) and Rudolph Peters, *Jihad in Classical and Modern Islam*. Princeton: Marcus Wiener, 1996.

[14] The collections of *hadith* are canonical accounts of the Prophet's deeds, words, and affirmations of consent organized by jurists for juridical purposes. Its corpus is shared by a chronologically-organized body of hagiographical material called the *Sira*, more closely resembling a biography.

[15] Zaiuddin Sardar, "The Other Jihad: Muslim Intellectuals and Their Responsibilities," *Inquiry* (London) 2, no. 10 (October 1985): 40-45, cited in Chaiwat Satha Anand, "The Nonviolent Crescent: Eight Theses on Muslim Nonviolent Actions," p. 23. Accessed at www.globalnonviolence.org October 5, 2004.

[16] See the discussion of this in Murat and Chittick, ibid. p. 20 ff. where the history of relating *jihad* to ascetical discipline is outlined. (*Mujahada* , asceticism is a word derived from the same root.)

[17] Annemarie Schimmel, *Mystical Dimensions of Islam*. Chapel Hill: University of North Carolina Press, 1975.

[18] Lings, ibid., 316-319.

advocates of violence conveniently exploit discourses and precedents of war in Islamic history to justify violence at odds with the spirit of the Prophet Muhammad. Certainly this is a perspective on *jihad* and nonviolence which is shared by the four leaders of nonviolent Islam we consider in this essay.

RUMI'S SUFI PERSPECTIVE ON THE PROPHET'S EXAMPLE AND THE NONVIOLENT JIHAD

Some further insight into the Prophet Muhammad as a model of nonviolence comes from the Sufi perspective of Mevlana Jalaluddin Rumi (1207-1273).[19] It is useful to bear in mind in our era of Wahhabism,[20] that Rumi's perspectives reflect what was once a predominant perspective particularly among Muslims of the Persian, Turkish, and Indian parts of the Islamic world.[21] Rumi articulates the *adab* (noble ettiquette) of the Prophet's pattern of restraint, forbearance, and patience in using good deeds and intentions to win opponents over by virtuous example. Observing that the Prophet's only intention was God's will and God's peace, Rumi describes the crucible of the Prophet's wars as the Prophet's "pivot of peace"[22] Rumi describes the Prophet's patience with attackers and patience in waiting to act only when God dictates:

> They [the hypocrites who broke trust with the Prophet] put their hands to the sword and continued to come and insult and molest his companions. The Prophet...said 'Be patient so that they may not say that they have prevailed over us. They desire by force to make the religion manifest. God will make manifest this religion.' For some time the companions prayed secretly and pronounced the name Mustafa [(Muhammad), the Divinely-Selected Pure [Prophet])...Then after a while the inspiration came: 'You too shall unsheathe the sword and make war.[23]

Forbearance with foes, restraint of action, patience in awaiting God's sign of permission – all these characteristics were central to the Prophet's mission and character. Rumi underscores the nonviolent nature of Muhammad's motives by asking if the Prophet who possessed the seven heavens would have been motivated by a desire to conquer the city of Mecca. For Rumi, the Prophet's sword *Dhu'l-Fiqar*, the sword of discernment, which was handed on to 'Ali becomes the symbol of spiritual maturity, not a weapon of violence. One who submits to a Friend of God (*Wali*) begins as a needle and transforms into a Dhu'l-Fiqar,

---

[19] Among the best introductions to this topic see Schimmel, ibid. and Carl Ernst, *The Shambhala Guide to Sufism*. Boston: Shambhala, 1996.

[20] Wahhabism is the insular doctrine the Saudi dynasty has promoted which seeks to root out anything considered "innovative." These alleged innovations include: much of the Muslim juridical tradition; mysticism (Sufism); philosophy; most artistic expression; and women's rights. Islamist groups such as the Taliban and al-Qaeda, as well as many movements agitating for the adoption of Islamic law and encouraging violent means have been influenced by Wahhabism. Its eponymous founder Muhammad 'Abd al-Wahhab (d, 1206/1792) reacted to perceived threats of the modern age by inventing a provincial and divisive form of Islam which has continued to be enforced and spread abroad through an alliance with the House of Saud and more recently fueled by the influx of oil money.

[21] For example a famous proverb states that in any Persian family's house one will be guaranteed to find these three books: the Qur'an, Rumi's *magnum opus*, *The Mathnawi*, and the *Diwan* of Hafiz.

[22] John Renard, *All the King's Falcons*. (Albany: SUNY, 1994, p. 112)

the discriminating sword of the Prophet and 'Ali. With that sword, Rumi encourages one to behead selfhood, slash the neck of sorrow with divine intoxication, and become ego-extinguished like a true dervish.[24]

In his vision of inner war, Rumi understands war as a process of reconciling, resolving, and integrating differences. He writes, "[I]n every religion ritual prayer is different, but faith does not change in any of them — its inward states, its kiblah [the orientation point of prayer], and so forth are all the same."[25]

Rumi describes spiritual warfare as including such activities as companionship with the Sufis; eating less; fasting; invoking, reciting, and remembering the Names of God; and keeping nightly vigils.[26] Thus for Rumi spiritual warfare means maintaining the constant remembrance of God by reciting and invoking the divine qualities of each of His Names so that one will come to know God the Beloved more fully and maintain continuous consciousness of His presence and so love Him more and more deeply and completely.

LESSONS FROM INDONESIA: PEACEFUL COEXISTENCE AS A FRAMEWORK FOR NONVIOLENCE

Before considering our four exemplars of nonviolence, let us lay a foundation for understanding how Islamic nonviolence fits into Islamic visions of society and justice. Non-violence is only one component of a broader matrix. Or as Abdurrahman Wahid asserts as quoted above, nonviolence emerges out of a framework which alleviates confrontational situations by addressing the dynamics of social change. And in the urgent context which requires the essays in this volume, a deeper question demands our attention: Does Islamic thought encourage peaceful co-existence, even extending to active respect for diversity of religion or lifestyle, or does it demand remonstrating against diversity, even to the point of violence?

We can frame this question by considering two types of Quranic quotes: What is the prevailing Quranic ethos? Are those verses definitive which condone warfare, or those verses more authoritative which establish the divine ordinance of peacefully co-existing multiple communities and the human duty to strive for righteousness (5. 48; 29.46; cf. 3.64)? Recognizing this framework of interreligious coexistence illuminates the universal significance of nonviolent discourse in Islam.

Although in an ideal sense the opposite of violence is peace, in everyday terms, the real alternative to violence is successful mutual co-existence which may lead to peace. This sense comes to light from some recent events in Indonesia. During Ramadhan 1425 (October 2004) Islamic radicals attacked nightclubs and restaurants serving alcohol and blockaded a Catholic school which they claimed was a center of conversion. The question which arose in public debate was whether this behavior could be reconciled with Islam. Is Islam more than merely a "religion of peace," within its own community, but a religion of tolerance accepting the rights of pluralistic communities as well, as some of the verses we have quoted here would suggest?

---

[23] ibid., p. 113.
[24] Ibid., 116
[25] ibid., 151.
[26] ibid., p. 151

(e.g., 3.64; 5.48; 29.46). When a crisis between Catholics and Muslims brewed in the neighborhood of the Sang Timur Catholic School, Abdurrahman stepped in to mediate to protect the peace. As he said at the time: "And where Muslims are the majority, they should protect the rights of minority groups."[27]

Abdurrahman's example in this intervention and his explanation of a framework for fostering nonviolence both attest to the prerequisite need for mutual coexistence – a just balance among people, communities and nations. Addressing the question of the meaning of peace, His Holiness the Dalai Lama emphasized this as well: "Peace in the sense of the absence of war is of little value to someone who is dying of hunger or cold... Peace can only last where human rights are respected, where the people are fed, and where individuals and nations are free."[28]

BADSHAH KHAN: SATYAGRAHA, SABR, AND ISLAMIC NONVIOLENCE

Badshah Khan[29] (1890-1988), known as "The Frontier Gandhi," was a Pathan,[30] and in terms of maintaining an unconditional resolve for the principle of nonviolence might be said to have been Gandhi's closest disciple. Among the leaders of the Indian Nationalist Movement, he was the only colleague of Gandhi's to join him in pledging unconditional nonviolence during World War II even if India were to be attacked. In the end, he also stood alone with Gandhi against the 1947 Partition. Though a Muslim, Khan Saheb, as he was called, was also a vegetarian. He spent half his life in jail and in 1962 was awarded Amnesty International's "Prisoner of the Year" Award. It was in jail that Khan perceived the connection between Gandhi's vision of nonviolence and the example of the Prophet Muhammad's life.

As a young boy, I had had violent tendencies; the hot blood of the Pathans was in my veins. But in jail [in 1926, the year he first heard Gandhi speak] I had nothing to do but to read the Koran. I read about the Prophet Muhammad in Mecca, about his patience, his suffering, his dedication. I had read it all before as a child, but now I read it in the light of what I was hearing all around me about Gandhiji's struggle against the British Raj....When I finally met

---

[27] "School's Wall Falls, Tensions Still High," *Jakarta Post* Tuesday October 26, 2004, p. 2. "All the nations groups" refers to the six recognized religious communities under Indonesia's constitution: Muslim, Protestant, Catholic, Hindu, Buddhist, and Confucian. A commentary on both sets of events by Muhammad Ali, a lecturer at UIN Syarif Hidayatullah State Islamic University with a similar appeal for peaceful coexistence appeared in the *Jakarta Post* Friday October 29, 2004. For the 12-year historical background leading up to this crisis (centering on the use of the school building for conducting mass since August 15, 1992) see Setiyardi, Y. Tomi Aryanto and Ayu Cipta, "God's Bitter Gate Keepers," *Tempo* (English edition) November 22, 2004, pp. 12-13.

[28] The Dalai Lama, *A Policy of Kindness*, ed. Sidney Pitburn (Ithaca: Snow Lion, 1990), p. 17, quoted in Omid Safi, "Introduction," *Progressive Muslims*, p. 25 where he discusses this in relation to the abuse of the equation "Islam means peace," and argues for the case that justice is prerequisite to peace.

[29] His full name was Khan 'Abd al-Ghaffar Khan. (The first "Khan" is his title as tribal chief). He was most often called Khan Saheb and sometimes Ghaffar Khan. Badshah Khan's older brother Abdul-Jabbar Khan (called similarly"Dr. Khan Saheb" [1883-1956]) was a leader in the Indian Congress and had served as a chief minister of the N.W. Frontier Province under the British Raj.

[30] The term "Pathan" is an English corruption of "Pushtun" and "Pukhtun," referring to people living in the Northern frontier between Kabul and the Indus River. The term "Afghan" is the Persian (Farsi) name for these same people. Current national boundaries (the Duran Line) divide Pushtun tribes – and even villages -- across Afghanistan and Pakistan.

Gandhi. I learned all about his ideas of non-violence and his Constructive Program. They changed my life forever.[31]

Neither was Khan the first Muslim whom Gandhi esteemed as a practitioner of nonviolence. In a list of exemplary *satyagrahi* (those who fight peacefully for truth and peacefully with truth) Gandhi once included the Prophet Muhammad's two martyred grandsons, the second and third Shi'i Imams Hasan and Husayn.

> The pursuit of truth is pure devotion (*bhakti*)....In this connection it would be well to ponder over the lives and examples of Harishchandra [Krishna], Prahlad [Vishnu devotee protected by Narasimha], Ramachandra [Rama], *Imam Hasan* and *Imam Husain*, the Christian Saints, etc.[32]

Badhsah Khan's achievement was that he raised a nonviolent army, the *Khudai Khidmatger*, (the "Servants of God") numbering about 100,000 men and women amongst a people steeped in a warrior culture. The scope of this accomplishment has to be measured against the Pushtun code of ethics (*Pushtunwali*): revenge (*badal*), hospitality (*melmastia*), and sanctuary (*nonawali*). It is the overturning of the first of these three which was remarkable. *Badal* the Pathan code of revenge, dictated that all harm and injustice must be avenged. Fueled by the romantic image of the avenging hero, the code of vengeance led to great and tragic losses of loved ones. The Khudai Kidmatger code called for the end to this cycle of revenge. And while Badshah Khan's father, Behram Khan, had earlier encouraged his people to abandon this mad code of violence and vengeance, it was his son inspired by Gandhi and the Prophet Muhammad who created a truly Muslim nonviolent movement.

SABR AND *SATYAGRAHA*: "NON-VIOLENCE" (*LA 'UNF*) IN ISLAM

Khan felt that the experience of the Prophet Muhammad's Meccan years demonstrated the political potential of *sabr* (usually translated as "patience, endurance, or forbearance"). He emphasized that *sabr*—which is also a divine attribute –characterized the Prophet and the nonviolent response of his nascent Muslim community to persecution, harassment, and oppression. Thus Khan concluded that *sabr* was equivalent to what Gandhi called *Satyagraha* (holding on to the truth; or, "truth force"). In Khan's interpretation, the Meccan surahs encourage holding on to the truth without retaliation or retreat and in perfect submission, i.e., Islam.[33] Khan described *sabr* as the "weapon of the Prophet" and observed that during the Prophet's Meccan years, the community practiced the Islamic "Satyagraha" of *sabr*. In this sense *sabr* also implies tenacity in a righteous cause, forsaking the right to revenge. Khan described *Sabr* as "bowing before the blow without a sound or a complaint," and would say, "Sabr is revealed at the first blow." Khan would quote Caliph Umar's saying, "We found the best of our life in *Sabr*."

---

[31] Khan in Ved Mehta. *Gandhi ad His Apostles*, 231, quoted in Eknath Easwaren, *A Man to Match His Mountains: Badshah Khan, Nonviolent Soldier of Islam*. Petaluma, CA, Nilgiri Press, 1984, 141
[32] Gandhi, *Selected Writings* (NY: Schocken, 1961), p. 39-40. Italics mine.
[33] Easwaren, ibid., p. 243

THE WEAPON OF THE PROPHET: PATIENCE AND RIGHTEOUSNESS

Khan offered his non-violent warrior-servants of God the weapon of the prophet as the practice of patience and righteousness:

> I am going to give you such a weapon that the police and the army will not be able to stand against it. It is the weapon of the Prophet [Muhammad], but you are not aware of it. That weapon is patience [*sabr*] and righteousness (*haqq*). No power on earth can stand against it. When you go back to your villages, tell your brethren that there is an army of God and its weapon is patience. Ask your brethren to join the army of God. Endure all hardships. If you can exercise patience, victory will be yours.[34]

Khan taught that nonviolence was the teaching of Prophet Muhammad:

> The Holy Prophet Muhammad came into this world and taught us "That man is a Muslim who never hurts anyone by word or deed, but who works for the benefit and happiness of God's creatures. Belief in God is to love one's fellow men."[35]

Khan described nonviolence in the spirit of Gandhi as the manner by which the Prophet Muhammad conducted himself:

> There is nothing surprising in a Muslim or a Pathan like me subscribing to the creed of non-violence. It is not a new creed. It was followed fourteen hundred years ago by the Prophet [Muhammad] all the time he was in Mecca, and it has since been followed by all those who wanted to throw off an oppressor's yoke. But we had so far forgotten it that when Gandhiji placed it before us, we thought he was sponsoring a novel creed.[36]

THE KHUDAI KIDMAGER OATH

Before dawn one morning in 1929 a young Pathan visited Khan and proposed creating an army of nonviolent soldiers. Khan saw that the Pathans could fulfill Gandhi's precept that true *satyagraha* is what Gandhi called the "non-violence of the strong," not the weak. In this pre-dawn conversation, over tea and bread, the concept of the "Servants of God" (*Khudai Kidmatger*) came into birth. All Pathans could join if they took this *Khudai Kidmager* oath:

> I am a Khudai Kidmatgar; and as God needs no service, but serving his creation is serving Him, I promise to serve humanity in the name of God.
> I promise to refrain from violence and from taking revenge. I promise to forgive those who oppress me or treat me with cruelty.
> I promise to refrain from taking part in feuds and quarrels and from creating enmity.
> I promise to treat every Pathan as my brother and friend.

---

[34] Badshah Khan, quoted in D.G. Tendulkar, *Mahatma: Life of Mohandas Karamchand Gandhi*, 2nd ed. 8 vols. Delhi: Publications Division, Ministry of Information and Broadcasting, 1962. Vol. 7, 1945-47, quoted in Easwaren, p. 117.

[35] Badshah Khan, *My Life and Struggle*, (1969: 231) quoted in Easwaran, p. 55.

[36] Badshah Khan, *My Life and Struggle*, (1969: 195) quoted in Easwaran, p. 103.

I promise to refrain from antisocial customs and practices.

I promise to live a simple life, to practice virtue and refrain from evil.

I promise to practice good manners and good behavior and not to lead a life of idleness. I promise to devote at least two hours a day to social work.

The first recruits were young men who'd graduated from Khan's school. They became a nonviolent "army" of volunteer soldiers – men and later, women—who served without pay. When a few of the men had their white shirts dyed brick red, the style was adopted. This led to their nickname "The Red Shirts." Brick red not only concealed soiling but also made a striking impression. Khan set up system of councils intended to reduce risk of infighting.

The Khudai Khitmager trained in drills at their camps, in long marches in the hills, and offered extensive social services. They opened schools in villages, helped on work projects, and maintained order at public gatherings. And in the spirit of their oath of nonviolence they carried no rifles, guns, or knives; instead they carried a walking stick. . Close to the 1947 partition Khan oversaw a weapons turn-in program.

Beginning in 1930 Khan, and the Khudai Khitmager endured the first of what would be a life-long series of political arrests, attacks, and jail sentences. By the 1950s the state of Pakistan eliminated the organization.

Observing Khan's saintly charisma and nonviolent demeanor, Gandhi wrote:

> I noticed wherever I went that every man, woman, and child knew him and loved him. They greeted him most familiarly. His touch seemed to soothe them. [He] was most gentle to whomever approached him. All this has filled me with boundless joy. A general merits such obedience. But [Ghaffar Khan] has it by right of love, unlike the ordinary general who exacts obedience through fear.[37]

On June 15, 1948, Khan was arrested and imprisoned for sedition for advocating a state of Pushtanistan; the Khudai Khidmatgar were banned and its headquarters razed. Since the 1950s, Pakistani regimes have engaged in a campaign of disinformation so that many Pakistanis and Pushtun misconstrue Khan as "merely a Nationalist agitator and subversive, and that he died a Hindu."[38]

It might be said that one of the correlates of nonviolence is justice and respect for women and their rights. Khan advocated women's equality and encouraged their involvement in the Khudai Khidmatger. Khan's sisters toured the Frontier unveiled and giving speeches. Khan denounced the practice of *purdah* (custom of veiling and secluding women). Articles in the movement's journal, *Pushtun* ("*The Pathan*") proclaimed, "...there is no place for *purdah*..." and that the only enemy to Pathan women are Pathan men who demand freedom for themselves while denying it to their own women.[39]

> God makes no distinction between men and women...In the Holy Koran , you have an equal share with men. You are today oppressed because we men have ignored the commands of God and the Prophet.[40]

---

[37] Gandhi, quoted in Easwaren, pp. 154-155; cf. quote on 162-163.

[38] Harris, ibid., 1998. p 103

[39] Easwaren, ibid., p. 105.

[40] Badshah Khan quoted in Tedulkar, 101-102, quoted in Easwaren. p. 133

Once he was asked about his English sister-in-law's religion. Khan explained that he didn't know, hadn't asked her, and reported that his older brother has not made her convert.

Khan lived at Gandhi's ashram and it was he whom Gandhi would often ask to recite Qur'an in the morning ecumenical prayer meetings.

Khan recognized and exemplified a thread of moral discourse and action in the Prophetic *sunna* which demonstrated nonviolence and peaceful coexistence – a phenomenon he recognized as both universal and Islamic.

MUHAMMAD RAHEEM BAWA MUHAIYADEEN (1884?-1986)[41]

Bawa Muhaiyaddeen is our only nonviolent visionary among these four who lived and taught in both the eastern and western hemispheres. As photos and film disclose, he was an extremely gentle and graceful man in his manner and speech. Although he looked youthful, legends surrounding him suggested he had lived beyond a hundred years. Like Badshah Khan, he carried his nonviolence to the point of being a vegetarian. He had, it was alleged, lived in the jungles of Sri Lanka and become there by deeply attuned to nature before emerging as a Pir or teacher of Sufism, Islam's inner or mystical dimension. His discourses reflected an inner knowledge more than an intellectual one; they are not laced with citations from the canons of the *'ulama*. And although Bawa technically belonged to the specific spiritual lineage of 'Abdul Qadir al-Gilani, Bawa's teachings were more inclusive and eclectic than sectarian. Among his books is an important one for our purposes, *Islam and World Peace* (1987). The Sri-Lankan Sufi master settled in America in 1971 until he was laid to rest outside of Philadelphia in a tomb which is today a pilgrimage site. Consistently, he described Islam as unconditional peace and love. For Bawa, Allah and the Prophet exclusively intended nonviolence:

> Praising Allah and then destroying others is not *jihad*. Some groups wage war against the children of Adam and call it holy war. But for man to raise his sword against man, for man to kill man is not holy war...Allah has no thought of killing or going to war. Why would Allah have sent His prophets if He had such thoughts? It was not to destroy men that Muhammad came; he was sent down as the wisdom that could show man how to destroy his own evil.[42]

This pacifist interpretation of *jihad* involves understanding Bawa's telling of the story of Adam and Satan as a framework "so you may better understand the meaning of *jihad*, or holy war."[43] Bawa narrates that because Adam had received the primordial light of Muhammad (Nur Muhammad), the leader of the jinns "became filled with jealousy, pride, and vengeance, and these qualities changed him into Satan....Then Satan spat on [Adam], and...Satan's poisonous qualities entered him." Though Gabriel removed most of the poison, some

---

[41] The claims of his birth year are advanced by Sharon Marcus in her "Introduction" to Bawa's book *The Triple Flame: The Inner Secrets of Sufism.* (Philadelphia Press, 2001) as reported in Gwendolyn Zoharah Simmons, "Are We Up To The Challenge? The Need for a Radical Reordering of the Islamic Discourse on Women," in Omid Safi, ed. *Progressive Muslims: on Justice, Gender, and Pluralism.* Oxford: One World, 2003, p. 245, n. 14. I have also heard claims of Bawa's longevity from many of his students.

[42] Bawa Muhaiyaddeen, *Islam and World Peace: Explanations of a Sufi.* Accessed at www.bmf.org/iswp/part2_holy_war.html October 2004, p. 4.

[43] Ibid., p. 1.

remained and was passed on to Adam's descendents. Bawa related this much of the story "to show you that the most important *jihad*, the holy war that each one of us must fight is the war against these qualities."[44] Thus for Bawa, the true *jihad*, an inner *jihad*, is directly related to this primordial predicament narrated of Adam and Eve:

> True *jihad* is to praise God and to cut away the inner satanic enemies. When wisdom and clarity come to us, we will understand that the enemies of truth are within our own hearts.[45]

And in this era of "religious"warfare run amok, Bawa's critique strikes perhaps even more deeply than when it was first given.

> My brothers, the holy wars that the children of Adam are waging today are not true holy wars. Taking other lives is not true *jihad*. We will have to answer for that kind of war when we are questioned in the grave.[46]

Uncompromisingly Bawa calls for nonviolence characterized by maternal guidance:

> We must not kill each other....And just as God does not kill His children because they have evil qualities, we must not murder or cut them down. Instead we must try to improve them by showing wisdom, love, compassion, and God's qualities, just as a mother teaches her mischievous child to change.[47]

In this war of nonviolence, the only weapons are divine qualities such as love and compassion:

> It is compassion that conquers. It is unity that conquers. It is Allah's good qualities, behavior and actions that conquer others. It is this state which is called Islam. The sword doesn't conquer; love is sharper than the sword. Love is an exalted, gentle sword.[48]

> For man to raise his sword against man is not holy war. True holy war is to praise God and to cut away the enemies of truth within our own hearts. We must cast out all that is evil within us, all that opposes God. This is the war that we must fight."[49]

Returning to Bawa's original starting point, the inner *jihad*, he promises, will bring us to "a direct connection to Allah, just as Adam had that original connection."[50] And with Bawa describing such warfare with the metaphor of a mother's way of correcting a child, Bawa emphasizes that his vision of "warfare" is fundamentally nonviolent.

---

[44] Ibid., pp. 1-2.

[45] Ibid., p. 2

[46] Ibid., p. 2

[47] Ibid., p. 3

[48] Ibid., p. 34

[49] Bawa Muhaiyaddeen, *Islam and World Peace: Explanations of a Sufi.* Philadelphia: Fellowship Press, 1986, p. 44. For a treatment of *jihad* as an essentially pacifist endeavor, see Rabia Harris, ibid, pp. 95-114.

[50] Ibid., www.bwf.org p. 4.

CHAIWAT SATHA-ANAND (1955 -) AND THE SEARCH FOR PEACE CULTURES

Chaiwat Satha Anand's witness and work in Thailand has become evermore relevant especially as Thailand's six million Muslims, predominantly Malay people living the south, have recently become embroiled in violent tensions with the Thai government of Prime Minister Thaksin Shinawatra. And while 2004 has been a particularly volatile year, with a death toll of 430 as of October,[51] the Malays of southern Thailand (Patani Raya, or Greater Patani) have struggled and revolted since the 18th century against various oppressive Thai rulers.[52]

Satha-Anand, sometimes known by his Muslim name Qader Muheiddeen, is a prominent contemporary Muslim scholar devoting himself to developing an Islamic theory of non-violence. He serves as the Director of the Peace Information Center, Foundation for Democracy and Development Studies at the Faculty of Political Science atThammasat University in Bangkok, Thailand. In an essay exploring the loss of humanity demonstrated by Muslims who killed Buddhist monks at knife point in January 2004, he examines the way a sense of community is shattered by such events. Raising this question belongs to a process of finding what he calls "peace cultures."[53] He cautions that to simply introduce state violence into an already-charged situation (as happened on "Bloody Monday," October 25, 2004) would increase the existing cultural rift.[54] Satha-Anand borrowed the concept of "peace cultures" from eminent peace researcher Elise Boulding. As he describes it, peace culture is a "mosiac" of "the historical memories of peaceful peoplehood, teachings and practice of communities of faith...and most relevant here, forms of governance that ensure justice and means of dealing with conflicts..."[55]

Satha-Anand then proceeds to outline the vision and method which is at once his own and that which he advocates. In doing this he turns to a particular paradigm of Islamic history, Abu Bakr.

From a Muslim's perspective, strengthening peace cultures would mean finding religious injunctions that would de-legitimize such senseless violence. In Islamic tradition, the companion of the Prophet Muhammad and the first Caliph, Abu Bakr, laid down ten rules as guidance in the battlefield. He said: "You must not mutilated dead bodies. Neither kill a child nor a woman, nor an aged man. Bring no harm to the trees, nor burn them with fire, especially those which are fruitful. Slay not any of the enemy's flock, save for your food. You are likely to pass by people who have devoted their lives to monastic services. Leave them alone."

Such a mandate argues clearly against the tragic violence of 9/11. In addition to setting clear limits on violence, Abu Bakr's mandate also requires interreligious harmony since the monks he refers to could not possibly be Muslim. Satha-Anand concludes, "This means that

---

[51] Andrew Perrin, "Thailand's Bloody Monday," *TIME* Asia Edition, p. 18-22.

[52] Farish A. Noor, "The Killings in Southern Thailand: A Long History of Persecution Unrecorded," *Muslim Wake Up.* April 30, 2004. Accessed at www.muslimwakeup.com October 2004.

[53] Chaiwat Satha-Anand, "Facing the Demon Within: Fighting Violence in Southern Thailand with Peace Cultures," Printed on the op-ed. Page of the Bagkok Post, http://www.bangkokpost.net January 30, 2004. Accessed at www.transnational.org/forum/meet/2004/Satha-Anand_Thailandpeace.html October 5, 2004.

[54] The tragic killing of 85 people in the Tak Bai district of Thailand's southern Narathiwat province is described in Perrin, ibid.

[55] Satha-Anand, "Facing the Demon Within."

in Islam, killing those who are innocent, unrelated to war, even trees and animals, and especially monks or priests or clergy are unacceptable."[56]

Acknowledging the severity of the current situation in Thailand, Satha-Anand suggests "more innovative cultural actions are needed....[which] should be carried out from within the existing civil society."[57] Satha-Anand turns to the role of civil society in arbitrating the heavily ideologically driven violence which seems unresolvable any other way. In this he shares a vision explicitly with Aburrahman Wahid and implicitly with Badshah Khan and Bawa Muhayideen that civil society is the viable locus of nonviolence.

In his book *The Nonviolent Crescent: Two Essays on Islamic Non-Violence* , he describes a particular successful case of Muslim non-violent (*la 'unf*) action in Thailand. From November 29, 1975, to January 10, 1976, Southern Thai Muslims demonstrated the massacre of five adult Malay Muslims and pressed for four demands. Satha-Anand calls the five conditions which made their demonstrations successful the "Five Pillars of Islamic Nonviolence." In summary they are as follows:

(1) The will to disobey. "The Muslims are willing to disobey because for them God alone is supreme. This total submission to Allah in turn means a rejection of any other form of absolute authority, including the state's." (Like the *shahadah*, this pillar allows no greater authority than God's.)

(2) Courage in the face of the state's severe repression rooted in the belief that God will take care of them. (This corresponds roughly to the *zakah*, by which members of the Islamic community are provided for.)

(3) Muslim discipline, born of long standing practice of five-times a day *salat* contributed to efficiency. Their long-cultivated communal discipline also surpassed the question of leadership by personalities. (Satha-Anand suggests this correlates to *salat.*)

(4) Community brotherhood (*ummah*), enjoined by the Qur'an and enjoined at many points in Islamic culture. (This is similar to the spirit of the *hajj*.)

(5) A willingness to take action in the spirit of *jihad.* (This corresponds roughly to the strenuous effort of fasting or *sawm*.)[58]

At his essay's conclusion, Satha-Anand systematically argues that the indiscriminate nature of modern warfare renders it religiously illicit (*haram*) by proposing eight theses on Islamic Nonviolence.

(1) For Islam, the problem of violence is an integral part of the Islamic moral sphere.

(2) Violence, if any, used by Muslims must be governed by rules prescribed in the Qur'an and Hadith.

(3) If violence [is] used [in a situation where one] cannot discriminate between combatants and non-combatants, then it is unacceptable in Islam.

---

[56] Ibid. p. 5
[57] ibid. p. 5
[58] Chaiwat Satha Anand, "The Nonviolent Crescent: Eight Theses on Muslim Nonviolent Actions." p. 23. Accessed at www.globalnonviolence.org October 5, 2004. Since Satha-Anand alludes to but does not indentify the correspondences between the classic Islamic pillars and these Five Pillars of Muslim Nonviolent Action, I have attempted here to deduce this set of correspondences.

(4) Modern technology of destruction renders discrimination virtually impossible at present.

(5) In the modern world, Muslims cannot use violence.

(6) Islam teaches Muslims to fight for justice with the understanding that human lives – as all parts of creation – are purposive and sacred.

(7) In order to be true to Islam, Muslims must utilize non-violent [la 'unf] action as a new mode of struggle.

(8) Islam itself is fertile soil for non-violence [la 'unf] because of its potential for disobedience, strong discipline, sharing and social responsibility, perseverance and self-sacrifice, and the belief in the unity of the Muslim community and the oneness of mankind.[59]

In the face of Thai Prime Minister Thaksin's recent attempts to create a sense of order and control, in both rhetoric and military action, Satha-Anand continues to voice caution concerning the risks of such violence.

> It reflects [Thai society's] desire for a decisive leadership. If I were a politician I would take that into account in my decision making. As a leader you should be concerned with what kind of society you are creating when you resort to violence. He's [Thaksin] playing into the hands of the extremists.[60]

Like Badshah Khan, Bawa Muhaiyadeen, and Abdurrahman Wahid, Chaiwat Satha-Anand , especially in his eighth thesis, links Islamic nonviolence to an underlying spiritual anthropology of the unity of humanity.

ABURRAHMAN "GUS DUR" WAHID (1941 -)

Abdurrahman became in 1999 the first elected president in Indonesia's history. This event placed Indonesia on the political map as the world's third largest democracy. Indonesia has long been the world's largest Muslim country with roughly 87% of its population of 220 million identifying themselves as Muslim. For the most part Indonesian Muslims have co-existed peacefully with the country's five other religious communities: Hindu, Buddhist, Catholic, Protestant, and Confucian. However this situation, democracy's flip side, has begun to deteriorate in the post-Suharto era. As evidenced in Indonesia's elections of September 2004, Indonesia has navigated a successful, if still precarious, course between Islamic ideals and democratic pluralism. While Abdurrahman is specifically committed to promoting nonviolence, it is his advocacy of pluralism which is the keystone to his building a society based on nonviolence.

Abdurrahman emerged to national prominence as the leader of Nahdatul Ulama (NU, the "Renaissance of Religious Scholars," a movement to which approximately 20% of Inodnesians belong). He was born of a prominent family of *pesantren* founders and

---

[59] Chaiwat Satha Anand, ibid., p. 23. Accessed at www.globalnonviolence.org October 5, 2004.
[60] Chaiwat Satha-Anand quoted in "Thailand's Bloody Monday," *Time Magazine* (Asia), November 8, 2004, p. 22.

teachers.[61] Abdurrahman's father, Wahid Hashim, minister of religious affairs from 1950 till his death by auto accident, was one of the formulators of Indonesia's constitutional foundation, centering around a pluralistic vision known as the *pancasila*, five principles.[62] After an Islamic education in Indonesian *pesantrens* and *madrasas* in Egypt (al-Azhar), as well as a secular education in Baghdad (University of Baghdad) and Europe, Abdurrahman became convinced of the "failure of formalizing Islam in the life of a state like Indonesia."[63] He also became convinced that Islam needed to be reinterpreted in line with contemporary scientific knowledge. After serving in a variety of capacities in the *pesantren* network he moved to Jakarta in 1977 where he participated in forums with other progressive Muslim thinkers such as Murcholish Madjid as well as with non-Muslims. Traveling to South America he met Brazilian liberation theologian Archbishop Oscar Camara and studied liberation theology, particularly the work of Leonardo Boff. In this, he shares with his counterparts in this essay, a willingness to cull ecumenical resources and associations contributing to cultures of justice and peace.

During the 1970s and 1980s Soeharto provoked a situation Abdurrahman perceived as dangerous. As student protestors were arrested, political dissenters turned to mosques as their centers. In this situation Islamic groups and Islamic discourse became the exclusive safe haven for dissent. In 1983, in conjunction with another prominent NU leader, Achmad Siddiq, Wahid successfully argued on Islamic lines that NU adopt *pancasila* as a vision of civil Islam.[64] Through this act Abdurrahman sought to create a framework to alleviate a potential confrontation with Soeharto's government. Inspired in part by the Islamic liberalism of Egyptian 'Abd al-Raziq, Abdurrahman chartered an accommodationist path based on the separation of religion and state: "there is no need for a nation-state with Islamic law."[65] In his view the current model of nation state is not essential to Islam. In taking this stance he has asserted an Islamic ideal of pluralism over an ideology of politicized Islam. As so many cases of the combining of *shari'ah* with a nation state suggest, this very act of relinquishing the demand for a *shar'ah* state charts in its own way a direct course toward peace.

In 1991, Soeharto established the Association for Indonesian Muslim Intellectuals (ICMI) and noticeably excluded Abdurrahman Wahid. Abdurrahman viewed ICMI as an attempt to re-Islamicize Indonesian politics in a way which would damage unity and pluralism and ultimately culminate in sectarian strife. In response Abdurrahman and 44 other prominent intellectuals from a variety of religious backgrounds established the Democratic Forum as a non-confessional discussion group on democracy and pluralism. Perceived by Soeharto as a threat, they were shut down; often their meetings were broken up forcibly. Abdurrahman continued to endure Soeharto's antipathy toward Indonesians' "mass support for his inclusivist Islam."[66]

---

[61] *Pesantren* are Islamic residential schools centered around a master who is a religious scholar and Sufi guide.
[62] *Pancasila*, literally, the "five ethical [principles]" stipulate: (1) Faith in one God; (2) humanitarianism; (3) nationalism; (4) democracy; and (5) justice. The first principle which requires profession of a religion (or belonging to a religious community) recognizes six religions (*agamas*) as valid: Muslim, Hindu, Buddhist, Catholic, Protestant, and Chinese. By defining Hindu and Chinese religious communities broadly, everyone becomes easily classifiable within one of these *agamas*.
[63] Abdurrahman Wahid, quoted in John Esposito and John O. Voll, *Makers of Contemporary Islam*. (Oxford, 2001) p. 200.
[64] Robert W. Hefner, *Civil Islam. Muslims and Democratization in Indonesia*. (Princeton, 2000), p. 160.
[65] Abdurrahman Wahid, quoted in Esposito and Voll, *Makers*., p. 205.
[66] Hefner, ibid., 163.

His pluralistic outreach continued. In 1994 he visited Israel and proposed that Indonesia and Israel establish relations. He also became a member of the Shimon Peres' Peace Foundation. In 1996 he published an article calling for official recognition of Confucianism as a state religion. He was also the first official to condemn the riots of 1996 even though NU members comprised the majority of rioters.

In 2003 when a crisis between Catholics and Muslims erupted in the neighborhood of the Sang Timur Catholic School, Abdurrahman literally stepped in to mediate. He proclaimed tolerance and dialogue as a priority among all the nation's different groups, and was quoted as affirming: "And where Muslims are the majority, they should protect the rights of minority groups." [67]

As he wrote of the perils of violence:

This willingness to use violence [by Islamic movements] will by necessity involve violence in their efforts. One act of violence begets further counterviolence and soon an uncontrollable escalation of violence ensues. To avoid the possibility of such an escalation, with its never-ending specter of a war of annihilatoin. Islamic movements should dedicate themselves to nonviolence as a way to achieve their objectives. [68]

Abdurrahman's example in the Sang Timor intervention and his explanation of a framework for fostering nonviolence both attest to the prerequisite need for mutual coexistence – a just balance among people, communities and nations as the foundation of nonviolence.

CONCLUSION

Arriving at an Islamic notion of nonviolence involves clarifying the following topics: identifying the terms of *jihad*; recognizing the relationship between the discourses of peace and war in the canonical sources; situating nonviolence as an outcome of a policy of peaceful co-existence between communities; and, assessing the relationship between religious and political authority. The four representatives of nonviolent theory and practice in this essay demonstrate a diversity of expression, while also sharing a consensus of ideals, ideas, and methods towards these ends.

The term *jihad* has caused confusion around the nature of Islamic nonviolence. Non-Muslims have too easily misread *jihad* as "warfare." Apologetic Muslims have sometimes been tempted to obscure and oversimplify *jihad* as only moral struggle. *Jihad* of the heart, and tongue are nonviolent; *jihad* by the hand, the *jihad* of the sword, is a last resort of self-defense. As we have seen, its permissibility is tempered by clearly-articulated restraints which both the Prophet Muhammad and Abu Bakr set forth.

---

[67] "School's Wall Falls. Tensions Still High." *Jakarta Post* Tuesday October 26, 2004, p. 2. "All the nations groups" refers to the six recognized religious communities under Indonesia's constitution: Muslim, Protestant, Catholic, Hindu, Buddhist, and Confucian. A commentary on both sets of events by Muhammad Ali, a lecturer at UIN Syarif Hidayatullah State Islamic University with a similar appeal for peaceful coexistence appeared in the *Jakarta Post* Friday October 29, 2004. For the 12-year historical background leading up to this crisis (centering on the use of the school building for conducting mass since August 15, 1992) see Setiyardi, Y.Tomi Aryanto and Ayu Cipta, "God's Bitter Gate Keepers." *Tempo* (English edition) November 22, 2004, pp. 12-13.

[68] Abdurrahman Wahid. "Islam, Nonviolence and National Transformation." in Paige, et al.

As we have tried to show at the beginning of this essay, the Qur'an very clearly addresses an ideal of peace and points to the terms of mutual co-existence between religious communities. The life of the Prophet Muhammad further exemplifies this ideal in practice. Because of war's inherent violence (the Qur'an says the death of one person is like the death of all humanity) war is always reserved as the last resort after every other means has been tried.[69] The intention of creating peace is regarded as paramount. Even in a war this standard is upheld. In the canonical model and early historical narratives captives are granted human rights, their lives spared, and captives are set free if they embrace Islam.[70]

Religions are not monolithic. Each has its threads of discourse of war; each its discourse of peace. In this essay I have tried to represent and examine four lives of witness to the thread of Islamic nonviolence and peace. While all four regard nonviolence and peace as paramount objectives per se, interreligious or pluralistic harmony serve as the foundation for realizing nonviolence and peace. In no way do these four representatives of nonviolence in this essay prove an essentialist point about the nature of Islam as understood in the oversimplified and overworked slogan "Islam means peace." What they do serve to show however is that in this tradition, as in many others, nonviolence and peace are integral to its legacy, its future, and among its most important resources. More deeply these living examples show that – and how—Muslims can practice nonviolence from a Muslim perspective and that nonviolence towers among the spectrum of Islamic ideals.

In all four cases we see a tendency to avoid politicizing religion. At one extreme Bawa was almost apolitical. Our two contemporary examples, Abdurrahman Wahid and Chaiwat Satha-Anand have advocated applying Islam in the context of a civil society. Rather than politicize Islam in a context of global nationalism, they have taken the vision of an Islamic *ummah* to refer to an inspiration for community and brotherhood. Further each has stressed the mandate entrusted to the *ummah* that diverse communities live together harmoniously in peace. It is this dimension of Islam, the Islamic discourse which protects and accommodates pluralism and refrains from transforming Islam into a political ideology, together with a core set of values surrounding peace and the sanctity of life, which gives voice to the practice of Islamic nonviolence.

BIBLIOGRAPHY

'Ali, Maulana Muhammad, *A Manual of Hadith*. New York: Olive Branch Press, 1977.

'Ali, 'Abdallah Yusuf. *The Meaning of the Holy Qur'an*. Baltimore: Amana Trust, 1983 (revised reprint).

Chittick, William. *The Sufi Path of Love: The Spiritual Teachings of Rumi*. Albany: SUNY, 1983.

Chittick, William and Sachiko Murata. *The Vision of Islam*. New York: Inner Traditions, 1994.

Cornell, Vincent, "Jihad, Islam's Struggle for Truth," *Gnosis* Fall 1991

---

[69] "For that cause [Cain's repentance over having murdered his brother Abel] We decreed for the children of Israel that whosoever killeth a human being for other than manslaughter or corruption on the earth, it shall be as if he had killed all mankind, and whoso saveth the life of one, it shall be as if he had saved the life of all mankind..." (Qur'an 5.32; Pickthall translation)

[70] Qur'an 8.70-72; Lings, ibid., p. 149.

Eknath Easwaren, *A Man to Match His Mountains: Badshah Khan, Nonviolent Soldier of Islam*. Petaluma, CA, Nilgiri Press, 1984.

Ernst, Carl. *The Shambhala Guide to Sufism*. Boston: Shambhala, 1996.

Guillaume, Alford. *The Life of Muhammad*. Oxford: Oxford, 1955, rpt. 1982.

Harris, Rabia, Terri. "Nonviolence in Islam: The Alternative Community Tradition." In Daniel L. Smith-Christopher, ed. *Subverting Hatred: The Challenge of Nonviolence in Religious Traditions*. Boston: Boston Research Center for the 21st Century, 1998.

Hefner, Robert W. Robert *Civil Islam: Muslims and Democratization in Indonesia*. Princeton, 2000.

Lings, Martin. *Muhammad: a Biography of the Prophet from the Earliest Sources*. Putney, Vermont: Inner Traditions, 1983.

Muhaiyaddeen, Bawa. *Islam and World Peace: Explanations of a Sufi*. Philadelphia: Fellowship Press, 1987. Also accessed on website: www.bwf.org October 2004.

Pickthall, Mohammed Marmaduke. *The Meaning of the Glorious Koran*. New York: Mentor, 1936, 1953.

Renard, John. *All the King's Falcons: Rumi on Prophets and Revelation*. New York: S.U.N.Y, 1994.

Safi, Omid. *Progressive Muslims: On Gender, Justice, and Pluralism*. Oxford: Oneworld, 2003.

Satha-Anand, Chaiwat. "Facing the Demon Within: Fighting Violence in Southern Thailand with Peace Cultures." *The Transnational Foundation for Peace and Future Research*. February 6, 2004. Accessed at www.transnational.org October 5, 2005. Printed on the op-ed page of *Bangkok Post* www.bangkokpost.net January 30, 2004.

Satha-Anand, Chaiwat. "The Non-Violent Crescent: Eight Theses on Muslim Non-Violent Actions," in Glenn D. Paige, Chaiwat Satha-Anand, and Sarah Gilliatt, eds. *Islam and Non-Violence*. Hawaii: Center for Global Nonviolence Inc, 1999. Accessed on website: www.globalnonviolence.org October 2004.

Schimmel, Annemarie. *Mystical Dimensions of Islam*. Chapel Hill: University of North Carolina Press, 1975.

Voll, John and John Esposito. *Makers of Contemporary Islam*. Oxford: Oxford University Press, 2001.

SECTION IV

In: Religion, Terrorism and Globalization
Editor: K.K. Kuriakose, pp.145-156

ISBN 1-59454-553-7
© 2006 Nova Science Publishers, Inc.

Chapter 9

"WAR AND CONSCIENTIZATION: CONCEPTUALIZING ALTERNATIVE APPROACHES TO HUMAN RELATIONS IN THE AGE OF EMPIRE"

Norberto Valdez

Department of Anthropology, Colorado State University

INTRODUCTION

Violence in human societies has a social basis, but the path to changing historical trends of aggression begins with individual reflection and a commitment to social change. This is my story of personal transformation from warrior/patriot to anti-war activist. The 37 years that have elapsed since I volunteered to participate in the U.S. wars in Southeast Asia, have been a continual process of learning and unlearning. What I witnessed and experienced during the period of 1968-70 during two "tours of duty" (as if I had been on vacation during that extraordinarily violent war in Viet Nam) resulted in a silent, internal struggle to understand myself, my family, my country, and the impacts of our militarist society on distant peoples and places. In reflecting on my personal transformation, I have determined to understand several aspects of my experiences. First, why did I volunteer to participate in a war that, according to some estimates, killed over three million Asian people? Second, how can I engage in the "ontological vocation" of rehumanization (P. Freire 1970) that fulfills the need for continuous creation rather than persistent destruction? Third, how might I contribute to social justice causes in the quest for non-violent solutions to local and global problems?

These three learning quests have been an important part of my reflexive endeavors and are integrally tied to both personal and professional aspects of my life in transformation. First, at the level of the personal, I am a multi-generational descendant of Chicano/Native heritage of the "manito" villages of southern Colorado and northern New Mexico whose historical experiences of conquest, colonization, and structural marginalization have informed my understanding of societal conflicts. Second, I have used my professional training and field work experiences in anthropology, ethnic studies, and related disciplines as the basis for obtaining a conceptual and theoretical basis for raising important questions about war and peace. Third, I have combined the personal and the professional in my commitment to learning and teaching about global conflicts in the classroom as well as in activism for social justice in the broader interest of building a more just and sustainable world.

One of the most astounding and impressive aspects of human history that I have come to appreciate in this project of transformation is the incredible capacity of human beings to perpetrate violence upon other human beings. One does not have to retreat very far back in time or space to cite cases of conquest, colonization, enslavement, and genocide to appreciate the depths of human depravity and our propensity for violence. The prevalence of such trends to the present has led to sociobiological explanations suggesting that this is merely a result of genetic programming, following the basic instinct for human survival. In many private debates about the role of aggression and war in human societies, popular intelligence boldly suggests that such violence is an adaptable aspect of human behavior and gives impulse to human improvement along the evolutionary trajectory of species survival, proliferation, and progress.

My purpose here is not to debate such explanations or to discuss the various anthropologies of violence and aggression. Rather, I propose at the outset a premise that human violence is not only an historical fact, given ample evidence, but that it finds its explanation in the historical circumstances which people in conflict help to create as conscious or unconscious agents of history. From this perspective, violence is not biologically-based and not necessarily inevitable. Furthermore, since I believe that any propensity toward violence is culturally and socially conditioned, human populations have the capacity to seek alternative solutions in times of conflict. Lastly, any potential for change in the patterns of conflict resolution must begin with individuals confronting their own values, their roles within society, and the impacts of their behaviors locally and globally. Only from this standpoint, it appears to me, can the consciousness, motivation, and commitment emerge through which people can engage in collective actions that will change the patterns of violence of the human past.

CONFLUENCE OF COSMOLOGY AND THEORY

Native American spiritual practice, in stark contrast to Judeo-Christian doctrine, is non-anthropocentric. It teaches that understanding the complexity of all our relations on this planet requires recognition of the ties among the seven directions. These include the four cardinal points with their color-coded symbolic representations of the (potential) unity among the so-called 'races' of humanity. Some Native traditions recognize two additional directions, the importance of Father Sky and Mother Earth that combine their cosmic energies to give us life. Finally, Native cosmology also includes a seventh direction, i.e., the individual who is the locus of energy that has the capacity to create the necessary conditions for the emergence of human agency and the potential for social change. Each of these characteristics exists in an interconnected and interdependent world within Native cosmologies and is symbolized in the notion of the "web of life" or "all my relations" ("mitakuye oyasin," in the language of the Lakota).

In my journey along the path of personal transformation, I have combined the Native notion of "all our relations" and the Freirian concept of the "ontological vocation" in order to wed the notion of the interconnectedness of humanity with the life-long pursuit of liberation from stultifying hierarchical human relations and structures. This suggests breaking free from the culture of silence that leads individuals and groups toward uncritical thinking and behaviors, thereby giving consent to violence perpetrated against other human beings. This means getting on the road to conscientization, obtaining the skills to learn about one's given socioeconomic and political situation, and becoming a Subject that interacts with the world in order to change it.

So it is from this conceptual and experiential base that my personal journey of transformation was incrementally launched. My Viet Nam experience provided the initial catalyst for years of post-Viet Nam reflection and engagement in what David Abalos has called "the core drama of life" (2002). I look back at my personal history and, subsequently, to the changes that have resulted from that reflection. I clearly see now that the early years of my youth were experiences of fractionization of a single human being into several "partial selves" (Abalos 2002:51) through various paternalistic and patriarchal influences. Men and institutions performed their 'normal' duties in the service of family and community in making an object out of a human being and shaping his mind to conform to the logic of a patriarchal and violent social system.

As suggested above, my early development was conditioned by patriarchal factors such as an authoritarian male parent and machista cultural inputs, priests and religious misogyny, coaches and disciplinarian violence, company commanders and militarization of the mind, etc. This resulted in what I now recognize as a fractionization of a human spirit. Patriarchy, sexism, racism, and classism dovetailed to create an individual who was conditioned to obey orders, to accept various kinds of oppression as "normal expressions of culture" or good citizenship, and to accept as normative behavior the uncritical silence and accommodation that are so important to the perpetuation of cross-generational cycles of oppression. It was on the basis of these factors and concerns that the countervailing need arose to engage in a rehumanizing vocation that challenges established dogmas and opens possibilities for alternative futures.

GETTING ON THE PATH OF REFLECTION AND CHANGE

Military service in Viet Nam was for me a powerful mirror that forced me to look into my family history and early schooling experiences for possible explanations of my rather naive volunteering for the violence of war. I began to engage in a radical project that is reflected in Audre Lorde's poignant assertion that "It is a waste of time hating a mirror or its reflection instead of stopping the hand that makes glass with distortion." This is a radical and positive step in the ontological vocation of rehumanization because it seeks to identify the root causes of the problem of deformation of individual selves and collective minds, and engages in actions to change them.

Lorde, like Freire, also recognized that an "imposed silence about any area of our lives is a tool for separation and powerlessness" (1980). Adrienne Rich, a close associate of Lorde, once said, "Responsibility to yourself means refusing to let others do your thinking, talking, and naming for you; it means learning to respect and use your own brains and instincts..." (1979). Freire emphasized that each individual, through dialogic engagement with the world around, empowers herself to name the worlds in which she lives and, on that basis, to interact with it in new ways with a new awareness of self and the capacity for creating social change. At the most personal level, my own life partner influenced my thinking and subsequent transformation by raising questions early in our relationship about my negative self-perception and particularly my actions that she detected were not in harmony with the person that she was beginning to know.

These powerful words from various sources resounded within me and initiated a very distinct phase in my life that can be characterized as a pedagogy of hope and human dignity. But I also began to realize that acknowledging the contradictions of one's life experiences is a slow and painful process. Entering new terrain of critical thinking and action is also fraught with fear (Freire 1970). I began to realize that engaging in the vocation of conscientization, liberation, and rehumanization is not based strictly on individualistic endeavor. The individual, as recognized in Native cosmologies, is clearly an important starting point for becoming a Subject of history but a primary aspect is interaction with the world in which one lives. Engagement in the ontological vocation of rehumanization inevitably leads down the path toward collective consciousness and the increasing awareness of the common conditions in which one's fellow human beings live. Particularly daunting is the realization that the ultimate goal of changing past historical trends is based on the individual taking responsibility for a meaningful role in collective actions.

REFLECTIONS ON SOCIAL MOTIVATIONS FOR WAR

I was not drafted into military service as the war intensified in 1967 and led to the Tet offensive by Vietnamese in early 1968. Nor was I subjected as an individual to "economic conscription" or the "poverty draft" which had been and continues to be a major factor in the decisions of lower-class youth to enter the military. I was not recruited through the military "buddy system" that encouraged two of my older brothers and their friends to find temporary security in group enlistment, if not in the distant location to which they were all sent. Actually, the thought of military service had not entered my mind prior to the summer of 1967. At that time, I had just completed my sophomore year at the University of Colorado, Boulder, where I was in good academic standing in anthropology. I was a live-in student in a Puerto Rican home where I assisted with the care for an elderly woman. As time permitted, I worked in her nephew's janitorial service and also in a biological sciences curriculum project at the university in order to pay for tuition and expenses. National Defense Student loans rounded out my budget. Thus, I did not have the kinds of concerns that typically lead lower class youth to consider the military as an employment option.

But during late summer 1967, I decided to forego my government-issued, 2-S student deferment and to enlist in the military. I've searched for reasons for having made this decision, since this was done very uncharacteristically, that is, unilaterally and without consultation with parents or family. Two older brothers had already enlisted and were serving on naval vessels on the "gun line" in Vietnamese coastal waters. One was assigned to the USS Ticonderoga in 1964, an aircraft carrier involved in the Tonkin Gulf incident that President Lyndon Johnson used as the pretext for deepening U.S. involvement in Viet Nam. The other brother was a quartermaster on a supply ship that transported Marine soldiers to

Vietnamese ports for deployment. Neither of my brothers communicated directly with me during their tours of duty. My four semesters in engineering and anthropology at Colorado offered me no preparation for understanding the increasing hostilities between the U.S. and Viet Nam during this period. Mainstream newspapers and the evening television newscasts were my main sources of global information. Finally, my having grown up in a small, economically-depressed, ranching and mining town in southern Colorado offered few resources with which to escape the provincialism of the region and to understand world events.

A partial explanation of my uncritical decision to enlist in the U.S. war against Viet Nam, about which I knew virtually nothing, has to do primarily with my family-orientedness, various authoritarian paternal figures in my adolescent development, and with government ideology propagated through the media. The latter provided me with information about Cold War "domino theory" of U.S. government officials suggesting that communism needed to be stopped before it infected the status of neighboring nation-states of southeast Asia. I understood my brothers' volunteering for military service in this context. I gave less importance to the lack of employment opportunities in our home town. I occasionally thought about our father's advice to them that it would be better to join the military than to get into trouble with the local police. Our father was a very strict disciplinarian who placed high value on family honor and punished any infractions that had even the remotest chance of reaching public attention. Family honor, for him, was coterminous with his personal honor and he took teenage indiscretions very personally. I had witnessed numerous forms of paternal punishments doled out to family members and I believe to this day that my volunteering to join them in warfare was an effort to protect them from harm, albeit in ways that I could neither comprehend nor implement at the time.

This blending of family loyalty, authoritarian paternalism, personal naivete, and Cold War ideology led to what might be seen, perhaps through today's U.S. nationalistic lens, as patriotism. Yet, family loyalty rather than patriotism was the single most important factor that influenced my decisions at that time. Further reflection on my past reveals another factor, that is, a progression of authoritarian personalities that conditioned my thinking and behavior. In addition to my father's authoritarian approach to child-rearing, I had important connections to Catholic teachings and priests. I prided myself as a very good student in a Catholic school where I was rewarded for obedience and rote memorization of texts. Obedience and conformity were taught through the awkward experience of the confessional where I could talk meekly to a shadow of a figure on the other side of a screen. I was also an acolyte who served at Catholic masses and other church functions, again being rewarded by priests who invited me to rural chapels in other towns to assist them. These small rewards were significant in the eyes of an impressionable youth with very few opportunities to travel, since my parents never owned an automobile. In fact, so influential were these interactions with priests that as I progressed through middle school, the thought of joining seminary became an increasingly important goal.

Another factor that preconditioned my thinking and reaction to the Viet Nam war was a strong desire to conform to the demands of the dominant society and, thereby, to achieve my share of the American Dream. This desire manifested itself in my attempts to do everything right, which meant White. My accomplishments as a class officer throughout my high school years, including student body president, a high grade point average, perfect school attendance, and flawless obedience weren't sufficient evidence of my desired assimilation into the mainstream. I also engaged in a silent, inner rejection of who I was culturally and ethnically. This occurred despite an overall positive family experience. My extended family relations throughout my young life had provided me with every opportunity to be proud of my heritage. Huge family reunions occurred regularly at family ranches and in town and were always occasions for youthful joy and sharing of family culture and history. Yet, in the context of my most important relations with mainstream society, I engaged in self-deception and denial that created the basis of several years of inner confusion over my ethnic identity. The selective reclaiming of aspects of this fractured and distorted identity is a critical component of the process of rehumanization through continuous re-creation and actualization of the self.

As I reflect on this experience today, I can see a trend of mental conditioning, provided by yet another set of authoritarian male figures, that is, my athletic coaches in high school and college. I was a four-sport letterman athlete who tended to establish close ties with coaches, not necessarily because there was bonding based on mentorship and friendship, but rather because I had a built-in conditioning to obtain their approval. Later, I was a member of the University of Colorado baseball team and I found in my coach's personality a close approximation of my father. Typically, coaches yell and demand conformity and obedience, and behind my relations with them were reflections of both my father and Catholic clergy.

Later, in the military, I found myself in company with superiors who shared many character traits and behaviors that were a smooth continuation of the authoritarianism, paternalism, and patriarchy of previous male figures in my life. Company commanders and platoon leaders, in their efforts to make a 'real soldier' out of me, carried the authoritarian character of my training to new levels, especially by adding a thoroughly sexist and homophobic aspect to my military experience. Orders yelled into one's face were frequently fraught with female sexual innuendo. The blatant and ugly misogyny was personally revolting since such trash talk had not been a part of my upbringing. I could not even remotely associate the negative stereotyping of women by company commanders to my experiences with female members of my maternal extended family who were not only nurturing but also strong women. Yet, my motivation to "do my job" properly and to do it effectively kept me definitively within the culture of silence and earned me accolades, much as in the past. In fact, such was my performance as a soldier that I was awarded the "American Spirit Award", the top award in my battalion. This was consistent with previous rewards for silence and obedience, such as the stack of holy pictures that I earned while studiously reciting prayers and other forms of Catholic indoctrination as rote memory exercises in middle school.

Gross assumptions about women as human beings and as members of society are part of the "archetypal drama of patriarchy" (Abalos 2002:53), an overarching way of life in which female stereotypes are deemed not only to exist in the real world but that they are determined to be true for all time. Thus, in the context of training men to become part of a project of military violence, a cog in the killing machine, they are taught not to question or doubt these eternal truths. "Their sense of justice is perverted to become the enforcement of revealed dogma. The cost they pay is the repression of the personal, political, historical, and sacred faces of their being" (ibid). As a result, they also suffer further fractionization of their personal selves. Rampant sexism in the military experience helped plant some of the seeds of transformation in my personal being.

Racism within the military is another archetypal structure that is rooted in stereotypes and perceptions of immutable hierarchies of human relations. I quickly became aware of the close correlations between rank, ratings, and race. Racial epithets of one kind or another abounded in casual talk and were shocking given the subtleties of the racism that had been a part of my youth. In the military, as in society at large, Blacks and Latinos were prominently in ratings or occupations that required little education or skills. For example, they were visible in the 'deck force' whose primary duties were to incessantly wield a chipping hammer, sand paper, and paint in a never-ending effort to maintain a rust-free appearance of the ship. The ranks of military brass was devoid of people of color. The treatment of Filipino personnel was particularly galling. They were permitted entry into few ratings and served most prominently as cooks and servants of military brass. They were blatantly segregated from other sailors and "f*****g Huks" was a common phrase hurled at Filipinos without much thought, although with plenty of malice. I never realized until much later that this epithet referred to members of a communist insurgency during the early 20th century in which Filipinos tried to expel the colonizing U.S. military forces from the Philippines following the appropriation of their independence movement against the Spanish.

I was particularly sensitized to intersections of racism and sexism in the port cities where soldiers and sailors went for RandR (rest and relaxation) after months on the gunline. These included the Philippines, Thailand, Japan, and Hong Kong. Testosterone-laced gossip about sexual exploits in different ports dominated conversations as "beach-time" approached. Comparisons of sexuality of women from different Third World countries were frequent and there seemed to be a consensus among many that the "little brown f*****g machines" of the Philippines were the best. Racism and misogyny were constant companions in the minds of the good military man.

In my previous experience, I had learned little about the insidiousness of racism and sexism, although I had numerous experiences that taught me that they existed. Because much of my youth was spent in close proximity with family and immediate neighbors, I had a refuge which shielded me from the deleterious effects of racism. Yet the contradictory messages regarding obedience, individual achievement, and success pushed me to overlook the negative messages that conflicted so strongly with family morals.

Despite the tendency for me to accommodate to the circumstances in which I was living in the military, there was one specific incident that forced me to think differently and to begin to evaluate more critically the paths that I was treading. This event occurred during an evening of revelry after spending more than forty days under stressful conditions in the I-Corp area near the demilitarized zone bordering North Viet Nam. Getting "on the beach" after such an ordeal typically meant bars, boozing to excess, and prostitutes. However, that particular night included a heavy political debate among a group of friends. One individual who became frustrated with his inability to out-duel me with words suddenly rose to his feet and yelled various unsavory epithets directly at me, and then punctuated his diatribe with "You f*****g gook!"

I had been stung by previous racist incidents in my life but this one was particularly biting in that "f*****g gooks" were the people that we were all trained to dehumanize and to kill. It was the unpredictable "gooks" whose little reed sampans we shot out of the water with 5-inch guns and proudly painted symbolic representations of another "confirmed kill" on the door of the communications command center. These were constant reminders that those little nameless men out fishing in the early morning to feed their families were threats to democracy and "our" way of life. It was the faceless "gooks" whose land and rice fields we pock-marked with over 2 million tons of bombs dropped courageously from B-52s at 30,000 feet or from fighter jets strafing hot spots. It was the black pajama-clad "gooks" whose villages and forests we laced with Agent Orange in order to expose a stubborn and invisible enemy. It was the ageless and sexless "gooks" whose skin we burned with napalm and maimed with wicked but smart technology that we euphemistically called "daisy cutters." It was stupid "gook" peasants who we could see toiling in their fields but who had no capacity to feel the pangs of human hunger and poverty. It was the stealthy and untrustworthy "gooks" whose capacity for resistance required "scorched earth" and "low intensity conflict" strategies in order to drain a metaphorical sea in which a people's resistance found succor. It was the voiceless "gooks" that we dehumanized in so many ways that their human worth became far less valuable than the time and effort, money and munitions that it took to incinerate and wipe them from the face of the earth. They were not Vietnamese children, women, and men with capacities to feel or express universal human emotions of love, grief, anger, desperation, and resistance. They were simply communist "gooks" who were a threat to someone else's national security interests.

Yet, in one brief moment of frustration, my angry friend placed me in the same category of devalued humanity into which we all had placed the Vietnamese and toward whom we all felt superior. This one flash of verbal violence stuffed me into a box of undesireables worthy of annihilation. I was transformed suddenly into an Object for dehumanization, ironically in the very presence of friends and co-combatants. I and the enemy became one and the same. This one seemingly insignificant incident brought together all of the negative social forces that had conditioned my thinking and behavior to that moment. I became a Vietnamese, a "gook" with no capacity to feel the sting of racism. I became the stereotype of everything the military mind believed Filipino, Japanese, Chinese, and Thai women to be. I became an Object within which all of the fractionated selves created by my past, molded by patriarchy, sexism, racism, homophobia, and classism, suddenly and unexpectedly clashed and violently shook both mind and body. Most importantly, I not only heard the stinging words that embodied my past, but also felt them in ways that I never had before.

From that moment on, I began to think more deeply about what such phrases as "all my relations" and "brothers under the skin" really meant. I was forced to realize that as a newly defined Other, I began to see my own mother, sisters, and other family members in the faces of "the enemy" and that we shared very basic human qualities and capacities. I had been violently shaken into the realization that poor people whose lifeways were different from those of an invading force had basic human needs and sensitivities to the environment and the world around them that were indeed shared with others. Importantly, I began to see the incongruities between stereotypes of the Other and the realities that people living in poverty embodied and lived on a daily basis.

The reality was that I and my own extended family, shared much with many Southeast Asian peoples who were the Objects of our dehumanization and aggression. My family, with deep Indigenous roots in the lands of the Southwestern U.S., had itself undergone various conquests by invading forces and colonization by newcomers who espoused strong notions of superiority and an imagined sense of providential guidance that made territorial expansion an inevitable consequence of their own destiny and progress. We also had experienced impoverishment, economic and political marginalization, and the expropriation of communal lands that are critical in subsistence-oriented economies. Sharing a common history in a different hemisphere, I in fact had suddenly become the enemy. Perhaps I had been all along.

COLONIALISM, CAPITALISM, AND IMPERIALISM

The previous discussion focuses on forms of oppression and reveals factors of dehumanization that occur primarily at personal levels. Finally, I must identify an additional overarching historical forces that, in similar fashion, condition human minds to accept and accommodate to the supposedly inevitable violence in human relations. While completing graduate studies at the University of Wisconsin, Madison, I came to appreciate the historical roles of colonialism, capitalism, and imperialism in the relationships among hegemonic powers and their subjects. These were critical years in the development of my understanding of world events and how the current hierarchies of global power were constructed. Interdisciplinary courses in history, political economy, sociology and anthropology provided me with a theoretical basis for understanding the contexts in which capitalist competition has operated for centuries, enriching relatively few countries and retarding the development of many peripheral ones.

Colonialism, in both its direct and indirect applications, set the stage for destruction of subsistence-oriented economies through the expropriation of land and resources. It became the principal mechanism for the rapacious extraction of raw materials that fueled the industrialization of the current global hegemons and gave impulse to the second important phase in the development of capitalism. In the process, it also created the violent ideological and physical modes for the systematic racialization, dehumanization, and subsequent brutal exploitation of the diverse peoples of most global societies.

Classic colonialism represents the early stages of the rise of capitalism which required that all the resources of the world, including human beings, be commodified and thrown into a common pool. Many matrilineal indigenous societies, in which kinship systems were determined through the female line of descent, and through which property and land was maintained in the hands of women, were forceably transformed into patriarchal ones which favored male prerogatives. Capitalism, thus, is an inherently violent and undemocratic system that creates hierarchies of power in order to function efficiently and condemns the vast majority of peoples and societies of the world to largely unremunerated sources of grossly cheap resources and human labor. Historically, this has been accomplished by the hegemons of power by any means necessary.

Gaining an understanding of these concepts within a framework of social theory provided a means through which I could appreciate why it was that the U.S. attempted to do what it did in Viet Nam. I also understood that nations with imperialist interests are loathe to use such concepts in their communications with their own people and the world. In fact, the hegemon desires to control the nature of discourse in order to explain and justify its actions by controlling modes of thinking and thereby manufacturing popular consent. Thus, notions of democracy, national interests, freedom, liberty, and Western civilization tend to be counterposed to their perceived polar opposites, such as communism, totalitarianism, godlessness, and state control. With the collaboration of corporate-controlled media, whose economic interests overlap significantly with those of the U.S. military-industrial complex, the basis is set for the ideological dovetailing of image fabrication and justifications for military interventionism. Regardless, in no case is there any serious discussion of social justice, despite the fact that issues of peace and justice are integrally intertwined (Barash:5ff).

My intention here is not to expound on the roles of each of the factors mentioned above in the U.S. war against the Vietnamese people. Suffice it to say that, contrary to its ideological positions, the U.S. has demonstrated for over a century an imperialistic view and a perceived self importance in the western Pacific that in country after country, it has intervened on behalf of its own national and capitalistic interests. In the process it has destroyed legitimate democratic movements through its choice of bringing to power and supporting despotic dictators such as Ngo Dinh Diem in Vietnam, Ferdinand Marcos in the Philippines, and Suharto in Indonesia. Prior to the rise of these dictatorial regimes, the imperialistic competition between the U.S. and Japan over China, Korea, and the Philippines triggered a chain of events that led to supposed 'surprise attack' at Pearl Harbor. A more objective and historical analysis of the U.S. conflict with the Japanese would reveal that the issues leading to war were not based on ideological matters of democracy and fascism. Rather, it was a conflict between imperial powers seeking domination over other countries in the region (Bello 1992:11).

Similarly, the Vietnamese, in seeking to free themselves of French colonial domination, found themselves in an imperialistic struggle among the three behemoths of China, the USSR, and the U.S. The unfortunate consequence for the Vietnamese people, impoverished by French colonialism, was as the old Malay saying stipulates: "When the elephants clash, the grass gets trampled." An understanding of the concepts of colonialism, capitalism, and imperialism proved tremendously useful in demystifying the complex social forces that led to the horrific destruction of people, environment, and resources not only of Viet Nam but also the trampling of neighboring countries of Laos and Cambodia who were drawn into the conflict.

PRAXIS AND PEACE ACTIVISM

In the post-Viet Nam period, the U.S. has engaged in many demonstrations of its militaristic and covert interventionist tendencies in many regions of the world, including the Latin American and Caribbean countries of Grenada, Jamaica, Cuba, El Salvador, Guatemala, Nicaragua, Honduras, Venezuela, and Colombia, to name only a few. These gave me many opportunities to test my own theoretical conclusions about U.S. aggression on a global basis. Importantly, confirmation of the roles of capitalist and imperialist interests and competition in U.S. wars led to my committed participation in community activism. As Freire (1970) suggested, one must take responsibility not only for one's own education but also for its application through dialogics and humanist (as contrasted with humanitarian) action. This is a vital part of the long-term commitment to the "ontological vocation" of rehumanization.

During the 1980s, U.S. hostilities against the tiny nation of El Salvador, where Ronald Reagan decided to "draw the line on communism," provided a watershed of experiences that allowed me to appropriate lessons from Viet Nam and to understand and apply them amongst Salvadorans, the new dehumanized Other. In a densely populated, agrarian nation where land is desperately needed by small farmers to satisfy their basic human needs, right-wing government despots were put in power through fraudulent demonstration elections to cater to the needs of transnational corporations such as Anderson Clayton, Hills Brothers Coffee, and capitalist cattle ranching firms. Their control of vast portions of the country for export production led to the formation of armed insurgencies that sought to amplify the silenced voice of millions of people with legitimate demands for land and also to defend their constitutional rights against state-sponsored terror.

Some of these conditions brought back distant memories of Viet Nam. In fact, some of the same people from the U.S. Agency for International Development who developed the land reform program to quell the revolutionary fervor of Vietnamese peasant farmers were assigned the same task in El Salvador. The same scorched earth policies and "low intensity warfare" tactics applied in Viet Nam were taught to Salvadoran military brass at the infamous School of the Americas at Fort Benning, Georgia. Also, to hide the role of the Salvadoran government in over 90% of the deaths and disappearances of more than 75,000 people, the government created externally-funded, private paramilitary death squads to carry out brutal terrorist atrocities. The brutality encouraged by the U.S. government in El Salvador was meant to overwhelm the Salvadoran resistance and to destroy the ghost of its humiliating defeat by a similarly determined people in Viet Nam.

I focused most of my efforts in solidarity with the Salvadoran people in collaboration with grass-roots and interfaith organizations in the U.S. But I also engaged in solidarity work with corresponding groups in Guatemala and Nicaragua where also during the 1980s the U.S. government was aiming to destroy the guerrilla insurgencies in the former and to overthrow the Sandinista government in the latter. My contributions, for the most part, consisted of community education presentations and fund raising. But I also participated in anti-interventionist demonstrations in the Baltimore-Washington area where I was living at the time. Anti-war activities in Washington, DC brought me many times in close proximity to the many monuments to U.S. capitalism and its heroes. I have also trod within a short distance of the Viet Nam War Memorial but, as with the many Hollywood films on that brutal war, I have chosen not to lay eyes on any of them. This monument, whose original intention created by its Asian designer was one of human compassion and remembrance, has been distorted by many to conform to and condone U.S. militarist and imperialist aims.

Additional efforts against U.S. militarism took me to Honduras to accompany Salvadoran refugees at Mesa Grande who were forced to flee the scorched earth devastation of their villages, fields, livestock, and livelihoods. I had learned much about low intensity conflict when my family in Baltimore hosted a peasant farmer who had brought his nine-year-old son from Mesa Grande for eye surgery. In Honduras, I heard many stories from traumatized individuals that put a human face on violence and suffering that I didn't have the capacity to fully appreciate in Viet Nam. I witnessed meetings and difficult debates among refugees who were organizing for a possible return to their bombed-out villages in the face of military repression and failing U.N. assistance "since our children and we are dying here anyway in a foreign land." Interestingly, the organizing and community empowerment efforts among the refugees were based on Paulo Freire's book *Pedagogy of the Oppressed* which I had been using in my own transformational experience. Some of our own stories from our internationalist perspective at Mesa Grande are documented in a book which we collectively wrote called *Going Home: The Story of Repatriation in El Salvador* (1992).

On other occasions, I helped maintain an international presence, complete with video cameras and other technology, to provide human shields against repression when some of the refugees decided to return to what was left of "home" in Chalatenango province in El Salvador. On one occasion, I spoke with a single mother whom I had met previously at Mesa Grande. She had a family of four who was divided in their decision to go home. She conceded to her daughter's wishes and embarked on the long walk home. Through tears she described how, just a week before my arrival in her village, a battle broke out between military and the guerrilla defenders of the villagers. The women and children rushed into the brick building which they had constructed not only for daily use of a power-driven maize grinder housed there, but also as a shelter in the event of danger. Two of her children were among several killed and she was wounded by shrapnel as a soldier directed mortar fire into the building from a hovering helicopter. She showed me pieces of flesh and brains stuck on the brick walls. Then she led me outside where she picked up a large piece of jagged shrapnel and pointed angrily to the yellow-on-green writing that said "Made in the USA."

At the sight of this action, I recall thinking immediately back to 1967 about a close military friend to whose aid I had rushed early one morning after a huge explosion near our base camp. I found him along with two others lying among some trees when he weakly called out for help. He had bad shrapnel wounds on his thigh and chest and I was traumatized by the sight of fatty tissue oozing through his dust-covered khaki uniform. I remembered the anger that I felt after he died. And that day in El Salvador, in a remote peasant village, I was able to empathize more closely than the average internationalist present with the anger expressed by this woman when she said, "Take a picture of this and when you go home, I want you to tell the truth to your fellow Americans about your government's actions here in my country."

These heart-felt words, despite the special circumstances in which they were spoken, are not unique. I have subsequently visited or worked in rural villages in Guatemala, Cuba, and in three different states in Mexico, and their messages have had a common thread. My professional work has involved primarily rural and Indigenous villages and, without exception, I have been deeply impressed by the kindness with which I as an internationalist has been welcomed into many a humble home. I have been even more impressed by their capacity to make an important distinction between citizens of the U.S. and the actions of their governments whose successive leaders are oftentimes undistinguishable in their militaristic objectives. More often, I'm puzzled by this capacity for understanding given that U.S. citizens seem incapable of seeking alternatives to their seriously flawed political system in which corporate money rather than people have control, not only over U.S. society but globally. These factors and the words of people such as the Salvadoran woman have deepened my commitment to social justice, to peace, and to the continuing ontological vocation of conscientization, liberation, and personal transformation.

REFERENCES

Abalos, David T. 2002. *The Latino Male: a Radical Redefinition*. Boulder: Lynn Rienner.
Barash, Paul. 1999. *Peace Studies*.
Bello, Walden. 1992. *People and Power in the Pacific*. San Francisco: Pluto Press.
Freire, Paulo. 1997 (1970). *Pedagogy of the Oppressed*. New York: Continuum Press.
Lorde, Audre. 1980. *The Cancer Journals*.
Rich, Adrienne. *1979. On Lies, Secrets and Silence*. New York: Norton.

In: Religion, Terrorism and Globalization
Editor: K.K. Kuriakose, pp.157-172

ISBN 1-59454-553-7
© 2006 Nova Science Publishers, Inc.

Chapter 10

"MAINTAINING HARMONY AND KEEPING THE PEACE:" NONVIOLENCE AND CONFLICT RESOLUTIONS IN NATIVE AMERICAN TRADITIONAL SYSTEMS OF JUSTICE

Charlotte Coté
University of Washington, Seattle, WA

There are rules in every society built on traditions and customs that regulate the behavior of its citizens. These rules became laws for each individual member of that society to abide by. When Europeans came to the "New World" (United States) they brought their own bodies of written or codified laws with them. Indigenous nations, the newcomers believed, did not have laws, only "barbaric customs and institutions,"[1] and a myth was developed that Indians had no law. This myth was reinforced to conquer and colonize indigenous nations and bring them under colonial rule and law.

Contrary to the "Indians have no law" myth indigenous nations living in North America had their own bodies of laws based on customs and beliefs that were passed down through their oral traditions. Their understanding of law and justice came from their philosophic understanding of the world. Their belief system recognized that confrontation and force were not needed to keep the peace. Indigenous societies had no concept of prisons, no police officers, and no legal institutions built on punishment and imprisonment. As a result, how crime was dealt with in indigenous law contrasted greatly with Euro-American concepts of law that focused on penalties, punishment, and incarceration.

In this article I will discuss indigenous ways of keeping peace and resolving conflicts and disputes in Indian communities through non-violent means, in contrast to American laws centered on force and physical oppression. I will also examine how tribes are revitalizing their justice systems today, returning to traditional peaceful ways in order to restore harmony, balance, and unity within their respective societies.

---

[1] Robert Yazzie, "Traditional Indian Law," *Tribal Court Record*, Special Edition, Vol.9, No.1, Spring/Summer, 1996, 8.

THE COLONIZATION OF THE INDIGENOUS POPULATIONS

The indigenous populations in what is now called the United States existed as separate and sovereign peoples long before this territory became a country. It has been estimated that there were between 80-100 million native people living here at the time of contact.

Today, there are over 562 recognized tribes and an estimated two and a half million Native Americans, including Alaska Natives, living in the United States today. Indians represent 0.9 percent of the total U.S. population.

In the early contact period the British colonial powers in North America recognized the sovereignty of Indian nations and entered into treaties with them as set out in the British *Royal Proclamation of 1763*. In the British Proclamation King George asserted that the several "nations" of Indians should be dealt with on a "nation to nation" level and that land "purchased" from them would be done through agreements (treaties) between the colonial powers and the tribes on a nation-to-nation basis.

The Royal Proclamation was designed to retain native goodwill by establishing a boundary between their lands and those of the whites. It enunciated the principle that Indian lands could be surrendered only to the Crown and for compensation in each instance. It "tacitly acknowledged aboriginal land title" and suggested procedures of surrender that were later incorporated into the treaty system.[2]

During the 17th century British and Spanish colonialists negotiated treaties with the Indian tribes in North America recognizing their sovereign status. These treaties also recognized tribe's ownership and occupation of the lands on which they resided. As the United States began to assert its domination over these lands, it continued the European practice of treaty-making with Indian tribes. The early treaties signed with the native tribes focused on establishing peace and friendship between the two parties. Before the War of 1812 the United States and the Indian tribes negotiated treaties as relative equals. The treaties were mutually beneficial. The United States acquired land and peace from the Indians in exchange for goods and services provided by the federal government. Under the U.S. Constitution, treaties with Indian tribes were as legally binding as agreements with other nations. But many of the treaties were broken as the increasing numbers of settlers entered lands reserved for the Indians.

After the War of 1812, which ended the threat of the British intervention in the U.S. internal affairs, friendship with Indians became less valuable. The United States was more concerned with Indian lands, which in many cases were taken by force. Indian treaties after the War of 1812 were rarely voluntary. These land cession treaties had two main provisions: first, Indians would relinquish land to the United States, and second, the United States would establish reservations for them to live on and that would be protected by the federal government. Some treaties promised Indians specific goods and services. The treaties declared that Indians could live on these reservation lands forever, hence the saying "as long as the water flows, or grass grows, or sun rises."[3] However, to this date, the United States has not fulfilled all the obligations in any of the treaties that have been ratified with Indian tribes.

---

[2] Brian E. Titley. *A Narrow Vision. Duncan Campbell Scott and the Administration of Indian Affairs in Canada* (Canada: University of British Columbia Press, 1992), 2.

[3] Sharon O'Brien. *American Indian Tribal Governments* (Norman: University of Oklahoma, 1993), 38.

As the United States asserted its power over this newly formed nation, it began systematically undermining indigenous political, economic, social, and spiritual systems.

Disease epidemics spread rapidly throughout the indigenous populations in the early contact period and weakened them making it easier for the new colonial governments to exercise control over the indigenous groups. Gibson notes how the smallpox disease, which decimated Indian societies because of its ability to spread quickly, "terrified the Indians."[4] Because of this fear and lack of understanding of the disease Indians became more susceptible to missionaries and government control, that is, to those individuals who were able to "cure" the disease with their medicines.[5] This also caused some indigenous people to doubt their own medicine people, undermining their own spiritual systems.

As Anglo settlement increased and spread across the United States the federal government began establishing policies to control and administer the indigenous population. Following the treaty process the U.S. government began setting up reservations for Indian tribes to keep them segregated from the white population. U.S. administrators envisioned reservations as holding tanks or assimilation centers where indigenous belief systems would ultimately be destroyed and Indians would eventually submit to Anglo values and culture. As federal administration over the Indian people increased, government employees were placed on each reservation, whereby the main job of these Indian Agents was to transform the tribal community into such that could eventually be integrated into American society.

Segregated onto these reservation lands native people were taught to read and write English, understand and accept Christianity, and develop the skills necessary to become small-scale farmers. The "Indian" represented to Anglo society what life was like in a natural or savage state. To bring indigenous people out of this state of barbarism they were to be "civilized" and "christianized," and, ultimately, colonized.

One of the key areas in the colonization process is the establishment of an education system to control and assimilate the "subordinate" cultures into the higher culture. The purpose of Western education instituted around the world was to make people useful in this new capitalist hierarchy of perpetual Eurocentric domination.[6] In his book *Pedagogy of the Oppressed,* Paulo Freire studies the effects of colonization on the groups being colonized. In his theory of antidialogical action, Freire states that "the invaders penetrate the cultural context of another group, in disrespect of the latter's potentialities; they impose their own view of the world upon those they invade and inhibit the creativity of the invading by curbing their expression."[7]

The U.S. policy of assimilation for Indian people was strengthened through a strictly enforced educational system. By 1874, attendance at government run schools was made compulsory. In 1879 the system of Indian Boarding Schools was established and Indian children, from ages five to fifteen, were removed from their homes and villages and forced to live in these boarding schools for ten to twelve months per year. It was here where indigenous people began their forced indoctrination in the Anglo language and value system with instruction based on individualism, competition, and a belief in the Christian faith. These schools were maintained through a very militaristic regime, where Indian children lived under

---

[4] James Gibson, "Small pox on the Northwest Coast: 1835-1838," *BC Studies*, No.5, 1982-83, 66.
[5] Gibson, 66.
[6] Jorge Noriega, "American Indian Education in the United States: Indoctrination for Subordination to Colonialism," in *The State of Native America*, ed. by Annette Jaimes (South End Press, 1992), 374.
[7] Paulo Freire, *Pedagogy of the Oppressed* (New York: The Continuum Publishing Company, 1994), 133.

unsanitary living conditions, were fed a poor diet, and educated by an inadequate curriculum. School administrators' racist notions of Indian culture and traditions further undermined tribal cultural values, as tribal languages and traditions were forbidden at schools.

Indigenous laws and customs were further destabilized as federal laws were enacted that destroyed indigenous governing systems, banned Indian religious ceremonies, prohibited traditional marriages, and imposed a western style of housing that encouraged a nuclear family unit and weakened the extended family system – thus, Indian tribes effectively came under the U.S. government control.

Indian peoples were not willing participants in this colonization process and tribes continually fought to hold onto their traditional way of life. Resulting constant clashes with the newcomers moving onto tribal lands frequently escalated local Indian-White wars. In the early contact period colonial governments established laws in an attempt to keep peace and order, especially between the new colonial settlers and the native people. These laws were utilized by the colonies and set the framework for the U.S. law. Eventually, these laws were extended over Indians and their lands as the United States instituted policies that ultimately undermined tribal authority over crimes committed on tribal lands.

The federal government began testing the limits to Indian sovereignty and various court cases emerged that both supported and challenged Indian tribes rights and jurisdiction over their lands and people. In the early 1800s the U.S. Supreme Court ruled in two significant court cases, *Cherokee Nation v. Georgia* (1831) and *Worcester v. Georgia* (1832), that Indian tribes possessed a nationhood status and retained inherent powers of self-government.[8] These rulings clearly recognized and affirmed Indian tribe's authority over Indian people on Indian lands.

Tribal jurisdiction over crimes occurring on Indian lands by Indians against Indians was upheld in the 1883 court case *Ex parte Crow Dog*. This case arose on Indian land and involved a Lakota Indian man, Crow Dog, who killed a fellow tribal member, Spotted Tail. The two men's tribes, the Brule Sioux, resolved this issued by utilizing traditional methods of dispute resolution that "required Crow Dog to provide restitution to Spotted Tail's family in the form of goods and provisions. Although the victim's family was satisfied with the resolution, in the eyes of the federal government, the tribal approach to justice did not inflict what it thought was appropriate punishment."[9]

U.S. officials placed Crow Dog in custody and charged him for murder. Crow Dog fought the conviction arguing that the U.S. courts had no jurisdiction over him and that he should be released from jail. The U.S. Supreme Court agreed with Crow Dog and ruled that since tribes were self-governing the offense should be handled by the Brule Sioux tribe. U.S. government officials were upset with this court ruling and two years later Congress passed the *Major Crimes Act* which transferred to the federal government criminal jurisdiction over seven major crimes committed by Indian on *Indian reservations, whether the victim was an Indian or non-Indian.*[10] The *Major Crimes Act* (1885) undermined tribal sovereignty by extending U.S. criminal jurisdiction over Indians and their lands.

---

[8] See David H. Getches et al, *Federal Indian Law. Cases and Materials*, 3rd edition (Minnesota: West Publishing Co.,1993), 131-155.
[9] "Tribal Court History," National Tribal Justice Research Center, internet article, www.tribalresourcecenter.org/ tribalcourts/history.asp
[10] William Canby, *American Indian Law* (Minnesota: West Publishing Co.), 104-105, 1998.

The constitutionality of the *Major Crimes Act* was tested the following year in the court case *United States v Kagama* (1886). Two Indian men were charged with murder of another Indian man in the Indian reservation. In *Kagama* the court ruled that the *Major Crimes Act* extended federal criminal jurisdiction over Indians committing major crimes on Indian lands.[11]

The U.S. government also established the "Court of Indian Offenses" in 1883, which was given jurisdiction over the less serious criminal offenses occurring in the Indian reservations. Tribal members where appointed as judges who resolved disputes between tribal members through the application of federal law and regulations. In some ways these courts benefited the tribes with judges being the members of the tribes who understood the customs of their people. The new courts, however, had the negative effect of pushing aside tribal law and justice based on restitution and retribution in favor of a more Euro-American notion of law based on punishment and imprisonment.[12]

These courts enforced the "Code of Federal Regulations" that was basically written to "civilize" and assimilate Indians into the mainstream U.S. society. Under the code, tribal ceremonies and traditions (such as the West Coast potlatch and Plains Indian Sun Dance) became criminal acts punishable by fines, loss of rations, or imprisonment. As Jackson notes,

> Far from being an instrument of self-determination, [the Courts of Indian Offenses] were conceived as an adjunct to the process of cultural assimilation. The establishment of these courts was part of the concerted effort to outlaw traditional cultural institutions, eliminate plural marriages, weaken the influence of the medicine men, promote law and order, civilize the Indians and teach them respect for private property by breaking up tribal land holdings into individual allotments. ... Customary law was ignored or outlawed as it represented a way of life that the court was designed to destroy.13

Indigenous people's understanding of law and justice was antithetical to the western concept of what constituted a crime and how the wrongdoing should be dealt with. In the United States the government is responsible for dealing with crime and the prescribed punishment. Central to this legal philosophy is that the individual criminal should feel the community's outrage over his or her crime. The punishments derived from this law came in the form of fines, public whippings, imprisonment, and death.[14] In indigenous societies laws are not made by an institution such as a legislative body but by the normative power of the entire society. Indigenous justice systems are centered on a holistic philosophy. Law is not an aspect of life, it is life itself, and therefore, justice is a central element of the life process. I will now discuss indigenous concepts of peace and justice.

---

[11] Getches et al, 185-187.

[12] O'Brien, 203.

[13] Michael Jackson, "In Search of the Pathways to Justice: Alternative Dispute Resolutions in Aboriginal Communities," *University of British Columbia Law Review* (special edition), 1992, 227.

[14] Larry Skogen, *Indian Depredation Claims: 1796-1920* (Norman: University of Oklahoma Press, 1996), 7.

INDIGENOUS CONCEPTS OF PEACE AND JUSTICE

The notion of peace and harmony is a constant theme in indigenous philosophies and world views. In his article, "Traditional law ways and the Spirit World," Rennard Strickland asserts that in the Cherokee worldview, law was the earthly representation of a divine spirit order. He says that the Cherokee did not think of law as a set of civil or secular rules limiting or requiring actions on their part. Public consensus and harmony rather than confrontation and dispute, were essential elements of Cherokee worldview, these reflected in their concepts of law and justice.[15] Strickland stresses that to Indian people, "Law is organic. Law speaks a language that reflects the ways of the people... Thus law is to Native Americans a part of a larger world view, an embodiment of a relationship of Earth and her people, a command from the spirit world."[16]

Establishing and maintaining peace was the central guiding principle of many indigenous nations in North America. One of the most well known indigenous governing systems is that of the Iroquois or Haudenosaunee people, the "People of the Longhouse." The Iroquois League or Confederacy was established between 1000 and 1500 A.D. when five indigenous nations came together (Mohawk, Oneida, Onondaga, Cayuga, and Seneca, and the sixth group, Tuscarora, joined in the early 1700s) to form a political alliance. It became one of the most powerful and most democratic Indian governing systems in North America. They lived in what is now upstate New York and Eastern Canada.

The government of the Haundenosaunee people is called "The Great Peace" and is still in existence today. It is founded on the five main principles: freedom, respect, tolerance, consensus, and brotherhood. "These values contrasted sharply with the principles that underlay European governments of the same time. In the 1500s, European governments were based on notions such as authoritarian rule by monarchs and the use of force and coercion to bring about unquestioning obedience."[17]

The Haudenosaunee resolved conflicts through the People's Council known as the Council of Fifty. Their Confederacy was established under democratic ideals and principles, based on equal suffrage, where both men and women solved community conflicts through consensus and diplomacy in an effort to maintain peace. Strong emphasis was placed on checks and balances, public debate, and consensus, with the ultimate goal that peace and unity be continually strengthened and maintained. Many scholars believe that the development of the U.S. government as it exists today was influenced by the Iroquois Confederacy.

In his book, Peace, *Power and Righteousness*, Kanien'kehaka (Mohawk) scholar Taiaiake Alfred, discusses the philosophies of the Confederacy and of his people the Kanien'kehaka (Mohawk) and how these principles that guided his ancestors can be utilized today. Alfred stresses the importance of native communities to return to their traditional values as a way for native people to move beyond their 500 year history of pain, loss and colonization. He believes that only a solid grounding in traditional values and principles of consensus-based

---

[15] Rennard Strickland, "Traditional Law Ways and the Spirit World," in *Fire and the Spirits* (University of Oklahoma Press, 1975), 10.

[16] Rennard Strickland, "The Eagle's Empire. Sovereignty, Survival, and Self-Governance in Native American Law and Constitutionalism," in *Studying Native America. Problems and Prospects*, Russell Thornton ed. (Madison: University of Wisconsin Press, 1998), 251.

[17] O'Brien, 18.

governance will enable native communities to heal their present divisions, resist assimilation, and forge new relationships of respect and equality with mainstream society.[18]

As Alfred discusses, the philosophy of his people was based on three principles: peace, power, and righteousness. Peace: that people must stay on the path to peace at all times. Power: that power must be maintained and that the tribal leaders must keep their hearts filled with peace and goodwill. Righteousness: that leaders must be good to all people and that their decisions must always be morally righteous.[19] The words of the great Mohawk prophet Deganwidah, who influenced the development of the "Great Peace," are still important to the Haudensaunee people and continue to guide their societies.

We bind ourselves together, for many purposes, members of one family, by taking hold of each other's hands so firmly and forming a circle so strong that if a tree should fall upon it, it would not shake nor break it, so that our people and grandchildren shall remain in the circle of security, peace, and happiness. Our strength shall be in union and our way the way of reason, righteousness, and peace.[20]

INDIGENOUS WOMEN

Indigenous societies were based on an egalitarian social system that provided indigenous women with considerable political, economic, social and spiritual power. Law, in the Western sense, was made and controlled by men who determined what would be defined as a crime and what type of punishment would be given to a person who was deemed a criminal. In Indigenous societies both men and women had the authority to determine what constituted a crime and what type of action would be taken if someone within the tribal community was guilty of a wrongdoing. For example, Strickland explains how women were an integral part of the traditional justice system in the traditional Cherokee society and "constituted a special class in the operation of Cherokee laws."[21]

In Cherokee political organization women were designated a special role as War Women. War women served in a position similar to judges, determining the fate of the captives and the prisoners caught during the warfare. Cherokee women also oversaw offenses that were made to other Cherokee women. "Women were granted the right to enforce these regulations, especially those relating to the obligations of widowhood and adultery."[22]

In the Haudenosaunee (Iroquois) Confederacy women were not eligible for seats on the Council of Fifty, but they did hold considerable power within the Iroquois League. The Iroquois were matrilineal, meaning that descent and property passed through the female line, thus giving Haudenosaunee women much political, social, and economic power.

The female elders, the clan mothers formed the women's council, which still operates today. The clan mothers were given the political power to nominate the leaders or chiefs of their tribe. The clan mother would do this after consulting with the other women of her clan. After the clan mother made her selection the entire tribe and Council of Fifty met to confirm

---

[18] Taiaiake Alfred, *Peace, Power and Righteousness. An Indigenous Manifesto* (New York: Oxford University Press, 1999), xi.

[19] Alfred, 97.

[20] Quoted in O'Brien, 18.

[21] Strickland, 26.

[22] Strickland, 26.

it. If the male she selected was very young, the clan mother would take him under her wing, while she served as his surrogate, until he reached the age to take over the position. These clan mothers also had the power to dispose of the leaders if they felt they were not doing their job or were guilty of some misconduct.[23]

In traditional indigenous societies Indian women had complete control over their lives and their bodies. In these tribal communities men, women, and children were viewed and respected as autonomous beings with the extended family or clan binding individuals together within a system of mutual obligations and respect.[24] But, while men and women were considered distinct, they also related to each other as complementary equals. The nature of this relationship created an environment that viewed violence toward women as deviant behavior. Because women were the lifegivers, they were greatly valued in their communities. As Strickland notes concerning Cherokee women, because of the deep respect the tribe had for their women, violence against a woman meant violence against the entire community.[25]

In Lakota society a man who battered his wife was considered by the other members of the tribe as irrational and thus could no longer lead a war party, a hunt, or participate in either. His actions were considered improper behavior and he "was thought of as contrary to Lakota law," therefore losing many of life's privileges and many roles open to men in the Lakota society.[26]

Many pre-contact indigenous societies were matrilineal whereby descent and property passed down through the female line. These matrilineages provided Indian women with authority over the tribes' economic production and land holdings. It also gave women authority over their own labor and the products of men's labor as they were the ones who distributed meals.

Consequently, the way male and female roles were traditionally structured made it unlikely for violence against women to occur. It was not until indigenous societies began to fall under colonial rule and a patriarchal and male-dominated social system was imposed on native societies, that violence against Indian women by Indian men started to occur. The dismantling of gender equality coincided with the colonization of Indian people. As Ojibway scholar, Calvin Morrisseau asserts, "from an Anishnabe perspective, striking out against a women is like striking out against everything we hold sacred, our life, our future, our customs, and beliefs, because our women represent the power which is contained within all these concepts. By weakening our women, we are weakening our people."[27]

IS PUNISHMENT NECESSARY FOR LAW?

Chief Justice of the Navajo Nation Robert Yazzie argues that, "Force, coercion and the ability to punish are not necessary to have law."[28] In pre-contact Native American societies justice philosophy and practice were based on healing and reintegrating individuals into their

---

[23] O'Brien, 19-20.

[24] Nancy Shoemaker. *Negotiators of Change* (US: Routledge, 1995), 7.

[25] Strickland, 26.

[26] Gloria Valencia-Weber and Christine Zuni, "Domestic Violence and Tribal Protection of Indigenous Women in the U.S.," *St. John's Law Review*, 69, 1995.

[27] In Kim Anderson, *A Recognition of Being. Reconstructuring Native Womenhood* (Toronto: Second Story Press, 2000), 94.

communities. This was seen as being more important than punishment. Indigenous societies did not have a penal system. Today, many Indian tribes utilize a peacemaking process to bring together victims and offenders in an effort to get to the root of the problem, with the ultimate goal to maintain and restore harmony and balance in their respective communities.[29]

In 1982 the Navajo Nation revived its traditional system of justice by creating its Peacemaker Court that blends the procedures of the Navajo common law with Anglo-American methods of dealing with crime and justice. The courts were established in response to the Navajo people's desire to use tradition and custom to resolve conflicts or disagreements addressed by law. This court system and judges support the longstanding Navajo tradition utilizing tribal headmen and community leaders to mediate and arbitrate local problems.[30]

A form of dealing with crimes or offenses within Indian societies was through mediation. Dispute resolution within a tribe was usually aimed to repair relationships. Repairing these relationships was best accomplished, not by a court or government, but by mediation of a chief, an elder, a clan mother, a medicine man or religious leader, or a respected relative. The idea behind this informal system of justice was to restore harmony and balance into the tribal community. The system of dispute resolution through mediation has been implemented in many tribal courts established in the Indian reservations throughout the United States.[31]

The Navajo justice process is known as hozhooji naat'aanii,[32] or in English, peacemaking, which is "a system of relationships where there is no need for force, coercion, or control." Chief Justice Yazzie says that there are no "good guys" or "bad guys" in this system. When a Navajo is charged with a crime, emphasis is placed not on punishing this person but the focus is on healing and reintegrating this person into the community with the end goal being to nourish relationships between the community members impacted by the offense. In the Navajo justice system the restoration of the society is deemed more important than the punishment of the criminal.[33]

The Navajo concept of justice centers on "hozho," or harmony, and restoring "good relations" within the community. As Mueller explains, "harmony, in the Navajo sense, is more profound than in the sense of its English usage, which denotes an internal calmness or sense of tranquility. The Navajo definition of harmony is closer to a quality of sense of natural and spiritual perfection."[34] The Navajo word "hozho" is often translated as harmony, although as Justice Yazzie points out, the English definition does not convey the deep meaning of the word. Literally, the word means "the perfect state." In the Navajo sense of the word, Yazzie says, it means that "there is a place for everything in reality, and there is hozho or harmony when everything is in its proper place."[35]

---

[28] Robert Yazzie, "Healing as Justice: The American Experience," *Justice as Healing Newsletter*, Spring, 1995.

[29] Laura Mirsky, "Restorative Justice Practices of Native American, First Nation and Other Indigenous People of North American: Part One," *International Institute for Restorative Practices*, April 27, 2004, 1.

[30] James Zion, "The Navajo Peacemaker Court: Deference to the Old and Accommodation to the New, in *American Indian Law Review*, 89 (1983), 89-90.

[31] Robert D. Cooter & Wolfgang Fikentscher, "Indian Common Law: The Role of Custom in American Indian Tribal Courts," *American Journal of Comparative Law*, Volume XLVI, Summer, 1998, N.3, 299.

[32] In Laura Mirsky, 1.

[33] Robert Yazzie, "Life Comes From It," *New Mexico Law Review*, Vol. 24, No.175, Spring, 1994, 179-183.

[34] J.R. Mueller, "Restoring Harmony Through *Nalyeeh*: Can the Navajo Common Law of Torts be Applied in State and Federal Forums" *Tribal Law Journal*, Vol.3, 2002/3, internet article, http:/tlj.unm.edu/articles/volume_2/Mueller/content.php

[35] Yazzie, 1995.

In his book, *The Problem of Justice. Tradition and Law in the Coast Salish World*, Bruce Miller examines the circumstances Native communities such as the Coast Salish people face in the process of revitalizing and reinvigorating their traditional justice systems. Miller says that this focus on traditional ways of administering justice has arisen as a result of three factors: tribes in both the United States and Canada have acknowledged the widespread failure of mainstream courts to appropriately administer justice to Native people; Native people in British Columbia are asserting their right to self-government, and this is part of the process; there is a society-wide interest in reparative justice, that allows the offender to acknowledge the harm done and to repair relations with the victim so that he/she can be reintegrated into his/her native community.[36]

In the Coast Salish world there is a lack of emphasis on guilt, intention, and precedent, connected to their notions of power, illness and control of will. There is an understanding that individuals can do harm to others through their failure to control their thoughts. "This harm can be unintentional or intentional ... and in some cases, a spirit helper or an individual has been said to act on the emotions of its human partner to harm enemies."[37] This explains the "de-emphasis on guilt and intention as guiding principles of justice since one is thought not to be at fault for such harm," as this could be the result of poor upbringing or a "failure to consolidate one's relationship with a spirit helper. Because spiritual power might be exercised inadvertently in some instances, justice practices typically focus on repairing relationships between families rather than punishing the individual."[38]

Traditionally, resolution of conflicts took place in an open forum, during public ceremonies. The emphasis was made on avoidance of conflict through proper training in the absence of coercive authority. Kinship groups were responsible for the behavior of their family members. Damage to a person or to a person's property constituted grounds for compensation. Senior members of the family worked out the details of the compensation. The offender had to leave the society and go through purification rituals that involved ceremonial bathing, cleansing to obtain purity so that he/she would once again become acceptable to his/her society.[39]

In his article "The Reemergence of Tribal Society and Traditional Justice Systems," Chief Judge of the Jicarilla Apache Tribe, Carey Vicenti discusses how the tribal courts have been working hard to reinstate and preserve traditions integral to native societies before Europeans disrupted their traditional life ways and undermined their traditional systems of justice.

> Before contact with non-Indians ever occurred, every tribe had its own institution for resolving problems. A "court," in many cases, never really existed ...even though transgressions against the social order occurred. We Apaches had a context against which the transgression could be read, interpreted, and resolved. We did not centralize all of their remedial powers into one institution. Rather, we would involve different elements of Apache

---

[36] Bruce Miller, *The Problem of Justice. Tradition and Law in the Coast Salish World* (Lincoln: University of Nebraska Press, 2000), 3-4.
[37] Miller, 68.
[38] Miller, 68.
[39] Miller, 64.

society—the chief. the warrior societies. the families. the clan. the medicine man. and so on—in the resolution of the problem.[40]

One of the principles guiding the Apache traditional justice system is the practice of restitution. Restitution, Vicenti says, is "symbolic of the remorse shown by the perpetrator. In the act of offering restitution, there is a transfer of power from the perpetrator to the victim. In offering restitution the perpetrator demonstrates the degree of remorse for having committed the intentional harm."[41]

In assessing correction action for a person causing a crime, a metaphysical exploration of the individual takes place. The "Apache concept of transgression does not necessarily assign to a person a degree of intent, be it mere negligence, gross negligence, spur of the moment intent, or intention backed by planning."[42] As Vicenti points out:

> Each individual may take actions resulting in the transgression of tribal norms or mores because of badness that is operating within his or her life. That badness can be, and often is, a badness of heart—what Western society might call sociopathic behavior—but the badness also may be explained by religious or spiritual reasons that have caused the state of heart, or by medical reasons that have caused momentary or periodic changes of behavior. So, in fashioning a remedy, much more attention has been placed upon determining other facts about the individual that can illuminate the metaphysical exploration of the individual undertaken by traditional participants.[43]

Apaches "value remorse as a state of mind to be accomplished by a perpetrator. But they consider it essential that the internal and external life of any perpetrator be examined to determine whether the individual is healthy or whole. And ultimately, they desire to reintegrate the individual back into tribal society."[44]

In Apache society importance is placed on accomplishing a state of remorse, not only to humble the perpetrator, but also to cure the victim. This is in contrast to justice in American society which does not place value on the principle of remorse. In American courts remorse is left to the victims and their families. A civil judgment is paid, a punishment is given and the criminal remains remorseless as he pays for his crime in prison.[45]

Indigenous systems of justice are based on a holistic philosophy that focuses on peace and harmony. Indigenous law is characterized as structural and procedural with importance placed on relationships, obligations, and group survival. In contrast, the American paradigm of justice is rooted in a European worldview based on a retributive philosophy that is hierarchical, adversarial, punitive, and guided by codified laws and written rules, procedures, and guidelines.[46]

In her article, "Indigenous Justice Systems and Tribal Society," Ada Pecos Melton examines the differences in indigenous and American justice systems. The retributive

---

[40] Carey Vicenti, "The Reemergence of Tribal Society and Traditional Justice Systems, " *Judicature*, Vol.79, No.3, Nov-Dec. 1995, 137.

[41] Vicenti, 138.

[42] Vicenti, 138.

[43] Vicenti, 138.

[44] Vicenti, 139.

[45] Vicenti, 139.

[46] Ada Pecos Melton, "Indigenous Justice Systems and Tribal Society," *Judicature*, Vol.79, No.3, Nov-Dec. 1995, 126.

philosophy of the American system of justice "holds that because the victim has suffered, the criminal should suffer as well."[47]

> It is premised on the notion that criminals are wicked people who are responsible for their actions and deserve to be punished. Punishment is used to appease the victim, to satisfy society's desire for revenge, and to reconcile the offender to the community by paying a debt to society. It does not offer a reduction in future crime or reparation to victims."[48]

Indigenous justice is based on a more holistic philosophy which can be described a "circle of justice" that connects all persons involved in a dispute or conflict on a continuum. Everyone involved in the conflict is focused on the same center. "The center of the circle represents the underlying issues that need to be resolved to attain peace and harmony for the individuals and the community. The continuum represents the entire process, from disclosure of problems, to discussion and resolution, to making amends and restoring relationships."[49]

Indigenous systems of justice utilize methods that are rooted in principles of restorative and reparative justice. The ideology guiding this system is based on the notions of healing and living in peace and harmony with all beings and with nature.

Restorative Principles

Restorative principles refer to the mending process that takes place within indigenous justice systems to renew damaged personal and communal relationships. The focus is on the victim and the aim is to heal and renew the victim's physical, emotional, mental, and spiritual well-being. The offender works at regaining dignity and trust so that he/she may also return to a healthy physical, emotional, mental, and spiritual state. These actions help both the victim and the offender to save face so that personal and communal peace and harmony will be restored.[50]

Verbal accountability by the offender and the offender's family is essential to express remorse to the victim and the victim's family. Face-to-face exchange of apology and forgiveness empowers victims to confront their offenders and convey their pain and anguish. Offenders are forced to be accountable for their behavior, to face the people whom they have hurt, to explain themselves, to ask for forgiveness, and to take full responsibility for making amends. Observing and hearing the apology enables the victim and family to discern its sincerity and move toward forgiveness and healing. Forgiveness is strongly suggested, but not essential for the victim to begin healing.[51]

The restorative aspect of indigenous justice often involves the utilization of ritual in order that the offender may cleanse his/her spirit and soul of the bad forces that caused him/her to behave offensively. These rituals include ceremonial sweats, fasting, and purifications that are used to "begin the healing and cleansing process necessary for the victim, the offender, and

---

[47] Melton, 126.
[48] Melton, 126.
[49] Melton, 126.
[50] Melton, 127.
[51] Melton, 132.

their families to regain mental, spiritual, and emotional well-being and to restore family and communal harmony."[52]

Reparative Principles

Reparative principles refer to the process of "making things right," not only for the offender but also for those persons affected by the offender's behavior. To repair relationships the offender makes amends by giving an apology, asking the victim for forgiveness, making restitution to the victim and the victim's family, and by engaging in certain acts that demonstrate to society that he/she is sincere in making things right.[53]

The communal aspect of this principle "allows for crime to be viewed as a natural human error that requires corrective intervention by families and elders or tribal leaders. Thus, offenders remain an integral part of the community because of their important role in defining the boundaries of appropriate and inappropriate behavior and the consequences associated with misconduct."[54]

In modern tribal court systems, tribes have established family and community forums where disputes and conflicts can be settled by talking things out. These forums draw on customary laws, sanctions, and practices, and involve all persons impacted by the crime or conflict. Historically, in Navajo society, "when someone harmed another, the party causing the injury compensated the victim or victim's family. The compensation was thought to be a symbolic gesture that would actually restore the community to a sense of harmony or wholeness... Restitution remedied bad feelings and restored good will."[55]

In Navajo society the person who claims the injury demands *nalyeeh*. *Nalyeeh* loosely translates as something similar to "restitution." Navajo tort law is *nalyeeh* and its sole purpose is to restore harmony to the community through a peaceful process. "*Nalyeeh* does not seek to point the finger of blame and fault ...Rather, *nalyeeh* seeks to encourage parties to talk things out, resolve differences, and restore balance to society. One can say that *nalyeeh* is healing or restorative justice."[56]

CONCLUSION

In this article I have examined the central differences between Anglo or American law and indigenous law. I discussed how indigenous societies in the United States had their own concepts of law and justice that were based on an understanding that force and violence were not needed to resolve disputes. Indigenous law "is built on relationships, traditions, emotions, and methods of dealing with each other in a good way," whereas Anglo or American law "is built on authority, rank, obedience in the face of punishment."[57] Today, most tribes in the United States have taken the initiative to take control of their justice system and started to

---

[52] Melton, 132.
[53] Melton, 127.
[54] Melton, 127.
[55] Mueller.
[56] Mueller.
[57] Yazzie, 1995, 4.

establish their own tribal courts, enacting their own laws and codes. Approximately 275 Indian nations have established formal tribal court systems. There is widespread variety of the types of forums and the laws applied to each court system, which is distinctly unique for each tribe. Some tribal courts resemble Western-style judiciaries where written laws and rules of court procedure are applied. But an increasing number of tribes are returning to their traditional means of resolving disputes through the use of peacemaking, elders' councils and sentencing circles.[58]

As Melton notes, these actions "stem from discontent with the efforts of modern tribal courts to address the crime, delinquency, social, and economic problems in tribal communities. It is joined by the dominant culture's current disillusionment with justice in this country, which causes doubt about retributive justice and a move toward a more restorative framework."[59] This emerging restorative perspective for the American justice system is illustrated by the following values:

> All parties should be included in the response to crime-offenders, victims, and the community. Government and local communities should play complementary roles in that response. Accountability is based on offenders understanding the harm caused by their offense, accepting responsibility for that harm, and repairing it ... [R]estorative justice guides professionals in the appropriate and equitable use of sanctions to ensure that offenders make amends to victims and the community.[60]

Keeping the peace through non-violent traditional means is being re-invigorated by tribal nations as a way to nourish and control violence and administer justice within their communities. Today, Native Indian communities are returning to an indigenous philosophical base that incorporates traditional values, concepts, and principles founded on peace, harmony, and unity. Justice Yazzie says the reason behind the revival of traditional peacekeeping is obvious: "life comes from it."[61]

BIBLIOGRAPHY

Alfred, Taiaiake, *Peace, Power and Righteousness. An Indigenous Manifesto*, New York: Oxford University Press, 1999.

Anderson, Kim, *A Recognition of Being. Reconstructuring Native Womenhood*, Toronto: Second Story Press, 2000.

Canby, William. *American Indian Law*, Minnesota: West Publishing Company, 1998.

Cooter, Robert D. and Wolfgang Fikentscher, "Indian Common Law: The Role of Custom in American Indian Tribal Courts," *American Journal of Comparative Law*, Volume XLVI, Summer, 1998, N.3.

Getches, David H., Charles F. Wilkinson and Robert A. Williams Jr., *Federal Indian Law. Cases and Materials*, Minnesota: West Publishing Company, 1993.

---

[58] "Tribal Court History." National Tribal Justice Research Center.
[59] Melton. 133.
[60] Melton. 133.
[61] Yazzie. 1994. 29.

Gibson, James R. "Smallpox on the Northwest Coast, 1835-1838." in *BC Studies*, No.5, (1982-83): 61-81.

Jackson, Michael, "In search of the pathways to justice: Alternative dispute resolution in Aboriginal communities," *University of British Columbia Law Review* (Special edition), 1992, pp.147-238.

Melton, Ada Pecos,"Indigenous Justice Systems and Tribal Society," *Judicature*, Vol.79, No.3 (Nov-Dec.1995).

Miller, Bruce, *The Problem of Justice. Tradition and Law in the Coast Salish World,* Lincoln: University of Nebraska Press, 2001.

Mirsky, Laura, "Restorative Justice Practices of Native American, First Nation and Other Indigenous Peoples of North America: Part One," *Restorative Practices E-Forum*, April 27, 2004, www.restorativepractices.org.

Mueller, J.R., "Restoring Harmony through *Nalyeeh*: Can the Navajo Common Law of Torts be Applied in State and Federal Forums?" *Tribal Law Journal,* Vol.3, New Mexico School of Law, September 16, 2004, http://tlj.unm.edu/articles/volume_2/mueller/content.php.

National Tribal Justice Research Center, "Tribal Court History," www.tribalresourcecenter.org/tribalcourts/history.asp

Noriega, Jose, " American Indian Education in the United States: Indoctrination for Subordination to Colonialism," in *The State of Native America*, ed by Annette Jaimes, Boston: South End Press, 1992.

O'Brien, Sharon, *American Indian Tribal Governments*, Norman: University of Oklahoma Press, 1989,1993.

Shoemaker, Nancy, *Negotiators of Change*, US: Routledge Press, 1995.

Skogen, Larry, *Indian Depredation Claims – 1790-1920,* Norman: University of Oklahoma Press, 1996.

Strickland, Rennard, "The Eagle's Empire. Sovereignty, Survival, and Self-governance in Native American Law and Constitutionalism," in *Studying Native America. Problems and Prospects*, University of Wisconsin Press, 1998.

Strickland, Rennard, "Traditional Law Ways and the Spirit World," in *Fire and the Spirits*, University of Oklahoma Press, 1975.

Titley, Brian E.. *A Narrow Vision. Duncan Campbell Scott and the Administration of Indian Affairs in Canada.* Canada: University of British Columbia Press, 1992.

Valencia-Weber, Gloria and Christine Zuni, "Domestic Violence and Tribal Protection of Indigenous Women in the U.S., *St. John's Law Review*, 69 (1995).

Vicenti, Carey, "The Reemergence of Tribal Society and Traditional Justice Systems," *Judicature*, Vol.79, No.3, Nov.-Dec., 1995.

Yazzie, Robert, "Healing as Justice: The American Experience," *Justice as Healing Newsletter*, Spring, 1995.

Yazzie, Robert, "Life Comes From It: Navajo Justice," *The Ecology of Justice*, Spring, 1994.

Yazzie, Robert, "Traditional Indian Law," *Tribal Court Record*, Special Edition, Vol.9, No.1, Spring/Summer, 1996.

Zion, James W., "The Navajo Peacemaker Court: Deference to the Old and Accommodation to the New," *American Indian Law Review,* 93 (1983).

SECTION V

In: Religion, Terrorism and Globalization
Editor: K.K. Kuriakose, pp.175-188

ISBN 1-59454-553-7
© 2006 Nova Science Publishers, Inc.

Chapter 11

FOUNDATION OF CHRISTIAN NONVIOLENCE

Paul Keim
Goshen College , IN

> The LORD said to Cain, "Where is your brother Abel?" And he said, "I do not know.
> Am I my brother's keeper?"
> Then He said, "What have you done? Hark, your brother's blood cries out to Me from the
> ground! (Gen 4:9-10, JPS Tanakh)

INTRODUCTION

Violence is killing us. Not just in the mundane sense that, every day, human lives are lost at an alarming rate at the hands of other human beings. Not just since the horrendous events of September 11, 2001, and the subsequent military retaliations that have plunged the U.S. into global conflict. But insofar as we persist in the idolatrous conviction that the use of lethal force can create justice, right wrongs, save the downtrodden, preserve dignity, protect honor, restore order, destroy evil, ensure security, and make peace – our humanity is undermined. We are soul sick and dying from the inside. Violence is killing us.

The shrill appeals to justice, courage, and freedom used to legitimize violence are often infused with religious significance and driven by religious zeal. Our political enemies of today bear a striking resemblance to the heathens, infidels and blasphemers of the past, and exhibit many of their stereotypical traits. We become convinced that only by the deaths of the evil ones can peace be restored.[1] Not until the passions of violent conflict have abated are we able to appreciate, in retrospect, their excesses. How might we keep this from happening again?

The biblical story of the killing of Abel by his brother Cain presents a primeval model of human conflict. Most of us, most of the time, prefer to live peaceful lives. But there is a

---

[1] The scapegoat mechanism alluded to here is derived from René Girard's seminal studies of violence and the sacred. Though I do not engage his ideas directly in this essay, I have found Girard's work extremely valuable for understanding the nature of violence and its intrinsic relationship to religion. I consider Girard's work to be indispensable for Christian peacemakers (see bibliography).

broadly shared moral assumption that we have the freedom, if not the responsibility, to resort to violence to protect ourselves and our loved ones from immanent danger, to oppose abject evil, or to punish moral outrage.

This chapter will attempt to describe an alternative Christian response to conflict. It is not intended to be a spirited defense of this position but rather a careful description of a set of beliefs and practices. It is hoped that in the telling something is also revealed about what motivates a commitment to peacemaking, what shapes and sustains an ethos of principled nonviolence, and what contribution such a commitment may make to the contemporary, inter-religious search for creative alternatives to violence.

TERMINOLOGY

The phenomenology of human violence is broader than the conventional terminology used to describe it. Certainly war is its most visible manifestation. But the position being expressed here cannot be reduced to an anti-war ideology. Certainly the types of violence most often sanctified by religious claims are those actions undertaken by nation states, or against states, that result in widespread injury, death and destruction. But it is necessary to expand this definition in order to understand its more insidious and corrosive aspects. Furthermore, the ethos of Christian nonviolence goes beyond an aversion to this kind of action. In his book, "Religion and Violence," Robert McAfee Brown presents a helpful typology that defines violence in terms of the underlying notion of violating one's personhood. As such, it may describe actions that are individual or corporate, overt or covert. Individual violence that is overt would encompass interpersonal conflicts and altercations. Corporate overt violence would be police action or open warfare. Individual violence that is covert may describe uses of coercive force. Corporate violence that is covert is what is often referred to as systemic violence.[2]

These distinctions allow for a deeper understanding of the nature of violence. The focus of concern here is with any human behavior that violates the personhood of another, and especially those violations perpetrated in the name of religious values. Approaching the problem of violence from this perspective also allows us to address hidden forms that may appear even in the context of otherwise peaceful communities.[3]

As for the designations commonly employed to identify those Christian traditions and practices that reject violence and compulsion in all its forms, a clarifying comment may be in order. Though often, and not improperly, referred to as type of Christian pacifism, this term may be misleading. Though expressing a common commitment to peace among pacifists, it may also obscure the real and substantial differences of motive, perspective and practice. Other terms that provide for greater precision in distinguishing among various pacifist orientations include "Christian peacemaking," "nonviolence," "nonretaliation," and

---

[2] Robert McAfee Brown (1973), p. 7.
[3] Thus, insofar as they are perpetuated with appeal to religious considerations, the inherent object of concern at issue here could include acts of domestic abuse, child neglect, or (tacit) support for systemic violence, even in communities otherwise committed to peacemaking.

"nonresistance." I will use the terms "Christian nonviolence," "Christian peacemaking," or "biblical nonviolence" to refer to the particular tradition being described in this chapter.[4]

VIOLENCE AS A HUMAN PROBLEM

According to the biblical witness, violence has been endemic to human experience since our expulsion from God's paradisiacal garden. The primeval history (Genesis 1-11) traces the successive stages of the earth's becoming filled with hubris and destructive behaviors. The first murder is an act of fratricide. The echo of Cain's attempt to distance himself rhetorically from responsibility for killing his brother haunts our collective conscience to the present day. Both the horror and the fascination of our violent impulses find expression in Cain's mocking, formulaic cry of self-justification: "Am I my brother's keeper?" (Gen 4:9).[5]

We are acutely aware of the problem of violence in our world. Conventional wars rage, as ever, with their spurious victories and collateral damage. But ours is becoming a world of "unconventional war." The most striking characteristic of this conflict is the weapon of suicide attacks against civilian targets. Since September 11, 2001, Americans and Europeans have experienced the terror of arbitrary violence in their own cities. In the so-called "war on terrorism" strategists struggle to come to grips with an enemy who seems perfectly willing to give his own life in the cause of taking the lives of others.

The incongruity of this conflict is sharpened by other factors, not least being the religious zeal and ideology of its proponents. A cultural breach between "East" and "West" and between modern and traditional mores is breaking out all over.

No less persistent a theme in human history is the profound desire for love, security, harmony, and peace. The paradise of Eden is both the starting point and the goal of the biblical mythos. Cycles of cursing and blessing, of dispersion and gathering, of estrangement and reconciliation, of wandering and return, trace an ever-so-slightly ascending spiral through biblical literature. In those days everyone did what was right in their own eyes (Jg 21:25). In the days to come, the wolf and the lamb shall graze together (Is 65:25).

From this perspective, the modern framing of the problem of violence is hardly adequate to give expression to this profound contradiction of our existence. In the convoluted logic of survival we are compelled to destroy life in order to preserve it. Beyond Eden scarcity binds us together and sets us at each other's throats. We envy what we cannot possess and our rivals who do.[6] But unlike Cain, when we stand in the field over the motionless corpse of Abel, we are inclined not so much to deny responsibility, as to deny that he is our brother at all. Having rendered him into something less than kin, less than human, Abel too becomes fair game. Violence is lurking at the door. How might we master it?

---

[4] The particular tradition represented here is unapologetically Anabaptist-Mennonite in orientation and perspective. Historically identified with "believers church" denominations such as Mennonites, Amish, Hutterites, Brethren, and Quakers, many of the tenets of Christian nonviolence articulated here have also been affirmed at various times and places by Adventists, Pentecostals, and other reforming and nonconformist traditions. Individuals and movements within Catholic, Orthodox and Reformation communions have also embraced forms of Christian peacemaking.

[5] Unless otherwise noted, all quotations and citations are taken from the New Revised Standard Version of the Bible (National Council of Churches, 1989).

[6] Another echo of René Girard's work, having to do here with "mimetic crisis."

VIOLENCE AS A RELIGIOUS PROBLEM

As a nonreductive symbol of the human dilemma however, violence may indeed serve to frame the ethical challenge of our day. We justify the lethal lunge that lurks at the edges of our broken relationships with appeals to expediency and honor, all sanctified by religious conviction. Our cause becomes God's cause (or vice versa). The victims too are God's. The escalation of conflict into violence seems to be compelled by a power not properly human – on their side demonic, on ours divine. In the cathartic maelstrom of clannish retribution, the principled eye-for-eye-tooth-for-toothness of in kind retaliation (*lex talionis*) is a revolutionary grace. In recognizing the ritual aspects of violence we begin to appreciate the deep linkage between believer and killer. The children of Adam may become aggressive for revenge, for justice, for cleansing, or for catharsis. Nevertheless, at the core of our being we recognize the taking of life as an awesome burden. Only the numbness of radical estrangement, from ourselves and others, makes the bloodletting bearable.[7]

Religion may provide a sanction for violence, an interpretive framework that can transform our aggression into service of God, and our antagonists into the personifications of evil. And yet, religion has also been the source of controls on our violent passions. Stunningly, the mark of Cain in the Bible is not the emblem of retributive justice that popular culture has made of it, but a sign of mercy. The paradigmatic father of fratricide is thereby protected from the tyranny of reciprocity. Though it comes at a cost (removal from the presence of God), God's mark of protection guarantees Cain's survival against the justice of the blood avenger (Gen 4:13-16).

VIOLENCE AS A CHRISTIAN PROBLEM

Whatever else it is, the problem of violence is also a Christian problem. As a ruling political ideology since the fourth century, Christianity has incited, supported and also set limits upon the employment of violence for the benefit of the Kingdom of Heaven. Because of its formative influence on Western culture, Christianity is associated with both the incredible progress and the unimaginable atrocities of the modern age. As the missional handmaiden of colonial hegemony, the Church has sent its Christian soldiers marching to the farthest corners of the globe in the name of its civilizing salvation. It is this legacy of Crusade and Manifest Destiny above all that makes violence a Christian problem.

In contrast, the tradition of Christian nonviolence is as old as the religion itself. It is based on the witness of Jesus of Nazareth, his life and teachings, his submission to death, and his overcoming of death in resurrection and the ongoing work of the reconciling church in the world. It is all the more ironic then that Christian nonviolence as an ethic of discipleship has been, from relatively early in the history of the church, the belief and practice of a minority of Christians. It remains so to this day.

The clear and consistent teaching of the early Church against the use of violence and participation in the military was only gradually eroded. First tolerated and legalized after years of bloody suppression, under the rule of Constantine in the 4th century, the church

---

[7] See the highly evocative conversation between René Girard and Wlater Burkert, along with Jonathan Z. Smith, in Hamerton-Kelly (1987).

became an established power of empire, and began to conquer by the sign of the cross.[8] The participation of Christians in the rank and file of the Roman imperial armies, rare in the first centuries because of the Church's peace teachings and the oath of allegiance to emperor required of soldiers, gradually became tolerated. Though renunciation of violence remained the teaching of the Church, it came to be more narrowly defined as an ethic of perfection reserved for monastic life, or an individual ethic not relevant to the conduct of statecraft. The consolidation of political identity in the Christianized Roman empire in the face of external threats led to a deeply compromising symbiosis between church and state. This unholy union between imperial and ecclesiastical authority led eventually to the horrors of the Crusades, implicating all of medieval Christian society in this ultimately ill-fated attempt to wrest the Holy Lands from the control of the "infidels."

But throughout the centuries there have been Christians, monastic and secular, clergy and lay, who have kept alive, or rediscovered, this central teaching of Jesus and the church. The lives of these saints have often been roads to martyrdom, not infrequently at the hands of other Christians. The personification of the recovery of the early Church's pacifism is St. Francis. As pointed out by Jane Russell, the mendicant movements that arose in response to the Franciscan embrace of peace and poverty had a profound impact on lay religious life in the medieval Church. One result was "a great surge in popular peace movements in the thirteenth century, which interrupted crusades and political wars with spontaneous demonstrations of people seeking alternatives to violence."[9]

In the midst of the religious wars of early modern Europe, a small group of radical Christian reformers recovered once again the peace teaching of Jesus and the early church. Called Anabaptists ("rebaptizers") by their opponents, this diverse movement spread rapidly throughout Europe. Leaders of the evangelical wing of the movement came together in the Swiss town of Schleitheim in 1527 to draw up the first known Anabaptist confession of faith. In its seven articles they expressed agreement on matters of faith and practice that included adult baptism, close communion, separation from the wickedness of the "world" (by which they meant the Christians of the establishment churches of their day!), and "the sword." The latter, which signified the divinely ordained function of secular rule, they considered "outside the perfection of Christ."[10] By committing themselves to live within the perfection of Christ, these Anabaptist Christians rejected the violence of "the sword" as well as participation in the offices of secular authority that wielded it.[11]

Walter Wink asserts, "It cannot be stressed too much: love of enemies has, for our time, become the litmus test of authentic Christian faith."[12] He continues: "I submit that the ultimate religious question today is no longer the Reformation's 'How can I find a gracious God?' It is instead, 'How can I find God in my enemy?'"[13] Put another way, "we can no more

---

[8] The pacifism of the early Christian Church and the rise of just war ideology in the Christian Roman empire is summarized by Bainton (1960), pp. 66-100. See also the discussion of Jane Elyse Russell in Hauerwas, et al., eds. (1999), 376-379.

[9] Russell, p. 380. She is dependent here on Ronald Musto's book, *The Catholic Peace Tradition* (Maryknoll, 1986).

[10] Quoted from Russell, op. cit., p. 383. See also the article "Bruderlich Vereinigung" in The Mennonite Encyclopedia (1955), vol. 1, pp. 447f.

[11] Not all Anabaptists of the 16th century were pacifists. For an thorough review of the issue, see Stayer, *Anabaptists and the Sword* (1976).

[12] Wink (2003), p. 58f.

[13] Ibid., p. 59.

save ourselves from our enemies than we can save ourselves from sin, but God's amazing grace offers to save us from both."[14]

BIBLICAL THEMES OF NONVIOLENCE

Christian nonviolence is rooted in biblical teaching. Its foundation is the life and words of Jesus as reflected in the apostolic witness of the New Testament. The teaching of Jesus is itself rooted in the scriptural tradition of ancient Israel. It was through Jesus, understood to be the messianic fulfillment of Torah and prophets, that the early church began to reread the First Testament as a record of God's healing strategy for the world.[15] The New Testament basis of Christian nonviolence will be reviewed first. Then, because certain texts of the Old Testament have often been evoked to justify the use of coercive and destructive force by Christians, or to support "just wars," we will also provide a brief rereading of selected texts from the Hebrew Bible that mitigate human violence. This overlooked and neglected aspect of Old Testament teaching points prophetically, as it were, towards Jesus' incarnation and his articulation of a persistent theological trajectory of peace in the Bible.

Love of Enemy

> "You have heard that is was said, 'You shall love your neighbor and hate your enemy.' But I say to you, Love your enemies and pray for those who persecute you, so that you may be children of your Father in heaven . . ." Matthew 5:43-45

Jesus' teaching is focused on the coming reign of God, breaking into history and transforming all human relationships. One can construe the entire corpus of Jesus' teachings and miracles as demonstrations of the characteristics of this inbreaking kingdom. Among the six central characteristics of the Kingdom of God discernable in the teachings of Jesus are the following:

a) The kingdom aims to make all one, for it transcends all human divisions which are in fact brought into unity in Christ.

b) The method of bringing about this unity is through reconciliation, not coercion, for the latter violates human freedom.

c) The creation of a new humanity takes place through the working of divine agape, an "energy of sheer goodness, going out towards its objects without regard to their deserts." Its characteristic form of expression is the forgiveness of sinners (which is, strictly speaking, unjust), and divine forgiveness is itself the power of its life.

---

[14] Quoting John Stoner, Ibid., p. 60.
[15] For a very accessible summary of the peace theology of the Bible see Ted Grimsrud, God's Healing Strategy (Pandora Press, 2000).

d) In the whole action of God in Christ this divine charity suffers even to death. Through Christ's resurrection God reigns from the tree. The manner of the kingdom is not power added to love but love manifesting itself as power to create.[16]

C. H. Dodd, who first articulated these characteristics of the kingdom in Jesus' teaching, summarizes, "War is fundamentally antagonistic to the kingdom and at this moment represents a concentration of all those things in human life which are most irreconcilably opposed to the will of God as shown in Christ. War itself is evil . . . We cannot Christianize war by taking part in it."[17]

Understood against this theological background, Christian nonviolence is not reducible to the mere rejection of violence and coercion. It is primarily an affirmation that the way to peace is peaceful, that the way to justice must be just, that the key to reconciliation is healing and hope. Of course, in the face of epidemic religious violence in our world, the simple, programmatic rejection of violence in all forms and situations may indeed be recognized as a virtue. But in and of itself it does not go far enough. There are many ways to harm others without using overt violence. Rejection of violence itself does not bring about reconciliation. It is not enough for one to refrain from killing one's enemy.

According to Jesus' teaching we are to love our enemies. This sets before us an even greater challenge. In order to love our enemy, in order to even understand what this might mean, we must not lose sight of the humanity of the enemy. The enemy never becomes a "thing," an "it," a problem to be solved, the personification of an abstract evil. The enemy, to be loved (agape), must remain a human being.[18]

Thus the moral center of biblical nonviolence is an ethic of love that is identified as a defining characteristic of the Christian community (1 John). The command to love is not a reference to a feeling or attitude. Rather it is a reference to an act or orientation that takes responsibility for the enemy, analogous to the way one's "love" for "loved ones" imposes responsibilities. This extension of kin-based obligations is the very essence of the legal fiction whereby contractual, treaty and covenant relations were articulated and conceived in antiquity.

Jesus' teaching about enemy love appears in two texts of the New Testament, Matthew 5:43-48, and Luke 6:27-36. It is best known, perhaps from its setting in the Sermon on the Mount (quoted at the heading of this section). In this particular section of the sermon, there are a series of reversals or radicalizations of conventional teaching. Love of enemy is set against the "natural" impulse to love those close to us (neighbor), and to hate our enemies, the paradigmatic "other." Jesus teaches his disciples here (Mt 5:1) that this conventional understanding exhibits no particular virtue. Such behavior is endemic to any culture. In our modern context we might even want to explain such behavior as instinctive, or driven by a subconscious evolutionary drive to preserve our own genetic legacy. Loving one's family and one's neighbors is not so much a cultural value as it is a natural inclination. Everybody does it!

In this passage, Jesus' teaching to love the enemy, and to pray for those who persecute, is grounded in a different kind of natural law. God causes the sun to shine on the evil and the

---

[16] Quoted from Klassen in Swartley (1992), pp. 2-3.
[17] Ibid., p. 3.
[18] Note the terms "dehumanization" and "enmification" elucidated in the study of the face of the enemy.

good, and the rain to fall on the righteous and the wicked (Matthew 5:45). In other words, Jesus teaches his disciples here to emulate an aspect of God's character. By loving our enemies, and by the principle of including all within a boundary by defining the boundary, i.e., everyone "outward" from ourselves to the enemy, we are living out an aspect of God's own nature, built into God's creation. It is a characteristic of the coming-and-already-in-your-midst kingdom of God. It is a hallmark of those who respond to the realization of God's reign on earth. It will not be like the rule of earthly sovereigns, whose job it is to define, isolate, move against, and destroy the enemy.

It is also not advocated in terms of effective outcomes. Loving enemies will not necessarily lead to greater security – even in the long term. We are to love our enemies because this is how we become children of the heavenly Father (Matthew 5:45). As with the other readings of the Sermon on the Mount, Christians may live with the conviction that loving others, including our enemies, will have a positive effect on the quality of life in the world. But there is no guarantee of it stated here. It is not the guiding principle. It is not the standard measure of our faithfulness. Our call is to live out "ultimate" values (teleios) just as the Father lives in ultimate (teleios) reality (Mt 5:48).

Luke's treatment of the same pericope emphasizes God's mercy as the model and motivation for this ethic:

> "But love your enemies, do good, and lend, expecting nothing in return. Your reward will be great, and you will be children of the Most High; for he is kind to the ungrateful and the wicked. Be merciful, just as your Father is merciful."
> (Luke 6:35-36)

The themes developed here in the "Sermon on the Plain" around the commandment to love the enemy tease out the ethical temperament of its application. Though some have referred to it as "nonretaliation" or the "renunciation of rights," Glen Stassen suggests that a more appropriate designation would be "transforming initiatives."[19] The expansion of the teaching to love the enemy found here is a litany of positive, creative, alternative responses to enmity that include a series of transformative actions, punctuated by the "golden rule":

- Do good to those who hate you
- Bless those who curse you
- Pray for those who abuse you
- If someone strikes you on the cheek, offer the other cheek
- If someone takes your coat, give your shirt also
- Give to everyone who begs from you
- If someone takes away your goods, don't ask for them again
- Do to others as you would have them do to you. (Luke 6:27-31)

---

[19] In Hauerwas, et al. (1999), p. 160. This discussion of the love command found in Luke is dependent on Stassen's discussion.

Love of Neighbor

Jesus' teaching about the Christian obligation to love the enemy appears to be an extension of another teaching, namely loving one's neighbor. Here the transformation or radicalization is not focused on a reorientation of our concern. Rather it involves a redefinition of the term "neighbor." It was long recognized as a fundamental principle of Torah (the "second" of the great commandments of the Old Testament), to love one's neighbor as oneself. But as so often happens, the definition of neighbor had become so narrow as to exclude most of those who might be labeled the "other." Jesus extends the obligation to include those who might resemble us, might be related to us even, but from whom we are estranged. For Jews of the 1st century nothing symbolized this more forcefully than the Samaritans. It is the recognition of virtue in the Samaritan (the "good" Samaritan – not the text's designation, as if this one Samaritan was the exception that proved the stereotyped rule) that is the key to understanding Jesus' teaching.

The parable of the virtuous Samaritan, found in Luke 10:25-37, extends the question asked Jesus by a certain lawyer, "Who is my neighbor?" to include the enemy. It is in recognizing the hospitality, the justice, the empathy, with the estranged neighbor, which may exceed that of professional purveyors of virtue – Scribes, Pharisees, etc., which provides the key to understanding Jesus' moral teaching here.

But the ethical principle of the parable of the "good Samaritan" is not only that one's neighbors include one's enemies. Here the "love of enemy" is not objective but subjective. In other words, it is not love for the conventionally detested Samaritan that is enjoined, but rather the love that the Samaritan, the enemy, had for the suffering victim. The teaching thus constitutes a re-humanization of the enemy by demonstrating that the enemy has virtues that may exceed one's own. In this respect it is reminiscent of the book of Ruth in the Old Testament, in which a Moabite woman, the very definition of the wholly other, exemplifies the virtues of character that reflect God's care and result in the saving of a family.

The love of neighbor is rooted in the "double love" command that Jesus refers to as the greatest. It requires love of God on the one hand,[20] and love of neighbor on the other.[21] According to Jesus, the ethos of the entire Torah, as well as that of the prophets, is summed up in this double love command. It is the standard by which other principles should be measured, and their interpretation guided.

The Discipleship of the Cross

It is not just in Jesus' teaching that we find a consistent and coherent ethic of love and nonviolence. Also in his life and death Jesus exemplifies the kind of way that leads to peace and reconciliation. He came "preaching peace" (Ephesians 2:17), and he died refusing to use the considerable powers at his disposal to save himself. This phrase from Ephesians does not indicate that Jesus was a preacher in the conventional sense, and that his message is reducible

---

[20] Mark 12:29-30, quoting Deuteronomy 6:5.
[21] Mark 12:31, quoting Leviticus 19:18.

to peace. "Rather, it says that his life and death incarnated a message – that his total being in the world heralded the new state of things which it describes as 'peace.'"[22]

The Doctrine of Nonretaliation

In the application of love of enemy there is the important principle of nonretaliation. Vengeance is left to God. In its place, Jesus' command is to forgive. It is a command for action, to live one's life in forgiveness. Instead of judging and condemning, Jesus' followers are instructed to forgive and give (Luke 6:37-38).

Most biblical scholars readily affirm that this essentially represents the ethical teaching of Jesus. The issue is not, apparently whether or not the gospels provide an accurate account of Jesus' life and teachings here. Or whether this unfairly discounts other teachings or episodes in Jesus' life that might complicate the picture. This is what Jesus taught, according to most Christians. The question is rather, is this what Jesus expects or requires of all Christians?

Here is where the opinions of Christian theologians and ethicists diverge. In his influential book, *The Politics of Jesus,* Mennonite theologian John Howard Yoder begins with a careful consideration of the question of the normativity of Jesus for Christian ethics. In his careful survey of Christian ethicists most deny that Jesus' life and teachings are an adequate or necessary basis for Christian ethics in the modern world. Yoder goes on to assert, at the end of that first chapter, his conviction that in fact Jesus is normative for Christian ethics. His study of the gospel of Luke and of Paul lays out an argument based on a close reading of NT texts, in support of this assertion.

Certainly there are different ways to interpret the central texts. But the question comes down not so much to that of how the teachings of Jesus are to be interpreted. On that most scholars agree. It comes down to the question of how one is to understand the moral imperative of these passages. Is Jesus the model for Christian ethics?

The other crucial set of texts in this regard has to do with an ethic of discipleship. Jesus calls his followers to "pick up their cross and follow him." Whatever else this may have meant, it was clearly understood by the leaders of the early Church that Christians should be prepared to give their lives for the gospel. The equation of the testimony of faithfulness to death gave us Christian "martyrdom," i.e., a witness to the truth of Jesus and faithfulness to his commandment.

Theologically, it is the reconciling work begun by Christ which the Church understands as its ongoing mission in the world. We are those who extend Christ's life and teachings, bring reconciliation to broken relationships, living the kinds of lives that help to mediate conflict, and who refuse to use violence, either in pursuit of praiseworthy goals, or in defense of the gospel. This is the theology of the cross and of discipleship. We take up our cross daily insofar as we extend healing and hope in a broken and hurting world.

The primary deviation from this commandment comes, not from a variant understanding of these texts. Rather, it comes from a particular way of understanding a later development in the history of the church, namely the relationship between the church and the state's exercise of earthly authority and power.

---

[22] Quoting from noted Mennonite theologian John Howard Yoder, from his provocative series of essays on biblical themes of peace entitled "He Came Preaching Peace" (1985), p. 11.

OLD TESTAMENT THEMES OF PEACE

In approaching the problem of war in the Old Testament, one of the oldest and most consistent arguments used by Christians to justify Christian participation in warfare and other forms of violence has been in reference to the so-called "holy wars" of the Old Testament. It has been taken as a test of God's sovereignty that an immutable God who once sanctioned warfare could not then later prohibit it altogether. Though this chapter cannot fully engage this problem, which numerous monographs have also addressed, it is worth making some observations about the ways that nonviolent Christians tend to read such accounts.

Millard Lind's careful reading of the "Yahweh is a Warrior" motif in the Hebrew Bible leads him to see the roots of an alternative political consciousness embedded in the events of Exodus.[23] "Holy war" in this tradition emphasizes the weakness and helplessness of God's people. Yahweh fights the battles with little or no human assistance. There is a biblical principle deeply ingrained in Old Testament theology that identifies trust in Yahweh as the counterpoint to trust in force. What the stories of reversed fortune and return from exile narrate, the prophets distill:

Not by might, nor by power, but by my spirit,
says the LORD of hosts. (Zechariah 4:6)

Against the background of Ancient Near Eastern political and religious ideology, the teachings of Torah provide an alternative consciousness and an alternative politics. The law of the Bible never becomes the king's law. It remains God's law, and to it all are subject, including the king. Barriers of separation are eventually overcome.

Reading the Hebrew Bible through the messianic revelation of Jesus' life and teachings, unencumbered by the logic of just war and the exigencies of Christian empire, it is possible to trace the development of an alternative consciousness of the community of faith, living as exiles within but not of the imperial domains of their sojourn. What follows is a representative sampling of such reading.

Isaiah 2:4

This passage was a favorite of Christian preachers of the early centuries. According to Russell, "the early Church fathers considered this prophecy fulfilled" and "the eschatological state of nonviolence and peace, prophesied by Isaiah, had become a reality in the church."[24] Its lines are among the most familiar texts of the Bible:

He shall judge between the nations,
And shall arbitrate for many peoples;
They shall beat their swords into plowshares,
And their spears into pruning hooks;

---

[23] Millard Lind, Yahweh is a Warrior (Herald Press, 1980). For an informative review of Christian attitudes towards war and the Bible see the chapter entitled "The Bible and War" in Willard Swartley's book, Slavery, Sabbath, War and Women (Swartley, 1983), pp. 96-149.

[24] In Hauerwas, et al., eds., p. 377.

Nation shall not lift up sword against nation.
Neither shall they learn war any more. (NRSV)

When we read this beautiful Zion hymn closely, with its inspiring vision of Jerusalem in the latter days, we can appreciate anew the qualitative impulse of its vision.[25] In the days to come the city on the hill will be reestablished. Nations and peoples will stream to Zion to be instructed in Torah. Yahweh himself will arbitrate among nations, since to be human and live in community is to have conflicts. The Jerusalem of the days to come does not promise a utopian paradise in which we all just get along. Rather, the master mediator is there among us, helping us to resolve our conflicts, to find nonviolent ways of living together in spite of our differences. The outcome of this is not so much a principled pacifism as an atrophy of interest in the anachronism of war. Discarded sword blades and spear tips get recycled for use in field, orchard and vineyard. Since nations no longer take up arms against each other, it makes more sense to study each other's languages and cultures and religions. The faculty of the war colleges will be the first to redo their curricula. They will call it: Walking in the Light of Yahweh.

Genesis 32-33

As the patriarch Jacob prepares himself for an encounter with his estranged brother Esau in Genesis 32-33, we note the reconciliatory power of face-to-face meetings. Set within this dramatic account is the ancient tradition of Jacob's tussle with a heavenly being. Jacob refuses to let go until he receives a blessing. He emerges with a limp, a new name, and an unexpected resource for encountering Esau. In Genesis 33 Jacob meets one who he believes to be his enemy. It is his brother Esau, whom he tricked out of his paternal birthright. But upon meeting him he receives an embrace instead of animosity. Overcome by this act of forgiveness, he exclaims, "truly to see your face is like seeing the face of God – since you have received me with such favor" (Gen 33:10). Esau's choice against retaliation transforms the potentially dangerous encounter, and shows Jacob/Israel the face of God in the face of the enemy.

THE THEOLOGY OF CHRISTIAN NONVIOLENCE

The central commitment of Christian peacemakers is ultimately derived from an understanding of who God is, what God has done, and what God requires of believers. This reconciling aspect of God's character is consistently portrayed in scripture and most fully revealed in Jesus. Through the example of Jesus' life and teachings, his violent death at the hands of Roman imperial authorities, and his resurrection, we are enabled to see the trajectory that runs through scripture and through the grain of the universe. This understanding is that

---

[25] For a fuller consideration of this passage within the context of biblical eschatology, see the author's article, "Watch Your Back: Ruminations on the Biblical Poetics of Hope," in *Crosscurrents* (Winter 2004), pp. 548-554.

God is love, and that those who claim to follow this God must similarly reflect the love that God has made available to us in a unique way through Jesus.

Creation is moving towards redemption. As disciples of Jesus, we are commanded to take up our cross and follow Jesus daily. This was the clear and consistent teaching of the Christian church for the first three centuries of its history. The second century catechism known as the "Didache," or "Teaching of the Twelve Apostles," begins with a nearly verbatim quote from the Sermon on the Mount's ethic of love and nonviolence:

> The way of life is this . . . [B]less those that curse you, and pray for your enemies; besides, fast for those that persecute you. For what thanks do you deserve when you love those that love you? Do not the heathen do as much? For your part, love those that hate you; in fact, have no enemy . . .[26]

BIBLIOGRAPHY

Bainton, Roland K., *Christian Attitudes Toward War and Peace* (Abingdon: 1960)

Bailie, Gil, *Violence Unveiled: Humanity at the Crossroads* (Crossroad Publishing: 1995)

Brown, Robert McAfee, *Religion and Violence* (Westminster Press: 1973)

Cahill, Lisa Sowle, *Love Your Enemies: Discipleship, Pacifism, and Just War Theory* (Fortress Press, 1997)

Carter, Craig A., *The Politics of the Cross: The Theology and Social Ethics of John Howard Yoder* (Brazos Press, 2001)

Chase, Kenneth R. and Alan Jacobs, eds., Must Christianity be Violent? *Reflections on History, Practice, and Theology* (Brazos Press, 2003)

Dombrowski, Daniel A., *Christian Pacifism* (Temple Univ Press: 1991)

Drescher, John M., *Why I Am a Conscientious Objector* (Herald Press: 1982)

Girard, René, *Violence and the* Sacred (Johns Hopkins, 1977)

Grimsrud, Ted, God's Healing Strategy (Pandora Press, 2000)

Hamerton-Kelly, Robert G., ed., Violent Origins: Walter Burkert, Rene Girard, and Jonathan Z. *Smith on Ritual Killing and Cultural Formation* (Standord Univ Press: 1987)

Hauerwas, Stanley, Chris K. Huebner, Harry J. Huebner, Mark Thiessen Nation, eds., *The Wisdom of the Cross* (Eerdmans, 1999)

Holmes, Robert L. and Barry L. Gan, *Nonviolence in Theory and Practice*, 2nd ed. (Waveland Press: 2005)

Hornus, Jean, *It Is Not Lawful for Me to Fight* (Herald Press, 1960)

Klassen, William, *Love Your Enemies: The Way to Peace* (Fortress Press, 1984)

Lind, Millard, *The Sound of Sheer Silence and the Killing State: The Death Penalty and the Bible* (Cascadia: 2004)

Lind, Millard, *Yahweh is a Warrior* (Herald Press: 1980)

Lohfink, Norbert, hrsg., *Gewalt und Gewaltlosigkeit im Alten Testament* (Herder: 1983)

McDonald, Patricia M., *God and Violence: Biblical Resources for Living in a Small World* (Herald Press, 2004)

---

[26] Quoted from the Franciscan sister Jane Elyse Russell, "Love Your Enemies: The Church as Community of Nonviolence," in Hauerwas, et al. (1999), p. 376.

MacGregor, G. H. C., *The New Testament Basis of Pacifism* (FOR: 1936)

Miller, William Robert, *Nonviolence: A Christian Interpretation* (Schocken: 1964)

Nelson-Pallmeyer, Jack, *Is Religion Killing Us? Violence in the Bible and the Quran* (Trinity Press International, 2003)

Niditch, Susan, *War in the Hebrew Bible: A Study in the Ethics of Violence* (Oxford, 1993)

Piper, John, *Love Your Enemies* (Cambridge, 1980)

Polner, M. and N. Goodman, *The Challenge of Shalom* (New Society Publishers: 1994)

Rieber, Robert W., ed., *The Psychology of War and Peace: The Image of the Enemy* (Plenum Press, 1991)

Smith-Christopher, Daniel L., ed., *Subverting Hatred: The Challenge of Nonviolence in Religious Traditions* (Orbis: 1998)

Stassen, Glen H., *Just Peacemaking: Transforming Initiatives for Justice and Peace* (Westminster/John Knox: 1992)

Stayer, James M., *Anabaptists and the Sword* (Coronado Press: 1972, 1976)

Swartley, Willard M., ed., *The Love of Enemy and Nonretaliation in the New Testament* (Westminster/John Knox: 1992)

Swartley, Willard M., *Slavery, Sabbath, War, and Women* (Herald Press: 1983)

Weaver, J. Denny and Gerald Biesecker-Mast, eds., *Teaching Peace: Nonviolence and the Liberal Arts* (Rowman and Littlefield: 2003)

Weinberg, Arthur and Lila, *Instead of Violence: Writings by the great advocates of peace and nonviolence through history* (Beacon Press: 1963)

Wink, Walter, *Jesus and Nonviolence: A Third Way* (Fortress Press: 2003)

Wink, Walter, ed., *Peace is the Way: Writings on Nonviolence from the Fellowship of Reconciliation* (Orbis: 2000)

Wood, John A., *Perspectives on War in the Bible* (Mercer Univ Press: 1998)

Yoder, John Howard, *He Came Preaching Peace* (Herald Press, 1985, Wipf and Stock, 1998)

Yoder, John Howard, *The Politics of Jesus: Behold the Man! Our Victorious Lamb*, 2nd ed. (Eerdmans: 1994)

Yoder, John Howard, *The Priestly Kingdom: Social Ethics as Gospel* (Univ of Notre Dame Press: 1984)

Yoder, John Howard, *What Would You Do?* (Herald Press: 1983, 1992)

Yoder, John Howard, *When War is Unjust: Being Honest in Just-War Thinking*, 2nd ed. (Wipf and Stock, 1996)

In: Religion, Terrorism and Globalization
Editor: K.K. Kuriakose, pp.189-202

ISBN 1-59454-553-7
© 2006 Nova Science Publishers, Inc.

Chapter 12

NON-VIOLENCE AND PEACE TRADITIONS IN EARLY AND EASTERN CHRISTIANITY

John A. McGuckin

Professor of Early Church History,
Union Theological Seminary, New York.
Professor of Byzantine Christianity, Columbia University,
Department of Religion.

IDEALS OF PEACE IN A VIOLENT WORLD

Christianity has had a very chequered history in terms of its peace tradition. It is often to images of Inquisition and Crusade that the popular imagination turns when considering the darker side of the Church's imposition of control over the personal and political worlds it has inhabited over long centuries. The figure of a pacific Jesus (the poet of the lilies of the fields and the advocator of peaceful resistance to evil, who so inspired Tolstoy and Gandhi, among others) is often contrasted with a Church of more brutish disciples who, when occasion presented itself, turned willingly and quickly enough to tactics of oppression and coercion— policies which they themselves had lamented as being against both divine and natural justice when applied to them in the earlier centuries of the Roman persecutions. The common version among church historians of this generic tale of a progressive sinking into the "brutal ways of the world" also points to regular cycles of renewal and repentance, when Christians are said to reappropriate the "real" meaning of their past and so renounce violent resistance in the cause of a "truly Christian" non-resistance. This, of course, is usually a matter of occasional academic protest from the sidelines or the wisdom of the aftermath, since in times of war the ranks of those who rush to defend the Christian defensibility of hostilities are rarely short of representatives, it would seem. The key academic studies of the Early Church's peace tradition, for example, had to wait until the 20th century. They appeared in two clusters, both of them the immediate aftermath of the great conflicts of 1914-18 and 1939-45, followed by a longer "tail" which was overshadowed by the Cold War's generic fears of nuclear holocaust and which produced a more thorough-going tenor of the "suspicion of war" in academic circles. Both the main clusters of post-war reassessments of Christian peace tradition in antiquity witnessed to a conflicted product in the tone of the literature. All lamented the fact and experience of war from a Christian perspective, but some justified the concept of limited war engagement (usually Catholic scholars defending the then-dominant Augustine-Aquinas theory of the Just War) while others were evidently more pacifist in tone (generally Protestant scholars calling for a "reform" of defective medievalist views). The more recent work, inspired by the public sight of several disastrously "failed" military interventions (such as Vietnam and Afghanistan) and the horrific record of genocidally tinged conflict at the end of the 20th century (one of the bloodiest and nastiest on human record, though we still like to regard the ancients as less civilized than us), have, again understandably, caused the Christian witness on war and violence to come under renewed scrutiny. Today the literature on war in early Christian tradition is extensive[1], and a synopsis of the primary sources has recently been collated in a useful ready-reference volume, with a good contextualizing discussion.[2]

While the common image of a militaristic Church is still, perhaps, prevalent in popular estimation, there are nevertheless a multitude of pacific figures who feature in the Church's exemplary stories of the lives of the saints. One such hagiography is the narrative on Abba Moses the Ethiopian in the Tales of the Desert Fathers, who, when warned in advance of the impending attack of marauding Blemmyes tribesmen in 5th century Lower Egypt, refused to leave his cell and (though famed as a strong man of previously violent temper) stayed quietly in prayer waiting for the fatal assault of the invading brigands. This story of his election of pacific martyrdom was celebrated as most unusual—a heroic and highly individualist spiritual act of a master (and thus not normative). All the other monks of Scete in his time were either slaughtered because they were surprised or else had much earlier fled before the face of the storm of invasion.

In terms of pacific saints, the Russian Church celebrates the 11th century princes Boris and Gleb—the sons of Vladimir, the first Christian ruler of ancient Rus (Kiev)—who, in order to avoid a civil war on the death of their father (when the third son, Svyatopolk, took up arms to assert his right to monarchical supremacy), are said to have adopted the role of "Passion Bearers." Refusing to bear arms for their own defence, and desiring to avoid bloodshed among their people, they followed the example of their new Lord, who suffered his own unjust Passion. The image and category of "passion-bearing martyr" is one that is dear to, and almost distinctive of, the Russian Church, so troubled has its history been. Nevertheless, even this celebrated example contrasts in many respects with the witness of other Russian saint-heroes, such as the great warrior-prince Alexander Nevsky; and it contrasts with the witness

---

[1] The chief sources in English are: RH Bainton. *Christian Attitudes to War and Peace: A Historical Survey and Critical Re-Evaluation.* Nashville. 1960; CJ Cadoux. *The Early Christian Attitude to War.* Oxford. 1919 (repr. NY. 1982); A von Harnack. *Militia Christi: The Christian Religion and the Military in the First Three Centuries.* (tr. DM Gracie. Philadelphia. 1980; original German edn. 1905; HA Deane. *The Political and Social Ideas of St. Augustine.* New York. 1963 (chs.5-6); J. Helgeland. *Christians and Military Service: AD 173-337.* PhD Diss. University of Chicago. 1973. (summarized in Idem. 'Christians and the Roman Army. AD. 173-337.' *Church History.* 43. June 1974. 149-161; JM Hornus. *It is Not Lawful for me to Fight: Early Christian Attitudes to War, Violence and the State.* (trs. A Kreider and O Coburn). Scottsdale. Pa. 1980; HT McElwain. *Augustine's Doctrine of War in Relation to Earlier Ecclesiastical Writers.* Rome. 1972; TS Miller and J Nesbitt (eds). *Peace and War in Byzantium. Essays in Honor of GT Dennis.* CUA Press. Washington. 1995; EA Ryan. 'The Rejection of Military Service by the Early Christians.' *Theological Studies.* 13. 1952. 1-32; WR. Stevenson. *Christian Love and Just War : Moral Paradox and Political Life in St. Augustine and his Modern Interpreters.* Macon. Ga. 1987.

of many other ancient Churches too (such as the Byzantine, Romanian, Serbian, Nubian, and Ethiopian) who had an equally fraught pilgrimage through history but who proudly elevated and honored the icons and examples of warrior-saints who resisted the onslaught militarily and died in the process. In the Romanian Church one of the great heroic founders was the warrior prince Petru Rares, who slaughtered the invading Turkish armies under the guidance of his spiritual father and confessor Saint Daniel the Hesychast. The saint commanded the prince to erect monasteries on the site of the great battles, to ensure mourning and prayer for the lost souls whose blood had been shed. This was an act that was seen as a necessary expiation of Petru's "equally necessary" violence. Both he and his spiritual mentor were heavily burdened by their perceived duty of defending the borders of Christendom; to this day Romania's most ancient and beautiful churches stand as mute witnesses to a bloody history where Islam's and Christianity's tectonic plates collided (as often they did in the history of the Christian East). The national perception in Romania of prince Vlad Dracul (the western bogeyman of Dracula) is diametrically opposed to the common perception of more or less everyone outside: within the country Vlad himself is regarded as a national hero and a great Christian warrior who assumed the duty of defending the Faith against the military attempts of Islam forcibly to convert Europe. Similarly, almost all the saints of Ethiopia are either monastic recluses or warriors. The saints of the (now lost) Church of Nubia[3] were also predominantly warriors. Likewise, the frescoes of saints on the walls of the ancient Stavronikita monastery on Mount Athos, on the Halkidiki peninsula, demonstrate serried ranks of martyr-protectors dressed in full Roman battle gear, in attendance on the Christ in Majesty.[4] The monks were not particularly warlike themselves but knew at first hand the terrors of living in the pirate-infested Mediterranean. Like the Nubians, a life entirely and permanently surrounded by hostile foes gave the Athonite monks a very practical attitude to violence, pacific resistance, and the need for defence in varieties of forms.

The Western Church also has its share of noble saint-warriors. In medieval English literature the warrior-saint was a highly romantic figure.[5] We can also think of the famed Crusading juggernaut Louis the Pious. These, however, are noticeably not any longer "popular saints" (as their counterparts remain in Eastern Christianity), though this may be laid to the door of a generic loss of interest in hagiography and the cultus of the saints in contemporary Western Christianity as much as to a sense of embarrassment that the ranks of saints included so many generals of armies. Along with its warriors the Western Church often appealed for an example of pacific lifestyle to the Christ-like image of Francis of Assisi (in preference, perhaps, to the more robust figure of Dominic and his inquisitional Order of Preachers), although one ought not to forget that the Franciscan order itself had from its early origins a foundational charge to evangelize Muslims in the Middle and Near East—its own form of potential "Inquisition" which never had the opportunity to flourish because of Ottoman power but which was often felt as real enough and resented greatly by the Eastern-rite Christians of those places.

---

[2] LJ Swift. *The Early Fathers on War and Military Service*. (Message of the Fathers of the Church. Vol. 19). 1983. Wilmington. De.
[3] Byzantine in foundation and structure, until its annihilation in the late 15th century.
[4] See M. Chatzidakis. *The Cretan Painter Theophanes: The Wall-Paintings of the Holy Monastery of Stavronikita*. Thessaloniki. (published on Mount Athos). 1986.
[5] Cf. JE Damon. *Soldier Saints and Holy Warriors : Warfare and Sanctity in the Literature of Early England*. (Ashgate press). Aldershot. 2003.

This macro-picture of Church history as a sclerotic decline (where simple origins are progressively corrupted into oppressive structures as the Church seizes an ever-larger foothold on the face of the earth) is so familiar, almost clichéd, that it hardly needs further amplification. It is perfectly exemplified in the general presumption that the Christian movement before the age of the emperor Constantine the Great (4th century) was mainly pacific in philosophy but afterwards began theologically to justify the use of coercive force, and so commenced the long slide into all manner of corruption of power and abandonment of the primitive spirit of the gentle Jesus.[6] The theory is problematized to some degree by the issue of "conflicted contextualization" for the notable resistance of the earliest Christian movement (2nd to early 4th centuries) to military service: whether this was predominantly pacifist in temperament, or was related to the military requirements to worship the pagan pantheon of gods, or was simply an aspect of the fear of an oppressed and persecuted group in the face of the state's arm of power. In early canon law the military profession had the same status as harlotry when it came to the seeking of baptism: before admission to the church was countenanced, an alternative career had to be sought. After the Pax Constantina that prohibition was relaxed as even the Christian emperors expected their fellow Christians to take up their station in the army. Recent historical study has progressively argued that the advancement of Christians to political and military power should not be seen as a surprisingly miraculous event (as the legend of Constantine would have it be) but as the result of more than a century of prior political and military infiltration of the higher offices of state by Christians bearing arms. The earliest materials (martyrial stories of how the poor resisted the Roman imperium) tend to come from the account of the churches of the local victims.[7] The full story (why, for example, Diocletian targeted Christians within his own court and army to initiate the Great Persecution of the early 4th century [8]) is less to the front, but clearly the great revolution of the 4th century which saw an internationally ascendant Church was not simply an altruistic "gift" of power to a pacific Christian movement but more in the terms of an acknowledgement by Constantine that his own path to monarchy lay with the powerful international lobby of Christians. The question as to "who patronized whom?"—Constantine the Church, or the Church Constantine? —remains one that is surely more evenly balanced than is commonly thought. The military and political involvement of Christians, therefore (as distinct from the "Church," shall we say) is something that is not so simply "switched" at the 4th century watershed of Constantine's "conversion."

Nevertheless, the story that from primitive and "pure" beginnings the Christian movement degenerated into a more warlike compromise with state power is a good story precisely because it is so cartoon-like in its crudity. It ought not to be forgotten, however, that it *is* a story, not a simple record of uncontested facts. It is a story, moreover, that took its origin as part of a whole dossier of similar stories meant to describe the movement of Christianity through history in terms of early promise, followed by rapid failure and succeeded by the age of reform and repristination of the primitive righteousness. In short, the

---

[6] Helgeland (1973. p. 17.) illustrates how both Harnack's and Cadoux's works progress from this shared presupposition despite their different perspectives on the issue of pacifism as a general Christian ideal (Cadoux regarded Harnack as having soft-pedaled the Church's early peace witness).

[7] The early martyrial acts are charged with the dramatic characterization of the martyr as the apocalyptic witness, and the condemning magistrate as eschatological servant of the Beast. The narratives often deliberately follow the literary paradigm of the Passion Story of the Gospels. The *Martyrdom of Polycarp* is one such example.

[8] Or how it might well be the case that Christian soldiers had already taken the imperial throne by force of arms in the mid 3rd century (in the case of Philip the Arab).

common view of Christianity's peace tradition, as sketched out above, is clearly a product of late-medieval Reformation apologetics. That so much of this early-modern propaganda has survived to form a substrate of presupposition in post-modern thought about Christian history is a testimony to the power of the apologetic stories themselves, and (doubtless) to the widespread distrust of the motives of the late medieval Church authorities in western Europe at the time of the Reformation. The common view about Christianity's peace tradition, however, is so hopelessly rooted in western, apologetic, and "retrospectivist" presuppositions (a thorough-going Protestant revision of the Catholic tradition on the morality of war and violence that had preceded it) that it is high time the issue should be considered afresh. The common histories of Christianity, even to this day, seem to pretend that its eastern forms (the Syrians, Byzantines, Armenians, Copts, Nubians, Indians, Ethiopians, and Cappadocians) never existed, or at least were never important enough to merit mention, or that western Europe is a normal and normative vantage point for considering the story. But this narrow perspective skews the evidence at the outset. Accordingly, the figures of Augustine of Hippo (the towering 5th century African theologian) and Thomas Aquinas (the greatest of the Latin medieval scholastic theologians) loom very large in the normative western form of the telling of the tale; both theologians were highly agentive in developing the Western Church's theory and principles of a "Just War." In the perspectives of the Eastern Christian tradition, not only do these two monumental figures not feature, but, needless to say, neither does their theory on the moral consideration of war and violence which has so dominated the western imagination. Eastern Christianity simply does not approach the issue from the perspective of "Just War" and endorses no formal doctrine advocating the possibility of a "Just War."

Its approach is ambivalent, more complex and nuanced; for that reason it has been largely overlooked in the annals of the history of Christianity, or even dismissed as self-contradictory. It is not self-contradictory, of course, having been proven by experience through centuries of political suffering and oppression. If it knows anything, the Eastern Church knows how to endure and hardly needs lessons on such a theme; but it is certainly not a linear theory of war and violence that it holds (as if war and violence *could be* imagined as susceptible of rational solution and packaging). Its presuppositions grow from a different soil than do modern and post-modern notions of political and moral principles. Christianity was, and remains at heart, an apocalyptic religion, and it is no accident that its numerous biblical references to war and violent destruction are generally apocalyptic ciphers—symbols that stand for something else, references to the "Eschaton" (the image of how the world will be rolled up and assessed once universal justice is imposed by God on his recalcitrant and rebellious creation). Biblical descriptions of violence and war in most of Christianity's classical exposition of its biblical heritage, rather than being straightforward depictions of the life and values of "This World Order," are thus eschatological allegories. To confound the two orders[9] (taking war images of the apocalyptic dimension for instances of how the world (here) ought to be managed)[10] is a gross distortion of the ancient literature. This has become

---

[9] What the ancient sources described as the "Two Ages": This Age of turmoil, which stands within the historical record and permits brutal oppression as the ultimate symbol of "the Beast," that is, evil personified; and the Other Age, which is the Transcendent "Kingdom of God," when peace will be established by the definitive ending of violent powers hostile to the good and the comforting of the poor.

[10] It is a major categorical mistake, therefore, for fundamentalist Christians to apply apocalyptically matrixed scriptural references to "war in the heavens spilling out on earth" as authoritative "justifications" from the Bible for Christians to engage in violent conflict for political ends. The essence of biblical apocalyptic doctrine is that the Two Ages must never be conflated or confused. The "Next Age" cannot be ushered in by political

increasingly a problem since the medieval period when allegorist readings of scripture have been progressively substituted (especially in Protestantism) for wholesale historicist and literalist readings of the ancient texts.[11] This is not to say that Eastern Christianity itself has not been guilty of its own misreadings of evidences in various times of its history or that it has no blood on its hands; for that would be to deny the brutal facts of a Church that has progressively been driven westwards, despite its own will, by a series of military disasters for the last thousand years. But Christian reflection in the Eastern Church has, I would suggest, been more careful than the West to remind itself of the apocalyptic and mysterious nature of the Church's place within history and on the world stage, and has stubbornly clung to a less congratulatory theory of the morality of war (despite its advocacy of "Christian imperium"), because it sensed that such a view was more in tune with the principles of the Gospels. What follows in this paper is largely a consideration of that peace tradition in the perspective of the eastern provinces of Christianity, the "patristic" foundation that went on to provide the underpinning of Byzantine canon law, and (after the fall of Byzantium) the system of law that still operates throughout the Churches of the East.

THE INFLUENCE OF ORIGEN AND EUSEBIUS

In the decades following the First World War, Adolf Von Harnack was one of the first among modern patristic theologians to assemble a whole dossier of materials on the subject of the Church's early traditions on war and violence.[12] In his macro-thesis he favored the theory of the "fall from grace" and argued that the Church progressively relaxed its earliest blanket hostility to bloodshed and the military profession in general. The relaxation of anti-war discipline he saw as part and parcel of a wider "corruption" of early Christian ideals by "Hellenism." And yet, no Eastern Christian attitudes to war, either before or after the Pax Constantina, have ever borne much relation to classic Hellenistic and Roman war theory[13], being constantly informed and conditioned by biblical paradigms (reined in by Jesus' strictures on the futility of violence) rather than by Hellenistic kingship theory or tribal theories of national pride. In the second part of his study (subtitled "The Christian Religion and the Military Profession"), Harnack went further to discuss the wide extent of biblical images of war and vengeance in the Christian foundational documents, suggesting that the imagery of "spiritual warfare," however removed it might be from the "real world" when it

---

victories gained in "This Age." By this means Christianity, in its foundational vision, undercut the principles that continue to inspire Judaism and Islam, with their (essentially) non-apocalyptic understandings of the spreading of the Kingdom of God on Earth in recognizable borders, and militarily if necessary.

[11] As if, for example, the biblical narratives of the Pentateuch where God commands Moses and Joshua to slaughter the Canaanite inhabitants in the process of seizing the "Promised Land" were to be read literalistically, as both vindicating war for "righteous reasons" and validating the forced appropriation of territories after conflict. Protestant fundamentalism would, of course, read the texts with that political slant (symbolically going further to adapt the text to justify Christianity's use of violence in a just cause); whereas the ancient Church consistently reads the narrative as allegorically symbolic of the perennial quest to overcome evil tendencies by virtuous action. The Canaanites assume the symbolic status of personal vice, the Israelite armies the status of the ethical struggle. While this allegorical symbolism still depends in large degree on a symbolic reading of violent images, it successfully defuses a wholesale biblical sanction for violence and war.

[12] A. Harnack. *Militia Christi. The Christian Religion and The Military in the First Three Centuries* (Tr. D. McI. Gracie). Philadelphia. 1981.

[13] Though Ambrose and Augustine take much of their views on the subject from Cicero.

was originally coined, must take some responsibility for advocating the sanctification of war theories within the Church in later ages.[14] For Harnack and many others following in his wake, Constantine was the villain of the piece; and not less so his apologist, the Christian bishop Eusebius of Caesarea. The latter finds no problem at all in comparing the deaths of the wicked as recounted in Old Testament narratives of holy war with Constantine's conquest and execution of his enemies in the Civil War of the early 4th century.[15] For Eusebius, writing in 336, the cessation of the war in 324 was a fulfilment of the Psalmic and Isaian prophecies of a golden age of peace.[16] Eusebius' fulsome rhetoric has had a great deal of weight placed upon it by those who favor the "theory of fall," even though on any sober consideration to extrapolate a court theologian such as Eusebius into a marker of general opinion in the Church of the early 4th century should have been more universally acknowledged to be a serious mistake. Eusebius' more sober thoughts on the expansion of the Church (as exemplified by Constantine's victory over persecuting emperors and his clear favoritism for the Christians) was really an intellectual heritage from that great theological teacher whose disciple he prided himself on being—Origen of Alexandria. It was certainly Origen who had put into his mind the juxtaposition of the ideas of the Pax Romana as being the providentially favorable environment for the rapid internationalization of the Gospel. Origen himself, however, was pacifist in his attitudes to war and world powers and was sternly against the notion of the Church's advocating its transmission and spread by force of arms.[17] In his wider exegesis Eusebius shows himself consistently to be a follower of his teacher's lead, and the Old Testament paradigms of the "downfall of the wicked" are what are generally at play in both Origen and Eusebius when they highlight biblical examples of vindication or military collapse. Several scholars misinterpret Eusebius radically, therefore, when they read his laudation of Constantine as some kind of proleptic justification of the Church as an asserter of rightful violence. His *Panegyric on Constantine* should not be given such theoretical weight, just as a collection of wedding congratulatory speeches today would hardly be perused for a cutting-edge analysis of the times. In applying biblical tropes and looking for fulfilments, Eusebius (certainly in the wider panoply if all his work is taken together, not simply his court laudations) is looking to the past, not to the future, and is intent only on celebrating what for most in his generation must have truly seemed miraculous—that their oppressors had fallen and that they themselves were now free from the fear of torture and death. Origen and Eusebius may have set a tone of later interpretation that could readily grow into a vision of the Church as the inheritor of the biblical promises about the Davidic kingdom (that the boundaries of Byzantine Christian power were concomitant with the Kingdom of God on earth, and thus that all those who lay outside those boundaries were the enemies of God); but there were still innumerable dissidents even in the long-lasting Byzantine Christian *politeia* (especially the monks) who consistently refused to relax the apocalyptic dimension of their

---

[14] He probably underestimated the extent to which the early Church was propelled, not by subservience to emperors, but more by the way in which the war theology of ancient Israel was passed on as an authoritative paradigm, simply by the force of ingesting so much of the Old Testament narratives in the structure of its prayers, liturgies, and doctrines. It is, nonetheless, worthy of note that formally, from early times, the war passages of the Old Testament were consistently preached as allegorical symbols of the battle to establish peaceful virtues in human hearts (not the advocating of conquest of specific territories). Harnack himself admitted (when considering the example of the Salvation Army) that this aspect of this thesis could limp badly.

[15] *Eusebius. Ecclesiastical History. 9.9. 5-8; Life of Constantine. 1.39.*

[16] Is.2.4; Ps.72.7-8.

theology and who resisted the notion that the Church and the Byzantine borders were one and the same thing.[18]

THE CANONICAL EPISTLES OF BASIL OF CAESAREA

Basil of Caesarea was a younger contemporary of Eusebius, and in the following generation of the Church of the late 4th century, he emerged as one of the leading theorists of the Christian movement. His letters and instructions on the ascetic life and his "Canons"[19] (ethical judgements, as from a ruling bishop to his flock) on morality and practical issues became highly influential in the wider Church because of his role as one of the major monastic theorists of early Christianity. His canonical epistles were transmitted wherever monasticism went; and in the Eastern Church of antiquity (because monasticism was the substructure of the spread of the Christian movement), that more or less meant his canonical views became the standard paradigm of Eastern Christianity's theoretical approach to the morality of war and violence, even though the writings were local[20] and occasional in origin. Basil's 92 Canonical Epistles were adapted by various Ecumenical Councils of the Church that followed his time: his writing is appealed to in Canon 1 of the 4th Ecumenical Council of Chalcedon (451) and in Canon 1 of the 7th Ecumenical Council of Nicaea (787), and it is literally cited in Canon 2 of the 6th Ecumenical Council of Constantinople (681), which paraphrases much else from his Canonical Epistles. By such affirmations eventually the entire corpus of the Basilian Epistles entered the Pandects of Canon Law of the Byzantine Eastern Church, and they remain authoritative to this day.

Basil has several things to say about violence and war in his diocese. It was a border territory of the empire, and his administration had known several incursions by "barbarian" forces. Canon 13 of the 92 considers war:

> Our fathers did not consider killings committed in the course of wars to be classifiable as murders at all, on the score, it seems to me, of allowing a pardon to men fighting in defense of sobriety and piety. Perhaps, though, it might be advisable to refuse them communion for three years, on the ground that their hands are not clean.[21]

The balance and sense of discretion is remarkable in this little comment, one that bears much weight in terms of Eastern Orthodox understandings of the morality of war. The "fathers" in question refers to Athanasius of Alexandria, the great Nicene Orthodox authority of the 4th century Church. Athanasius' defense of the Nicene creed and the divine status of

---

[17] See N McLynn. "Roman Empire," pp. 185-187 in: J.A. McGuckin (ed). *The Westminster Handbook to Origen of Alexandria.* Louisville. Ky. 2004.

[18] For a further elaboration of the argument, see J.A.McGuckin. *The Legacy of the Thirteenth Apostle : Origins of the East- Christian Conceptions of Church-State Relation.* St. Vladimir's Theological Quarterly. 47. Nos. 3-4. 2003. 251-288.

[19] The "Canonical Epistles of St. Basil," otherwise known as the "92 canons." They can be found in English translation in *The Pedalion or Rudder of the Orthodox Catholic Church : The Compilation of the Holy Canons by Saints Nicodemus and Agapius.* Tr. D Cummings. (Orthodox Christian Educational Society). Chicago. 1957 (repr. NY. 1983). pp. 772-864.

[20] Basil was the Bishop of Caesarea in Cappadocia, now a city (Kaisariye) of Eastern Turkey.

[21] Basil. Ep. 188. 13; Pedalion. p. 801.

Christ had won him immense prestige by the end of the 4th century, and as his works were being collated and disseminated (in his own lifetime his reputation had been highly conflicted, his person exiled numerous times, and his writings proscribed by imperial censors), Basil seems to wish to add a cautionary note: not everything a "father" has to say is equally momentous or universally authoritative. In his Letter to Amun, Athanasius had apparently come out quite straightforwardly about the legitimacy of killing in time of war, saying:

> Although one is not supposed to kill, the killing of the enemy in time of war is both a lawful and praiseworthy thing. This is why we consider individuals who have distinguished themselves in war as being worthy of great honours, and indeed public monuments are set up to celebrate their achievements. It is evident, therefore, that at one particular time, and under one set of circumstances, an act is not permissible, but when time and circumstances are right, it is both allowed and condoned.[22]

This saying was being circulated and given authority as a "patristic witness" simply because it had come from Athanasius. In fact, the original letter had nothing whatsoever to do with war. The very example of the "war hero" is a sardonic reference *ad hominem* since the letter was addressed to an aged leader of the Egyptian monks, who described themselves as *Asketes*, that is, those who labored and "fought" for the virtuous life. The military image is entirely incidental, and Athanasius in context merely uses it to illustrate his chief point in the letter—which is to discuss the query Amun had sent on to him as Archbishop: "Did nocturnal emissions count as sins for desert celibates?" Athanasius replies to the effect that with human sexuality, as with all sorts of other things, the context of the activity determines what is moral, not some absolute standard which is superimposed on moral discussion from the outset. Many ancients, Christian and pagan, regarded sexual activity as inherently defiling, and here Athanasius decidedly takes leave of them. His argument, therefore, is falsely attributed when (as is often the case) read out of context as an apparent justification of killing in time of war; he is not actually condoning the practice at all, merely using the rhetorical example of current opinion to show Amun that contextual variability is very important in making moral judgements.

In his turn, Basil wishes to make it abundantly clear for his Christian audience that such a reading, if applied to the Church's tradition on war, is simplistic and that is it is just plain wrong-headedness to conclude that the issue ceases to be problematic if one is able to dig up a justificatory "proof text" from scripture or patristic tradition (as some seem to have been doing with these words of Athanasius). And so, Basil sets out a nuanced corrective exegesis of what the Church's canon law *should really be* in terms of fighting in time of hostilities. One of the ways he does this is to attribute this aphorism of Athanasius to indeterminate "fathers," who can then be legitimately corrected by taking a stricter view than they appeared to allow. He also carefully sets his own context: what he speaks about is the canonical regulation of war in which a Christian can engage and be "amerced"[23]; all other armed

---

[22] Athanasius Epistle 48. *To Amun.* full text in A Robertson (tr). *St. Athanasius Select Works and Letters.* Nicene and Post Nicene Fathers of the Church. Vol. 4. (1891). repr. Eerdmans. Grand Rapids. 1980. pp. 556-557.

[23] That is, find canonical forgiveness for the act of shedding blood, which is canonically prohibited. The background context of the canons which forbid the shedding of blood are important to Basil's thought and are presumed throughout. He takes it for granted that clergy are absolutely forbidden to shed blood and, even if they do so accidentally, will be prohibited from celebrating the Eucharist mysteries afterwards. In this case, just as with

conflicts are implicitly excluded as not being appropriate to Christian morality. Basil's text on war needs, therefore, to be understood in terms of an "economic" (*ad hominem*) reflection on the ancient canons that forbade the shedding of blood in blanket terms. This tension between the ideal standard (no bloodshed) and the complexities of the context in which a local church finds itself thrown in times of conflict and war is witnessed in several other ancient laws, such as Canon 14 of Hippolytus (also from the 4th century).[24] The reasons Basil gives for suggesting that killing in time of hostilities could be distinguished from voluntary murder pure and simple (for which the canonical penalty was a lifelong ban from admission to the churches and from the sacraments) is set out as the "defense of sobriety and piety." This is code language for the defense of Christian borders from the ravages of pagan marauders. The difficulty Basil had to deal with was not war on the large scale but local tribal insurgents who were mounting attacks on Roman border towns, with extensive rapinage. In such circumstances Basil has little patience for those who do not feel they can fight because of religious scruples. His sentiment is more that a passive non-involvement betrays the Christian family (especially its weaker members, who cannot defend themselves but need others to help them) to the ravages of men without heart or conscience to restrain them. The implication of his argument, then, is that the provocation to fighting that Christians ought at some stage to accept (to defend the honor and safety of the weak) will be inherently a limited and adequate response, mainly because the honor and tradition of the Christian faith (piety and sobriety) in the hearts and minds of the warriors will restrict the bloodshed to a necessary minimum. His "economic" solution nevertheless makes it abundantly clear that the absolute standard of Christian morality turns away from war as an unmitigated evil. This is why we can note that the primary reason Basil gives that previous "fathers" had distinguished killing in time of war from the case of simple murder was "on the score of allowing a pardon." There was no distinction made here in terms of the qualitative horror of the deed itself, rather in terms of the way in which the deed could be "cleansed" by the Church's system of penance.

Is it logical to expect a Christian of his diocese to engage in the defense of the homeland while simultaneously penalizing him if he spills blood in the process? Well, one needs to contextualize the debarment from the Sacrament in the generic 4th century practice of the reception of the Eucharist, which did not expect regular communication to begin with (ritual preparation was extensive and involved fasting and almsgiving and prayer), and where a sizeable majority of adult Christians in a given church would not have yet been initiated by means of baptism and were thus not bound to keep all the canons of the Church. By his regulation and by the ritual exclusion of the illumined warrior from the Sacrament (the

---

the Church's canonical rules relating to the prohibition of second marriages, what began as a general rule was relaxed in its application to wider society, although the clergy were required to sustain the original strict interpretation (see *Apostolical Canons* 66. *Pedalion*. pp. 113-116.) Today in Orthodoxy, marriage is described as a one-time occurrence; but if the marriage is broken, a second (and even third) marriage can be contracted "as an economy" to human conditions and relational failures. The clergy, however, are not allowed to contract second marriages (even if the first wife has died); the economy is not permitted to them. Clergy in the eastern tradition are still canonically forbidden from engaging in any violence beyond the minimum necessary to defend their life (*Apostolic Canon* 66.), though they are censured if they do not vigorously defend a third party being attacked in their presence. For both things (use of excessive violence in self-defence and refusal to use violence in defence of another) they are given the penalty of deposition from orders.

[24] "A Christian should not volunteer to become a soldier, unless he is compelled to do this by someone in authority. He can have a sword, but he should not be commanded to shed blood. If it can be shown that he has shed blood he should stay away from the mysteries (sacraments) at least until he has been purified through tears and lamentation." *Canons of Hippolytus* 14.74. Text in Swift (1983) p. 93. See also *Apostolic Tradition* 16.

returning "victor" presumably would have received many other public honors and the gratitude of the local folk), Basil is making sure that at least one public sign is given to the entire community that the Gospel standard has no place for war, violence, and organized death. He is trying to sustain an eschatological balance: war is not part of the Kingdom of God (signified in the Eucharistic ritual as arriving in the present) but is part of the bloody and greed-driven reality of world affairs, which is the "Kingdom-Not-Arrived." By moving in and out of Eucharistic reception, Basil's faithful Christian (returning from his duty with blood on his hands) is now in the modality of expressing his dedication to the values of peace and innocence by means of the lamentation and repentance for life that has been taken, albeit the blood of the violent. Basil's arrangement that the returning "noble warrior" should stand in the church (not in the narthex where the other public sinners were allocated spaces) but refrain from communion makes the statement that a truly honorable termination of war, for a Christian, has to be an honorable repentance.

Several commentators (not least many of the later western Church fathers) have regarded this as "fudge," but it seems to me to express, in a finely tuned "economic" way, the tension in the basic Christian message that there is an unresolvable shortfall between the ideal and the real in an apocalyptically charged religion. What this Basilian canon does most effectively is to set a "No Entry" sign to any potential theory of Just War within Christian theology[25], and it should set up a decided refusal of post-war, church-sponsored self congratulations for victory.[26] All violence— local, individual, or nationally sanctioned—is here stated to be an expression of *hubris* that is inconsistent with the values of the Kingdom of God; and while in many circumstances that violence may be "necessary" or "unavoidable" (Basil states the only legitimate reasons as the defense of the weak and innocent), it is never "justifiable." Even for the best motives in the world, the shedding of blood remains a defilement, such that the true Christian afterwards would wish to undergo the kathartic experience of temporary return to the lifestyle of penance, that is, "be penitent." Basil's restriction of the time of penance to three years (seemingly harsh to us moderns) was actually a commonly recognized sign of merciful leniency in the ancient rulebook of the early Church.[27]

CONCLUDING REFLECTIONS

We might today regard such early attempts by Christians as quaintly naïve. They are wired through the early penitential system, clearly, and have a fundamentally "economic" character about them. By "economy" the early Church meant the art of doing what was

---

[25] As developed especially (out of Cicero) by Ambrose of Milan in *On Duties*. 1. 176; and Augustine (*Epistle* 183.15; *Against Faustus* 22. 69-76; also see Swift :1983. pp. 110-149). But Ambrose (ibid. 1. 35.175) specifically commands his priests to have no involvement (inciting or approving) whatsoever in the practice of war or judicial punishments: "Interest in matters of war," he says, "seems to me to be alien to our role as priests."

[26] Many churches have uneasily juggled this responsibility in times past. Prime Minister Margaret Thatcher famously denounced the Archbishop of Canterbury's post-Falklands-War service in 80's London (St. Paul's cathedral) as "far too wet," while other critics in the country were hard on him for not stating at the outset that the Falklands invasion did not fulfill the requirements of a "Just War" in terms of classical western theory and thus should have been more severely denounced by the Church.

[27] Ordinary murder was given a 20-year debarment from the Church's sacraments, as well as all accruing civic penalties (Basil's Canon 56. *Pedalion*. p. 827). Manslaughter received a ten year debarment (Basil's Canon 57. *Pedalion*. p. 828).

possible when a higher ideal standard was not sustained. In the case of war, Basil and the canonical tradition are tacitly saying that when the Kingdom ideals of peace and reconciliation collapse, especially in times of conflict, when decisive and unusual action is required, and when the ideals of reconciliation and forgiveness fall into chaos in the very heart of the Church itself[28] as members go off to fight, then the ideal must be reasserted as soon as possible—with limitations to the hostilities a primary concern, and a profound desire to mark the occasion retrospectively with a public "cleansing." While the honor of the combatants is celebrated by Basil (even demanded as an act of protection for the weak), one essential aspect of that honor is also listed as being the public acceptance of the status of penitent shedder of blood. The clergy (as with other economic concessions of morality operative in the Church's canons) are the only ones not allowed this "benefit of necessity". In no case is violent action permitted to one who stands at the altar of God: even if a cleric spills blood accidentally (such as in an involuntary manslaughter), such a person would be deposed from active presbyteral office. The sight of "warrior-bishops" in full military regalia passing through the streets of Constantinople in the Fourth Crusade left its mark on contemporary Greek sources as one of the greatest "shocks" to the system and as one of the incidentals that were taken by the Greeks as proof positive that Latin Christianity in the 13th century had a serious illness at its center.

More than naïve, perhaps, might we regard such a morality of war as seriously "under-developed"? Can such an important issue really be dealt with by so few canons of the ancient Eastern Church, and even then by regulations that are so evidently local and occasional in character? Well, the charges of inconsistency (praising a noble warrior, then subjecting him to penance) and muddle-headedness were raised in early times, especially by Latin theologians who wanted to press the envelope and arrive at a more coherent and all-embracing theory of war, one that balanced the apparent biblical justifications of hostility on the part of the chosen people with the need to limit the obvious blood lust of our species. The Latin theory of Just War was one result. Considered primarily (as it was meant to be) as a theory of the limitation of hostilities in the ancient context (hand-to-hand fighting of massed armies whose very size limited the time of possible engagement to a matter of months at most), it, too, was an "economic" theory that had much merit. Its usefulness became moot in the medieval period when armament manufacture took ancient warfare into a new age, and it has become utterly useless in the modern age of mechanized warfare, where it could not stop the fatal transition (on which modernized mechanical warfare depends—both that sponsored by states, and that sponsored by smaller groups which we call "terrorism") to the centrally important role of the murder of non-combatants. Be that as it may, it is not the purpose of the present essay to offer a sustained critique on Just War theory—merely to raise up a mainline Christian tradition of the ancient East, which has never believed in Just War, and to offer, instead of an elegant theory, a poor and threadbare suggestion of old saints: that war is never justified or justifiable, but is *de facto* a sign and witness of evil and sin.

When it falls across the threshold of the Church in an unavoidable way, it sometimes becomes our duty (so the old canons say) to take up arms—though when that is the case is to be determined in trepidation by the elect who understand the value of peace and

---

[28] Note that they are not querying the collapse of peace ideals outside the Church, as they regard the spread of hubris and violence on the earth as a clear mark of all those dark forces hostile to the heavenly Kingdom. The advocacy of a war that is not a direct response to a clear and present threat of aggression is thus permanently ruled out of the court of morality in this system.

reconciliation, not in self-glorifying battle cries from the voices of the bloodthirsty and foolish. But in no case is the shedding of blood, even against a manifestly wicked foe, ever a "Just Violence." The eastern canons, for all their tentativeness, retain that primitive force of Christian experience on that front. It may be the "Violence of the Just," but in that case the hostility will necessarily be ended with the minimal expenditure of force and be marked in retrospect by the last act of the "Violent Just," which will be repentance that finally resolves the untenable paradox. Ambivalent and "occasional" such a theory of war might be. But if it had been followed with fidelity, the Church's hands might have been cleaner than they have been across many centuries; and it might yet do a service on the wider front in helping western Christianity to dismantle its own "economic" structures of war theory which are so patently in need of radical rethinking. Perhaps the place to begin, as is usually the case, is here and now: with "Christian America" at the dawn of a new millennium, in which we seem to have learned nothing at all from generations of bitter experience of hostility—except the *hubris* that international conflicts can be undertaken "safely" now that other super-powers are currently out of commission. Such is the wisdom of the most powerful nation on earth, currently in an illegal state of war[29] that it wishes to disguise even from itself and even as the American military deaths at this time of writing exceeded 1000, with a pervasive silence all that it has to offer in relation to all figures of the deaths of those who were *not* American troops. Such is the wisdom under a leadership which is itself apparently eager to line up for a "righteous struggle" with the "forces of evil," which so many others in the world outside have seen as more in the line of a determined dominance of Islamic sensibilities by Super Power secularism of the crassest order. In such a strange new millennium, perhaps the ancient wisdom of the need to be tentative finds a new power and authority?

SHORT BIOGRAPHICAL NOTE

John Anthony McGuckin, a priest of the Orthodox Church (Patriarchate of Romania), came to America from England in 1997, where he was a Reader in Patristic and Byzantine Theology at the University of Leeds, to assume the Chair in Early Church History at the renowned school of Union Theological Seminary in New York. His academic career began with the study of Philosophical Theology at Heythrop College, a Pontifical Athenaeum, from 1970-72, and from there he read for a Divinity degree at the University of London, graduating with First Class Honors in 1975. For his doctoral researches at Durham University (1980), he studied the politics and theology of the early Constantinian era, with a thesis on the thought of Lucius Caecilius Lactantius, the emperor Constantine's pacifist Christian tutor and political advisor. Prof. McGuckin was elected a Fellow of the Royal Society of Arts in 1986, and a Fellow of the Royal Historical Society in 1996. He is the author of seventeen books on historical theology, including: *The Transfiguration of Christ in Scripture and Tradition* (Mellen. 1986); *St. Cyril of Alexandria: The Christological Controversy* (Brill. 1994); *At the Lighting of the Lamps: Hymns from the Ancient Church* (1995, and repr. Morehouse.1997); *St. Gregory of Nazianzus: An Intellectual Biography* (SVS.2000)—Nominated for the 2002

---

[29] The conflict in Iraq: an invasion not given sanction of international law through the medium of the United Nations, but initiated to overthrow the dictatorship of Saddam Hussein on the pretext that he was manufacturing weapons of mass destruction.

Pollock Biography Prize; *Standing in God's Holy Fire: The Spiritual Tradition of Byzantium* (Orbis, 2001); *The Book of Mystical Chapters* (Shambhala, 2002); and *The Westminster Handbook To Patristic Theology* (WJK. 2004).

He has published numerous research articles in scholarly journals ranging in subject matter from New Testament Exegesis to Byzantine Iconography, mainly centered on the thought of Origen of Alexandria and the fourth to fifth century Greek Christian theologians. In 1994 his first collection of poetry, *Byzantium and Other Poems*, was published. Prof. McGuckin has served as visiting professor and guest lecturer in many universities and colleges in England, Ireland, Greece, Romania, Ukraine, Italy, and the United States. In 2003 he was invited by the Royal Norwegian Academy to serve as an International Research Fellow at the Academy's "Center For Higher Studies" in Oslo. There he formed part of a team of international specialists considering the elaboration and development of principles of aesthetics in early Christian culture-formation. He is currently working on a study of the history and teachings of the eastern Orthodox Church. He recently won the prestigious Henry Luce III Fellowship in Historical Theology. He teaches Graduate-level courses as a faculty member of both Columbia University's Religion Department, and Union Theological Seminary, and also serves as a priest in a small Orthodox parish in upper Manhattan.

In: Religion, Terrorism and Globalization   ISBN 1-59454-553-7
Editor: K.K. Kuriakose, pp.203-214   © 2006 Nova Science Publishers, Inc.

Chapter 13

ROMAN CATHOLIC TRADITION AND PASSIVE RESISTANCE

*Gabriel Moran**
New York University, New York, NY

Catholic tradition has always embodied a precarious tension between condemnations of violence based on the teachings of Jesus of Nazareth and a philosophical/political tradition that has grappled with the reality of force, violence and war. In the earliest part of church history, non-cooperation with the war making powers was emphasized. After the fourth century, the church became part of the political, economic and military power of the Roman empire and its successors. Voices of dissent against the use of violence were never stilled but they have been in the minority.

This essay recounts the rebirth and expansion of traditional protesting against violence. I will comment briefly on Jesus' teachings and on the approach to nonviolence today. My main focus is on the past Century, more specifically on those who have witnessed nonviolence as a way of life. While Roman Catholic protest is rooted in New Testament teaching, it usually has a philosophical side. For better, and for worse, the last 2000 years of history is part of the tradition. Invoking Jesus' teaching and trying to bypass the past 2000 years will not work.

THE BIBLE AND NONVIOLENCE

The Christian version of the Bible includes what Christians call the Old Testament as well as the books of the New Testament. The life, death and resurrection of Jesus are set within the context of this complex literature. Each Christian group gives primary emphasis to

---

* Gabriel Moran is Director of the Program in Philosophy of Education at New York University. He also teaches international ethics in the International Education Program. He has a PhD in religious education from the Catholic University of America. For the past forty years he has been a leading author in the field of religious education. His works have been translated into many languages. He has written essays on force, violence and war for several edited collections and journals. His books include *A Grammar of Responsibility* (1996) and *Both Sides: The Story of Revelation* (2002)

some parts of the Bible, thereby arriving at various interpretations on how a Christian should live. While all Christians would claim to be followers of Jesus, the interpretive prism of St. Paul's letters or the importance of the fourth gospel may be determinative of how the Christian group or individual is defined as a follower.

During the 2000 presidential campaign, George W. Bush was asked who his favorite philosopher is. He answered, Jesus Christ. The response caused ridicule or horror in many places. But if one asks what is wrong with the answer, I think it is the second of the two words. If Bush had simply answered "Jesus", he would have found himself in the company of Gandhi or Martin Luther King Jr. The reason for suspicion about Bush's answer is his addition of "Christ" which is a Christian liturgical term. Although it is common to refer to "Jesus Christ", anyone sensitive to the meaning of "Jesus (the) Christ" would not refer to a philosopher named Jesus Christ. If philosophers are the question, then the teachings of Jesus of Nazareth have to be placed in comparison with other thinkers rather than cited as words of God. That is a risk Christians take if they wish to enter the political arena in order to persuade people who are not Christians on the value of these teachings (Yoder 1972).

When Christians do believe, live and present the challenging teachings of Jesus, they find a positive response from many Jews, Muslims, Buddhists and people with no religion. Jewish scholars are particularly helpful in explaining the essence of Jesus' teaching. Jesus' Sermon on the Mount, which includes the Beatitudes, is often taken to be a summary of Jesus' teaching (Lapide 1986).

There is little doubt that Jesus belonged to the peace party in the reformations of his day (Theissen 1964, 64). He opposed both Zealots who made war on the opposing Roman forces, as well as the Roman authorities who tried to appropriate a halo of divine approbation. The Sermon on the Mount is regularly given faint praise as a personal ideal but one that no state can live by. It is a practice common to both Christian and non-Christian to dismiss the Sermon on the Mount as irrelevant to the practice of "realistic" government policies.

The dismissers often show little knowledge of the teaching beyond a few phrases taken out of context. Jesus' teaching needs to be set within a temporal and geographical context, wherein he was commenting on the texts of his people. He was not rejecting that tradition but emphasizing aspects of it. The assumption that he was advocating a supine attitude in the face of oppressors is not borne out by the Sermon as a whole, nor the tradition of which it is a part. The purpose of the teaching, as careful students through the centuries have recognized, is to de-hostilize enemies in order to win them over. "Do good to those who hate you" is a political strategy requiring skill, courage and persistence. Jesus recognized that there is no way out of an escalation of mutual retaliation unless someone refuses to act violently and instead responds asymmetrically. Reconciliation will benefit the hater as well as the hated.

"Love your neighbor," so often repeated without much thought, would be better translated as "love to your neighbor." Jesus commented on Leviticus 19:18: "Love your neighbor as yourself; I am the Lord". Christian love is neither selfish nor altruistic; it is a love of both neighbor and self, grounded in recognition of God's love for every creature. Special attention is given to victims of human unkindness, the disadvantaged, and those who come last. But, the fundamental attitude is not pity, Nietzsche's complaint about Christianity, but a rousing call to action. Martin Luther King Jr. described his "nonviolent army" by saying that to be accepted in the armies that maim and kill, one must be physically sound, possessed of straight limbs and accurate vision. But in Birmingham, Alabama., the lame and the halt and the crippled could, and did, join up (King 1964, 38). Gandhi, another activist inspired by

Jesus' teaching, found that "individuals who neither submit passively nor retaliate to violence find in themselves a new sense of strength, dignity and courage" (Gustafson 1999,101).

POST-BIBLICAL TRADITION

The early Christian church believed that Christians should not take up arms in any war. The Greek Fathers of the Church were generally united in their attitude against war. Clement of Alexandria, Justin Martyr and Cyprian were among the outspoken opponents of Christian participation in war. The greatest of these writers, Origen, set out a theory in which he argued that Christians should not serve in the military but that they are still responsible for serving the commonwealth (Origen 1980).

The Christian writer's name most closely associated with the term "just war" is Augustine, an African bishop of the late fourth century who set the direction for much of Western Christianity. Augustine was no enthusiast for war (Wills 1999). He thought that the Christian, in imitation of Jesus, should not use violence to defend himself. However, he believed the Christian had a responsibility to aid a victim under attack. (Marcus 1983) It is difficult to argue with Augustine's principle. But it is even more difficult to move from the image of a man protecting his wife or child to the reality of a nation-state at war in the 21st century (Augustine 1972, 4:15, 19:7, 1:21). Thomas Aquinas, who always tried to avoid directly contradicting Augustine, worked at subtly adding changes in Augustinian teaching. Disappointingly, Aquinas raised little challenge to what became "just war" theory. He outlined six conditions for going to war and three conditions for how war is to be fought (Thomas Aquinas 1966, 1a, 2ae, 90-97).

Opposition to war survived in the Christian Middle Ages mainly in the mystical tradition. The mystics sought a unity beyond conflict. Mysticism is often dismissed as apolitical and "otherworldly". While mysticism does not fit in with ordinary politics, its political reverberations are considerable. As the Marxist, Ernst Bloch phrased it, "He who believes that he is in union with the Lord of Lords does not, when it comes down to it, make a very good serf" (Bloch 1986, 127). Cut loose from the moorings of ordinary life, mysticism can easily turn violent, as often happened in the late Middle Ages (Ozment 1973). For the same reason, mysticism could also provide peaceful unity at the end, and peace as the means.

The greatest mystic of the Middle Ages was the fourteenth-century preacher, Meister Eckhart. His pleas for peaceful reconciliation went unheeded in his own day. However, Eckhart's writings continue to inspire people. At times, Eckhart has been pictured as a misplaced Buddhist but he was firmly rooted in the New Testament and Christian tradition. He was keenly aware that passionate preaching of justice for the poor might unleash more conflict but he was convinced that there was no true peace without justice (McGinn 1986).

The most outstanding medieval essay on peace, *Peace Protests*, belongs to Desiderius Erasmus. Erasmus was a great humanist of the 16th century, one of the world's first cosmopolitans. Erasmus was dissatisfied with a choice between "just war theory" and "pacifism". He was opposed to war but thought that simply stating that one is for peace is inadequate to the violence all around us. Erasmus presciently saw the need for structures of mediation that could work through international conflict. Almost four centuries later the world is slowly coming to accept what Erasmus saw as indispensable for peace making. (Chapiro 1950).

THE 20TH CENTURY

The story of the Roman Catholic Church in the 20th century is one of a gradual shift towards skepticism about claims for any war being just. Some impetus for a Catholic Peace Party was provided by papal statements and individual bishops. More often, official statements lagged behind Catholic groups who were willing to take a radical stand against war.

Pope Leo XIII in his encyclical *Rerum Novarum* (1891) asserted the need for a new international order in which peace would be based on justice rather than military defense. He also raised the question of whether new technology made any just war unlikely. Pope Benedict XV in *Ad Beatissimum* (1916) outlined the causes of war and methods for obtaining peace. He condemned class warfare and gross materialism as underlying the failure to achieve a peaceful order.

When Pope John XXIII was elected pope at age 79, he was widely assumed to be a caretaker. He startled the world by moving swiftly to engage the Roman Catholic Church within the political and economic realities of the 20th century. Two of his outstanding accomplishments were the calling of an ecumenical council in 1959 and the publishing of an encyclical on peace in 1962.

Pope John XXIII's elegant plea for peace is entitled *Pacem in Terris* (Peace on Earth). In this document, the pope expressed a hatred of nationalism and condemned the arms race. His emphasis on nonviolence was an attempt to transcend the opposition of just war theory and pacifism. He called for structural reform of the international political and legal systems. Notably missing from the document is an endorsement of the right of self-defense for peoples and states, a doctrine commonly put forward as justification for war. Pope John concluded that in an age such as ours, which prides itself on its atomic energy, it is contrary to reason to hold that war is now a suitable way to restore rights which have been violated (Pope John XXIII 1968, 127).

A year after the publication of *Pacem in Terris*, 2,500 bishops of the Roman Catholic Church met in Rome for what is known as the *Second Vatican Council*. A council, overseen by the pope, represents the highest teaching authority of the Church. Included on the agenda for Vatican II was the issue of peace and war. The topic was dealt with in one of the Council's most important documents, *The Pastoral Constitution on the Church in the Modern World* (Second Vatican Council 1968).

A discussion of the ethics of war took place during the Council's third session in 1964. A condemnation of "total war" was accepted without debate. However, a similar condemnation of nuclear weapons initiated a vigorous debate that continued into the fourth session in 1965 (Anderson 1966). Conservative Catholic groups from the United States argued that the condemnation of nuclear weapons would put U.S. Catholics in the difficult position of opposing either their church or their government. The peace activists, however, had their own lobby (along with prayer and fasting) to convince the bishops that a radical stand for an ethic of peace was called for.

At the fourth session, several prominent U.S. bishops, including Cardinals Francis Spellman of New York and Patrick O'Boyle of Washington, criticized the proposed condemnation of total war. Bishop Philip Hannan was most vociferous in defending the controllability in the use of nuclear arms. The Council rejected their plea, noting "all these considerations compel us to undertake an evaluation of war with an entirely new attitude" (98). This new attitude included a recognition of nonviolence in resisting war: "We cannot fail to praise those who renounce the use of violence in the vindication of their rights and who resort to methods of defense which are otherwise available to weaker parties, too, provided this can be done without injury to the rights and duties of others or of the community itself". (85). This praise was hardly a rousing call to the whole church to pursue a policy of nonviolence. Nonetheless, it represented progress in that direction.

At the final session of the Council, Cardinal Joseph Ritter of St. Louis, spoke out against the possession of nuclear arms. (Douglass 1966,118-19). The Council, accepting the right of a nation to defend itself, would not condemn war outright or the possession of nuclear weapons. (87). But it did condemn total war, the use of nuclear and other weapons that cause indiscriminate killing. In previous councils, the Church was often ready to pronounce condemnation of any perceived heresy. At the Second Vatican Council, the word condemnation was used only once: "Any act of war aimed indiscriminately at the destruction of entire cities...merits unequivocal and unhesitating condemnation "(Second Vatican Council 1968, 87).

INDIVIDUAL LEADERS

In the United States, Catholic opposition to war slowly developed from the time of World War II. The opposition took the form of a communal movement in which individual protest was sustained by participation in a community's beliefs, rituals and mutual support. Nevertheless, it is helpful to focus on a few individuals who inspired these Catholic communities. During the second half of the twentieth century, small groups of people dedicated to nonviolent opposition to war eventually influenced the larger structures of the Catholic church.

Dorothy Day is a touchstone for all the groups who subsequently emerged in the U. S. Catholic church. Thomas Merton was and still is a strong literary voice from within the monastic tradition. Daniel Berrigan, since the 1960s, has represented direct, active protest against the war making powers of the government. The movement is not without its internal tensions regarding what constitutes violence and what are the limits in the methods used to oppose violence.

Dorothy Day. Together with Peter Maurin, Dorothy Day founded the Catholic Worker movement in 1933. Day was born of Scot-Irish Calvinist parents. She worked with the Anti-Conscription League in World War I and the women's suffrage movement, for which she was arrested and jailed in 1917. After conversion to Catholicism in 1927, Day wrote for several Catholic magazines (Day 1981).

The Catholic Worker movement began as a struggle for social justice and for the rights of the poor. Day took on voluntary poverty to side with workers and launch a social and moral regeneration. From 1933 to 1941, thirty-two Worker houses were founded. The houses were hospices for volunteers, soup kitchens, meeting rooms, clothing centers and schools rolled into a single "revolutionary headquarters." To spread the word, Day began *The Catholic Worker* which sold for a penny a copy and continues with the same price until today. Its circulation during the 1930s grew to 185, 000. (Cornell and Forest 1968).

People sometimes confused Day with isolationists (most notoriously with Father Coughlin who slid into anti-semitism) but Day was an internationalist or transnationalist. She based her convictions on the Christian gospel and maintained her opposition to war throughout World War II (Miller 1982).

In August of 1940, Dorothy Day wrote an open letter in *The Catholic Worker* opposing all preparation for war (McNeal 1974, 75-77). She called for opposition to the manufacture of munitions and to the purchasing of defense bonds. Day had always seen the connection between the oppression of the poor and the destruction from war. However, many people who were ready to join with her in the fight against poverty were not prepared to stand against the United States government's call to arms.

The immediate results of Day's uncompromising pacifism were disastrous.

Twenty of the thirty-two Worker houses were closed. *The Catholic Worker* lost over 100,000 subscribers (Piehl 1982, 195-98). The movement might have appeared finished, but instead Dorothy Day's integrity and consistency under the most trying conditions provided a foundation both for a Catholic Worker movement that still attracts bright and dedicated people and for other communities that are trying to sustain a nonviolent way of life.

Some people within the Catholic Worker movement tried to articulate a "just war pacifism," which did not reject "just war" theory but concluded that it was no longer applicable. While the Catholic Worker excluded that view after World War II, it became the position toward which many bishops and moralists slowly moved.

Day's stands against the government were thought to be outlandish by most Catholics, including most bishops. But Day never portrayed herself as a radical Church reformer. She respectfully disagreed with bishops, but did not make them the enemy. She was not a theorizer of nonviolence but someone dedicated to living nonviolently and inspiring others to follow the same path.

Very few Catholics opposed the United State's part in World War II. The war seemed to fulfill the traditional criteria for a just war. Toward the end of the war, however, as the United States engaged in"obliteration bombs," some Catholics, including a few bishops, condemned these actions. The policy of firebombing Japanese cities reached its culmination with the bombing of Hiroshima and Nagasaki. For most people at the time, the use of atomic bombs did not seem to cross any new boundary. A moral consensus against the use of nuclear weapons took several decades to develop among Catholic Church leaders.

The Vietnam War was the occasion for a significant shift in the attitude of Catholics toward war. At the start of the Vietnam War, Catholics were more hawkish than other U.S. citizens; at the end of the war, they were more dovish, and remained so (Gallup and Castelli 1987, 82). In contrast, U.S. bishops lagged behind the people and were resistant to condemning the war as immoral.

Thomas Merton. One of the leading voices of protest against the war was that of Thomas Merton, a Cistercian monk. Like Dorothy Day, Thomas Merton came to the Catholic peace movement in the United States from an unusual background. He was born in France of a Quaker mother. After studying at Cambridge University, he came to the United States and completed a master's degree in English at Columbia University. He became a Catholic in 1938 and entered a Trappist monastery in 1942.

Merton's autobiography and his books on spirituality had inspired many Catholics during the 1950s (Merton 1952). Cloistered in a Kentucky monastery, Merton was an unlikely candidate to lead a peace movement. But he drew upon a long Catholic tradition that he appropriated with critical intelligence. He provided a calm but penetrating view of the turbulent 1960s. Merton's writings have continued to inspire generations of Catholics.

Thomas Merton described the paradox of his being a "peace activist" in his monastic cell with these words: "To adopt a life that is essentially non-assertive, non-violent, a life of humility and peace is in itself a statement of one's position ... It is my intention to make my entire life a rejection of, a protest against the crimes and injustices of war and political tyranny which threaten to destroy the whole race of man and the world with him"(Twomey 1978, 33).

In 1964, Thomas Merton wrote an open letter to the bishops of the Second Vatican Council. His two chief concerns were the right of Catholics to be conscientious objectors and the moral problem of using nuclear weapons. He found implicit support for his positions in the statements of Pope Pius XII and Pope John XXIII. Merton was instrumental in bringing the Council to condemn what it called "total war" (Zahn 1971, 257).

Merton did not live long enough to develop a complete theory of peace making. He was highly critical of the Augustinian theory with its stress on the subjective purity of intention. He also found it impossible to call himself a pacifist because of the term's connotations, including sole dependence on the conscience of the individual and a lack of concern for the oppressed. (Merton 1964, 151,115). Toward the end of his life, Merton had begun a dialogue with Zen Buddhism and found support for nonviolence in traditional Eastern thinkers.

While he passionately pleaded for justice and peace, Merton refused to dabble in the hatred that often affected the 1960's movements. Inspired by Dorothy Day's gentle but unyielding stance and aware of Martin Luther King Jr.'s evolving tactics in the 1960s, Merton never lost sight of the aim of peace, which requires a method of peace. Without criticizing by name some Catholic activists and their tactics during the protests of the late 1960s, Merton worried that direct political action against violence inevitably becomes entangled in violence. In one of the last statements of his life, he said: "The language of spurious nonviolence is merely another, more equivocal form of the language of power ... Nonviolence is not for power but for truth. It is not pragmatic but prophetic. It is not aimed at immediate political results but at the manifestation of fundamental and critically important truth"(Zahn 1971,75).

In a letter commenting approvingly on this statement, Gordon Zahn notes Merton's "insistence that the action not be measured by results." (Meconis 1979, 38). I do not think that is quite right. The most crucial word in Merton's statement is *immediate*. Like anyone passionately dedicated to a cause, Merton wanted results but he was not prepared to sacrifice a disciplined and patient approach for the sake of getting instantaneous and impressive results. He was properly suspicious of how modern news media that can be used by protesters to get attention can also become an obstacle to a quiet, determined and long-range search for peace.

Merton, in the company of Dorothy Day, was willing to stay with a course that many people dismiss as too passive. Like Day, Merton was not inclined to divide the world into friend and enemy. He wrote: "A test of our sincerity in the practice of nonviolence is this: are we willing to learn something from our adversary? If a new truth is made known to us by him, will we admit it? Are we willing to admit that he is not totally inhumane, wrong, unreasonable, cruel?" (Merton 1970, 23). The Catholic Church lost one of its strongest advocates of nonviolence when Merton was accidentally killed in 1967.

Daniel Berrigan. The Jesuit priest, Daniel Berrigan, is associated with the activist side of anti-war protest. With his brother, Philip, he will always be remembered for bold actions that directly confronted the United States government and sent both men to prison for long stretches. It should nonetheless be noted that Dan Berrigan was a poet and a theologian before becoming a peace activist. And he never became a simple political activist. He maintained a serenity and a sense of humor in the midst of conflicts with the government and with his own church. He was sustained by his religious devotion to the scriptures and the religious practices of his community. It is an unusual activist who once said: "Don't just do something; stand there."

It cannot be denied, however, that the community of peace advocates, in which Dan Berrigan was prominent, tested the limits of what constitutes nonviolent protest. The question of legitimate means of protest is a perennial one but shaped by contemporary circumstances. The Vietnam War has often been called the first televised war. Television brought the horrors of war into the living room at home. It may also have deadened sensibilities by the nightly news repetition of images of suffering tucked between automobile ads and the latest Hollywood scandal. Protesters against the war tried to use the very institutions they were attacking to help them spread their message. A tiny band of people can get great publicity from the news media and the justice department, but the attempt to exploit these institutions can undermine the trust and integrity of communities professing peace.

What the news media called "the Catholic Left," had a brief history, emerging into public view with a break in of a government facility at Catonsville, Maryland in May 1968, and effectively ending with the conclusion of a trial in Camden, New Jersey, in May 1973. It is easy to see the whole period as a clumsy and unsuccessful attempt to stop a disastrous war (Greeley, 1971). But while most of the "radical left" in politics disappeared with the end of the Vietnam War, the Catholic peace movement has continued in communities of resistance, peace organizations, and an episcopal leadership that shifted its teaching on war and peace.

The favored form of protest during the Vietnam War was to break in to government offices and pour blood on draft records. This highly symbolic act, derived from the church's sacramental practice, was dramatically effective and caught the attention of the news media. But breaking into a building and destroying property raised serious problems, legally, ethically and strategically. Many passionate opponents of the war thought that such concerns were irrelevant but for people sensitive to how any violence can undermine a commitment to peace the issue has to be carefully addressed.

One way to justify destroying property is to limit the term violence to actions directed against human beings. However, "property" is a term that takes its origin from the integrity of the human organism; at least some forms of property (food, clothing, shelter) are integrally tied to the human self. Some further distinctions concerning property are therefore needed. John Swomley of the Fellowship of Reconciliation tried to isolate a meaning of property that would not have the protection of nonviolence. He wrote: "It is necessary to recognize that property whose sole purpose is to degrade or destroy human beings has disvalue rather than value. Some who would agree to its disvalue would argue for action that ...uses the destruction of such property to expose the nature of the government" (Swomley 1972,181).

Many religious pacifists were skeptical about a manner of protest that was in danger of generating violence, whether intended or not. Both Dorothy Day and Thomas Merton expressed qualified support for the action of Dan Berrigan and his associates. Thomas Merton wrote of Catonsville: "This was an attempt at prophetic nonviolent provocation. It bordered on violence and was violent to the extent that it meant pushing some good ladies around and destroying some government property. On a long term basis, I think the peace movement needs to really study, practice and use nonviolence in its classic form with all that implies of religious and ethical grounds."(Zahn 1971, 231).

The Catonsville break in got the attention of the government and much of the country. Dan Berrigan composed a play, *The Trial of the Catonsville Nine*, based on the transcript of the trial in which the defendants were allowed to state their case against the government (Berrigan 2004). The government, and J. Edgar Hoover in particular, became infuriated at the tactics and the publicity of the group. Prosecutor William Lynch said that the government considered the Catholic Left to be a more serious threat to the country than organized crime (Meconis 1979, 101). For several months during 1970, Daniel Berrigan went underground and playfully mocked the FBI's determination to arrest him. He was finally captured when an FBI informer infiltrated the overly trusting community.

The FBI was several times successful in planting informers. In the government's most ambitious trial against the protesters, the case relied almost entirely on an informer, Robert Handy. Strangely, however, Handy ended up testifying for the defense. He said that FBI policy in making arrests was first "to make sure the defendants commit as many crimes as possible and destroy the draft files." (New York Times 1973, 1) Handy also said of the people he informed on that "they are the finest group of Christian people I have ever been associated with. They are not even capable of hurting anyone." But he concluded his description: "As far as mechanical skills and abilities, they were totally inept ... It definitely wouldn't have happened without me."(Handy 1973, 7) When the protesters were set up and captured in the Camden government office, J. Edgar Hoover and Attorney General John Mitchell exulted: "We have broken the back of the Catholic Left" (Washington Post 1971, 1).

What the news media had called the Catholic Left may have come to an end in the early 1970s but numerous small groups continued to protest against the further militarization of the United States and a policy of nuclear retaliation. Basing their organization on the biblical text, "they shall beat their swords into plowshares" (Is. 2:4), the groups called themselves the Plowshares. Starting with a break in of the General Electric plant in King of Prussia, Pennsylvania on September 9, 1980, the group, led by Dan and Phil Berrigan, initiated a series of "plowshare actions" in Groton, Connecticut, Wilmington, Delaware , and Orlando, Florida. The pouring of blood and the symbolic hammering of the missiles was the usual gesture of protest (Musto 1986, 259).

In less dramatic fashion, organizations such as Pax Christi, USA, have continued to awaken opposition to war and violence. Pax Christi was founded in France at the end of World War II; a U. S. branch was begun in 1973. Respectful of church tradition and sensitive to the range of feelings among Catholic believers, Pax Christi's mission is to educate Catholics to the realities of violence and to form alliances with other peace making groups. By 1981, the group had five thousand members, forty-six of whom were bishops. It openly criticized U. S. military policy and called for the end of draft legislation. Pax Christi has continued to be a strong voice for Catholics and an influence on the bishops even after the militarization that began in September, 2001 (Musto 1986, 260).

U. S. Bishops

The National Conference of Catholic Bishops trailed behind some of the more radical Catholic communities. But the bishops had been moving toward a more critical stance on military policies since the 1970s. Pastoral letters in 1976, 1978, and 1979 condemned the threatened use of nuclear weapons and called for a test ban treaty between the United States and the Soviet Union. In 1982, the United States Catholic Conference issued *Statement on Central America*, affirming the call for liberation and peace. The bishops opposed the U.S. government's anti-communist crusade, declaring that "the dominant challenge is the internal condition of poverty and the denial of human rights"(U.S. Catholic Bishops 1982).

The bishops' pastoral letter in 1983 should not, therefore, have been a total surprise. But much of the country, including the White House, were taken aback by *The Challenge of Peace* (U.S. Catholic Bishops 1983) and what seemed a drastic change of course. The government had counted on the staunch anti-communism of the bishops as a support for U.S. policy. The White House tried to influence the bishops in their writing of the letter. The government was concerned because the bishops were not young radicals who might reverse themselves when fashion dictated. The bishops had slowly and agonizingly argued themselves into the firm conviction that "just war theory" is inadequate in the age of nuclear weapons. Thomas Gumbleton was one of the most important voices in the bishops' stand on peace. Bishop Gumbleton gave credit to Dan Berrigan and his associates for the evolution of his own thinking: "I have to face the question they faced: Is the war moral or immoral? I think people who are ready to put their whole lives on the line forced me to do some thinking"(National Catholic Reporter 1971).

During the composition of *The Challenge of Peace*, the document underwent three drafts, including a first draft published in *The National Catholic Reporter.* It produced widespread debate in the Catholic community, especially over the inclusion of pacifism. The bishops acknowledged that "the nonviolent witness of such figures as Dorothy Day and Martin Luther King Jr. has had a profound impact upon the life of the church in the United States" (U. S. Catholic Bishops 1983,117).

The bishops edged away from their traditional reliance on just war theory, admitting "pacifism" as a complementary theory in the tradition. They concluded that "peacemaking is not an optional commitment. It is a requirement of our faith … The content and context of our peacemaking is set, not by some political agenda or ideological program, but by the teaching of the Church "(U.S. Catholic Bishops 1983, 333). The bishops condemned all use of nuclear weapons.

The bishops received praise for their document although they were not given the credit they deserved for their contribution to the emerging thaw in the Gorbachev-Reagan dialogue of the late 1980s. The bishops' letter has continued to influence the thinking of U.S. Catholics about the issues of violence and war. The Catholic Church has tried to develop what Cardinal Joseph Bernadin named "a consistent ethic of life." (Steinfels, 2003, 17-39). An opposition to war has been tied to opposition against the death penalty and abortion. For most of the country, including many Roman Catholics, the bishops are so obsessed with the abortion question that they do not pay enough attention to violence outside the womb. However, if liberal critics of war invite the support of the Roman Catholic Church, they are going to have to pay attention to the bishops' concern with abortion.

CONCLUSION

The overall record of the Roman Catholic Church in opposing war and advocating nonviolent tactics does not fare well when measured against the Sermon on the Mount. Starting with St. Augustine, the attempt to control the number of wars and the injustices inherent to war was well intentioned and may have had some good effects in earlier times. The Geneva Conventions are a modern variation on this tradition. But we are past the time when war itself should be declared illegal.

In the United States, Catholic anxiety about not being thought sufficiently patriotic often took precedence over the demands of the gospel. The Catholic bishops and clergy were all too ready to endorse the policies of the U.S. government, including its twentieth-century military build up. A population composed mainly of immigrants wanted to avoid the taint of being insufficiently American. Only a few brave souls protested the World Wars and the policies of the Cold War.

The expectation of a "peace dividend," common at the beginning of the 1990s, now seems quaint and naïve. In 2001, the nation shifted into a war mentality that seems to be without end. In the Roman Catholic Church it can at least be said that the party of nonviolence is no longer relegated to the margin. Roman Catholics have to be restrained in their claim to be the party of peace but the testimony of Dorothy Day, Thomas Merton and Daniel Berrigan continues to sound in the land and call the nation to recognize that violence has to be resisted if the nation is to have a future at all.

REFERENCES

Anderson, Floyd, ed. (1966). *The Council Daybook*, Session III. Washington: National Catholic Welfare Conference.

Augustine (1972). *Concerning the City of God*. Baltimore: Penguin.

Berrigan, Daniel (2004). *The Trial of the Catonsville Nine*. New York: Fordham University Press.

Bloc, Ernst (1986). *The Principle of Hope*. Cambridge: MIT Press.

Chapiro, Jose (1950). *Erasmus and Our Struggle for Peace*. Boston: Beacon Press.

Cornell, Thomas and Forest, James (1968). *A Penny a Copy: Readings from the Catholic Worker*. New York: Macmillan.

Day, Dorothy (1981). *The Long Loneliness*. San Francisco: Harper SanFrancisco.

Douglass, James (1966). *The Non-Violent Cross*. New York: Macmillan.

Gallup, George and Castelli, Jim (1987). *The American Catholic People*. New York: Doubleday.

Greeley, Andrew (1971, Feb. 19). *L'Affaire Berrigan*. New York Times.

Gustafson, Carrie (1999). *Religion and Human Rights*. Armonk: M.E. Sharpe.

Handy, Robert (1973, April 7). *An Affidavit*. American Report.

King, Martin Luther Jr (1964). Why We Can't Wait. New York: Harper and Row, Lapide, Pinchas (1986). *The Sermon on the Mount*. Maryknoll: Orbis Books, 1986.

McGinn, Bernard (1986). *Meister Eckhart: Teacher and Preacher*. New York: Paulist Press.

Marcus, R.A. (1983). *Saint Augustine's Views on the Just War*. The Church and War. Ed.W.J. Sheils. Oxford: Blackwell.

Meconis, Charles (1979). *With Clumsy Grace: The American Catholic Left*. New York: Seabury Press.

McNeal, Patricia (1974). *The American Catholic Peace Movement*. Philadelphia: Temple University Press.

Merton, Thomas (1948). *The Seven Storey Mountain*. New York: Harcourt Brace.

Merton, Thomas (1964). *Seeds of Destruction*. New York: Farrar, Straus and Giroux.

Merton, Thomas (1968). *Faith and Violence*. Notre Dame: University of Notre Dame Press.

Miller, William (1982). *Dorothy Day: A Biography*. New York: Harper and Row.

Musto, Ronald (1986). *The Catholic Peace Tradition*. Orbis Books.

National Catholic Reporter (1972, February 11). Interview with Thomas Gumbleton.

New York Times (1973, April 1).

Origen (1980). *Contra Celsus*. Cambridge: Cambridge University Press.

Ozment, Steven (1973). *Mysticism and Dissent*. New Haven: Yale University Press.

Pope John XXIII (1968). *Pacem in Terris*. New York: Macmillan.

Second Vatican Council (1968). *Pastoral Constitution of the Church in the Modern World*. Huntington: Our Sunday Visitor.

Steinfels, Peter (2003). *A People Adrift: The Crisis of the Roman Catholic Church in America*. New York: Simon and Schuster

Swomley, John (1972). *Liberation Ethics*. New York: Macmillan.

Theissen, Gerd (1964). *Sociology of Early Palestinian Christianity*. Philadelphia: Fortress Press.

Thomas Aquinas (1966). *Summa Theologiae*. New York: McGraw-Hill.

Twomey, Gerard (1978). *Thomas Merton: Prophet in the Belly of a Paradox*. New York: Paulist Press.

U.S. Catholic Bishops (1982). *Statement on Central America*. Washington: United States Catholic Conference;

U.S. Catholic Bishops (1983). *The Challenge of Peace*. Washington: United States Catholic Conference.

Washington Post (1971, April 23).

Wills, Garry (1999). *St. Augustine*. New York: Viking.

Yoder, John Howard (1972). *The Politics of Jesus*. Grand Rapids: Eerdmans.

Zahn, Gordon (1971). *Thomas Merton on Peace*. New York: McCall.

In: Religion, Terrorism and Globalization
Editor: K.K. Kuriakose, pp.215-226

ISBN 1-59454-553-7

Chapter 14

"A HEART AS WIDE AS THE WORLD:"[1] A CHRISTIAN SPIRITUALITY OF NONVIOLENCE

Daniel Groody
University of Notre Dame

In the fall of 1991, I was living in northern California, and I decided to attend a lecture by the then-president of Peru, Alberto Fujimori. About two-thirds of the way into his presentation, there was a loud and uproarious outburst in the audience which disrupted everything. After the protesters were escorted out of the auditorium, I was curious to find out who these detractors were and why they were there. When I walked outside, I discovered that they were some young people, mostly college-aged students, who affiliated themselves with a group known as the Shining Path or *Sendero Luminoso.*

I was quite familiar with the Shining Path because I had just returned from Peru myself. The Shining Path is a revolutionary, communist movement committed to the armed and violent overthrow of the Peruvian government. They have waged guerilla warfare and terrorized towns, villages, and cities since 1980. They occupied cities, killed police officers, blew up the cars of political leaders, and sliced open dogs, hanging their bodies from city light posts. They targeted not only government leaders and police forces, but even unarmed civilians. They drew their name from José Carlos Mariátegui, who wrote "Marxism-Leninism will open the shining path to revolution." Since 1980, the Shining Path has killed more than 25,000 people and has cost the country billions of dollars in damage to its infrastructure.

Wondering why anyone would want to join this group, I went up to one of the protesters and wanted to try to understand her point of view. She explained to me all of the familiar abuses of the U.S. government in Peru, and she tried to enlighten me about the crimes being committed by the U.S. government there. More of an ideological monologue than a conversation, I listened to her for fifteen minutes. Without denying some of the valid observations she made, I then asked her, "do you have any idea of the seeds of destruction that your organization is sowing through outright violence?" Unimpressed by my question,

---

[1] I am grateful to LaReine- Marie Mosely, SND for part of this title, who also has used it in an essay in a forthcoming book edited by Daniel Groody. The title of her essay is "A Heart as Wide as the World: Particularizing and Concretizing the Preferential Option for the Poor."

she said, "We're fighting for justice, and if you don't believe me, then go down and talk to the people at the Revolutionary Bookstore! They will set you straight!"

After some thought, I took her advice. I decided to pay a visit to "Revolutionary Bookstore," not because I felt capable of breaking through the iron-bars of their ideological mindset but because I wanted to understand the rationale for joining a group that promoted and planned deliberate violence. When I entered the store, I said I would like to know something about the Shining Path. Hopeful of gaining a new recruit, the man enthusiastically took out the constitutional manifesto of the group, and he proceeded to explain to me the different goals and methods of the organization.

Surprisingly, we actually agreed on the first step. As we looked at the current socio-economic situation of Peru, we both agreed that it was a mess and that things needed to change. But the next step in his reasoning process was more complicated. He said the Shining Path's next goal was to destroy existing Peruvian institutions. This was more problematic. I was in partial agreement, especially because of the many structural injustices in the country. But a total elimination of Peruvian institutions seemed like it would only open the way to social chaos, so I asked, "what do you propose to put in its place?" He explained, "We would establish our own communist regimes and create institutions accordingly." Having just witnessed the collapse of the communist system in Russia, I asked what would make the institutions he suggested more stable and less prone to human corruption? He did not have an answer. I could feel the ground beneath us begin to drift in different directions. "Then," he said, "we would get rid of the foreign bourgeois and establish the local bourgeois." "What is the difference between the foreign and the local bourgeois?" I asked. "Don't both of them oppress the poor?" Again, nothing of substance came back. And then he said, "we are committed to revolutionary change even if we have to cross a river of blood to achieve our objectives." "And what does this mean," I asked. "It means that it doesn't matter how many people die in the process," he said, "or what the violence, as long as we achieve our goals. That is what is most important." Then there was a long pause as I recognized a complete break in our positions. To him, human life was utterly dispensable, as long as the goals of the organization were accomplished. To me, human life must be protected as a sacred gift of God, regardless of the challenges. Reflecting on the wake of discord, division, and destruction that such a fanatical mentality leaves behind, I asked, "Do you really think you can build a peaceful society on violence?" He said, "Death and violence are the costs of revolution." Unconvinced by his argument and convinced there has to be a better alternative to social change, I looked at him and asked, "Do you have any books on non-violent revolution?" He said, "No, we don't believe in nonviolence; it is impractical and a complete waste of time."

This experience at the Revolutionary Bookstore brought me face to face with the contrast between the spirit of violence and the spirit of nonviolence. It challenged me to understand not only the logic of groups like the Shining Path that advocate violence as a means of social change, but it also challenged me to articulate why I believe violence is not an answer, and why nonviolence is the only viable alternative for social protest. In contrast to those who subscribe to the ideology of groups like the Shining Path, nonviolence rejects violence in favor of peaceful methods as a way of being faithful to one's core religious convictions, and as a way of effecting political and social reform. This experience also challenged me to examine not only some of the ideas and principles but above all some of the underlying *values* that shape both a stance of violence and nonviolence. In the pages that follow, I would like to look at the notion of nonviolence and examine some of its underlying values from the perspective of spirituality. First, I want to look at nonviolence as it emerges from the perspective of Christian spirituality. Second, I would like to look at the life of Jesus of Nazareth, particularly at some of the texts that shape our understanding of him, some of the options he faced in his own day, and the particular non-violent choices he made. Third, I would like to look at some specific individuals who have espoused nonviolence in recent history and have explicitly drawn their strength and inspiration from Christian spirituality. Finally, I will offer some concluding reflections on a Christian spirituality of nonviolence.

WHAT IS SPIRITUALITY?

Few words today are as important, yet as complex and controversial, as the word spirituality. While there are many fine works that look at the meaning of spirituality in our contemporary context, I would like to say at the outset that spirituality is not limited to religion nor is it limited to theology. Rather, spirituality draws on experience and it encompasses the entirety of one's life, including the political, the social, the economic, the cultural, and many other dimensions of life that shape it. In other words, spirituality deals with one's experience of God within the totality of one's life experience.

Defining spirituality, however, and studying it from an academic perspective is one of the great, contemporary, intellectual challenges.[2] For the purposes of this essay, I would like to say that spirituality deals with how one experiences, understands, and enacts their relationship with God within their specific cultural context.[3] God in this context is that to which one gives ultimate value, that to which one gives one's complete attention, that to which one gives one's heart and treasure. While in this essay I will look at spirituality as it relates to the God of Jesus Christ, "god" can take on other forms. C.S. Lewis once noted, and I paraphrase, "it is not so much if one believes in God, but it is a matter of which god one believes in." Spirituality, then, deals with living out that which one values. From this standpoint, everyone has a spirituality. One could say from this standpoint that the Shining Path has a spirituality that expresses itself by achieving the value of justice for Peruvians.

If spirituality deals with how one lives out that which one most values, Christian spirituality is a particular kind and a particular expression of spirituality. It involves not only one's own values but those of Jesus of Nazareth. It means making one's own the values of Jesus through openness to the work of the Holy Spirit in one's life. In other words, Christian spirituality deals with following Jesus and therefore living out that which Jesus most valued.

Lastly, Christian spirituality addresses that which is most central to a person. One way of conceptualizing this is to say that Christian spirituality goes to the "heart" of the person. From a biblical perspective, the heart is not just the center of emotion and sentimentality, as is often perceived in our western, post-modern culture, but the heart goes to the core of what is most human and most real in a person.[4] In addition, Christian spirituality affirms that it is fundamentally in the heart that one encounters God. It also affirms that Jesus of Nazareth

[2] Sandra Schneiders defines spirituality as "the experience of conscious involvement in the project of life integration through self-transcendence toward the ultimate value one perceives." See "The Study of Christian Spirituality: The Contours and Dynamics of a Discipline." Christian Spirituality Bulletin 1 (Spring 1998): 1, 3-12.
[3] I am grateful to Simon Hendry, who has greatly contributed to my understanding of spirituality in this way.
[4] Jean de Fraine and Albert Vanhoye, "Heart," in *Dictionary of Biblical Theology*, ed. Xavier Leon-Defour (Paris: Desclée Company, 1967), 200-02.

reveals not only the truth about God, but the truth about what it means to be a human being. The task of spirituality is to probe the depths of one's life (or one's heart) as one also probes the depth of God's life (or God's heart). In other words, Christian spirituality takes its reference point above all from the radical love manifested in the life, teachings, death, and resurrection of Jesus Christ. Christian spirituality affirms that in Jesus we witness a love as wide as the world, and a God who invites others to love in the same way.

JESUS OF NAZARETH AND THE GOSPEL OF NONVIOLENCE

While some people today, including contemporary Christians, look at the early days of Christianity as the "golden years" of humanity, on closer examination, we see that Jesus and the early Christians faced many of the same problems we are facing today. Jesus too lived in a world marked by wars, terrorism, injustices, oppression, and violence. Accordingly, even while Jesus says, "my kingdom does not belong to this world" (Jn. 18:36, NAB), this does not mean that Jesus was not at all concerned with this world. Christian spirituality is not a form of escapism but is a form of commitment to God and others. It expresses itself here and now by creating a more just world through a spirit of nonviolence.

While the United States, for good reasons, distinguishes the State from the Church, it is impossible to separate God from the world or spirituality from politics.[5] If spirituality deals with living out one's values, politics deals with how those values are negotiated and implemented in human society. Spirituality influences everything, and it is out of one's spirituality that one lives what one ultimately values. Human beings are social beings, and spirituality is about interaction with other human beings and ultimately with God. Believing that Jesus is "non-political" or "a-political" is in itself a political statement, one that even many contemporary Christians would like to make.[6] But Liberation theologians in the last forty years have helped remind us of the integral link between the life of Jesus and the politics of his day, and the life of contemporary Christians and the key socio-political issues that they face.[7]

The story of Christianity begins with the nonviolent Jesus.[8] This is not to say that the Church has always practiced nonviolence nor witnessed to it, but as one goes to the source of Christianity, namely to the life of Jesus—especially as it is recorded in the gospels--we can see that the heart of Jesus reveals a non-violent God.

One of the ways we can appreciate the non-violent stance of Jesus is to look more closely at his own historical context. It is helpful to examine some of the options Jesus had available to him as he faced violence in his own day, and some of the teachings and practices he

---

[5] For more on this topic, see Jim Wallis, *The Soul of Politics: A Practical and Prophetic Vision for Change* (Maryknoll, N.Y.: Orbis Books, 1994).

[6] For more on this topic, see Johannes Baptist Metz, *A Passion for God*, trans. James Matthew Ashley (New York: Paulist Press, 1998).

[7] See in particular Gustavo Gutierrez, A Theology of Liberation: History, Politics, and Salvation (Maryknoll, N.Y.: Orbis Books, 1973); Jon Sobrino, *Spirituality of Liberation* (Maryknoll, N.Y.: Orbis Books, 1988); and Ignacio Ellacuriia and Jon Sobrino, *Mysterium liberationis* (Maryknoll, N.Y.: Orbis Books, 1993).

[8] The foremost theologian on a spirituality of nonviolence is John Dear, who is the author of more than thirty books. See in particular *The God of Peace* (Maryknoll, N.Y.: Orbis Books, 1994); *Our God is Non-violent* (New York: Pilgrim Press, 1990); *Seeds of Nonviolence* (Baltimore, MD: Fortkamp, 1992); *Living peace* (New York: Doubleday, 2001).

advocated, particularly as these are expressed in the Scriptures. From these reflections we can look at some of the particular contributions that Christian spirituality makes to the larger reflection on nonviolence.

In order to understand Jesus and his option for nonviolence, it helps to situate his choices within the overall context of his vision and mission. In the Gospel of Luke we read about this framework as follows:

> [Jesus] came to Nazareth, where he had grown up, and went according to his custom into the synagogue on the Sabbath day. He stood up to read and was handed a scroll of the prophet Isaiah. He unrolled the scroll and found the passage where it was written:

> 'The Spirit of the Lord is upon me,
> because he has anointed me
> to bring glad tidings to the poor.
> He has sent me to proclaim liberty to captives
> and recovery of sight to the blind,
> to let the oppressed go free,
> and to proclaim a year acceptable to the Lord.'

> Rolling up the scroll, he handed it back to the attendant and sat down, and the eyes of all in the synagogue looked intently at him. He said to them, "Today this scripture passage is fulfilled in your hearing" (Lk. 4:16-21, NAB).

Much of Jesus' mission is an unfolding of this passage. Nonetheless, Jesus' contemporaries did not greet his message with universal enthusiasm. Bringing glad tidings to the poor, proclaiming liberty to captives, recovery of sight to the blind, letting the oppressed go free, and announcing the irruption of God's reign in history, brought Jesus into conflict with not only the political but also the religious leaders of his day. If Jesus inaugurated God's reign in history, then that meant that somebody else was no longer going to be ruler. This regime change brought about violence on many levels.

On the one hand, lest we mistake Jesus for a person who simply preached "love one another" in a radical-hippie, late-1960's, flower-child kind of way, this passage reveals Jesus as challenging all humanly-constructed empires, especially those that maintained their power through violence. From a spiritual perspective, Jesus directly confronted the kingdom of evil. There was even an element of fighting in Jesus' message: "Do not think that I have come to bring peace upon the earth. I have come to bring not peace but the sword" (Mt. 10:34-39). On the other hand, lest this passage distort Jesus into a flag-waving, armed guerilla, violent activist, elsewhere, when Jesus is arrested, his very actions challenge those who seek resolution through violence:

> His disciples realized what was about to happen, and they asked, "Lord, shall we strike with a sword?" And one of them struck the high priest's servant and cut off his right ear. But Jesus said in reply, "Stop, no more of this!" Then he touched the servant's ear and healed him (Lk. 22:49-52).

Rather than inflict wounds through violence, Jesus reveals a healing that is accomplished through nonviolence, even when his enemies were set on destroying him. Jesus did not come to bring a superficial peace that glosses over deep injustices. Conflict did arise between Jesus and his adversaries. But what is striking is not the fact that there is fighting and conflict; what is striking is that Jesus faced the conflict and fought for a transformed world through nonviolence.

THE RADICAL OPTION OF JESUS: CHOOSING NONVIOLENCE AMID THE VIOLENCE OF THE WORLD

In the face of many conflicts, Jesus, as a Jew, had different options available to him. The choices he made are even more striking when we look his own particular context, where there were options other than nonviolence available to him. Palestine was under Roman rule in Jesus' day, replete with abuses that came with the empire. Jews had little political, economic, religious, or cultural independence, and people responded to this repression in a variety of ways. Three groups worth noting were the Pharisees, the Sadducees and Herodians, and the Zealots.[9]

The Pharisees were a religiously and politically *conservative* group, who defined themselves over and against Roman rule. They zealously followed the Old Testament laws, as well as their own religious traditions. By and large they did not participate in political affairs except in those things that affected them directly. Nonetheless, they were the largest and most influential religious-political party during New Testament times.

The Sadducees and Herodians were liberals who *collaborated* with Roman rule. The Sadducees were a wealthy, upper class, Jewish priestly party, who did not believe in the resurrection and therefore invested their energies in political and social affairs. The Herodians were a Jewish political party of King Herod's supporters, and they hated Jesus as well because Jesus challenged their political ambitions.

The Zealots were a group of fanatical Jewish *crusaders* determined to end Roman rule in Israel, even by violence if necessary. Concerned about the future of Israel, they believed in a Messiah but did not believe in Jesus as the one sent by God. They hoped for a political leader who would restore Israel to power. As "freedom fighters" they shared much in common with what today we call "terrorists," and they were dedicated to overthrowing Roman rule.

John Howard Yoder in his groundbreaking book, *The Politics of Jesus,* says that Jesus rejected all three of these options. Jesus was not a conservative, for he did not subscribe to the teachings of the Pharisees but took the understanding of the law to a new level (Mt. 5:21-48). He was not a liberal in the sense that he collaborated with the state and legitimized the Roman Empire. He was not a crusader and he did not advocate the use of armed violence to effect political change. As an alternative, Jesus chose the option of nonviolence, which opened up many new possibilities than those of his time period, and allowed him to relate to all people, regardless of their religious or political affiliations.

Jesus expands on what nonviolence means when he says,

> But to you who hear I say, love your enemies, do good to those who hate you, bless those who curse you, pray for those who mistreat you. To the person who strikes you on one cheek, offer the other one as well, and from the person who takes your cloak, do not withhold even your

---

[9] For more on these three positions, see John Howard Yoder, *The Politics of Jesus,* 2nd ed. (Grand Rapids, MI: Eerdmans, 1994).

tunic. Give to everyone who asks of you, and from the one who takes what is yours do not demand it back. Do to others as you would have them do to you. For if you love those who love you, what credit is that to you? Even sinners love those who love them. And if you do good to those who do good to you, what credit is that to you? Even sinners do the same. If you lend money to those from whom you expect repayment, what credit (is) that to you? Even sinners lend to sinners, and get back the same amount. But rather, love your enemies and do good to them, and lend expecting nothing back; then your reward will be great and you will be children of the Most High, for he himself is kind to the ungrateful and the wicked. Be merciful, just as (also) your Father is merciful (Lk. 6:27-36, NAB).

As Rob Yule notes, Jesus, in contrast to the conventional logic of his day, is proposing here "not an ethic of retaliation ('You hit me, and I'll hit you'), or even an ethic of reciprocity ('You scratch my back, and I'll scratch yours'); it is an ethic of responsiveness, an ethic of response to God's grace, an ethic of mercy ('God loves the undeserving, so we love the undeserving too')."[10] Jesus was concerned with eliminating oppression, but what we see here is that the sword which ultimately defeats violence is not military strength but radical love. This kind of love, which is the fruit of a Christian spirituality, is not that of warm feelings and romantic sentimentality but the decision to love all people, even one's enemies and those who do harm, even when it means that one must undergo suffering. In every instance, Jesus is saying that Christians must go way beyond the conventional expressions of love, taking love to a new level. Imitating Jesus, they must literally lay down their lives, whatever the cost, trusting in God and in his justice. Nonviolence, in this regard, is nothing other than an act of heroic virtue; it is a decision to conquer violence not through counter violence but through love; it is a decision to not let violence win but to overcome it through a love that knows no limits, that not even death can defeat, that is as wide as the world.

CROSS AND RESURRECTION LOGIC

From a practical perspective, however, the life of Jesus and that of his followers, echoing the words of the man in the Revolutionary Bookstore, seems terribly impractical, and in the short term, inefficacious. Jesus was nailed to a cross. Rome continued in power for centuries. People continued to be exploited. Injustices continued to take place. And many of the early Christians were persecuted or killed. On the surface, the life of Jesus and those who followed him seemed to end in total failure. Did Jesus' death, resurrection, and absolute commitment to nonviolence even make a difference?

Here, Christian spirituality adopts a different logic than that of contemporary political pragmatism. Unlike some international leaders, who—even while holding to "Christian" convictions—believe that war and violence is a solution to international conflict, Christian spirituality asserts that faithfulness is more important than effectiveness. In contrast to such pragmatic logic, Christian spirituality, expressed as following Jesus, deals not with cause and effect logic but cross and resurrection logic.[11] In fact, Christian spirituality lived as following Jesus accepts suffering as part of the cost of commitment to truth. And such suffering is not a

---

[10] Yoder, *The Politics of Jesus*, 89-92. See also Rob Yule's comments on the ideas of Yoder at the following web site: http://www.stalbans.org.nz/teachings/rob_yule/jesus/jesus3-6th.htm:10/11/2004.
[11] John Howard. Yoder, *The Original Revolution*, Christian Peace Shelf Series 3 (Scottdale, Pa: Herald Press, 1972).

passive resignation or a fatalism, but a firm belief that the ultimate effectiveness will come through faithfulness, even if one does not live to see the results. Nonviolence in this sense means active resistance to evil, but it does so on its own terms and with its own weapons. It recognizes that it is better to undergo suffering than to inflict suffering on another. One does not accept suffering because of masochism but because of a firm belief that in the end God's justice will reign, as was expressed in the life, death, and resurrection of Jesus of Nazareth. Even though the leaders of the world sentenced Jesus to death, God's verdict on Jesus—and therefore the way he lived and his message of nonviolence—was life (Acts 2:32).[12] The resurrection is the ultimate victory of life over all the forces of death that threaten human beings, including violence.

The heart of the Christian witness to nonviolence lies in the fact that even while Jesus suffered rejection, injustice, and violence, he did not retaliate in return with the same kind of violence. In other words, the cross is the ultimate expression of God's love, even to the end! As Jon Sobrino put it,

> On the cross of Jesus God himself is crucified. The Father suffers the death of the Son and takes upon himself all the pain and suffering of history. In this ultimate solidarity with humanity he reveals himself as the God of love, who opens up a hope and a future through the most negative side of history. Thus, Christian existence is nothing else but a process of participating in this same process whereby God loves the world, and hence is the very life of God.[13]

Jesus loved all people to the end, even to the point of loving his persecutors and enemies, rather than retaliating in turn with the same measures of violence against them. Here is the ultimate act of nonviolence offered in the face of the ultimate injustice and the ultimate act of violence. Jesus' nonviolence opened the way to a new vision of life and a new spirituality that gave one a capacity to see the interconnectedness of all people and a new capacity to love others as he loved them. Since then, those committed to live out a Christian spirituality have staked their lives on texts like the beatitudes, where Jesus says,

> Blessed are the peacemakers, for they will be called children of God. Blessed are they who are persecuted for the sake of righteousness, for theirs is the kingdom of heaven. Blessed are you when they insult you and persecute you and utter every kind of evil against you (falsely) because of me. Rejoice and be glad, for your reward will be great in heaven" (Mt. 5:10-12, NAB).

THE WITNESS OF NONVIOLENCE: CHRISTIAN SPIRITUALITY IN CONTEMPORARY PRACTICE

Since the first century when the foundational events of the Christian mystery took place, countless followers of Jesus have staked their lives on Jesus' non-violent vision, such as the early Christian martyrs, the Desert Fathers and Mothers, and others like St. Francis of Assisi. The length of this essay does not permit me to go into their respective contributions to

---

[12] See in particular, Virgilio P. Elizondo, *Galilean Journey* (Maryknoll, N.Y.: Orbis Books, 1983).
[13] Jon Sobrino, *Christology at the Crossroads* (Maryknoll, N.Y.: Orbis, 1994), 224.

nonviolence, but in the space remaining, I would like to highlight four contemporary examples which give expression to the Christian witness of nonviolence, namely, Martin Luther King, Jr., Dorothy Day, Oscar Romero, and John Paul II.

Most people are familiar with the life and death of Martin Luther King, Jr., his struggle to overcome the racial injustices of his day, and his vision of a universal family and racial integration. What is particularly important in our discussion is the central spirituality that governed his vision. Influenced also by Ghandi's philosophy of nonviolence and his own Christian spirituality, King's active nonviolence through sit-ins and marches put Civil rights at the center of the national agenda. Even while others in the civil rights movement adopted violent responses to injustices, he never wavered in his insistence that nonviolence was the only way to achieve lasting reform and genuine peace. Like Jesus, his death was a testimony to the power of love even against forces of violence that threaten life. In his letter from the Birmingham Jail, he rejected even those black nationalists who advocated violence as the means to social change: "...we need emulate neither the "do-nothingism" of the complacent nor the hatred and despair of the black nationalist. For there is the more excellent way of love and nonviolent protest. I am grateful to God that, through the influence of the Negro church, the way of nonviolence became an integral part of our struggle."[14]

Martin Luther King, Jr. noted that violence in the end is not only contrary to the will of God revealed in Jesus, but it is also, in the long run, futile. Throughout the King Memorial in Atlanta, one is reminded of this vision when one reads statements like, "Let no man pull you so low that you hate him. Always avoid violence. If you sow the seeds of violence in your struggle, unborn generations will reap the whirlwind of social disintegration." And, "Hatred and bitterness can never cure the disease of fear; only love can do that. Hatred paralyzes life, love releases it. Hatred confuses it. Love harmonizes it. Hatred darkens life; love illuminates it." And, "We must forever conduct our struggle on the high plain of dignity and discipline. We must not allow our creative protest to degenerate into physical violence. We must rise to the majestic heights of meeting physical force with soul force." Spirituality shaped the heart of King's vision, and this spirituality led him to a social protest that did not ignore injustice nor passively accept it. When he was given the Nobel Peace Prize in 1964, he said,

> Violence is impractical because it is a descending spiral ending in destruction for all. It is immoral because it seeks to humiliate the opponent rather than win his understanding: it seeks to annihilate rather than convert. Violence is immoral because it thrives on hatred rather than love. It destroys community and makes brotherhood impossible. It leaves society in monologue rather than dialogue. Violence ends up defeating itself. It creates bitterness in the survivors and brutality in the destroyers.[15]

Like Jesus, he fought injustice by taking his fight to a higher level, by enacting his vision of the Gospel, by going to the heart of truth, by living out his Christian spirituality. To look at Martin Luther King's social vision without the spirituality that engendered it is to look only at the fruit of his efforts and not the root system that nourished it.

As Martin Luther King's non-violent vision became embodied in the Civil Rights movement, Dorothy Day's (1897 – 1980) vision became embodied in the Catholic Worker

---

[14] Martin Luther King, *Letter from Birmingham Jail.* http://nobelprizes.com/nobel/peace/MLK-jail.html: 10/15/2004

[15] For a complete copy of King's speech, see http://nobelprize.org/peace/laureates/1964/king-lecture.html.

Movement.[16] In 1933, Dorothy Day and Peter Maurin founded the Catholic Worker Movement in New York City, leading a life of voluntary poverty and active nonviolence as they protested the evils of the day. Day's vision of nonviolence began in 1936 when she advocated a pacifist response to the Spanish Civil War, and later World War II and Vietnam. She remained deeply convinced that those who professed to live as Christians could not in good conscience kill their brothers and sisters. Even while many American Catholics supported the notion of "just war," Day supported neither this position nor her Marxist position of earlier years. Her conviction emerged fundamentally from her insight in the Scriptures, quoting St. Peter, "It is better to obey God than human beings," (Acts 5:29) and her own experience of Christian spirituality, "We believe that Christ went beyond natural ethics and the Old Dispensation in this matter of force and war and taught nonviolence as *a way of life*."[17] She lived nonviolence in such tactics as strikes, pickets, boycotts, the nonpayment of federal taxes that supported war, the refusal to register for the draft, and civil disobedience.

Day's interest in nonviolence stemmed principally from her life long interest in religious truth. She based her conviction on the beatitudes of Jesus, as noted above. She wanted Catholic workers to learn not only to love with compassion, but to overcome fear, which generates violence. Overall, she wanted people to love their enemies not because of the fear of war but because God loves them.[18] As she wrote,

> I can write no other than this: unless we use the weapons of the spirit, denying ourselves and taking up our cross and following Jesus, dying with Him and rising with Him, men (sic) will go on fighting, and often from the highest motives, believing that they are fighting defensive wars for justice and in self-defense against present or future aggression.[19]

One cannot but find her words illuminating even in our present day as leaders look to war to resolve the complex and pressing problems of national security.

In recent decades, another compelling witness to the power of nonviolent love in the context of a violent society is Oscar Romero. Romero became the archbishop of San Salvador during the turbulent Civil War of El Salvador, beginning in the 1970's, when military death squads, in the name of national security, assassinated tens of thousands of poor peasants. While some social movements took up arms to combat this violence, Romero recognized that such an approach directly contradicted the Christian gospel and only further perpetuated the cycle of violence. Romero profoundly believed that at the root of many injustices in society were unjust social structures, which violently oppressed the poor. He knew that Christians must work towards the transformation of these structures, but Romero believed that violence must be conquered within the depths of one's soul. In a homily on March 14, 1977, he said, "As long as one does not live a conversion in one's heart, a teaching enlightened by faith to

---

[16]For more on Dorothy Day, see Robert Ellsberg, ed. *Dorothy Day: Selected Writings* (Maryknoll, N.Y.: Orbis, 1992).

[17] Stephen J. Krupa. "Celebrating Dorothy Day," *America*, August 27, 2002.

[18] For more on Dorothy Day and her philosophy of non-violence see Ira Churnus, *American Nonviolence: The History of an Idea*. Maryknoll, NY: Orbis Books, 2004, 145-160.

[19]*Dorothy Day, Peter Maurin and the Catholic Worker Movement: Dorothy Day, Prophet of Pacifism for the Catholic Church*, Houston Catholic Worker, Vol. XVII, No. 5, September-October 1997. Also available online at: http://www.cjd.org/paper/pacifism.html:10/15/2004.

organize life according to the heart of God, all will be feeble, revolutionary, passing, violent. None of these is Christian."[20]

Romero sought not only the conversion of society but also the conversion of one's enemy through love: "We will be firm in defending our rights, but with a great love in our hearts, because when we defend ourselves with love we are also seeking sinners' conversion. That is the Christian's vengeance."[21] Nonetheless, like King, commitment to nonviolence eventually led to a violent death for Romero. In 1980 he was assassinated while celebrating the Eucharist. For Romero, this martyrdom was not an end but a beginning, because he grounded his own life on the conviction that violence cannot ultimately kill love, which he expressed in the laying down of his own life for the people he loved and served. He said, "Martyrdom is a grace that I don't believe I merit. But if God accepts the sacrifice of my life, may my blood be the seed of liberty and a sign that this hope will soon become a reality. May my death, if it is accepted by God, be for the liberation of my people and a testimony of hope in the future."[22] Days before he died, Romero said, "I should tell you that, as a Christian, I don't believe in death without resurrection. If they kill me, I will be resurrected in the Salvadoran people."[23] Grounded on a profound Christian spirituality that led to the imitation of the nonviolent Christ, he poured out his own life on the altar for the crucified peoples of his own country, in the hopes of creating a more humane society.

In addition to King, Day, and Romero, John Paul II also reiterated the futility of violence in his own writings. He recognized that war leads to further wars. He believed that Christian spirituality puts us in touch with this core vision of Jesus, who reveals the truth. He believed that only when people unite their own sufferings, for the sake of truth and freedom, to the sufferings of Christ on the cross, can they find the way to lasting peace. He rejected cowardice in the face of evil and violent reaction to it, which only makes things worse.[24] John Paul also brought out how Christian spirituality bears fruit in nonviolence, but he also brought insight into the human condition. By implication, he challenged those groups like the Shining Path who naïvely believe that hope in human progress alone is futile. He notes in *Centissimus Annus*,

> Moreover, man, who was created for freedom, bears within himself the wound of original sin, which constantly draws him towards evil and puts him in need of redemption. Not only is this doctrine an integral part of Christian revelation: it also has great hermeneutical value insofar as it helps one to understand human reality.[25]

Recognizing the frailty of human beings helps one understand the limitations of setting one's hope on any social organization committed to reform, and especially those who seek this reform through violent methods:

---

[20] Oscar Romero, Homily on March 17, 1977, quoted in, Oscar Romero, *The Violence of Love*, Maryknoll, NY, Orbis Books, 2004, 1.

[21] Oscar Romero, Homily on June 19, 1977, quoted in, quoted in, Oscar Romero, *The Violence of Love*, Maryknoll, NY, Orbis Books, 2004, 2.

[22] Oscar Romero, *La voz de los sin voz* (San Salvador: UCA Editores, 1987), March 19, 1980 interview, 461.

[23] Oscar Romero, *La voz de los sin voz* (San Salvador: UCA Editores, 1987), March 19, 1980 interview, 461.

[24] John Paul II, "Centesimus Annus" in *The Encyclicals of John Paul II*, J. Michael Miller, ed and intro (Huntington, IN: Our Sunday Visitor, 1996), 612.

[25] Ibid., 613.

When people think they possess the secret of a perfect social organization which makes evil impossible, they also think that they can use any means, including violence and deceit, in order to bring that organization into being. Politics then becomes a "secular religion" which operates under the illusion of creating paradise in this world. But no political society which possesses its own autonomy and laws can ever be confused with the Kingdom of God.[26]

Martin Luther King, Jr., Dorothy Day, Oscar Romero, and John Paul II offer the world alternatives to the human propensity towards violence and its destructive consequences. Figures such as these, who drew their strength on the teachings of Jesus Christ and who lived them out in fidelity to their spirituality, are distinguished representatives of the power of nonviolence. They are the great figures who have broken the spiral of violence through the radical option of love, which reveals in its own way the infinite love of God.

A HEART AS WIDE AS THE WORLD

It is not that the great figures of history who testify to the power of nonviolence know nothing of the violence of their own hearts. On the contrary, spirituality, as such, cultivates those values of radical love even in the face of one's sinful inclination to choose violence. Walter Wink brought out this point clearly when he recalled the story of a Native American grandfather who was talking to his grandson about the tragedy on September 11th. The grandfather said, "I feel as if I have two wolves fighting in my heart. One wolf is vengeful, angry, and violent. The other one is loving and compassionate." The grandson asked, "Which wolf will win the fight in your heart?" The grandfather answered, "The one I feed."[27] Christian spirituality cultivates nonviolence by nourishing its vision on the life of Christ, who loved others to the end, even in the face of violence and hatred. A spirituality of nonviolence, in the end, is about magnanimity. It is about loving all people, and, with the help of God's grace, loving even one's enemies. Following in the footsteps of Jesus, nonviolence ultimately is about choosing to love to the utmost extreme, and, in doing so, to love so completely and universally that one's own life reflects God's love, a love so deep and powerful that it knows no bounds because it is as wide as the world.

---

[26] Ibid.
[27] Walter Wink, "Edifying Tales of Nonviolence," in *Radial Grace* (Center for Action and Contemplation, c 2003), 3

SECTION VI

In: Religion, Terrorism and Globalization
Editor: K.K. Kuriakose, pp.229-239

ISBN 1-59454-553-7
© 2006 Nova Science Publishers, Inc.

Chapter 15

NONVIOLENCE AND THE "WAR" ON TERRORISM

Thomas R. Mockaitis
DePaul University

The words "war" and "nonviolence" certainly appear incongruous in the same sentence. "War," as the philosopher soldier Karl von Clausewitz wrote over two hundred years ago, "is a violent act to compel an enemy to do our will."[1] In the West such conflict has been, since the seventeenth century, the preserve of organized states constrained only by what mainstream Christianity has dubbed "Just War Theory." Succinctly put, Just War Theory requires that war be waged in the service of a just cause, declared by legitimate authority, and waged in a human manner.[2] The final stricture was to place some limits on the degree of violence and to distinguish between soldiers and civilians. Sadly, the long history of warfare does not speak well for the success of such restraint. On the contrary, warfare has become increasingly more deadly and the distinction between combatant and noncombatant has all but disappeared.

What hope then can there be for restraint in a global war on terrorism? In the conventional war model, very little. Fortunately, however, a better approach deserves consideration. Leaving aside for the time being consideration of the dubious assertion that the struggle against Al Qaeda should be dubbed a war, an unconventional approach to opposing terrorism, an approach based on the counter-insurgency and peacekeeping experience of several nations, should be considered. The prophet of this approach is not the Prussian General but the ancient Chinese writer, Sun Tzu. "To fight and conquer in all your battles is

---

[1] "*Der Krieg ist also ein Akt der Gewalt, um den Gegner zur Erfüllung unseres Willens zu zwingen.*" Karl von Clausewitz, *Vom Krieg* (Berlin: Dümmlers Verlag, 1832); http://www.clausewitz.com/CWZHOME/Vom Kriege/VKTOC.htm. The Translation is my own.

[2] For a brief overview of the evolution of Just War Theory see my chapter, "God and Caesar," in Barbara Batten and Thomas R. Mockaitis, *Just Peacemaking Study Guide* (Louisville, KY: Presbyterian Church (USA), 2003): 11-22. Contrary to prevailing myths about the inherent violence of Islam, this world religion has its own version of just war theory. This article will, however, focus on the U.S. response to the global terrorist threat.

not supreme excellence," he declared over 1000 years ago, "Supreme excellence consists in breaking the enemy's resistance without fighting."[3]

Consideration of the efficacy of a new approach to countering terrorism requires analysis of the U.S. approach to both conventional and unconventional war over the last half century, an approach that has come to be called "the American way of war."[4] Analysis of this approach reveals its limitations, both moral and practical. These limitations in turn suggest an alternative strategy, one that addresses the root causes of terrorism while employing selective and limited force against only the most ardent terrorists based on sound, timely intelligence.

THE AMERICAN WAY OF WAR

Culturally, historically, and in particular militarily, the United States has never been given to half measures. President Theodore Roosevelt's admonition to "speak softly and carry a big stick" might be considered a national mantra. Spoken in the era of gunboat diplomacy, this approach came to fruition during the Second World War. The near totality of the conflict allowed the U.S. to bring its enormous industrial might to bear on both Germany and Japan while suffering no attacks on its home land. Overwhelming force backed by seemingly inexhaustible supplies of men and material provided the apparent formula for victory.[5] This strategy of abundance carried over into the unconventional conflicts of the Cold War.

In the late 1940s the U.S. enabled the Greek government to destroy a Communist insurgency. The insurgents' decision to concentrate their forces for conventional operations coupled with Marshall Tito's decision to seal the Yugoslav border against them enabled America's conventional approach to succeed and further encouraged a false confidence in the efficacy of overwhelming force.[6] In the 1950s the U.S. conducted similar successful campaigns against fifth columns in Korea and the Hukbula revolt in the Philippines, again under what would later be appreciated as highly unusual circumstances.[7] At the time, however, the efficacy of the American approach went largely unchallenged.

Not surprisingly, the U.S. military applied the same approach to the complex situation in Vietnam that had apparently served it so well in the past. Asked what the appropriate response to insurgency ought to be, General William Westmoreland, Commander of Military Assistance Command Vietnam replied tersely, "firepower."[8] Suggestions that insurgency could only be defeated by the painstaking process of "winning hearts and minds" were often dismissed with variations of the now infamous cliché, "Get 'em by the balls, and their hearts and minds will follow." The emphasis on overwhelming force backfired as collateral damage

---

[3] Sun Tzu, *Sun Tzu on the Art of War: The Oldest Military Treatise in the World*, translated with introduction and critical notes by Lionel Giles (London: 1910); *Taosim Information Web Page*, http://www.clas.ufl.edu/users/gthursby/taoism/suntext.htm

[4] *Conventional war* refers to conflicts between regular armed forces on behalf of the states they represent, operating in uniform and according to generally accepted conventions. Unconventional war is broad category covering various forms of conflict conducted by irregular forces operating of uniform and often independent of recognized states. Examples include, insurgency, partisan warfare, and terrorism.

[5] Cold War rhetoric obscured the fact that the worst fighting, the highest casualties, and the best German forces were on the Eastern front.

[6] McClintock

[7] Cable

[8] Cited in Andrew Krepinevich Jr., *The Army and the Vietnam War* (Baltimore, MD: Johns Hopkins University Press, 1986), pp. 194-97

made more enemies than it won friends. Neither U.S. political culture nor the military it spawned were suited to a protracted and costly struggle in a cause that seemed increasingly dubious. Under the think cloaks of "peace with honor" and "Vietnamization," America withdrew from the war in 1973. Saigon fell two years later.

Unfortunately, the Vietnam War provided just enough extenuating circumstances to shield the U.S. military from the full weight of the defeat. While some officers took the lessons of the conflict to heart, others avoided them by blaming politicians for micro-managing the war, the media for distorting the reality of the struggle, and kids on the streets of Chicago and Berkley for undermining support for the war at home. A consensus emerged that unconventional wars should be avoided. Counter-insurgency fell under the doctrinal category of "foreign aid for internal defense," according to which the U.S. would train, supply, and support (primarily through its special forces) states threatened by Marxist revolution.[9] The U.S. thus avoided the high casualties and unacceptable political fallout of Vietnam but reaped a bitter harvest of bloodshed and ill will in El Salvador and Nicaragua, where forces America trained but could not control often ran amuck.

In the aftermath of Vietnam faith in the efficacy of overwhelming force to solve almost any problem lay dormant but never disappeared from the core of military thinking.

It reasserted itself dramatically during the administration of Ronald Reagan. In conjunction with a massive military build up and reorganization of the Defense Department to produce the new joint approach to war fighting, Secretary of Defense Casper Weinberger articulated guidelines for choosing which wars to fight and principles for winning them:

- Do not commit forces unless [the objective is] deemed vital to our national interests.
- Intend to win and commit the necessary resources to do so.
- Have clearly defined political and military objectives.
- Continuously reassess the relationship between objectives and forces committed.
- Have reasonable assurance of public support.
- Force should be the last resort.[10]

Under the leadership of General Colin Powell, Chairman of the Joint Chiefs of Staff during the administration of former President George H. Bush, these principles morphed into the Powell Doctrine. The doctrine came to fruition in America's overwhelming victory during the first Gulf War, 1990-91. Optimists proclaimed that the demon of Vietnam had finally been exorcised, the President spoke of a "new world order," and as the last remaining super power the U.S. seemed willing to take on any task.

The abundance of failed states and the consequent humanitarian crises, including genocide and famine, beckoned for intervention. The U.S. answered the United Nations' call for new, more robust style of peace operation to restore order and end suffering, by force if necessary. Enthusiasm for these new missions dissipated in a hale of bullets on the streets of Mogadishu, Somalia in 1993. When CNN broadcast images of an American body being dragged through the streets of Mogadishu, the U.S. folded its tents, came home, and tried to

---

[9] For a discussion of this shift see Thomas R. Mockaitis, "Unconventional War," in Sam C. Sarkesian and Robert E. Connor, Jr., *America's Armed Forces: A Handbook of Current and Future Capabilities* (Westport, CT: Greenwood Press, 1996), pp. 404-6.

[10] Roundtable/Study Group Report, "The Weinberger/Powell Doctrine: Still relevant or fit for the dust bin of history?," Council on Foreign Relations, October 28, 2002, http://www.cfr.org/publication.php?id=5147.

shy away from humanitarian intervention. Everyone in Washington seemed to recall Weinberger's key dictum, "vital to our national interest." And yet for all of its reluctance to get involved, the U.S. could not remain idle as harsh criticism over its failure to prevent the Rwandan Genocide (1994) demonstrated.

The U.S. thus found itself dragged into the worsening situation in Bosnia, first promising to help extract the embattle United Nations Protection Force and, following the massacre at Srebrenica, agreeing to halt Bosnian Serb Aggression with force. Intervention would, however, be on American terms and keeping with the historic commitment to firepower. Following alleged shelling of the Sarajevo marketplace in August 1995, the U.S. led a North Atlantic Treaty Organization (NATO) air assault against the Bosnian Serb Army. The air strikes combined with the suppressing fire of the Rapid Reaction Force on Mount Igman forced the Serbs to the Bargaining table. The Dayton accords ended the conflict and provided for deployment of a heavily armed Implementation Force and its successor the Stabilization Force, which remains in place to this day.

Although it stopped the war in Bosnia, Dayton did not, however, put an end to ethnic strife in the former Yugoslavia. Two years later NATO, led the by U.S., found itself once again engaged in a Balkan war, this time to end ethnic cleansing in the Serbian province of Kosovo. Once again President Clinton insisted upon, and got, a U.S.-style operation: an air war with the guarantee that ground forces (which would suffer casualties) would not be used. Contrary to American expectations, Serbia did not capitulate after a few days of bombing; it took seventy-eight days of increasingly intense air attacks and the realization that NATO's viability as an alliance was at stake to produce the desired result.[11]

THE AMERICAN WAY AND THE "WAR" ON TERRORISM

U.S. history and American values shaped the response to the September 11, 2001 tragedy in New York City in a predictable way. Within a week of the attacks, President George W. Bush declared a global war on terrorism and vowed to spare no effort or cost in eradicating Al Qaeda and its affiliates. He further asserted that states that sponsored, harbored, or abetted terrorist organizations would suffer the same fate as the terrorists themselves. As a metaphor for rallying public behind a long and difficult struggle, "global war on terrorism" has worked well. However, the administration does not mean it to be a metaphor, and the "war" has created the mistaken notion that the struggle is primarily a military one.

That mistaken assumption aside, the U.S. has engaged in two conventional conflicts under the broader umbrella of the global war on terrorism. With broad NATO support the U.S. invaded Afghanistan in November 2001 using a skillful combination of conventional air strikes, Special Forces operations, and assistance from Northern Alliance Forces opposed to the Taliban. The mission did not follow the traditional U.S. approach, in no small measure because the Pentagon had no contingency plan for invading Iraq. With Special Forces and Central Intelligence Agency operatives acting as forward air controllers, the U.S. used force selectively and effectively. The follow-on mission to capture Osama bin Laden and destroy his organization along with what remains of the Taliban has been less successful. The U.S.

---

[11] Ivo Daalder and Michael O'Hanlon, *Winning Ugly: NATO's war to Save Kosovo* (Washington, DC: Brookings Institute Press, 2001).

also made the mistake of not making greater use of NATO allies willing to help during the war.

Having removed the Taliban, the U.S. turned next to Iraq. Unlike the attack upon Afghanistan, which enjoyed widespread support among the NATO allies, the invasion of Iraq has divided the alliance. Even those nations willing to join the U.S.-led coalition may have perceived that they had little choice. The ten new members admitted to the alliance at the Prague summit needed ratification of the proposed expansion for their membership to become official. The Senate did not take up the matter until *after* the invasion. Needless to say, all ten members supported the U.S. Whether people on the streets of Bucharest, Sofia, and Lubliana share the enthusiasm of their governments is far less clear. Some of America's closest allies (most notably Germany and Canada) have refused to send troops. They, and even some members who have contributed, remain skeptical of claims that Saddam Hussein had weapons of mass destruction or links to Al Qaeda.

Undeterred by hesitant allies or lack of evidence to make the case for preemption, the Bush administration forged ahead with "Operation Iraqi Freedom." The American way of war reasserted itself in its most recent emanation as "shock and awe," a concentrated but focused air assault followed by a blitzkrieg race to Baghdad. An almost gleeful Tommy Franks boasts in his memoirs of finally having all the assets and political backing needed to do the job, a thinly veiled reference to military frustration over Vietnam.[12] Franks explains that he designed the lightening campaign to prevent Saddam from setting his oil wells ablaze. To the General's credit, the Air Force made every effort to avoid civilian casualties. Less commendable (perhaps even unconscionable) was Franks' willingness to fight with fewer than the 200,000 troops. General Eric Shenseki, Army Chief of Staff, said it would take more than 200,000 troops, not to beat the Iraqi army, but to stabilize the country. The Rumsfeld Pentagon forced Shenseki into retirement for his candor and in so doing promoted an atmosphere in which criticism is tantamount to disloyalty.

As expected, the U.S.-led coalition easily defeated the Iraqi army, but was woefully unprepared for the protracted insurgency that flared up in the aftermath of victory. Understaffed and overextended, the U.S. military has understandably fallen back on what it knows best and does well: conventional maneuver warfare supported by firepower. Despite efforts to minimize civilian casualties, such "collateral damage" inevitably occurs when using air strikes and artillery against insurgent positions in urban areas like Fallujah. The failure is, however, primarily strategic rather than tactical. Without a comprehensive plan for combating unrest and providing long-term stability, soldiers on the ground have an impossible task and are forced to improvise. A series of ad hoc responses, however, do not redeem poor planning.

CRITIQUING THE U.S. TACTICS OF FORCE IN COUNTERING TERRORISM

Leaving aside its efficacy in conventional war, serious moral and practical objections must be raised to the use of force in the current campaign against terrorism. Just war theory not only sets rigorous ethical standards for going to war but requires that the manner of

---

[12] Tommy Franks. *American Soldier* (Reagan Books. 2004).

waging war also be just. These criteria are succinctly captured in the Latin phrase, "*Jus ad Bellem; jus in Bello*" (just war and justice in war). Wars must be fought for a just cause using just means. The Catholic Theologian Thomas Aquinas established three criteria for going to war: 1. War must be declared by legitimate authority; 2. the cause for which the war is fought must be just; 3. the belligerents must have right intentions, seeking to work for good and oppose evil.[13] The requirement to wage war justly also hinges on three broad principles: 1. discrimination; 2. proportionality; 3. responsibility.[14] Every effort must be made to focus the use of force on military targets to avoid civilian casualties. The amount of force employed must be proportional to the threat, and those using force must be held responsible for their actions.[15] The exacting standards run counter to trends in the evolution of modern warfare during which weapons have generally become more deadly and less discriminating and the distinction between combatant and non-combatant has but disappeared. Unconventional warfare further complicates matters since the belligerents usually operate out of uniform and hide within civilian populations.

Critiquing how well U.S. actions comply with the requirements of Just War Theory requires separation of military actions since the September 11, 2001 terrorist attacks. I have always been doubtful that there can truly be a "global war on terrorism," and the term has been seriously abused to cover a host of political agendas unrelated to national security. It is, however, possible to discuss the war in Afghanistan, the war in Iraq, and the more defuse series of actions that may be taken against Al Qaeda and its affiliates.

Afghanistan: Immediately after the September 11 attacks, U.S. attention turned to the Taliban regime in Afghanistan. Despite disingenuous denials from Kabul, few doubted that governments direct support for Osama bin Laden and Al Qaeda. The U.S. immediately set in motion military plans to topple the regime and pursue the terrorists within Afghanistan. American actions clearly met the *Jus ad Bellem* requirements for going to war. The nation had been attacked and according to the U.N. Charter had a right to defend itself. NATO strengthened this legitimacy by declaring the invasion of Afghanistan an "Article 5" operation: an attack on one member nation is an attack on all, requiring the alliance as whole to act.[16] Even critics of the war shed few tears at the thought of seeing the Taliban removed from power.

In conducting the war, the U.S. also adhered as closely as possible to *Jus in Bello* criteria. An air campaign unavoidably produces casualties, no matter how many "precision" weapons the belligerents use. Taliban had no qualms about operating in urban areas and locating military assets in mosques, knowing the U.S. would be reluctant to bomb them. Mishaps did occur and civilians were killed, but to its credit the U.S. military tried to exercise restraint. The one area in which its strategy might be criticized has more to do with bad judgment than

---

[13]   Thomas Aquinas, *Summa Theologica*, Part II, Question 40 (Benziger Bros., ed., 1947), http://ethics.acusd.edu/Books/Texts/Aquinas/JustWar.html

[14]   "Just War Theory," *Internet Encyclopedia of Philosophy*, http://www.iep.utm.edu/j/justwar.htm#The%20 Principles%20Of%20<I>Jus%20In%20Bello</I>

[15]   Ibid.

[16]   Article 5 declares: "The Parties agree that an armed attack against one or more of them in Europe or North America shall be considered an attack against them all and consequently they agree that, if such an armed attack occurs, each of them, in exercise of the right of individual or collective self-defence recognised by Article 51 of the Charter of the United Nations, will assist the Party or Parties so attacked by taking forthwith, individually and in concert with the other Parties, such action as it deems necessary, including the use of armed force, to restore and maintain the security of the North Atlantic area." Washington Treaty, 4 April 1949, http://www.nato.int/docu/basictxt/treaty.htm

willful abuse of power. Because of the difficulty of rapidly deploying American troops to Afghanistan, the U.S. made effective use of Northern Alliance forces opposed to the Taliban. Leavened by Special Forces and CIA agents and backed by American air power, the Northern Alliance carried the bulk of the fighting in the war to oust the Taliban. The strategy worked so well that it made sense to continue to employ the Alliance in the ongoing hunt for Osama bin Laden, Mullah Mohamed Omar, and their followers that ensued. Offering cash rewards for captured "terrorists," however, appears to have led to at least some detentions based on personal vendetta or just for pecuniary gain.

Iraq: The war in Afghanistan had barely finished and the situation in the vast, decentralized and inhospitable country was far from stable. The new President, Mohamed Karzi, was derisively referred to as the "mayor of Kabul and then only until dark," and Al Qaeda still operated along the border with Pakistan. Despite these challenges the Bush administration determined to force a showdown with Saddam Hussein and invaded Iraq in March 2003. Since the war continues as a festering insurgency, analyses cannot be complete. However, both the motives and conduct of the war to date can be assessed using traditional just war theory.

The decision to invade Iraq falls woefully short of the *Jus ad Bellem* criteria. Despite disingenuous efforts to link the Hussein regime to terrorist attacks, no clear connection has ever been established. Claims that the dictator possessed weapons of mass destruction capable of harming the U.S. also remain unsubstantiated. The U.S. had not been attacked by Iraq unless one stretches the definition of "attack" to include firing on U.S. aircraft over the no-fly zones in which no U.S. flyer was killed or injured and no manned aircraft had been downed in twelve years. The war could hardly be called defensive. Even if one were to grant that pre-emption can be justified, an imminent threat such as troops massing on a border would have to be presented to make the case. The fact that then governor George Bush campaigned in 2000 criticizing the Clinton administration for failing to remove Saddam from power lends credence to claims that the invasion never was about terrorism.[17]

The Bush administration also fell woefully short on the criteria of legitimate authority. Despite repeated efforts to gain UN approval, neither the Security Council nor the General Assembly would approve military action. NATO, which had supported the U.S. in Afghanistan, refused to dub the invasion of Iraq an article five operation. Individual countries, most new members from Central and Eastern Europe plus stalwart Britain, supported the U.S., but few contributed significant numbers of troops. In the end, the Bush administration had scraped together a coalition of the reluctant, the coerced, and the cajoled, while much of the world considered the invasion a unilateral act of aggression. Finally, military action did not meet the "last resort requirement" of *Jus ad Bellum*. As the subsequent invasion clearly demonstrated, the Iraqi military had deteriorated since the first Gulf War (1991) and, with no outside support in sight, it would probably have continued to decline. The international arms inspectors also failed to establish that Saddam's chemical, biological, or nuclear programs posed any immediate or even long term threat. To the Bush administration's claim that Saddam Hussein had violated thirteen UN resolutions, the Arab world could respond that Israel had violated more. By almost any standard, the U.S. decision to invade Iraq fails to meet any of the just war criteria.

---

[17] Richard Clarke asserts that the administration discussed invading Iraq even before 91/11.

On the matter of *Jus in Bello*, the U.S. coalition fairs considerably better, at least during the conventional war. Using a different approach than that employed during the first Gulf War, General Tommy Franks did prepare the ground offensive with an extended and sustained bombing campaign. Opting instead for "shock and awe," he launched intensive but focused attacks on Iraqi command, control, and communications facilities and against Iraqi units. He sought both to minimize civilian casualties and to prevent the destruction of Iraq's oil wells.[18] In both objectives, he largely succeeded. Franks conducted the ground assault with similar focus and restraint, keeping civilian casualties to a minimum. However unjustified the invasion of Iraq may have been, its conduct conformed as closely to *Jus in Bello* criteria as could reasonably be expected of a modern conventional war.

The same cannot, unfortunately, be said of the counterinsurgency campaign that followed, although even in this effort U.S. and coalition soldiers have struggled to make the best of a bad situation. The real fault for excesses that have occurred lies with a fundamental flaw in U.S. strategy. The vast majority of American troops were in no way prepared for a protracted irregular war for which they had not adequately trained. Nor had they been deployed in the requisite numbers necessary to conduct such a campaign. When Army Chief of Staff Eric Shenseki had suggested that it would take more than 200,000 troops to successfully invade and occupy a country the size of Iraq, the Rumsfeld Pentagon pushed him into retirement. The invasion went ahead with around 150,000, more than enough troops to defeat the Iraq army, but not enough to secure Iraq's long porous borders, across which *mujahadin* from all over the Muslim world came to augment the growing resistance to occupation. Nor were their enough to occupy and maintain order within all areas of the country. To compound this strategic flaw, the first U.S. administrator, Paul Bremmer over-ruled the generals in deciding not to keep the Iraqi military and police already acting as such but to rebuild them from scratch instead.[19] The shortage of security forces, especially trained police, contributed to an atmosphere of lawlessness and created a power vacuum easily filled by insurgents.

Once the initial euphoria over liberation passed, and Iraqis faced a country in ruin and liberators who looked increasingly like occupiers. The U.S. faced violent opposition from a number of sources that coalesced into a general insurgency. Loosely organized but defuse and pervasive, the armed opposition has a single objective: to get the U.S. and its allies out. This goal gives them considerable legitimacy as freedom fighters throughout the Arab and Muslim worlds. To their credit, U.S. forces did their best to keep the use of force limited to the point of suffering more casualties than they might have taken with a greater reliance of firepower. As the situation in places like Faluja deteriorated, however, the troops could not overcome the troop shortages without resorting to air attacks and artillery. Even with the best of intentions, which they certainly had, the forces could not spare the innocent in combating the guilty with such weapons, especially when insurgents willingly used those civilians and their homes as cover. Following the reoccupation of the city, claims that the troops used only the minimum force necessary to achieve the objective offered cold comfort to thousands of people whose homes had been destroyed.

America's moral credibility suffered a further blow, with the prisoner abuse scandal at Abu Ghraib prison in Baghdad. U.S. personnel not only engaged in prisoner abuse that ranged

---

[18] See General Tommy Franks. *American Soldier* (New York: Regan Books, 2004) for a description of the invasion.
[19] Michael Gordon, "Debate Lingering on Decision to Dissolve Iraqi Military," *New York Times*, 21 Oct. 2004.

from degradation to inflicting physical pain and psychological torment, but even filmed their behavior. The military disciplined a handful of relatively low ranking soldiers, both men and women, but could allay suspicion that the culpability went much higher. An April 2002, a Justice Department memorandum narrowly defined torture and argued that President Bush could ignore international norms and definitions in the interest of national security.[20]

As of this writing, the U.S. remains bogged down in a desultory war that promises to drag on for some time. While the outcome of the struggle is not in doubt, the manner in which it is being conducted suggests that the cost in lives and treasure will be higher than it might have been with better preparation. It remains to be seen whether the invasion and occupation of Iraq will improve international security and decrease the risk of terrorism. Considerable evidence suggests that it may make things worse.

THE WIDER "WAR" ON TERRORISM

While I do not agree that the struggle against terrorism is a war, for the purpose of analyzing the administration's actions against Al Qaeda, its affiliates and supporters, the term has some value. Taken as whole, the actions against terrorism (in addition to Afghanistan and Iraq previously discussed) can be critiqued, at least to some degree, using traditional just war theory. In applying this critique, it may be useful to accept NATO's division of the struggle into three operational categories: anti-terrorism (actions taken to prevent terrorism), consequence management (actions taken in response to an actual terrorist attack), and counter-terrorism (offensive action taken against terrorists and terrorist organizations).[21] Since consequence management deals primarily with steps taken to mitigate the effects of an attack and resemble those taken in response to natural disaster, they need not concern us here. Moral issues surrounding anti-terrorist measures have primarily to do with civil liberties while counter-terrorism remains the most morally controversial aspect of the strategy.

The issue of *Jus ad Bellum* in the war on terrorism can be easily addressed. Terrorist acts have been universally and unequivocally condemned by all respected international organizations, including the UN and NATO. After the September 11 attacks, Congress and the vast majority of the American people stood behind the President's "declaration of war" against terrorism. Without giving the U.S. a blank check, the UN made an unequivocally strong statement condemning terrorism and calling for international cooperation to combat. Interestingly though, the Security Council Resolution passed in response to the Al Qaeda attack on the U.S. viewed terrorism as more a law enforcement than a military problem.[22] Nonetheless, the decision to attack terrorism clearly met the just war requirements for going to war.

Considerably great moral ambiguity surrounds actions taken within that war. To begin, while many anti-terrorism measures pose few problems, others are far more controversial. "Target hardening," measures taken to protect sites physically from terrorist attack, fall into the first category. Concrete barriers, metal detectors, and park restrictions inconvenience

---

[20] Neil Lewis, "U.S. Spells Out New Definition Curbing Torture," *New York Times,* 1 January 2005, p. 1. The Justice Department has under pressure amended its earlier position.
[21] *NATO's Military Concept for Defense Against Terrorism,* adopted Oct. 2003, updated 15 Dec. 2003, http://www.nato.int/ims/docu/terrorism.htm
[22] Security Council Resolution, 28 Sept. 2001, UN document S/RES/1373 (2001).

everyone equally, pose no ethical dilemmas, and are perfectly justifiable responses to a perceived threat. Random searches of airline passengers and "behavior profiling," closer scrutiny of passengers based on suspicious actions such as paying cash for a one-way ticket on the day of travel is also just. Expanding wire tap warrants to include all phones used by a suspect adjusts regulations from the era of the rotary dial to the age of the cell phone.

Beyond these and similar security measures, many steps taken to prevent terrorism either violate civil liberties or represent a potential threat to them. While violations of civil rights do not represent nor even necessarily lead to actual physical violence, the distance between the two is easily crossed. Given the increase in threats, and in some cases assaults, against Muslims (or those perceived to be Muslim) in the aftermath of September 11 makes the connection disturbingly clear. Add to these incidents the officially sanctioned but questionable legal detention of thousand of others and the connection becomes even clearer. Threats to civil liberties must be taken seriously in any country but especially in one already racially polarized. Secret search warrants, relatively unfettered access to financial, medical, and library records, and similar measures threaten the very security they propose to protect. They contribute to further encouraging an already dangerous latitude Americans allow police in the conduct of their duties. Under extreme circumstances, such as during an actual attack or its immediate aftermath (measured in days or weeks, not months or years), it may be necessary to temporarily suspend some civil liberties but only for definite and limited periods of time.

The moral issues surrounding anti-terrorist measures pale in comparison to those associated with counter-terrorism. Offensive action against elusive terrorists operating within civilian populations blurs the nice distinctions between law enforcement and military action and creates ample opportunity for crossing the line into vigilantism. To begin with, counter-terrorism requires intelligence, which if not freely given, must be gotten from captured terrorists. Since these prisoners rarely volunteer information, the temptation to coerce it from them may prove irresistible. Such was the case at Abu Ghrab and also Guantanamo Bay detention centers. How to use intelligence that has been gathered can be more complicated than might be imagined. The immediate reaction is to kill terrorists identified, but if doing so merely produces more terrorists then doing so may be counterproductive. The tit for tat killings in Northern Ireland and Israel/Palestine illustrate this point all to well.

AN ALTERNATIVE APPROACH?

An essay titled "Non-violence and the 'War' on Terrorism," might neatly conclude that violence is never justified even against such odious people as Osama bin Laden and his henchmen. For a pacifist this essay could have no other ending. I am, however, not a pacifist. Like Dietrich Bonhoeffer, I believe that although always wrong, taking human life is sometimes the lesser of two evils, but only when killing will save more lives than not killing. In combating a global terrorism network, deadly force will be necessary against the hard core leadership of an organization that will under no circumstances be talked out of their extreme ideology and who believe that ideology justifies mass slaughter by any means.

That being said, great care must be taken not to exaggerate the size of that core. The majority of those supporting terrorism do so for issues that have more to do with quality of life issues than religious or ideological fanaticism. No matter how well off or educated the bin Ladens of the terrorist world may be, they draw considerable support and most of their manpower from poor, underdeveloped countries like Egypt and Afghanistan. Even affluent Saudi Arabia has its pockets of relative deprivation, neighborhoods filled with young people with little hope for the future and rife for recruitment into extremist organizations. Only by attacking the root causes of terrorism can we hope to defeat it. Addressing these causes, however, requires the nation to face uncomfortable questions about the exploitive aspects of globalization, the one sided nature of U.S. policy towards Israel and the Palestinians, and uncritical support for a host of oppressive regimes.[23] Beyond that, fighting terrorism should become a matter for law enforcement on an international scale. As for anti-terrorism, we would do well to have a frank discussion of the level of risk we are willing to accept as the price of living in a free society. Only after we have had this sobering conversation can we get on with life. The alternative is to live in a state of constant, debilitating fear.

This pragmatic approach would be painful and expensive, but in the long run might prove more fruitful than any number of invasions or pre-emptive strikes. In the short run (and, sadly, politicians live in the world of the short run), however, declaring war is terribly convenient. It covers a multitude of sins, literally and figuratively and allows an administration to rally support for a host of policies dubiously connected to fighting terrorism in the name of patriotism.

---

[23] I argue this point in my chapter, "Winning Hearts and Minds in the War on terrorism," in Thomas R. Mockaitis and Paul Rich, eds., *Grand Strategy in the War on Terrorism* (London: Frank Cass, 2003).

SECTION VII

In: Religion, Terrorism and Globalization
Editor: K.K. Kuriakose, pp.243-263

ISBN 1-59454-553-7
© 2006 Nova Science Publishers, Inc.

Chapter 16

GLOBALIZATION, RELIGION, AND NONVIOLENCE

K.K. Kuriakose

Teachers College, Columbia University, New York

We are living in a tide of "globalization" that reaches to the urban and rural humans alike, to all corners of the earth, for pro or con, without exception. The process of globalization enhances technological culture where everything is directed to accumulate wealth, and that humanity globally experiences immense change and upheaval in social consensus and is being reshaped with new fabrics. The technological culture and market-based globalization fail to satisfy the full spectrum of human needs, as well as satisfy emotional, spiritual and creative dimensions of human aspiration. On the other hand, this consensus of economic development and the process of globalization deepen material scarcity and poverty that translate directly into human suffering. The concepts and behavioural patterns that impact religions and religious experiences of people around the world are rapidly changing. One irony at this religious and historical turning point of humanity is that it failed to understand the essence or core values of religions. Instead of receiving the values and rich heritages of religions it is being used for vested interest, and such a consensus leads many to involve violence. Religions are also used for finding justification for war and violence. Thus, terrorism and violence exist in the modern arena and challenge the peaceful existence of people around the globe.

In this article I will, first, address the range of issues that advance through globalization and its effect on religions and human behaviour in the struggle for a better humanity. Secondly, I will discuss the consequences of technology on culture and the economic-centered globalization that caused the spread of a violent culture. The central concern of my inquiry is to explore the concept of peace and non-violence in world religions and its significant role for a new world order. Also I would like to that inquire as to how non-violence has to be accepted with priority in the globalization agenda for the transformation of communities and building up peaceful communities along with justice.

GLOBALIZATION

Globalization represents different factors and it is as old as human history going back to the nomadic age, while the understanding of the word is different in its modern connotation. In early human history it was considered the habitation of people in different regions, while in the post-modern age it is characterized by "economic globalization," and a growing consciousness that all humanity share the same planet. In a study on globalization in history, A. G. Hopkins pointed out that the use of the word "modernization" in the 1950s and "globalization" in the 1990s had an intriguing relationship comparing "the wave of globalization" with "the development of global consciousness." He contended that, "This wave was different, however, in that the global consciousness flowered in peacetime rather than in the shadow of war"(Manning, p. 165). Hopkins' argument that global consciousness forms in peacetime rather than times of conflict and disruption is contrary to the observation of historical thinkers like Carl Becker and Emery Borgadus. According to Becker, "The climate of opinion of an age is not something disembodied and self-generating but rather is enmeshed in the concrete social and historical context in which it comes into being"(Ancher, p.3). Becker visualized that the rise of ideas and ideological development in an age would be a result of the inter-linked development that happens in a society such as political, economical, social, scientific, educational and industrial. Bogardus, going one step further, suggests that social thought does not find its expression at all times and in all contexts, but usually during social disturbances or during a time of social crisis and tension (Bogardus, p. 8). Historically, new ideas are at an ebb tide in a period of prosperity and harmony. Contrary to this, when the social conditions are severe or a society suffers from injustice, oppression or disturbance, in such contexts of turbulence, human thinking is highly stimulated and new ideas or ideologies originate.

In the post-modern period from the Second World War, the decline of post-war colonialism, the spread of democracy, mass migration to foreign lands, human struggle to combat poverty of the masses, segregation experiences, social and economic inequality, development of terrorism and the like catalyzed global consciousness. The advent of television followed by the Internet brought a revolution in communication across nations. The statistics on global realities, and issues like human rights violations, were brought to light to the world by the organizations like the United Nations and Amnesty International.

After the 1970s the forces of globalization had greater significance in many areas that included new technologies, cultures, economic exchanges, and political movements. "The final shift to a globally integrated world was achieved after 1990"(Williams, (2003), p. 62), and it has been centralized in the shifting economic structure with the production-dominated world economy. The process progressed with modernization, along with the advancement of science and technology. "A significant part of global prosperity of the 1990s came from new technologies such as cellular phones and genetic engineering" (Carnes, p.890). A British physicist Tim Berners-Lee, in early 1990s, succeeded to devise "the software grammar" or "the Internet language," the basis for the World Wide Web, the electronic impulses that paved the way of finding many windows in computer world. Social scientists commented on the pros and cons of globalization and of the development of a single global technological culture. The proponents observed globalization as spreading a culture of efficiency, coined with free trade. While critics argued that the process is a re-colonization of the world by industrialized nations (Ghosh, p.87). Globalization promotes a single technological culture spread by multicultural organizations and international organizations like World Bank, IMF, WTO, and NAFTA. This single technological culture damages local and traditional cultures. While the world communities accepted technological changes, cultural change was feared and resisted. According to L.S. Stavrianos "But technological change customarily has been accepted and welcomed because it normally raises living standards, while cultural change has been feared and resisted because it threatens traditional and comfortable values and practices." (p. 657). This critical distinction will inform our discussion.

IMPACT OF GLOBALIZATION ON POLITICAL CULTURES AND RELIGIONS

In world religions globalization is associated with mission, the propagation of their faith. "The first activity to be globalized in its reach was Christianity which, although widespread in all the other continents, did not reach large parts of central and East Africa until after 1870"(Williams, (2003), p. 61). In the colonial world, the Roman Catholic mission had far reaching evangelist activity. In modern times, that is replaced by the evangelical Christian's missionary activity across the nations. Evangelical Christianity, with a loose network of "global evangelism" programs has produced a wide appeal in developing countries, especially in South America and sub-Saharan Africa.

Ethnic, linguistic, cultural, and economic disparity in many communities has resulted in the changing of many social and political attitudes, leading to a more secular worldview and a decline in traditional cultures in Africa and Asia. The affluent middle class of these lands copy the lifestyle of their counterparts in Western countries. A major factor behind such a change is the influence of Western music, television, and movies in these regions. In the changing political and economic situation, the influence of traditional religions took new shape. In East Asian cultures globalism reflects with a mixed impact from the deep-rooted Confucian fabrics. A loosened tie from Confucian elements became evident in early 21st-century life in Tokyo, Seoul, Beijing, Taipei, and Hong Kong because of globalization. It has been affected more through family systems than any other social systems. Confucianism, with its ancestral roots and patriarchal authority, has adjusted to the Western lifestyle and single-child families with a concurrent revolution in family values. China also loosened her traditional systems and embraced the Internet and rapidly connected schools and businesses through digitization. In India, information technology advanced many middle class people to millionaire status, people with the brain power to break the rigid caste and land heredity. While in the United States and Europe, "globalization" fatigue is evident. In countries like China and India the concern is more with economic development.

The process of globalization has far reaching impact on religions and national communities. According to Samuel Huntington, "In the emerging era, clashes of civilizations are the greatest threat to world peace"(Suarez-Orozco, p. 163). He contends that the world is dissolving into fragments on the basis of "religious beliefs and historical attachments to different civilizations." The growing concerns of human rights and international peace are identified in many countries as being due to globalization. "Indeed very often religion has provided a way to re-imagine the nation-state, just as globalization has been undermining national autonomy" (Tignore, p.456). It is also noted that a rapid diffusion of religious and cultural systems is taking place in some regions due to multi-religious phenomenon. Muslims, in France, the United States, and Germany, constitute a growing population. Turkish Muslims are the fastest growing population in Berlin, and the descendants of Pakistani and Indian Muslims are being revitalized in northern England. The challenge brought by the internal dissenters as well as the external enemies are the outcome of emerging multi-religious communities around the world. This is a silent feature happening in world regions across the cultures. "In Huntington's view, the progress of globalization will be severely constrained by religio-political barriers, leading to a multi-polar world as opposed to a standardized, global culture predicted by Internet pioneers and proponents of virtual state" (Suarez-Orozco, p. 162).

Because of globalization and international co-operation, more people live outside their home country than ever before. The roles and rights of the people who live temporarily or permanently outside their homelands and the growing pressure on them from the host nations, are also reasons for conflicts with regards to personally held beliefs, morals or religious practices. When both countries, the origin and host, are similar in culture and political and religious tradition, there may not arise any major problems; however, when both countries have different orientation in beliefs and practices, problems arise that must be addressed. While the European and American cultural traditions do not conflict too drastically, someone from Western culture moving to an Eastern country, or vice versa, may make temporary or permanent religious assumptions about the other's freedom, and their religious behaviour will certainly differ. This is true for a Hindu, Muslim, or Christian when moved from their dominant area to another tradition. As a matter of fact, clashes may occur in human behaviour pattern.

In some regions the arrival of foreign religious communities brings issues to the local political agenda. A good example of this is in an American public school system in Dearborn, Michigan, where 35 percent of students in 2001 were Muslims. Providing *Halal* (lawful under Islam) at the lunch meal raised issues such as violation of religious rights in local politics.

In China and Russia the activities of evangelical Christians has raised some religious rights issues. The growing evangelical groups and the lawful "house churches" are considered a form of subversion to the Chinese government who wants to control all religious activities. In 1997, Russian President Boris Yeltsin enacted legislation to ban Western evangelical activities that have no religious roots fewer than 15 years in its country.

Simultaneously, with the rapid globalization forces on economic and social change, in India a communal identity has developed with Hindu nationalists. The dominant traditional elites were suddenly challenged by the newly formed economic class and traditional caste members. The Hindu militants argued that secular nationalism failed to establish economic justice and that religion could fill the role once occupied by a secular state. The Hindu nationalists also demanded that India be described as a nation of Hindus and that minorities only be given a lesser status in political involvement. Their political target of the Hindu nationalist was to establish a nation-state and they formed the Bhartya Janata Party (BJP), or Indian People's party. Since the 1970s this communally supported BJP became powerful and played a key role in Indian politics and eroded many advancements of the Congress Party, which had worked for a secular state since India's independence in 1947. The tactics of the BJP succeeded with the overthrow of the Indian National Congress party, and it then came into power under the leadership of A. B. Vajpayee in mid-1990s. The BJP government's policy was to transform secular India to a Hindu religious controlled country. Hinduism spirited BJP favoured a Hindu domination in the country. As a matter of fact, Christians and Muslims were mistreated, and several human rights violations occurred in different areas, especially in northern India. But the national election, in 2004, displaced the BJP government and the United Progressive Alliance government headed by the Congress party came in power. The new government announced that their main agenda will be to keep India as a "secular state," and that protecting the rights of minorities will be a crucial concern in their political agenda.

The situation of the Muslims in the Islamic belt of the Middle East and in other continents is a different story. For many Muslims, "*sunna*" is supreme in their life and must be followed in their daily life. They believe it is according to Muhammad's life and teaching. Islamic governments either adopted "*sunna*" as a model legal system or "*sharia*" in their countries. According to "*sharia*," Muslim law, religion and political government stay apart. "But many Muslims believe that their faith governs every aspect of life" (Said, p .45). However, there is an ongoing debate among Muslim scholars regarding how much control religion should have over law, government, and daily life. Some argue that Islam should be the basis of jurisprudence as well as individual daily life. For them the Prophet Mohammed was involved in politics as well as being a religious leader. In many Muslim countries the government is ruled by "summa," the way or path of a Muslim, as a legal system. Some others enforce Islamic religious practices as law, that effect political and social life, as well as in some cases individual life. In some African and Middle Eastern countries the practice of female circumcision was legally enforced as a means to deprive the victim of sexual feelings. The Egyptian high court, in 1997, granted a petition of women and commented that the practice of female circumcision was not authorized by the Koran.

The developments of modern Muslim cultures can be categorized in two ways. The first one is evident in the developments that we see in Iran, and the assumed leadership of Ayatollah Ruhollah Khomeini. The traditional clerics led an explosive and revolutionary movement in Iran by criticizing the modernizing processes in the 1970s as globalism. These social changes undermined the moral principles of Islamic teaching. And in 1979 the people overthrew their political head, Shah Mohammad Reza Pahlavi. Many people felt that modernizing and westernizing the region would lead them towards rampant materialism and unchecked individualism. Islamic revolutionaries were satisfied with Islamist government rules by the Islamic laws. Khomeini along with a council of Islamic clerics established a theocratic state which reduced the status of women, ruptured the relations with the West and supported the arbitrariness of the leaders. They also wanted to spread their ideals with strict Islamist governments to other nations. Religious terrorists, groups such as "Hezbollah," were behind Iranian leaders to spread these ideals.

Second, the development of terrorists is a new sect among religions. Communalists in the name of religion, the so-called religious terrorists, have created an alarming political situation which has affected global security in recent years. Terrorist groups are formed with a belief in the justification of violence, and their terrorism is motivated by firm faith and commitment to their religion. Terrorism grew in Palestine, with terrorist attacks mounting by the mid 20th century. Troubles in Northern Ireland also have a long history, where Roman Catholics and Protestants rebelled against each other with mutual terrorism. Terrorism had political or national motives in many regions, and terrorism labelled its newest form as being religiously motivated. The attack of militant religious terrorist group on Americans in Lebanon in the early 1980s, prompted a new era in the history of terrorism. The terrorist group called Hezbolla, in Arabic "Party of God," killed 241 U.S. soldiers. The young Muslims formed terrorist links to many different countries for a planned attack and used modern technological advances for their targets. Al Queda, a network formed by Osama bin Laden, a billionaire, has members in over 60 countries, and they believe they are in a holy war between good and evil.

Bin Laden issued a fatwa, a religious edict, in 1998, addressed to Islamic followers across the nations stating, "To kill Americans and their allies, both civil and military, is an individual duty of every Muslim who is able"(Carnes, p. 894). Al Qaeda "also wants to overthrow any government in a Muslim country that does not rule by what it believes are Islamic principles" (Frank, p. 33). Bin Laden, leader of the Al Qaeda, motivates his followers with his charismatic speech and inspires them to believe and obey his ideas. He defines everything he does by his religion and his speech is filled with Quranic references, which are meant to justify the violence. The Afghan-ruled Taliban fell in line with bin Laden and other extremist groups known for their terrorist activities terrorism. They targeted the World Trade Center in New York City on September 11, 2001. Four U.S. commercial airlines were hijacked that morning by members of Al Qaeda. One plane crashed in the Pennsylvania countryside, while another crashed into the Pentagon in Washington DC, a symbol of US military might, killing more than a thousand people. Two other jets targeted the twin towers of the World Trade Center, a symbol of U.S. capitalism. "The twin towers were destroyed, more than 3,000 people were killed, and fighting terrorism became the priority of governments around the world"(Andrea and Overfield, p. 545).

Globalization has posed far-reaching challenges in different regions, along with their economic activity, mixed social, cultural political and religious behaviour system. "In many regions people have sought to give a new role to religions to define the moral fabric of political communities"(Tignore, p. 456). People failed to understand the essence of their religion which speaks about peace and co-existence. As a result, religions are used to justify their narrow claim for their national identity. Identity and community conflict go hand in hand. Therefore, fundamentalism led to communalism, and religions were used to justify struggles for national identity that resulted in political terrorism. "Although terrorists are vilified as murderers and cowards by those who are their targets, they are considered idealists and heroes by those who share their views" (Andrea and Overfield, p. 545). The irony is that religious communities are being demonized for their terrorist activities. As a matter of fact, we have to recognize that the so called "religious terrorists" are neither nationalists nor religious terrorists, but are fundamentalists who had been co-opted as "communal terrorists." Hence we could see that religion and globalization were in conflict and religions are reacting to globalization by "circling the wagon" and redefining the nation-state in a dangerous way. The revolutionary activity of some radicals has made it clear that this is an improper exercise of religion or use of religion.

RELIGIOUS TERRORISTS OR COMMUNAL TERRORISTS?

As far as an individual or group working for the communal interest, they are not qualified to be called religious terrorists because their concerns are purely communal. Their interest is more in acquiring popularity in the society, rather than commitment to a religion or practice of faith in life. When religion is used for vested interest and forgetting the essential teachings, it cannot be called a "holy war." No religion teaches or supports violence, and a "holy war" is applicable only for reasons of faith.

While the political foundations of Islam have shaped different faces in globalism, especially in the Middle East, as mentioned above, the social and cultural aspects of Islamic life in the Middle East also have had their fair share of criticism. For some, adopting Western customs and values can be inspiring and considered a sign of progress. "To others, they are destructive of indigenous traditions and a barrier to the growth of a genuine national identity based on history and culture" (Duiker, p. 881). It became a strong conviction among Middle Eastern Muslims that their collaboration with America brings Western values to the Islamic community and that only served to weaken them. "And many of the Muslims who believe this also believe it is America's fault that they ever turned from Islam: that America's actions--our meddling, our trade, our relations with them--are a modern crusade designed to weaken and destroy Islam"(Frank, p. 63). They also bring an ideological concept that the success of life is based on earning plenty of money. In addition, the American presence in the Middle East challenged them as they created an economic system that could not support them for economic success. Further, to a Muslim faith should be primary to the individual and success and wealth are far less important. As a matter of fact, they have to turn back to the Islamic faith and keep Islamic values.

The Taliban influence in Afghanistan (1996-2001) brought another face to the influence of religion on people who believed in the militant teachings about the evil of non-Muslim nations. Furthermore, they taught that modern culture is evil, with music and art being part of this evil culture. And they advocated that women must be kept away from men to avoid temptation. The Taliban used religion to justify violence and intolerance. Until the Taliban became a controlling force in Afghan life, religion was not a major concern for the state. "But the Taliban who believed that a more radical, strict version of Islam was the only way to save the country from destruction, brought a new, harsh tone to a Afghan religious life" (Frank, p. 86). The Taliban imposed such a harsh form of religion when they took political power in the country that it was a difficult form of religion for the Afghan people. The Taliban government issued laws one after another to regulate the civic life and to force the people into submission, rather than to understand any deeper religious meaning. Any men or women who disobeyed Taliban were considered infidel or deserving of punishment.

The Taliban regime brought a horrible life to women and girls in Afghanistan. However, some girls violated the edicts by attending secret underground schools. Female teachers taught small group of girls in private apartments. As the Quran was the only book they had permission to study, young girls always carried a copy with them. Kitchens were also used for instruction, under the pretence that they were having a cooking class. After the Taliban lost power in 2001, Afghani girls rushed back to schools and hundreds of them signed up for classes at Kabul University. But by that time, an entire generation of young girls was left without hope of education and were married as early teens, many with children.

The religious impact of politics has been widespread; it has different forms in different cultures. For instance, religion became an even more powerful force in politics in the Untied States and Eastern Europe by the 1980s. In Poland, the spreading of Communist ideology not only was crushed, but was undermined by the role of the Papacy. Pope John Paul II gave unwavering support to the Polish people in order to encourage them to resist the Communist regimes of that region. Ultimately this political climate swept the communist regime in the Soviet Union and Eastern Europe in one decade (New York Times, April 3, 2005, p. N39). While in the Untied States the overt and covert support of the "Christian fundamentalists" became more predominant. And in the war against Iraq, these "fundamentalists'" offered blind support of the Bush administration and the criticism from many Christians was that "Insisting on the literal interpretation of the Bible, Protestant fundamentalists have long railed against secularising trends in American society" (Tignor, p. 458). Serious criticism on the secularization trends of Western, as well as modern Christianity from the traditional religious minded are also there. Because of post-modernism, for the church became a major "service organization," a place for the consumers, a place of caring the needy. Church, "a religious institution," functioned as a business organization, and a place for periodic interaction. Thus "Church" moved away from the traditional religious activities, where attending Divine Liturgy, observing lent and fasting, repentance and confession(among Roman Catholic and Orthodox traditions), and spiritual development had priority in church practice. But in modern times the Church assembly and activities focus on the social aspects more than in the moral and philosophical aspects of religion. The traditions are shaky. Many, especially youth, ask the question: "Why traditional religious practice?" However, they raise questions about religion. Digital information has had much impact, but its value is measured quantitatively. This limits our assessment of reality as to what can be quantified because spirituality is not quantifiable.

GLOBALISM, CULTURAL CONFLICTS, SOCIAL AND GENDER EQUITY, AND RELIGIONS

The decline of colonialism after the Second World War and the rise of widespread awakening for democratization across the nations, not only led to seismic waves around the world, but also a demand for economic and social justice along with globalization. Robert F. Arnove and others observed in the African region because of globalization that a consciousness "Intensified inequality is both a barrier to broad participation in democratic governance and a breeding ground for socially disruptive discontent"(p. 421). No one should be denied opportunities because of racial, ethnic, socioeconomic, or gender discrimination.

The globalization process and its impact on political, economic, and social life of other regions inspired Africans in reshaping their country. The concerns were electrified in South Africa with Nelson Mandela's democratic election and by drawing the curtain on 56 years of apartheid. The new situation very soon reflected in the political, economic and social systems, for, "It was secure in its political authority, enjoyed huge good will around the world, and operated from the moral high ground of having replaced a regime that had created one of the most heinous and racially inequitable economic and social systems of the 20th century"(Fiske and Ladd, p. 52). They copied from other advanced countries concerns like promotion of educational equity with a national priority in the fundamental rights of people.

A new global consciousness and concern to let women participate, along with other social and cultural justice concerns, was one of the positive results of this post-modernism. One area affected by this consciousness during the post-modern period is the cultural and social subordination of women. Feminist curiosity and creativity, along with globalization and a feminist philosophy have been growing since the 1970s (Card, p. 3). Modern research in social sciences and cultural studies provided an incentive to recognize the subhuman treatment of women and to resolve cultural conflicts related to them.

Among all the social movements that have been witnessed in the second half of the 20th century, the women's equity movement hit a higher point than any other movement across religions and cultures. Judaism, Islam and traditional Christianity devalued women in many ways. Although in ancient religious cultures the female goddesses were leading religious figures. Hinduism still continues that consensus. However, when it comes to social status women are treated in subhuman ways regardless of religious affiliation. In Hindu, traditional male figures like Shiva are always accompanied by female counterparts like Parvati, Kali or Durga. Confucianism is acquainted with patriarchy and Daoism and Shinto makes little distinction between male and female duties. And the Buddhist tradition recognizes female deities. For instance, in Japan, women seek intersession from Kuan Yin. In modern globalization, the concern of equal status for women includes equality in jobs, wages and opportunity for success and life opportunities. In the United States the struggle has a long history. "In 1841, when the first arts degree was awarded to a woman, there were seven major occupations open to her sex: needle trades, keeping boarders, cotton mill work, bookbinding, typesetting, and domestic service" (Merriam, p.13). Later women opened their own businesses targeting other women's desires, like the Ladies Oyster Shop and Ladies Bowling Alley and the Ladies Reading Room in several places.

The national movements of women for political participation are reflected as well in their religious life. First, it is reflected in the global democratic process when women began to be included in franchises in national elections. By 1950 it was only in 69 countries and it grew to 129 countries in 1975. Another change in the status of women in the last decades has been the opening of educational opportunities to them across the nations. The worldwide rate for women's literacy was only 59 percent in 1960, but by 1985 this number went up to 68 percent. However, it has been proved that women have more adaptability than men in the changing global situation, especially in the migration history with language, customs and practices. In the early days women engaged in general education but the percentage of women who got professional training began to increase in the post-modern era, as well as their participation in national productivity and wealth. Education and economic stability increased their status as well as their self-esteem and enabled them to defend their equity in social life. The view on women changed when women began not only take part in the political affairs, but as leaders of their nations. In three neighbouring countries in South Asia, Indira Gandhi in India, Benazir Bhutto in Pakistan, and Srimivao Bandaranaike in Sri Lank, women became prime ministers.

While the non-Western feminist struggle focused on equal status with men, Western women pleaded for equal recognition in religion, workplace, media, and home. Our academic institutions have not fully examined the close link between religion and gender, neither have they given sufficient attention to the impact of religion on gender politics. As Meade observes "Only relatively recently has religion become recognized as a distinct element that has to be reckoned with in its own right when investigating history and gender; it cannot be fully accounted for by simply speaking about general cultural influences" (Meade, p. 71). In all cultures, especially traditional cultures, religion and patriarchy governed all and that not only affected individual development but also contributed to family, community and national ideals.

Feminist activists were concerned with a liberating alternative to establish a faith system with a role for women. The question arose across the cultures: Why are women off the mark from equal opportunity in religious activity? This became a serious concern in Christianity by late the 1960s. Christian denominations attempted to resolve many feminist views, along with concerns in social justice, birth control, and women in the priesthood. Female participation in church activities increased rapidly in this period and many Protestant denominations responded to the uproar by putting women in the church pulpit and then ordaining them as ministers.

One can certainly see the transformation of women's participation in civic life along with globalization. The number of women in the workforce in Great Britain remarkably increased from 32 to 44 percent between 1970 and 1990. While in the Soviet Union 70 percent of doctors and teachers were women during this period. According to the United States Census Bureau in 1998, after the 1970s the fastest growing group of female workers were mothers of young children. And by the 1990s, over 55 percent of working mothers went back to work before their child was even a year old. Today over 56.5 million women are in the workforce in the United States. On the other hand, Janet Zollinger Giele and others observed from a study that Third World women and minorities' situations are discouraging, for "cotemporary development, rather than fostering equality, thus appears to deepen inequality by exploiting to most vulnerable people on the economic periphery while it serves the interest of those with wealth or education who inhabit the modern core"(p.6). Women's situation was worsened in past decades, neither status nor safety improved. Because the globalization of the world economy only aggravated the poverty of women and policy such as privatization of public services and liberalization of trade that damage home industries. Further, they were forced off the land by the need to earn wages and they moved with migration groups and joined in the urban labor force.

Women adopted various ways of transforming their living conditions and after 1970 numerous activists groups were formed in many countries to communicate these women's issues. Their hope was to overturn legal restrictions, first on both sides of the Atlantic Ocean, and then it followed in other lands. In Britain many women aligned themselves with antinuclear protesters, catching the attention of the world and establishing themselves as a powerful political force. Women not only fought for their rights but also increased their involvement in social issues in their region and throughout the world.

Two charismatic leaders in religious traditions, Mother Theresa and Matha Amritanandamayi Devi, not only inspired women's participation in social issues but increased the self-esteem of traditional Asian women. Born in Yugoslavia, Mother Theresa moved to Calcutta, India, where she chose to minister to the poor, unwanted, needy and ailing where she saw the love of God. While Matha Amritanandamayi Devi also received world attention because of her concern for the poor and underprivileged. She inspired the masses from the Vedic teaching of ancient India and emphasized the consensus of peace, unity and love in human progress. In a speech addressing the Interfaith Celebration in honour of the 50th Anniversary of the United Nations in1995, she said, "The real flow of life lies in unity, in the oneness that arises out of love" (www.mothersbooks.com). Women who became active in public life in modern times increased the self-esteem of women in general and reversed many of the effects of the subordination of women in past generations. Also, many female leaders emerged in political and social movements with concerns for building up peace communities around the world. Religion may oppose some aspects of globalization, but, as we can see, it also agrees with many positive aspects of globalization. This shows that essential beliefs support or may help give globalization a positive direction.

COSMIC VIEW OF RELIGIONS: KARMA, DHARMA AND JUST WAR THEORY

Confucianism, which has a deep root in Chinese social fabric, was intended to build up a better society based on social values, institutions and transcendent ideals. The supreme goal of Kung Confucius (551-479 BCE) was to build a civilized human society. According to this religion, values, norms and behavior patterns build human relationships. In addition, this religion has a transcendent dimension too, but it is not as one sees in other world religions especially concerning life after death. For Confucius the transcendent nature did not mean otherworldly or heavenly realm, but perfection of transcendent ideals. His moral teachings were grounded in the family, school, society and state. Confucius did not identify separate priests because parents, teachers and officials were the priests or educators. This philosophy formed a deep heritage in the Chinese social fabric and way of life.

Asian religions, Judaism, Christianity, and Islam advocate that humans, as well as nature, are the creation of God and accept the natural world as good. The authorship of cosmos goes to the Godhead (Genesis 1:1-27) and the doctrine of cosmos "God calls into existence the things that do not exist" (Romans 4:17). Hinduism, Buddhism and Jainism developed and shared the beliefs that the universe is created and destroyed in endless cycles, the world is transitory and the appearance of permanence is *maya*, illusion. While Christianity emphasizes the power of sin in humanity and creation, that idea has less importance in Asian religions. Bad behavior might be punished in this world and the next. Christians subscribe to good deeds in life, for according to the scripture a Christian is rewarded in the last judgement. "For we must all appear before the judgement seat of Christ, so that each one may receive good or evil, according to what he has done in the body"(II Corinthians 5:10).

Islamic teaching makes no compartmental division between "church" and "state," but it finds unity between the two. Further, Islam advocates that "one of the objectives of Muslim life is to make this unity a real experience of human beings." And also content that "One of the major obstacles to the human experience of a unity of faith and life is the presence of injustice" (Said et.al., p.228). God is just and merciful and those who repent and purify while on earth can return to paradise after death. A person should, therefore, try their best to be good and help others, above all, trusting in God's justice and awaiting the reward that is God's mercy. Islam teaches that this worldly life is a period of testing and preparation for the life to come. Its followers also believe that there will be a last day, or judgment day, when everyone will be rewarded according to their deeds on earth. As all World Religions adhere and has a basic presumption that human beings are born intrinsically good but have an imperfect human nature. Also, the religions recommend that it is redeemable. In Confucianism the teaching and models of elders and superiors in society provide this redemption. Renewed effort and right behaviour and, through different religious or ritual practices, including piety, meditation, and arms giving, one can find redemption in Hinduism. While Buddhism teaches that the eight fold path of principles including right actions, speech, and livelihood can negate hatred, greed, and ignorance in this struggle for a renewed society.

In Hinduism human destiny is governed by the *karma* and *dharma* of each person, and by *purushartha,* which is the basis of life. The legitimate four goals for human life are defined within the doctrine of *purusharthas.* The four goals in life are: *dharma,* pointing to a moral life; *artha,* possession of wealth; *kama,* enjoyment of the senses; and *moksha,* seeking liberation. "The ultimate goal for the individual that underlies all of these four goals is, of course, the quest for perfection, but the focus of this goal in Hinduism is on the process rather than on the product "(Reagan, p. 99). According to *Mahabharatha,* the quest for the perfection of man is the pursuit of *Brahman* or self-knowledge and that will lead to immortality. Further, the basic concept of human life and its perfection is defined with a formula called *Satcitanand. Sat* means being, *Cit* means intelligence, and *Anand* means bliss. This philosophical formula states that *dharma* can flourish by *satya,* and is adhered to at every stage. Being intelligent and blissful constitutes the very nature of *Brahman* and not its attributes. *Brahman* is to understand as '*cit*' intelligence or consciousness. *Brahman* is being, '*sat,*' self-luminous, and in one nature it illumines all other things and in the other it is also.

Actions of non-violence are considered a supreme good in moral matters. According to *karma* theory, we reap what we sow. Human beings reap the fruits of his or her deeds, whether good or bad, right or wrong. Bad deeds result in unpleasant consequences in the same way good deeds result in pleasant consequences. Good actions provide happiness and result in the birth into a higher caste in the next life. On the other hand, acts of violence are morally bad and cause re-birth in a lower-category. The *Chandogya Upanishad* defined the concept with *ahimsa* in the list of religious virtues. According to this list, the supreme virtues are truthfulness, non-violence, austerity, straightforwardness, and charity. The *Bhagavadgita,* the famous philosophical text in Hindu scriptures, supports war to remove injustice and evil forces from society, and the intention is to purify society. "A warrior may kill his enemies on the battlefield because it is his duty to defend the country and to protect the people" (Christopher, p.79). However, Sri Shankaracharya, the enlightened Hindu philosopher, when commenting on the *Bhagavadgita,* said "that a yogi should be non-violent towards others and should identify the self of all beings with his own. Also, he should do only to others that which is desirable and pleasant to his own self, but should refrain from doing that to others which is undesirable and unpleasant for himself"(Christopher. 74).

However, the concept of "just war theory" has brought up critical issues for religious people as an escape for keeping many in engaging in wars, for political and social issues. In Islamic scriptures, as Said notes, there is "no license in Islam for any war (indeed, for any human enterprise) that falls outside the bounds of the divine commandments and prophetic practice"(p.229). Muslims always look to Muhammad and what he did in critical situations and call it "jihad". In Western Christianity, the idea of the "just war theory" developed as a consensus to justify war, contrary to Jesus' teaching practice, and the witness of early Christians. For Christians, the New Testament and Jesus' teachings and practice are significant as well as authoritative. Jesus taught a new principle of loving the enemy: "I say to you, Do not resist one who is evil, but if any one strikes you on the right cheek, turn to him the other also"(Matthew 5:39). Jesus' teaching of the Sermon on the Mount became significant as a call for peaceful human co-existence. Peter, a disciple of Jesus, took a sword and cut the ear of Malchus, the servant of the high priest who had come along with the soldiers to arrest Jesus. Jesus said to Peter "Put up thy sword into the sheath"(John 18:11). Obviously, Jesus opposed violence even for self defense. He was extremely clear what to profess and do. For it mattered, "But Jesus said, 'No more of this!' And he touched his ear and healed him (Luke 22: 51)." This scene at Gethsemane is foundational for Christian pacifism. Jesus chose the Cross and defended himself using the Way of the Cross to oppose his enemies. His arrest in Gethsemane proved his non-violent teaching and he moved to Golgotha to endure that principle. There is no permission to. perform acts of violence or support for war, for either establishing a worldly kingdom, or otherwise, according to Jesus' teaching and practice. Paul reminded believers that "For we are not contending against flesh and blood, but against the principalities, against the powers, against the world rulers of this present darkness, against the spiritual hosts of wickedness in the heavenly places" (Ephesians 6:12). As Peter Riga puts it "Christianity's origins were non-violent for three hundred years and spread non violently through the preaching and proclamations even amidst terrible persecutions"(p. 51). Contrary to the witness of Jesus and the early church, Christians of the later centuries involved in violence.

While all world religions do not completely prohibit violence, we can see that violence is inconsistent with their core beliefs. Apparently, the religious reaction against globalism is not necessarily based on religious beliefs. And reacting with violence is contrary to these beliefs and reflects bitterness to assimilating to cultural fabrics.

GLOBALISM, MATERIAL, CULTURAL AND SPIRITUAL CRISIS

The market ideology and the ideology of nationalism are the two critical issues of the modern technological culture. They counter the religious impulse of humankind. Both are grounded in individualism and spell disaster to the global community. The two forces that influence modern technological culture are the market and the nation. In post-modern societies everything is directed to accumulating material wealth. Therefore the technological culture fails to satisfy the full spectrum of human needs, including the emotional, spiritual and creative dimensions of human aspirations. In spite of human progress and achievements and further possibilities of scientific and technological advancements based on development in globalism, humanity has reached a relatively fragmented and ecologically endangered global village.

Humanity faces a crisis in our individual lives, in families, and behavioural patterns in human relationships and the natural ecosystem. Cornel West calls this phenomenon as a "walking nihilism" or "the peoples lived experiences of hopelessness and meaninglessness", as a cultural-spiritual crisis. In the *Prophetic Fragments*, West recommends for a meaningful response from faith communities at this desperate situation of humans in their struggle and their hopeless and meaningless life. "For West, a crucial response must begin with the notion of struggle and hope in a world in desperate need of hope"(Wimberly, p. 280).

The emphasis on accumulation of wealth disregards religious -oriented cultures and values, but seeks secular values. The cultural crisis, with its "individualism" notion, has reached an acute stage in the modern industrial-technological culture. The "individualism" that originated in colonial America damaged the "jeremiad" of the British Puritans (Gabbard, p. 18). God had called on them to build an ideal community, headed by John Winthrop, which was rooted in the Biblical teaching of "love your neighbour as yourself." For the establishment of an ideal life people must restrain their greed for the benefits of others and for the good of the community, which should exist in peace and harmony. Winthrop's attempt to reconcile the key concepts of his time, "status, property, and God," and to create a secular heaven on earth failed in an acquisitive community. As historian Alexander Callow observed, "The seed of individualism shattered the notion of collective responsibility and the opportunities of the new world broke the spine of the ideal community" (p. 38).

The national character of the American settlers and the moral-cultural crisis that the American society addresses today is a continuation of the colonial past. More than anything else, individualism was a force that motivated American culture, according to the authors of the book *Habits of the Heart* by Robert Bellah and others. And this individualist ideology has brought American culture to a destructive point. The modern American society, government and corporations are the most powerful structures and effect culture, character and daily practices of life. It seems the bureaucratic individualism of today is the latest expression of American middle class culture. The authors commented that today universities are under the pressure of poplar culture and the crisis in intellectual culture is growing day by day, and as Callow contented, industrial revolution and the technological culture that followed yielded to secular values.

The modern concept of development and the technological culture create and perpetuate biotic and cultural poverty and scarcity. The advancement of science and technology with its counterpart of modern industrialized societies promoted a highly materialistic lifestyle undermining the natural power to renew and sustain life. The modern technology that is used for farming, building construction, clothing manufacturing, production of energy, and waste disposal results in environmental damage. Moreover, it has been noted that industrialized technologies causes alteration of weather patterns and ozone destruction, upon (due to), the combustion of fossil. This kind of damage leads to imminent decline of ecological balance and is not easy to correct or replace neither by nature or human. Along with such damages and crises, globalization deepens material scarcity and poverty. Different statistics reveals this fact, for instance "In 1960 the poorest 20% of the world's population had just 2.3% of the wealth of the world. Today this has shrunk to just barely 1%"(Bigelow, p. 9). Also, globalization destroys farm communities in both industrialized and third world countries. In Europe alone 200,000 farmers and 600,000 beef producers gave up agriculture, in 1999, as they were not getting enough income to cover their costs. In China, half of its agricultural farmers have been uprooted due to modernization in the last two decades. Cheap meat imports from Europe displaced West African farm business, and in India traditional oil seeds like sesame, linseed, and mustard are replaced by the soya imported from the United States. According to a US Department of Agriculture study, the price of many major commodities, like cotton and soybeans, was lower in 2000 than it has been in more than 25 years. "This economic disaster is translating directly into human suffering: Suicide is now the leading cause of death among American farmers, occurring at a rate three times higher than in the general population" (Bigelow, p. 245). This aspect of globalism must be addressed by the values at the core of religious beliefs. At that core is non-violence and unless this concept is embraced across cultures, globalization is headed for disaster.

FOR A NEW WORLD ORDER

Humanity's journey has come a long way, and we are at the most crucial stage of that journey. "It can 'lead to the Bomb or the Buddha' i.e., to utter annihilation brought about by the Bomb (or environmental destruction) or to peace" (Zachariah, p. 44). Today, with globalism, we face critical questions about the fate of the earth, and the future of humankind. The concerns are the ecology of peace, and are a moral and religious problem. The challenge today to all sensitive people on earth is that we turn away from the act of destroying the lovely world whether in fear, greed or anger, and keep it as a beautiful place to live.

Preventing mass killing, preserving peace, and strengthening human rights concerns became the top agenda for humanitarian agencies. However, these agencies could play only a limited role. Eighty-three armed conflicts erupted between 1989 and 1992 and 90 percent of the casualties were civilian. "By 1995 the world had 42 million displaced people, another 160 million were victims of disaster, and 2 billion lived in conditions of abject poverty"(Tignor, p. 455). Internal conflicts in the nations grew in many regions and the main reason behind the restlessness was due to increasing economic integration among nations and resulted in casualties of civilians. Disparity in social and economic inequality among citizens and the attempts to bring social justice among them is a basic concern of democratic countries around the world. Also, issues such as inequality on the basis of gender, race, origin of nationality, became top concerns in the search for a global community.

The post-war world was divided into two heavily armed camps in a balance of terror. Eastern European states adapted Western models of economic development to establish there freedom, and expected to create a new undivided Europe. However, the ethnic hatreds and tensions brought these nations to divisiveness.

In Africa and Asia, the newly declared independent countries had the difficulty of transitioning from a traditional to a modern society. The transition from an agrarian economy to an industrial one needed time as well as a substantial amount of economic and technological assistance, without which, such a transition will only be a myth. Furthermore, Asia and Africa are facing economic and technological issues. "As the new century dawns, internal conflicts spawned by deep-rooted historical and ethnic hatreds are proliferating throughout the world, leading to a vast new movement of people across state boundaries unequal to any that has occurred since the great population migrations of the thirteenth and fourteenth centuries"(Duiker, p. 881). In many non-Western regions, Western cultural values and customs are resisted. Because of such conflicting attitudes, people engage in conflict and violence, as they may feel such transitions undermine the stability of their noble traditional heritage. Also remarkable, is the comment of "Some observers, like the U.S. Scholar Francis Fukuyama, argue that capitalism and the Western concept of liberal democracy have vanquished all of their rivals and will ultimately be applied universally through out the globe"(Duiker, p. 883).

The United Nations declared that the Universal Declaration of Human Rights in 1948 optimized the possibility of a better human existence on the earth. However, after 50 years the human rights abuses are more serious than ever in some regions, while in other regions they have indeed improved. In different regions there are violations of basic rights in the form of discrimination, censorship, political imprisonment, torture, slavery, kidnapping, genocide, poverty, refugees, abuse of women and children, and overall, their rights continue to be ignored. In 1998 a poll called the Human Rights Index was conducted by the *Observer*, a British newspaper. The study was created in order to rank 194 nation-states and to complete a record of human rights abuses. The poll was based on the basis of human rights violations and the index included items such as: extra-judicial killings, use of torture, use of the death penalty, disappearances, denial of free speech, denial of political rights, denial of child rights, and denial of religious freedom. The violation index ranked Algeria first and then North Korea, while China was ranked 10th, with the United States 92[nd.] and United Kingdom 141st (O'Byrne, p. 5).

Safeguarding citizens in their new environment is another issue emerging with globalization. Mass migration due to globalization poses different human rights concerns across the nations. "The wider international acceptance of basic human rights has allowed such migrants to insist more readily on their rights in their new home areas which are often prescribed in law, while they retain very different assumptions about their citizenship responsibilities"(Williams, (2003), p. 66). The conflicts grow between migrants and indigenous people in different regions. Evidence of this intolerance can be seen in Fiji because of Indian migration, with Jewish settlers in Israel/Palestine, with Arab Christians and Muslims, and between Serbs and Albanians in Kosovo. Hence governments have to address two kinds of problems one is with its own citizens and then the problems arising with the new inhabitants.

There is no doubt that there is a need for a new world order with common interests that transcend national boundaries. Fear of domination and fear of loss of national economic and political sovereignty have been barriers to the success of international economic or political associations. Such fears may be allayed if mass participation by disarmament and environmental movements is used to foster such trans-national associations. The globalization process has to seek for a workable new order based on increased democratization in developing countries, and on sustainable growth and development of the world economy.

SPREADING A CULTURE OF NON-VIOLENCE

In 1939 Albert Einstein wrote a historic letter to President Franklin Roosevelt. In it, Einstein warned of the possibilities of atomic warfare. Einstein did not believe that a nation's security could be assured through "national armament." Indeed a nuclear build-up, or arms race, would only lead to intimidation and "mutual fear and distrust" (Einstein, p.145). Disregarding such warnings, inventions continued and military technology made unprecedented advances acquainted with the wars. "Einstein had warned when the first nuclear bombs were detonated, that 'we drift to unparalleled catastrophe,' nevertheless an arms race proliferated, with each new invention triggering counter-inventions" (Stavrianos, p. 652).

As Einstein predicted the arms race competition continued between the super powers of the United States and the Soviet Union. In 1945 Americans built an A-bomb and the Soviets followed with their model in 1949. By 1952 America had created the H-bomb, with the Soviets creating theirs just one year later. The attempt was to update military technologies, but it resulted in a rush to stockpile nuclear weapons on both sides. By 1960 the super powers reached a point where nuclear war could potentially destroy the world "without a soldier firing a shot." The final result of this race ended with the accumulation of a global arsenal of 50,000 nuclear weapons.

It is ironic to note that past advances in technology led humans to violence. When humans were nomadic and food gatherers, the incentive for, or means for, violence was little. . When the technology advanced, both the incentive and habits of violence increased. "This occurred with the agricultural and industrial revolutions, which increased productivity dramatically and created affluent civilizations fundamentally different from all the preceding subsistence societies"(Stavrianos, p. 653). Another paradox of our age is that as the agricultural and industrial revolutions of the past made war a profitable endeavor, globalization made it unprofitable and suicidal. For modern terrorists, such as the attackers of the World Trade Center, in New York City, the nuclear bomb was not, or need not be, a means to killing one or many. "This is why Einstein warned us that we now face the choice of new 'ways of thinking,' or 'unparalleled catastrophe"(Stavrianos, p.653).

The critical challenge today is nothing but to use our own brains once again to adapt to a new environment, to our own human needs, to launch a comfortable and peaceful living for the community. At this point the educational system has an important moral challenge to help students understand the corrupting and destructing influence of war, not only on humans, but on all living species in nature.

Human behavior can be changed according to the situation. For instance, in his research among the Senio tribe in Malay Peninsula, psychologist Kilton Stewart discovered fascinating information regarding their long inhabitation in that region. The focus of his research was human dreams and thinking development especially in comparison to other cultures. Stewart lived with and studied the tribe for 15 years. One of the most prominent findings was that the Senio tribe had no conflict with their neighboring tribes, nor had any record of violent crimes for nearly 300 years (Lawrence, p. 37). He also observed that the way these individuals interacted with each other improved their quality of living. After his study, Stewart concluded that, "Observing the lives of the Senoi, it occurred to me that modern civilization may be sick because people have sloughed off, or failed to develop, half their power to think" (Lawrence, p. 38). Stewart found that those living in modern civilization had an inability to engage in reflective thinking or the creative process. In addition he noted that modern culture neglects social forms of education. The modern educational system has not taken note of Stewart's study and a curriculum of social education has not been widely launched.

CHALLENGING EXPERIMENTS OF NON-VIOLENCE IN THE 20TH CENTURY

In the modern age Mahatma Gandhi and Martin Luther King, Jr. top the list of being advocates of non-violence in human endeavours. Both applied religious ideals in political life. Gandhi grasped the essence of all World Religions, assumed a leadership role and applied himself to build a better world with the principles of non-violence. He did not limit the practice of non-violence in a particular realm or for political reasons. He found non-violence to be the noblest virtue, and accepted it as a lifestyle, first in family, then in communities, both in South Africa and India. He applied religious ideals in political life, and laboriously in the Indian independence struggle against British imperialism. Like Gandhi, Martin Luther

King, brought the principle of non-violence to the civil rights struggle in the United States, to fight against the social segregation of the African Americans. As Mark C. Carnes explains "The Reverend Martin Luther King, Jr.'s nonviolent approach was essentially religious, his oratory deeply felt, passionate, but always dignified and controlled"(p. 830). He won the heart of many not only in the United States, but he also stood up for oppressed people around the world, and was concerned for the freedom and transformation of them (Phillips, p. 53). With this concern he visited other regions in Africa, Europe and Asia.

CONCLUSION

Globalism could be seen not as all bad or all good, it is a mixture of experience for the world population. While globalism benefited from its technological advancement to global economy with social progress, at the expense of damaging the global ecosystem, it failed to satisfy human emotional, moral and spiritual needs and nourished only an "individualistic" culture.

The tragedy of globalization is that it is rooted in the market -oriented development and individualist possession, in contrast to the community-oriented concept of development. Globalization brings ecological harm to an industrialized world and Third World people alike. In addition, Third World countries face many obstacles to building their economic infrastructures. Although there are several economic schemes to combat Third World poverty and misery, the economic disparity widens between the rich and poor and globalization only helps to promote a new class—the neo-capitalist. This new class comes at the expense of globalization by cutting the edges of traditional structures, patriarchy or caste and class boundaries. Instead of safeguarding the human rights of people, violations of rights and growth of economic and social injustice increased in many regions. As a reaction to globalization the political culture turned and supported revolution or terrorism as an alternative to safeguard there religion and economy. The irony is that a widespread notion that terrorism and war have roots in the scriptures. This flawed understanding of people from different corners of world is a great challenge to global security as well as to the heritage of religions.

It is a moral challenge to religious people to communicate to the world that religions teach peace and non-violence and it is a core concern of world religions. Religion supports globalization and globalization supports non-violence. Unfortunately, this is misunderstood by many religious groups.

The concept of peace and non-violence has to be brought to the forefront of the globalization agenda. The spreading of non-violence along with the establishment of democracy should be the central concern of world governments in their search for a new world order where religious heritages should be recognized. As the Buddhist eight-fold path insists, the matrix of mutual interdependence is a key formula for the establishment of peaceful community. Principles such as right actions, speech, and livelihood can negate hatred, greed, and ignorance in this struggle for a renewed society.

BIBLIOGRAPHY

Anchor, Robert. (1979), *The Enlightenment Tradition.* Berkeley, The University of California Press.

Andrea, J. Alfred, and Overfield, H James, (2005), *The Human Record: Sources of Global History*, Fifth Edition, /Volume 11, Since 1500, New York, Houghton Mifflin Company.

Arnove, F Robert and Torres, Alberto Carlos, (2003), *Comparative Education: the Dialectic of the Global and the Local*, Lanham Marryland, Rowman and Littlefield

Balmer, Randal, (2001), *Religion in the Twentieth Century America*, New York, Oxford University Press.

Bellah, N Robert, Madsen, Richard, Sullivan, M William, Swidler, Ann and Tipton, Steven, (1985),*Habits of the Heart: Individualism and Commitment in American Life,* New York, Perennial library.

Berndt, Hagen, (1998), *Nonviolence in the World Religions*, London, SCM Press.

Bigelow, Bill and Peterson, Bob (Eds.) (2002), *Rethinking Globalization: Teaching for Justice in an Unjust World*, Milwaukee, Wisconsin, Rethinking Schools Press.

Bogardus, Emory S (1960), *The Development of Social Thought* New York, Longman's Green and Co., Inc.

Callow, B. Alexander, Jr.(Ed), (1982) *American Urban History: An Interpretative reader with Commentaries,* New York, Oxford University Press.

Card, Claudia (1991*), Feminist Ethics*, Lawrence, Kansas, University Press of Kansas

Carnes, Mark C.(2006), The *American Nation: A History of the United Stat*es, New York, Pearson Education, Inc.

Carnes, Mark C and Garraty, John A (2006), *The American Nation, A History of the United States,* New York, Pearson.

Daun, Holger and Walford, Geoffrey (2004), *Educational Strategies among Muslims in the Contexts of Globalization*, Boston, Brill Publishers.

Distefano, Anna, Rudestam, Erik Kjell, Silverman, J Robert (Eds.), 2004, *Encyclopedia of Distributed Learning,* Thousand Oaks, California, Sage Publications.

Duiker, William and Spielvogel, J Jackson, (2004), New York, Thomson/ Wadsworth.

Eisler, Riane and Miller, Ron, (2004), *Educating for a Culture of Peace*, Portsmouth, NH, Heinemann.

Ferguson, John (1977), *War and Peace in the World's Religions*, London, Sheldon Press

Fiske, B Edward and Ladd, F Helen, *Learning From South Africa*, Education Week, vol. 24, No. 27, March 16, 2005

Frank, Mitch, (2002), U*nderstanding September 11th: Answering Questions About the Attacks on America,* New York, Viking

Gabbard, A David, (2000), *Knowledge and Power in the Global Economy" Politics and the Rhetoric of School Reform*, Mahwah, NJ, Lawrence Erlbaum Associates Publishers

Ghosh, Ratna, Ontario, Canada, McGill Journal of Education, Vol, 39, No.1, Winter 2004

Giele, Zollinger Janet and Stebbins, F. Leslie, (2003), *Women and Equality in Workplace: A Reference Handbook*, Santa Barbara, Ca. ABC Clio, Inc.

Gopin, Marc, (2000), *Between Eden And Armageddon: The Future f World Religions, Violence and Peacemaking*, New York, Oxford University Press.

Gubler, Arnulf, (1998), *Technology and Global Change*, New York: Cambridge University Press.

Holmes, L Robert (Ed.), (1990), *Nonviolence in Theory and Practice* , Belmont, California, Wadsworth Publishing Company.

Hooks, Bell, 2003, *Teaching Community: A Pedagogy of Hope*, New York, Routhledge

Keyser, H Catherine, (Ed.) (1991), *China A Teaching Workbook*, New York, Columbia University.

Kumar, Anil, *Efforts for Promoting a Culture of Peace in Indian Education, New Era of Education,* Vol, 84, No.3, December 2003, Gipping Press, Suffolk, UK.

Kuriakose, K Karikottuchira, (2004), *Nonviolence: The Way of the Cross*, Longwood, Fl. Xulon Press.

Landau Elaine, (2002), *Osama bin Laden: A war Against the West*, Brookfield, Connecticut, Twenty-First Century Books.

Lawrence, Gordon, (Ed.) (1998), *Social Dreaming Work*, London, Karnac Books.

Logue, McLead Calvin (Ed*.), (1997), Representative American Speeches 1937-1997,* Einstein, Albert, Peace in the atomic Era, New York, H. H. Wilson.

Mahadevan, T.N. P (1938), The Philosophy of Advaida, London: Luzac and Company, 1.

Manning, Patrick, (2003), *Navigating World History: Historians Create A Global Past*, New York, Palgrave.

McFadden, Robert D, Pope John Paul 11, Church Shepherd And a Catalyst for World Change, *New York Times* (Daily), New York, April 3, 2005.

McNamara E. Thomas, (2004), *Evolution, Culture and Consciousness: The Discovery of the Preconscious Mind*, Lanham, Maryland, University Press of America, Inc.

Meade, A Teresa and Wiesner-Hanks, E Merry (Eds.), (2004), *A Companion To Gender History,* Malden, MA, Blackwell Publishing Ltd.

Merriam, Eve, (1971), *Growing Up Female in America*, Boston, Beacon Press.

Murphey, Rhoades, (2003), *A History of Asia*, New York, Longman.

O'Byrne, J Darren, (2003), *Human Rights An Introduction*, Harlow, England, Longman.

Phillips, T. Donald,(1999), *Martin Luther King, Jr. On Leadership: Inspiration and Wisdom For Challenging Times*, New York, Warner Books.

Pope John Paul II: Giant of the Age, Malayla Manorama (Daily), English Edition, Kottayam, India, April 2, 2005.

Reagan, Timothy, (1996), *Non-Western Educational Traditions: Alternative Approaches to Educational Thought and Practice, Mahwah, New Jersey, Lawrence Erlbaum Associates Publishers.*

Riga, J Peter, *Radical Differences Between Islam And Christianity, Social Justice Review*, Vol 96, March-April 2005, No. 3-4.

Said Aziz Abdul, Funk, C Nathan, Kadayifci S Ayse (Eds.) (2001), *Peace and Conflict in Islam:Perceepts and Practice*, Lanham, University Press of America, Inc.

Saito, Naoko, *Education for Global Understanding: Learning From Dewey's Visit to Japan, Teachers College Record*, Teachers College, Columbia University, New York, vol 105, No. 9, December 2003.

Schaie, K Warner, Krause, Neal, Booth, Alan (Eds.), (2004)*, Religious Influences on Health and Well-Being in the Elderly*, New York, Springer Publishing Company.

Smith-Chritopher, L Daniel, (Ed.), (1998), *Subverting Hatred: The Challenge of Nonviolence in Religious Traditions,* New York, Orbis Books.

Stavrianos. Leften. Starvos (1999), A *Global History: From Prehistory to the 21st Century*, upper saddle River, New Jersey, Prentice Hall Sandra, Harris et. al. (2004), *Winning Women: Stories of Award-Winning Educators*, Lanham, MD Rowman and Littlefield.

Suarez-Orozco, Marcelo and Qin-Hillard, Desiree Baollan, (2004), *Globalization: Culture And Education In The New Millennium*, Berkeley, University of California Press.

Thomas, M.M, (1971), *Salvation and Humanization*, The Christian Literature Society, Madras, India.

Tignor, Robert etl.al , (2002), *Worlds Together, Worlds Apart: A History of The Modern World from The Mongol Empire To The Present*, London: WW Norton Company.

West, Cornel (1988), *Prophetic Fragments*, Grand Rapids, Michigan, William B. Eerdmans Publishing Company.

Wilkinson, Philip, (2003), *Buddhism: Explore the Teachings and Traditions of This Ancient Religion*, New York: DK Publishing, Inc.

Willims, Michael and Humphrys, Graham (Eds.), (2003), Citizenship Education And Lifelong Learning: Power And Place, New York, Nova Science Publishers.

Williams, Raymond, (1983), *Keywords: A Vocabulary of Culture and Society*, New York, Oxford University Press.

Williams, Rosalind, (1996), Anti-Discriminatory Practice, London, Cassel Zachariah, Mathai, (2004), *Ecology Peace and the Future of Humanity*, Nagpur, India, India Peace Centre.

Wimberly, Ann E Streaty, "Daring to Lead With Hope," *Religious Education*, Vol. 98, Number 3, Summer 2003.

In: Religion, Terrorism and Globalization
Editor: K.K. Kuriakose, pp.265-277

ISBN 1-59454-553-7
© 2006 Nova Science Publishers, Inc.

Chapter 17

NONVIOLENCE IN SOCIAL AND GLOBAL EDUCATION: A PEDAGOGY FOR PEACE

Tony L. Talbert and Perry L. Glanzer
Baylor University, Texas

VIOLENCE IS JUST A PAGE AWAY

Educators and parents often lament the fact that children are fed daily doses of violence through television, theater, video game and music video images and descriptions. Some may even meet on a regular basis to discuss and design ways to insulate children and teenagers from the violence that threatens the safety of their homes, schools and communities. In their attempts to attach blame and seek answers to the complex questions surrounding violence, parents and educators may not hesitate to cry for censorship of violent images and content pedaled to children and teenagers by the media producers of the television, film, music and video industries. With frantic reaction to violence educators and legislators enact zero-tolerance rules, establish safe school zones, erect metal detectors, eliminate Internet access and enumerate a litany of rules that standardize dress and curriculum (Ayers, 2001; Casella, 2001). In some cases, instead of seeking to attach blame, schools and communities have responded proactively to threats and incidences of violence by creating violence prevention programs. These programs typically include training in empathy skills, anger management, conflict resolution, peer mediation, cooperative games, and social skills (Haft, 2000; Dovey, 1996; Noguera, 1995).

Yet, while educators and parents may act and react to the most overt examples of violence in their schools, communities, homes and world, students are often exposed to violence wrapped in the victorious descriptions and glorified images of conquest, warfare and coup de' tats. What is the source of these violent depictions? Who is the purveyor of this material? All one must do to find the answers to these questions is to survey the pages of print, examine the grainy and glossy photographs and peruse the bold titles in the typical Social Education textbooks, curricula and educational media resources that occupy a prominent place in Social Education classrooms in most any democratic nation. Often the violence carried out by the nation-state is implicitly or explicitly justified as an appropriate defense of goals such as democracy and/or freedom. Thus, while educators, parents and concerned citizens often seek external influences for the causes of violence they may fail to challenge the narratives about and justifications of violence in Social Education curricula. The assumption appears to be: it is not really problematic violence when it is promoting democracy, freedom or the interests of the nation-state.

In this essay, we argue that the dominance of violence in defense of democracy, freedom or other national interest in Social Education curricula creates two problems. First, making violence in defense of a nation-state a major theme of textbooks or curricula undermines a number of the purposes commonly associated with public education, especially education in a liberal democracy. Instead of creating critical-thinking students it encourages dangerous forms of nationalism and patriotism. Second, it fails to demonstrate respect for citizens from communities, either secular or religious, who espouse nonviolence.

Interestingly, Bengt Thelin (1996) notes that one of the distinctive features of early peace education was its effort to reform the teaching of a nation's history. "The cleansing and ennobling of patriotism" was considered a primary task for the school that would primarily be brought about through the reform of what we today consider Social Education. In line with this tradition we set forth specific strategies for providing students with peace education in both Social and Global education that both fulfills the purposes of democratic public education and demonstrates respect for communities of nonviolence.

LIBERAL DEMOCRACY AND VIOLENCE

Social Education curricula, textbooks and media resources in the United States are typically organized along a war-centric scope and sequence that provides descriptions of a nation's involvement in both domestic and international warfare and conflict. For example, in American texts, militaristic imagery and language of domestic and international conquests are organized around the three central themes of (1) land; (2) enemy; and (3) hero (Sheety, 1999).[1] For every thousand pages published on the causes of various wars there is less than one page directly on the causes of peace (Blainey, 1988). In other words, American public school social education texts give neither an "objective" picture of the world nor a "balanced" picture of history. In fact, most public school social studies texts rarely attempt to do any such thing. As William Reid has argued, curriculum never succeeded in providing universal, objective knowledge or even a balanced view of different issues. Instead, "Curriculum became a place where people would tell themselves what it meant to be American, to be English, to be German, and so on."[2] If a nation examines its public school curriculum it will likely communicate that the people are a warlike, conquering people.

Still, a parent or educator might ask, why shouldn't militaristic language and descriptions be a central part of the text? For example, in America why shouldn't the battles of the

---

[1] Throughout this paper, we will use numerous examples from the North American environment because this is our educational context. Since we agree with Brock-Utne (1996) that peace education is actually best developed by indigenous communities of a nation-state who understand their traditions, we will rarely suggest examples that might be used in other contexts in which we have not lived and worked. Nonetheless, we do hope that peace educators from other countries may find creative connections with our essay.

[2] William R. Reid, "Curriculum as an Expression of National Identity," *Journal of Curriculum and Supervision* 15 (2000): 113-22.

American Revolution, the War of 1812, the Western Indian Campaigns, and the Civil War serve as symbolic vocabulary of democratic prowess through conquest for American Social Education students? What's wrong with the tales of the storming of San Juan Hill, the overpowering of Iwo Jima, the campaign of Normandy, the battle for Pork Chop Hill and the seizing of Panama as the context in which American Social Education students embrace the concept of America's dominance on the world stage? Is there any inherent wrong in depicting the bombing of Hiroshima, Nagasaki, Saigon, and Iraq as justifiable acts to protect American lives and promote the principles of democracy to the men, women and children beyond the American shores? Why shouldn't the scope and sequence of American Social Education curricula, textbooks and media resources be organized around the images, descriptions, depictions, legends and cherished myths of American military dominance and conquest of the west and beyond? Is this not America's heritage? Should public school texts eliminate the descriptions of America's past involvement in warfare, exploration, conquest and territorial protection?

There is certainly credence to Liddell Hart's memorable motto, "If you want peace, understand war" (Howard, 1983). Thus, the problem is not so much the presence of war in the curriculum as two other things. First, the curriculum often fails to examine a nation's use of violence in defense of national interests in critical ways. The constant representation of war, conflict and violence as the pathway to a nation's rise to prowess must certainly influence students' attitudes toward war and peace. There is the subtle and ubiquitous representation that democracy, freedom, justice, equality or various other national goals are the pearls of great price that can only be achieved and preserved through war. Yet, the result is that liberal democracies act little different than authoritarian regimes in how they approach threats to the nation-state. For instance, John Synott (1996) notes, "In the contemporary world, whether in Burma, against the Karen, Mon and Lahu peoples; in Chile in the oppression of the Mapuche; or in the valley of the Narmada River in India, the resistance of indigenous peoples is portrayed by the oppressors and invaders as the actions of criminals and subversives" (p. 84). Yet, if liberal democracy is to be noted for anything it is its sensitivity to the rights and concerns of those in the minority. If children in liberal democracies are not taught to examine their own country's use of violence in critical ways, they will continue the oppression of minority groups and their interests.

The second problem is the absence of peace and the glorification of war. If the texts do not offer examples of peace, alternatives to violence and solutions to armed conflict, then the cognitive power of Liddell's notion of comparing and contrasting peace and war is lost. Little attention is given to peaceful alternatives. In particular, there is a failure to give attention to the communities and individuals offering examples of peace, especially religious communities and individuals.

The Lack of Critical Perspective

The fact that military actions and engagements are usually not held up for critique or questioning undermines the purpose of education in a liberal democracy. For instance, some of the most striking examples of militaristic images and glorification of armed conquest, with little discussion of the human cost and alternative peace initiatives, are regularly found occupying United States' public school fourth through twelfth grade Social Education classrooms. While many of the Social Education textbooks, curricula and media resources present some condemnations of dictators and megalomaniac tyrants, there are few examples of how U.S. foreign policy supported the regimes of these undemocratic leaders.

A typical example of the militaristic images and glorification of armed conflict that comprise the bulk of U.S. Social Education textbooks, curricula, and media resources can be found in the Macmillan/McGraw-Hill Social Education textbook, curricula and media series entitled, *Latin America and Canada: Adventures in Time and Place*. In this Social Education series democracy movements in Latin American nations are presented as embryonic outgrowths of American largess. Most chilling is the absence of specific examples of how U.S. foreign policy supported coup de' tats over freely elected leaders in the name of "democracy building." A policy which sought to ensure the rise or maintenance of a dictator's political and social power in order to ensure geo-political and economic stability for those western political and economic entities that had invested heavily in the hopes of reaping the benefits of raw materials, cheap labor and finished products deriving from a faux democracy.

One of the most blatant examples of the Macmillan/McGraw-Hill resources' sterilized depiction of the U.S. role supporting dictators in Central America can be found in the discussion of Augusto Pinochet, the former Chilean tyrant whose U.S. supported regime perpetrated decades of terror that led to the death and disappearance of thousands of adults, children and nameless innocent victims. Pinochet is presented in a mixed bag of terms when the text offers: "Pinochet was able to rebuild Chile's economy. But he also established a brutal dictatorship. People who disagreed with him were arrested, tortured and often killed. Pinochet's dictatorship marked the end of Chile's long democratic tradition" (Banks, et al., 1998, p. 355). Yet, despite this recognition that his rule was marred by violence and executions, the text avoids mentioning that the United States supported Pinochet while he collaborated with multinational corporations under the guise of "democracy building." Equally neglected is the role the United States played in toppling Pinochet when he could no longer be trusted to ensure economic expansion. Strikingly, the first reference to Pinochet is his ability to rebuild the Chilean economy. While the text does offer two sentences admonishing Pinochet's dictatorial rule, there is no discussion of the U.S.'s role in supporting Pinochet's decades-long assault on the democratic principles of life, liberty, justice, equality and pursuit of happiness through the torture and death of thousands of men, women and children.

A study conducted by Dan Fleming (1982) analyzing 45 Social Education textbooks, grades 8-12 found that the "overall textbook coverage of U.S./Latin American relations was poor" (p. 168). While nearly all Social Education textbooks, curricula and media resources offer some criticism of U.S. policies, "the perspective of Latin American countries was given little mention and the cultures of the region were ignored" (Fleming, 1982, p. 169).

Promoting Peace Education

Thinking critically about a nation's violence in defense of democracy is not enough. Students must be given alternatives. In other words, there must be a concerted effort on the part of Social educators to seek alternative approaches to the militaristic democracy as presented by textbook authors, curriculum developers and media producers. Mary-Wynne Ashford's research on peace education concluded that when students seek alternatives to prevent war and violence they develop new attitudes about themselves and others (1996). In addition, Ashford's research indicates that students who are actively seeking solutions to war and violence seemed "less likely to suffer anxiety and helplessness, and the actions of these children and youth contributed to changing public opinion about war" (1996).

To provide peace education we must give equal representation in presenting the characters, concepts, events and activities of persons who challenged militarism and conquest through local, state, national and international peace movements. Social Education teachers, students, parents and community leaders must work to develop textbook, curriculum and media alternatives which honestly address the outcomes of war, armed conflict and violent coup de' tats. Social Education content, concepts, themes and issues that promote the advantages of peace must be incorporated by offering examples of persons, organizations, and events that worked collaboratively to ensure peaceful solutions on the local, state, national and global arenas. The glorification of violence as the only alternative to resolving conflict must be countered by images and descriptions that promote human interactions that bridge the social, political, cultural and economic divide between nations and their people.

This is why multiculturalism can only be a partial answer to the glorification of violence. For example, attention to the American government's violent abuses against Native Americans, African Americans, and Latinos may provide critical thinking. It shows the hypocrisy of American values and violence—although Americans promote the idea that democracy provides the mechanism for the protection of rights and the means for nonviolent conversations about the common good, our violence often betrays our ideals. Yet, multiculturalism still has its limitations. It may become merely another way to tell stories of violence, although the important point is that they often reveal to us the ugliness of violence in supposed defense of democracy. Nonetheless, we must ask the question, are we more interested in stories about a diversity of people than a diversity of ideas and practices? What is often needed is not only attention to how Social Education texts give attention to different ethnic and racial groups but how the texts can show justice to a diversity of ideas and practices. This is particularly true when it comes to the practices of violence and nonviolence.

For instance, in discussions about American foreign policy in Latin America there are seldom discussions, images or description of Oliver La Farge, William R. Lingo, Ralph B. Guinness, David Starr Jordan and William C. Carr all prominent characters and leaders in peace movements who challenged U.S. involvement in supporting these dictators, revolutions, coup de' tats and armed conflicts.

Perhaps the fact that nonviolence receives little attention in American history likely stems from the fact that religious history has received little attention in American history texts. Since religious beliefs provide one of the major sources for nonviolent perspectives, excluding it from the curriculum tends to involve excluding nonviolent perspectives and examples. For example, Warren Nord (1995) found in his survey of public school textbooks that the texts largely ignore religion. He noted, "one text gives more space to farming in the colonies than it does to religion; another gives more pages to cowboys and cattle drives at the end of the nineteenth century than to all of post 1800 religion" (p. 141). Influential religious pacifists, such as the Quakers, are seldom discussed or if they are mentioned the importance is considered for religious freedom and not pacifism. The same is true with modern day figures or groups. Nord found only two of the five American history texts he studied related Martin Luther King's views on nonviolence to his religious convictions and none of them mentioned the nonviolent role of the black churches in the civil rights movement. Even peace education suffers from this defect. Thelin (1996) notes that recognizing the important linkages between peace education and religion is something that has often been overlooked in the secularized peace education movement.

Integrating Nonviolence into the Social Education Curriculum

There are a variety of ways that educators can incorporate attention to nonviolence in the curriculum. While many peace education programs exist outside the U.S. and the need for input by global peace educators is important, we should note that our examples draw mainly upon the North American experience. This stems not from our belief that North American models are best but from the belief that methods of peace education must be derived and implemented within the local context. As Brock-Utne (1996) noted with regard to African peace educators, "It is important that African peace educators do not derive their theories mostly from Western peace educators but search in their own heritage for an African way to deal with conflicts" (p. 10in).[3] Thus, we offer our three examples arising out of the North American context that may spur local creativity and development in this area and that draw upon prominent developments in education or unique methods as ways to incorporate attention to nonviolence in the U.S. Social Education curriculum.

1. CRITICAL THINKING ABOUT THE NATIONAL NARRATIVES OF VIOLENCE

An example of an alternative method to approaching violent events in a nation's history can be found in James Juhnke and Carol Hunter's book, *The Missing Peace: The Search for Nonviolent Alternatives in United States History* (2001). Their book challenges traditional interpretations found in many American textbooks that justify "redemptive violence." It also offers alternative interpretations of American historical events that question whether the use of violence was justified or whether nonviolent alternatives were adequately explored in a critical fashion.

A specific example of how such a critical thinking exercise might be employed concerns the coverage of World War II in American Social Education curriculum. Without question World War II occupies the most prominent place in American Social Education textbooks, curricula and media resource materials. It is therefore no surprise that the events between 1941 and 1945 represent an important body of knowledge in which Social Education students are expected to develop in-depth knowledge, skills, attitudes and values concerning the U.S. and its relationship with the rest of the world. Social Education textbooks, curricula and media resources typically offer a litany of descriptions and images of battles, victims of warfare, conventional and atomic destruction, military personalities, citizens of Allied nations unified by the war, and the defeat of Nazi, Fascist and Imperial dictators through the collective efforts of a democratic initiative.

---

[3] Our one concern though with Brock-Utne's suggestion is that it may fail to recognize that Africans may now consider their heritage to include certain traditions commonly understood as "Western" but are actually quite close to Africa's heritage and are increasingly being appropriated by Africans (e.g., Christianity, Islam).

Most often the text and subtext of these discussions and images are brought to a crescendo with a familiar photo and a simplistic statement describing the U.S. dropping of two atomic bombs on the Japanese cities of Hiroshima and Nagasaki. Frequently, the focus of these descriptions centers on the events that took place on August 6th, 1945 in the Japanese city of Hiroshima. Typically, the depiction is accentuated by pictures of the airplane that delivered the bomb and the city in the aftermath of the explosion. In some instances, the textbooks' authors offer brief commentary on the American and Japanese publics' surprise of such destruction caused by a single atomic weapon. However, textbook treatments of Hiroshima bombing inadequately convey this event's horrors and complexities (Kazemek, 1994). Most often the commentary of America's decision to unleash atomic destruction on the Japanese people is simplistically juxtaposed between the idea of retaliation for the Japanese attack on Pearl Harbor in 1941 and the justification for saving human life by avoiding a prolonged ground war in Japan. In both instances, the only alternatives are couched in militaristic terms. Democracy can only be won through an act of total annihilation.

Are there alternative viewpoints to the series of events that comprise the bombing of Nagasaki and Hiroshima? Were there persons in the U.S. and around the globe who actively engaged in discussion and protests against the use of atomic weapons? Were there alternatives to the military's and Truman's policy that swift use of an atomic weapon would bring peace?.

These are the questions that begin to form the structure of openness to other solutions. For example, openness to other solutions can be achieved in the teaching and learning of this event by including the description of the Hibakusha, the survivors of the Hiroshima destruction, that offer the stories of how this single act of warfare led to both the immediate and slow death of 130,000 and 150,000 people by the end of that year (Whig, 1990). In addition, the diaries of men and women who either survived or were the loved ones of those who were killed in Pearl Harbor should be read in addition to the Hibakusha descriptions. Through the comparing and contrasting of these events utilizing dialogue circles and discussion clusters, openness of exploration and expression can be achieved. Moreover, an understanding of the cause and effect relationships that promote revenge, hatred and acts of violence can be examined as students develop their own diaries describing times when they were either the victims or the perpetrators of violence born from anger and misunderstanding.

An understanding of different options can be achieved by students engaging in a scenario that places them in the situation of serving as advisors to U.S. President Harry S. Truman. Students can develop a position paper or graphic representation that offers the President alternatives to using an atomic weapon against the people of Japan. Additionally, students can participate in a panel discussion as they research and represent the diverse responses of world leaders in 1945 to the American decision to drop atomic bombs on Nagasaki and Hiroshima. By exploring, analyzing and representing the diverse responses of world leaders, students move into the realm of understanding the cause and effect relationships and meaning of the events. Students also step outside of the one dimensional square of two bombs dropped on two cities in 1945, as presented in traditional Social Education textbooks, curricula and media resources, into the three dimensional cube which examines the multiple levels of understanding, cause and effect relationships, similar and different perceptions and the ripple effect of violence that crosses generations of time and space that comprise the events which unleashed the destructive possibilities of a nuclear age on humanity.

Americans could also be taught to question some of their responses to this action. David Weaver Zercher (2004) observed that Americans have short memories in this area. While humorist Dave Barry's claimed after the events of September 11, 2001, "But I know this about Americans: we don't set out to kill innocent people. We don't cheer when innocent people die," the reality is that after the atomic bombs were dropped, one American newspaper ran a cartoon captioned "Land of the Rising Sons," which "depicted bodies flying through the air over the Hiroshima landscape" (p. 104). Being taught to think critically about a nation's violent history involves holding up a mirror to a country's past so that students may be more willing to think creatively about nonviolent solutions.

We believe that every country has its own history of violence that can be examined in a similar way. For instance, Synott (1996) outlines how the Australian Aboriginal history of genocide is now gaining more scholarly attention and an Aboriginal view of history has started to emerge. Thus, we believe that every country or community will need to develop its own pedagogy that will explore acts of violence that have been legitimated on the basis of pressing national ends.

2. THE VOICE OF CIVIL SOCIETY: NATIONAL VIOLENCE AGAINST PACIFIST INDIVIDUALS AND COMMUNITIES

One way that democratic nation-states can gain a critical perspective on their story is to pay attention to the stories of nonviolent communities in civil society. Most any country's history could also be expanded and enriched by focusing on stories of nonviolent communities. The history of the nonviolent Bruderhof Community in Africa, America and England could be included. Likewise, Gandhian communities that Gandhi started in South Africa and then in India could be depicted in these country's texts.

We will provide one example from the American context. The story of the Hutterite community that settled in the Dakota Territory provides a good example of the kind of multicultural education that could also provide insight into pacifism, America's history of conscientious objection and the violence sometimes employed against pacifists. The Hutterites originated from a group of Austrian Anabaptists that formed during the Reformation. They take their origins from Joseph Hutter who was chosen as pastor of the community in 1533 and burned at the stake for heresy in 1536 (Janzen, 1999; Hostetler, 1997). They believed that Jesus taught pacifism and that Christians should not own private property. Persecuted for their religious beliefs they emigrated to Moravia, Slovakia, and Transylvania and finally settled in Ukraine where they received exemption from military service. In 1870, however, Tsar Alexander II rescinded the military exemption of the Hutterites. As a consequence, a group of Hutterites left the Ukraine to visit North America as a possible refuge where they could practice their nonviolent ways.

The 1873 visit to North America proved noteworthy for a number of reasons. The group visiting Canada experienced violent reaction to their possible emigration to Manitoba which required the Lt. Governor to send 50 troops to let the Hutterites escape. America proved more welcoming. The Hutterites actually received an audience with President Ulysses S. Grant and asked for exemption from military service. Secretary of State Hamilton Fish later told the Hutterites that the federal government did not have the power to grant military exemption but he concluded, "For the next fifty years we will not be entangled in another war in which military service will be necessary" (Janzen, 1999, p. 26). Later, Congress even considered what was termed a "Mennonite Bill" which would have allowed a large settlement of Mennonites to be given land and military exemption in what is now North Dakota. The bill was later defeated.

Despite the bill's failure and the uncertain promises of protection against military service, a large group of Hutterites immigrated to the United States. The immigrants attracted little attention, although they were always wary of what America might require of them. When the 1898 Spanish-American war began, they established a colony in Manitoba, Canada in case military conscription became required of them. The outbreak of World War I was what eventually created a crisis in the community.

When Congress passed the Selective Service Act of May 18, 1917, no provision was made for conscientious objectors except that they could be placed in noncombatant positions. They would still be required to join the military and wear the military uniform. The Hutterites proved to be some of the most stubborn about military service. While some Mennonites performed work at military camps, the Hutterite men refused all such participation. Instead, they were subjected to numerous forms of punishment. One historian summarizes the treatment:

> They were bayoneted, beaten, and tortured by various forms of water "cure."...the men were often thrown out of a window and dragged along the ground by their hair and feet by soldiers who were waiting outside. Their beards were disfigured to make them appear ridiculous. One night, eighteen men were aroused from their sleep and held under cold showers until one of them became hysterical. Others were hung by their feet above tanks of water until they almost choked to death. On many days they were made to stand at attention on the cold side of their barracks, in scant clothing, while those who passed by scoffed at them in abusive and foul language. They were chased across the fields by guards on motorcycles under the guise of taking exercise, until they dropped from sheer exhaustion. In the guardhouse they were usually put on a diet of bread and water. (Hostetler, 1997, p. 127)

Four Hutterites were sentenced to thirty-seven years in prison and sent to Alcatraz. There they were placed in solitary confinement with a military uniform in the cell. They slept in only their underwear and were given only a glass of water to drink. Eventually, they were transferred to Fort Leavenworth, Kansas where after even more brutal mistreatment two of them died.

Meanwhile, back in the colonies, local settlers painted Hutterite churches yellow and forced young Hutterite men to kiss the American flag. When a Hutterite colony refused to buy war bonds, a group of locals came and drove away a hundred steers and a thousand sheep without resistance from the Hutterites.

The colonists eventually had enough and all but one of the colonies in South Dakota immigrated to Canada. Yet, even the sale of their land proved to be an issue. The South Dakota State Council for Defense wanted five percent of money for the sale of the land to be given to war bonds and five percent to the Red Cross. The Hutterites responded by lowering their price by 10 percent (Hostetler, 1997).

Overall, the story of the Hutterites in South Dakota can be told and related as another multicultural story in America. Yet, it can also do much more. It can illuminate the fact that part of a culture may involve the very notion of nonviolence. It also reveals part of America's ugly use of violence in defense of Democracy in such a way that the use of violence undermined the very principles of liberal democracy (in this case religious freedom) for which America was supposedly fighting.

3. PEACEFUL ALTERNATIVES AND CHARACTER EDUCATION

Two separate popular trends have emerged in the past two decades that educators could draw upon to give attention to nonviolence in the Social Education curriculum. First, the growth in school violence has led to the implementation of violence prevention programs throughout schools. In America, fifteen states now have violence prevention legislation addressing violence prevention in schools.

Second, character education, or the teaching of particular virtues to students, has also emerged in the past decade and a half as a popular movement in public schools. The Council for Global Education identifies more than three dozen virtues that it believes can be taught around the world. Evidence of this movement's success in America comes from the fact that from 1993 to 2004, almost half of the American states (23) either passed new laws requiring public schools to teach students character qualities or modified old laws (Glanzer and Milson, 2004). Almost all of the states list the virtues they require or suggest that educators teach to students. Yet, nonviolence has not received extensive attention in this movement. Nonviolence is not included as a virtue in the Council for Global Education's list of virtues. In addition, in only one American state (Indiana) is nonviolence a listed virtue.

If the topic is addressed, most character education and violence prevention programs as well as scholarly discussions of nonviolence tend to focus on these matters at the individual or classroom level. For example, Thomas Lickona's (1991) well-known book on character education devotes a chapter to teaching children to solve conflicts in nonviolent ways. While such an emphasis upon character education and nonviolent practices are welcomed by many, doubts and criticisms have been raised about the effectiveness of both character education and violence prevention programs (Noddings, 2002; Nash, 1997; Posner, 1994). Noddings (2002) observes that part of the problem is that separate programs fail to transform the whole school climate. What is needed instead, with regard to both character education and violence prevention programs, she argues, are approaches that attempt to address these matters throughout the school culture.

We agree with Noddings that in order for character education and violence prevention to be effective, these programs must move into the broader curriculum and transform the whole school culture. Thus, educators must consider various ways to incorporate the application of virtues or violence prevention into the social studies curriculum (e.g., Milson and Null, 2003).

One way to undertake this sort of approach is to make sure that discussing virtues such as self-control or nonviolence or various techniques for conflict resolution extends to the Social Education curriculum. For example, these virtues and methods have been demonstrated by various figures such as those mentioned earlier who not only demonstrated self-control at a personal level, but sought to encourage an entire community or nation to address conflict in a nonviolent and peaceful way.

We contend that where there are stories and images of generals leading their men into harms way on domestic battlefields and foreign shores, there must be equally prominent descriptions and depictions of the role of conscientious objectors, scientists, political leaders and activist citizens whose collective efforts challenged the conventional wisdom of militaristic fervor during periods of war by promoting peace, social justice, democratic rights, and the responsible development and use of technology. To use an American example, when the names of George Washington, Ulysses S. Grant, Pershing, George Patton, Westmoreland, Schwarzkopf and Colin Powell are prominently displayed as examples of American heroism, should there not be equal representation of Linus Pauling, Dorothy Day, Bella Abzug, Leo Szilard, Norman Cousins, A.J. Muste, A.J. Lelyveld, Arnold Beichman, Jane Addams, William Jennings Bryan, Martin Luther King, Jr., and other pacifists who challenged militarism throughout America's history?

The problem though with some of this character education, as James Davison Hunter points out (2000), is that it often attempts to teach character education apart from the practices, communal context and communal memories and sources of authority that help form character. For example, with regard to nonviolence, schools attempt to incorporate the practices of nonviolence apart from the communal contexts and narratives that actually give these practices motivational power and meaning for those who practice them. As some of the essays in this volume make clear, the practices of nonviolence often exist and are difficult to extricate from religious or secular worldviews and the communities that attempt to embody those views.

Social Education can make this point clear by discussing the ways that nonviolent responses are supported by a broader community. One of the best moral models of nonviolent reaction that would help demonstrate this point to children is Ruby Bridges. The story of Ruby Bridges has been chronicled by Robert Coles (1986). The daughter of poor sharecroppers, at the age of six she helped initiate school desegregation in New Orleans. Every day, escorted by federal marshals, she would be escorted through a mob hurling threats and slurs at her. Coles wondered "about the continuing ability of such a child to bear such adversity, and with few apparent assets in her family background" (p. 22). What Coles later realized he missed was that she possessed a wealth of resources that his eyes failed to initially see. As she told him, "I go to church...every Sunday, and we're told to pray for everyone, even the bad people, and so I do" (Coles, 1986, p. 23). Later she would say,

> The minister said God is watching and He won't forget, because He never does. The minister says if I forgive the people and smile at them and pray for them, God will keep a good eye on everything and he'll be our protection...He may not rush to do anything, not right away. But there will come a day, like you hear in church (p. 24).

What resources Ruby had were clearly drawn from the community of character in which she was involved and the practices and story it taught her. The practices of prayer, forgiveness and hope, supported by the story of God's involvement in the world, helped sustain her to react peacefully and lovingly toward her enemies.

These same truths hold for how many other nonviolent religious communities sustain themselves. What would help balance Social and Global Education is a recognition and teaching about such individuals and communities in a way that makes students aware of the alternatives associated with peaceful lives and communities.

SOMEDAY

If the most recent horrific acts of school violence in Littleton, Colorado, the terrorist killing of 300 children in Russia and a seemingly endless list of other schools and communities around this world have taught us any thing, we know that our children will need to be taught nonviolent responses to violent conflict. How do we help students seek solutions to conflict? How do we promote collaboration? How do we teach nonviolence? How do we equip students with the skills that lead to constructive solutions?

A different type of Social and Global Education can help. The alternatives proposed may inspire the Social and Global Education student to initiate a letter campaign or a petition drive that calls upon local, state, national and international leaders to rebuild the homes of those who have been victims of natural or human violence and destruction; to design programs that feed the hungry and impoverished whose means of sustenance have been destroyed by domestic and international violence; to run for local, state and national elected office on a social justice platform; to organize and lead protest movements that target political and corporate leaders whose environmentally irresponsible policies, practices and production of goods endanger the lives of human and animal species across the globe; to seek peaceful solutions to the conflicts that arise from misunderstanding, intolerance, avarice and prejudice at home, school and in society.

An approach to Social and Global Education that employs the strategies we suggest doesn't just inform, but it also prepares students to reform and transform the way they think, act and feel about themselves and the world around them. It inspires them to create movements that change the way Social and Global Education is represented in the next generation of Social and Global Education textbooks, curricula and media resources. Thinking locally and acting globally will become mantras instead of mottos.

BIBLIOGRAPHY

Ashford, M.W. (1996). Peace education after the cold war. *Canadian Social Education, 30* (Summer), 178-181.

Ayers, W., Dohrn, B., and Ayers, R., eds. (2001). *Zero tolerance: Resisting the drive for punishment in our schools.* New York: The New Press.

Banks, J., Beyer, B. K., Contreras, G., Craven, J., Ladsen-Billings, G., McFarland, M. S., and Parker, W.C. (1998). *Latin America and Canada: Adventures in time and place.* New York: MacMillian/McGraw-Hill School Division.

Blainey, G. (1988). *The causes of war (3rd ed.).* New York: Free Press.

Brock-Utne, Brigit. (1996). Peace education in postcolonial Africa. *Peabody Journal of Education 71* (3), 170-90.

Casella, R. (2001). *At zero tolerance: Punishment, prevention, and school violence.* New York: Peter Lang.

Coles, R. (1986). *The moral lives of children.* Boston: Houghton Mifflin Company.

Dovey, V. (1996). Exploring peace education in South African settings. *Peabody Journal of Education, 71*(3), 128-50.

Fleming, D.B. (1982). Latin America and the United States: What Do United States History Textbooks Tell Us?" *The Social Studies* 73 (July/August),168-171.

Haft, W. (2000). More than zero: The cost of zero tolerance and the case for restorative justice in schools. *Denver University Law Review*, 77, 795-812.

Harris, I.M. (1996). Editor's introduction. *Peabody Journal of Education, 71*(3), 1-11.

Hostetler, J.A. (1997). *Hutterite society*. Baltimore: John Hopkins University Press.

Howard, M. (1983). The causes of wars and other essays (2nd ed.). Cambridge, MA: Harvard University Press.

Hunter, J.D. (2000) *The death of character: Moral education in an age without good or evil* (New York: Basic Books).

Janzen, R. (1999). *The prairie people: Forgotten Anabaptists*. Hanover, NH: University Press of New England.

Juhnke, J. and Hunter, C. (2001), *The missing peace: The search for nonviolent alternatives in United States history*. Kitchener, Ontario: Pandora Press.

Kazemek, F.E. (1994). Two handfuls of bone and ash: Teaching our children about Hiroshima. *Phi Delta Kappan, 75 (7)*, 531-34.

Lickona, T. (1991). *Educating for character: How our schools can teach respect and responsibility*. New York: Bantam Books.

Nash, R.J. (1997). *Answering the 'virtuecrats': A moral conversation on character education*. New York: Teachers College Press.

Noddings, N. (2002). *Educating moral people: A caring alternative to character education*. New York: Teachers College Press.

Noguera, P.N. (1995). Preventing and producing violence. *Harvard Education Review 65*, 189-207.

Null, J. W. and Milson, A. J. (2003). Beyond marquee morality: Virtue in the social studies. *The Social Studies, 94* (3), 119-122.

Posner, M. (1994). Research raises troubling questions about violence prevention programs. *Harvard Education Letter, 10* (3), 1-4.

Reardon, B.A. (1988). *Comprehensive peace education: Educating for global responsibility*. New York: Teachers College Press.

Sheety, A. (1999). *Curriculum and peace in the Middle East*. (ERIC Document Reproduction Service No. ED433265).

Synott, J. (1996). Australian construction of humans, society and nature in relation to peace education. *Peabody Journal of Education 71* (3), 84-94.

Talbert, T. and C. White (2003). *Lives in the balance: Controversy, Militarism, and Social Efficacy*. In C. White's *True confessions: Popular culture, social efficacy, and the struggle in schools*. Cresskill, NJ: Hampton Press.

Thelin, Bengt. (1996). Early tendencies of peace education in Sweden. *Peabody Journal of Education 71* (3), 95-110.

Turner, J. (1999). Every day, a new chance for peace. *Montessori Life, 11(1)*, 18-22.

Weaver-Zercher, David L. (2004). A modest (though not particularly humble) claim for scholarship in the Anabaptist tradition. In D. Jacobsen and R.H. Jacobsen, *Scholarship and Christian Faith: Enlarging the Conversation*. New York: Oxford University Press.

Whig, L. (Executive Producer). (1990, August 8). *Voices of Hibakusaha: Hiroshima Witness*. Produced by the Hiroshima Peace Cultural Center and NHK, the public broadcasting company of Japan.

GLOSSARY

Ahiṃsā (Ahiṃs, Ahimsa): Non-injury, non-killing, non-violence. This is an important virtue in the Indian religions, particularly of Hinduism, Jainism and Buddhism. Although it is a negative term, indicating what one should not do, it also has a positive meaning, involving positive acts of kindness, compassion and love. Gandhi also called it love-force, truth-force and soul-force. It is all comprehensive and includes physical, verbal and mental non-violence and love, and is to be extended also towards sub-human beings.

Al Qaeda: It means "the base" in Arabic. The terrorist network started in Afghanistan, led by Osama bin Laden.

Badal: the Pathan code of revenge fueled by the romantic image of the avenging hero which dictated that all harm and injustice must be avenged. (See Pathan)

Dhu'l-Fiqar: the two-bladed sword of 'Ali ibn. Talib (597-661) the Prophet Muhammad's cousin and son-in-law. The sword is not only a symbol of 'Ali's courage and chivalry, but since its shape resembles the first word *la* ('no") of the profession of faith (*shahadah*), it also symbolizes the cutting away of idolatry. (See *shahadah*)

Hadith: collections of canonical accounts of the Prophet's deeds, words, and affirmations of consent organized by jurists for juridical purposes. A single account is a hadith; the entire corpus is sometimes collectively referred to as *hadith*, or more properly by the plural *ahadith*. Together with the Qur'an, these accounts are the textual basis for the *sunna* (see below). Its corpus is shared by a chronologically-organized body of hagiographical material called the *Sira*, more closely resembling a biography. (See "Qur'an," "Sunna")

Harb: an Arabic word literally meaning warfare used in the Qur'an (see Jihad)

Harijans: People of Hari or Viṣṇu. Gandhi was born in a Vaiṣṇavite family. Harijan was the name he gave to the untouchables or outcastes or scheduled castes. *The Harijan* is also the name of the Weekly that he edited.

Hajj: the annual pilgrimage to the Ka'ba or House of God and other sacred sites in Mecca during the eighth through fourteenth days of the 12th lunar month of the Islamic calendar. As one of Islam's five pillars of worship, it is required that those who are eligible perform it at least once in a lifetime. The hajj commemorates points of sacred history in the lives of Abraham, Hagar, Ishmael, and the Prophet Muhammad. As the Islamic community (*umma*) grew to global proportions, the *hajj* became increasingly a force of solidarity and a forum for the exchange of knowledge. Many who perform the hajj then typically proceed to the mausoleum and mosque of the Prophet in Medina.

Hanbali: A tradition of Islamic legal interpretation (*fiqh*), based on the work of Ahmad ibn Hanbal (780-855) which emphasizes reliance on the primary sources of Qur'an and Sunna over judicial reasoning.

Haqq: a broad term, listed among God's Beautiful Names meaning righteousness, reality, truth, and rightfulness. Some Sufis have invoked this name to suggest that God's qualities are "realized" in and through their actions.

Haram: "forbidden" One of five broad categories in Islamic jurisprudence (*fiqh*): required (*halal*), recommended (*mansub*), accepted (*munbah*), discouraged (*makruh*), and forbidden (*haram*).

Hiṃsā (*Himsa*): Injury, violence.

Hudaybiya, Treaty of: While on the way to Mecca in 628, with the intention of performing the Hajj, the Prophet stopped at Hudaybiyah, a valley below Mecca at the edge of the sacred precinct, and instructed his companions to take an oath of fealty to him. With everyone's consent, he negotiated a 10-year treaty with his Meccan adversaries (the Quraysh) rather than complete the hajj. Many Muslim interpret this as a victory of political recognition gained through peaceful diplomacy. The terms of the treaty, and the way in which Muhammad's adversaries violated it two years later, made it possible for the Muslims to enter and conquer Mecca peacefully.

Islam: In Arabic the word means submission (to God). Islam is based on the teachings of Muhammad and the Quranic teachings. The religion was started in Arabia in the seventh century.

Jain: A person belonging to the Indian religion called Jainism, which gives special emphasis to non-violence.

Jihad: Defined as holy war, and the word is used in Arabic for "striving for Islam".

Katriya: The warrior class, the second of the four classes (*varṇa*) in the Indian class-cum-caste system.

Khudai Khidmatgar: The Servants of God, a non-violent movement, founded by Khan Abdul Ghaffar Khan in the Northwest Frontier Provinces of India, among the Pathans.

Jihad: literally "effort," or "struggle," describes vigilence in the practice or defense of faith. The Qur'an refers to jihad as an effort with one's means, but not as an act of war. Though the term was first used to describe defensive warfare in the lifetime of the prophet, the word jihad is not itself a word for warfare. (See *"Harb"* and *"Qatl"*). Hanbali jurist Ibn Taymiyya classified four types of jihad: with the heart, the tongue, the pen, and the hand (sword), and urged that jihad be carried out with patience and kindness. In instructions given on the conduct of jihad as warfare, the Prophet, Abu Bakr, and others stipulated stringent conditions of nonviolence to protect all noncombatants, including non-human creatures. (See *"Jihad al-akbar"* and *"Nafs"*)

Jihad al-akbar: a *jihad* against one's lower self (*nafs*). The *jihad* fought against an inner opponent distinguished from the lesser *jihad* (*jihad al-asghar*) a military *jihad* fought against a religio-political opponent. (See *"Jihad"* and *"Nafs"*)

Jinn: "genies," or spirits made of smokeless fire referred to in the Qur'an as including both submitted (Muslim) *jinn* and unsubmitted *jinn*. Some *jinn* attentatively listened to the Prophet recite Qur'an, as is attested in the chapter titled "Jinn." The Qur'an also narrates that numerous *jinn* assisted Solomon in building the Temple. The Qur'an refers to Iblis (Diablos) as one of the jinn and the Qur'an's final verse makes clear that the Qur'an was sent to both "humanity and jinn." In popular understanding jinn are often the source of ailments and problems. A common word for "crazy," *majnun*, derives from the word *jinn* and literally means "jinn-possessed."

Madrasah: as referred to in this essay, an Islamic day school in Indonesia, usually a high school (see "Pesantren")

Mahatma (Mahtm): Great Soul. An honorific title used by Rabindranath Thakur to refer to Gandhi.

Makara Sankrnti: A Hindu solar festival of North India, referring to the crossing (*sankrnti*) of the Sun into the zodiac sign of Makara (Capricorn). In South India the corresponding festival is called Pongal.

Mysticism: It is a form of religious experience in which the believer finds union with the ultimate principle of the universe. In its Christian form, mysticism has been a continuous tradition but it was especially prominent in the fourteenth and fifteenth centuries. Emphasising an absorption of the human by the divine, Christian mystics have had to fend off accusations of heresy. They appeal to Jesus as the model of divine-human union in which the Christian can participate.

Nafs: the soul or self, often the "lower self," or "ego," as opposed to the higher functions of the intellect (*'aql*) and spirit (*ruh*). Borrowing key terms from the Qur'an, the Sufis describe the soul's progress toward peacefulness in three stages. First, *nafs al-ammarah* (the dominating self) is a soul which has succumbed to the influences of the body, world, and *jinn*. Such forces eclipse the natural and pure tendencies of both one's inner spirit (*ruh*) as well as the assistance of one's guardian angel in leading a person to goodness. The *nafs al-lawwamah* (the self-reproaching self) represents the awakening of conscience to this condition and the beginning of an inner *jihad*. As victory is gained one reaches *nafs al-mutma'innah* (the tranquil self) leading subsequently to stages of the self in which one is both "satisfied with" and "satisfying to" God. (See "*Jihad*," "*Jihad al-akbar*," "*Nafs al-muhasaba*")

Nafs al-muhasaba: the reckoning or accounting of the soul. A practice of introspection, self-scrutiny, or self-examination in which one reviews one's thoughts, words, and deeds and evaluates the underlying intentions. This process of bringing these movements of the soul to the light of conscience serves as a preliminary step to *tawba* (repentance) and *istighfar* (seeking forgiveness).

N gapa cami: A Hindu festival pertaining to the cult of snakes (*n ga*), celebrated on the fifth lunar day (*pa cami*) of the bright half of the month of Śr vana or M rgaśirṣa.

Pancasila: literally, the "five ethical [principles]" of the Indonesian Constitution stipulate: (1) Faith in one God; (2) humanitarianism; (3) nationalism; (4) democracy; and (5) justice. The first principle which requires profession of a religion (or belonging to a religious community) recognizes six religions (*agamas*) as valid: Muslim, Hindu, Buddhist, Catholic, Protestant, and Chinese. By defining Hindu and Chinese religious communities broadly, everyone becomes easily classifiable within one of these *agamas*.

Pathan: The term "Pathan" is an English corruption of "Pushtun" and "Pukhtun," referring to people living in the former Northwest Frontier Province bordered by the Kabul River (on the Northwest) and the Indus River (on the Southeast). Those living north of the Kabul River pronounce their tribal name as "Pakhtun." Those living Southeast of the Kabul say "Pushtun." The term "Afghan" is the Persian (Farsi) name for these same people. Current national boundaries (the Duran Line) divide Pushtun tribes – and even villages -- across Afghanistan and Pakistan.

Pesantren are Islamic residential schools centered around a master who is a religious scholar and Sufi guide.(see "Madrasas")

Partition: as a result of the granting of independence to the former British colony of India on August 15, 1947, the division into India, West Pakistan, and East Pakistan which resulted in the relocation of 8.4 million people and over a million deaths.

Purdah: the custom of veiling and secluding women. This practice (*hijab* in Arabic) was prescribed for the Prophet's wives in Medina, but the question of how universal a practice this was or is meant to be is a subject of much controversy.

Qatl: an Arabic word for killing which is used in Qur'anic dicourse on warfare (see, "Jihad")

Qur'an: the Islamic scripture revealed to the Prophet Muhammad which is used as liturgy, a source of law, and a reading for inspiration and devotion. In the first five-verse portion revealed in 610 CE, the reading (96.1-5) emphasizes God's graciousness in two areas: as creator who brings the human being to life from an embryo and as the giver of knowledge by the pen. Revealed over the course of 23 Islamic lunar years and arranged in 114 chapters totaling almost the length of the New Testament,, the title, "Qur'an," literally means "recitation," and "reading" alluding to the practice of reciting the Qur'an in ritual prayer (*salat*) as well as its pervasive teaching of reading the universal signs (*ayat*) thoughout creation and history. Since the ninth century Islamic theologians have subscribed to a consensus that the Qur'an is the eternal uncreated word of God.

Ramadan: the ninth lunar month of the Islamic calendar, which symbolizes the month in which the Qur'an was first revealed and during which a month-long dawn-to-sunset fast is observed every day. Although the days of fasting can be challenging, the nights of Ramadan and the three-day festival following its end (*'Id al-Fitri*) are festive and hopeful occasions. The nights of Ramadan are characterized by joyful celebrations involving family and community meals, extra prayers, and even shopping. (See "*Sawm*")

Sabr: Patience, Forbearance, Endurance. Also one of God's Beautiful Names. Badshah Khan recognized the quality of *sabr* as practiced by the Prophet to be equivalent to Gandhi's *satygraha*. (see *Satyagraha*)

Salat: the ritual form of prayer prescribed to be repeated five-times a day. After ablution, the prayer continues with cycles of standing for Qur'an recitation, bowing, prostrating, and sitting for silent or softly chanted prayers. Of the five pillars, salat is the most frequently referred to in the Qur'an which says that every Prophet has done – and even every creature has its own form of – salat. (See Qur'an)

Satya: Truth, which for Gandhi, was not only truth, but *the* name of (a non-sectarian) God or Supreme Being.

Saty graha: Holding on to, i.e., insisting on, truth. A strategy, founded on truth, self-suffering and non-violence, that Gandhi developed in order to bring about social and political reform, through fasting, or civil disobedience or non-violent resistance.

Svadeśī: That which belongs or pertains to one's own region or country. For Gandhi *svadeśī* was a part of non-violence and consisted in giving preference to one's country's or region's products for the sake of the progress of its inhabitants and for the promotion of self-reliance, and national or local pride and dignity.

Untouchability: The Hindu practice of higher castes not touching, in their eyes, the degraded lower castes or outcastes in order not to get polluted

Satyagraha: "truth force," the moral and spiritual power which Gandhi taught and practiced in his nonviolent campaign for Indian National Independence. Gandhi spelled out its main features as: truth (*sat*); love (*ahimsa*); chastity (*brahmacarya*) and non-possession (*vairagya*).

Sawm: *Fasting. The fast from dawn-to-sunset every day of the month of Ramadan is a pillar of Islamic worship and precludes eating, drinking, smoking, gum chewing, or ingesting any other substances. The sick, pregnant mothers, and travelers are exempted and encouraged to make up their lost days. The purposes of the fast include training the soul (*nafs) and developing compassion. The Prophet identified a deeper degree of fasting performed with the ear, eye, tongue, hand and every limb. In this sense the jurist and theologian al-Ghazali (1058-1111) and others have identified the interior fast which includes fasting from such inner forces as anger and resentment. (See "Ramadan," "Nafs")*

Shahadah: the testimony of faith or witness which is the first pillar of Islamic worship: *la ilaha illa Allah:* there is no deity beside the only God. More broadly the *shahadah* includes its counterpart profession: *wa Muhammadan Rasul Allah* and Muhammad is the Messnger of God. For Muslims the *shahada* is a natural recognition of God's unity and His Mercy in providing continuous prophecy. By sincerely pronouncing these two ideas before two adult witnesses, one has "embraced" (converted to) Islam.

Shari'ah: a conception of revealed law and the right path of religion and morality as mediated through the two primary sources of revelation: Qur'an and Sunna. Particular interpretations of shari'ah are derived through such Islamic disiplines as scriptural interpretation (*tafsir*); jurisprudence (*fiqh*); hadith studies (*'ulum al-hadith*); theology (*kalam*); and Sufism (*'ilm al-tasawwuf*). (See "*Qur'an,*" "*Sunna,*" and "*Hadith,*")

Sufism (tasawwuf): often translated as, "mysticism," a broad term covering a variety of religious orientations, including asceticism, training at the hands of a spiritual master, veneration of saints, and the study of texts in the fields of spiritual psychology and metaphysics. Since the term was adopted retroactively and began to be used in the 11th century, it has since then most often connoted practice in a spiritual community (*tariqa*) whose teacher's authority is established by a chain of transmission going back directly to the Prophet Muhammad. The legitimate etymology of the word *suf* (wool) points to the ascetic garb (a patched woolen frock) associated with Sufism's imputed origins, but manuals on Sufism also list alternative etymologies equally useful in understanding Sufism's intended goals: purification (*saf*); exclusive devotion to prayer and study (from *Ahl a-Saff*); the foremost in piety (*Ashab al-Saff*); and sometimes even wisdom (*sufiya,* from the Greek *sofia*). In the vision of Sufism's most universally known teacher and poet, Jalaluddin Rumi (1207-1273), the essence of Sufism is expressed in passionate love for the Divine Beloved especially as embodied in one's spiitual master.

Sunna: the exemplary precedent of the life of the Prophet Muhammad, particularly as codified in the collections of hadith and serving as a basis for etiquette, ethics, and ritual.

Vaisnavite: A Hindu who worships Visnu, or some other Deity (like Krsna) associated with Visnu, as the Supreme Being.

Visnu: A major Hindu God.

Vegan: A shortened form of the word Vegetarian, it refers to one who is stricter than a vegetarian in that this person would also refrain from any dairy products and any other animal by-products.

Wahhabi, Wahhabism: a reformist, literalist, and strict doctrine developed in the 18th century and promoted by the Saudi dynasty which claims to restore the original pristine

Islamic belief and practice of the first three Islamic centuries. Its eponymous founder Muhammad 'Abd al-Wahhab (1703-1792) aimed to root out all forms of covert "polytheism" (*shirk*) as well as anything considered "innovative ." Such alleged innovations (*bid'a*) include: much of the Muslim juridical tradition; Sufism; philosophy; most artistic expression; and women's rights. Originally the movement was especially opposed to modernity and Ottoman hegemony. Currently Islamist groups such as the Taliban and al-Qaeda, as well as many movements seeking to make Islamic law the basis of a nation-state by violent means if necessary have been influenced by Wahhabism. Wahhabism has continued to be enforced and disseminated by the House of Saud as fueled by the influx of oil money.

Wali: one of the principle Islamic terms for saint, literally meaning "friend [of God]," in the sense of a powerful patron. The Qur'an frequently refers to the "friends of God" (*'awliya' Allah*).

Zaqat: the alms-tax of $1/40^{th}$ of most household income which is one of the Islamic pillars of worship. (The rate of taxation is higher for agricultural produce.) Designated recipients of *zakat* include the poor, debtors, slaves to be freed, scholars. Since the word *zakat* means "purification," the practice is understood as purifying the giver and the money from which it is given.

INDEX

B

C

F

S

U

V

W

X

Y